*The Practice of the Bible in the Middle Ages*

# The Practice of the Bible

# in the Middle Ages

Production,

Reception,

& Performance

in Western

Christianity

EDITED BY

Susan Boynton and Diane J. Reilly

COLUMBIA UNIVERSITY PRESS    NEW YORK

COLUMBIA UNIVERSITY PRESS
*Publishers Since 1893*
New York Chichester, West Sussex
Copyright © 2011 Columbia University Press
All rights reserved

Library of Congress Cataloging-in-Publication Data
The practice of the Bible in the Middle Ages: production, reception, and
performance in Western Christianity / edited by Susan Boynton and
Diane J. Reilly.
    p.  cm.
    Includes bibliographical references and index.
    ISBN 978-0-231-14826-9 (cloth: alk. paper) — ISBN 978-0-231-14827-6
(pbk.: alk. paper) — ISBN 978-0-231-52739-2 (e-book)
    1. Bible — Influence — Medieval civilization.    2. Bible — History.
I.  Boynton, Susan, 1966–    II.  Reilly, Diane J.
    BS538.7.P725    2011
    220.094′0902 — dc22

                                                            2010038350

Casebound editions of Columbia University Press books
    are printed on permanent and durable acid-free paper.
Printed in the United States of America

c 10 9 8 7 6 5 4 3 2 1
p 10 9 8 7 6 5 4 3 2 1

References to Internet Web sites (URLs) were accurate at the time of writing. Neither the author nor Columbia University Press is responsible for
Web sites that may have expired or changed since the book was prepared.

# Contents

# Acknowledgments

As with all such projects, this book could not have been completed without the assistance and advice of a great many scholars. First, we are grateful to Jennifer A. Harris, of the University of Saint Michael's College, and Greti Dinkova-Bruun, of the Pontifical Institute of Mediaeval Studies, who together first conceived of the idea of a volume dedicated to the Bible in the Middle Ages. Although that project had a different focus and broader parameters, many of the same scholars ultimately contributed to *The Practice of the Bible*, including Jennifer Harris herself. Second, we must thank our contributors, many of whom reworked already laboriously produced and edited essays for our new project, while others answered the call to contribute quickly, enthusiastically, and sometimes at short notice. All have cheerfully submitted to repeated rounds of editing as we sought to iron out subtle inconsistencies in terminology between chapters and render them understandable to the broadest possible audience. Next we would like to acknowledge Karen Hiles's expert editing, Lauren Mancia's help in compiling the glossary, and Jane Huber's vital critique of the introduction. We would also like to express our gratitude to the editorial team at Columbia University Press, Wendy Lochner, senior executive editor, and Christine Mort-lock, assistant editor, who saw our project from proposal to completion, and to the four anonymous referees who provided observations and critiques that strengthened the volume in innumerable ways. Susan Boynton's work during an early stage of the project was aided by an ACLS Fellowship from the American Council of Learned Societies as well as by a Membership in the School of Historical Studies, Institute for Advanced Study (Princeton), which was made possible by the National Endowment for the Humanities through its Fellowship Programs at Independent Research Institutions.

# *Abbreviations*

CCM = *Corpus consuetudinum monasticarum.* Siegburg: Franz Schmitt, 1963–.

CCCM = *Corpus Christianorum,* continuatio mediaeualis. Turnhout: Brepols, 1971–.

CCSL = *Corpus Christianorum,* series latina. Turnhout: Brepols, 1954–.

CSEL = *Corpus scriptorum ecclesiasticorum latinorum.* Vienna: Gerold, 1866–.

MGH = *Monumenta Germaniae Historica.* Berlin: Weidmann, 1877–.

PL = *Patrologiae cursus completus, series Latina*, edited by Jacques-Paul Migne. 221 vols. Paris: Migne, 1844–66.

SC = *Sources chrétiennes.* Paris: Editions du Cerf, 1942–.

*The Practice of the Bible in the Middle Ages*

## Orientation for the Reader

*Susan Boynton and Diane J. Reilly*

I n the Middle Ages, practices of biblical reading, performance, and interpretation yielded a large and varied manuscript tradition and provided material for all levels of education. Just as commentary on the Bible was a central activity of contemplative and scholarly life, so manuscripts of Scripture formed the core collections of monastic libraries and were also central to university studies. Biblical texts were the foundation of the medieval Latin and vernacular sermons that were preached to both the clergy and the laity. The Christian Bible was also one of the earliest texts to be translated into postclassical languages, a process from which new interpretations emerged in response to contemporary political and religious needs. The results influenced the development of the vernacular languages. In addition, as the basis for the medieval tradition of history writing, the Bible framed the worldview of the literate. Even those who never saw a written Bible would have heard biblical texts read, sung, and synthesized in the liturgy and sermons.

What we understand today as the Christian Bible is made up of Hebrew sacred texts and texts written in the first century CE about the life of Jesus and the early Christian community. The concept of the

Christian Bible as a unit is, however, a medieval invention. The Hebrew Bible (Tanakh) was not a book (despite the fact that the term Bible is derived from the Greek *biblia* for "books"), but rather a complex body of texts that was in large part a product of ancient Near Eastern scribal culture, as Karel van der Toorn has argued.[1] Early Christians wrestled with the definition and format of their Scriptures, while assuming that the received tradition of the Hebrew Bible was authoritative. According to the Gospel authors, Jesus had cited the Tanakh continually;[2] Paul also drew on it in his Epistles. Yet, in late antiquity, two factors argued against immediately adopting the texts of the old and new dispensations as a unit. First, they had never previously traveled together. Even though the Pentateuch, Prophets, Kings, and historical works had been grouped as a canonical Jewish Scripture by the end of the first century CE, they were preserved separately.[3] Conversely, in the first decades of Christianity, the story of Jesus and his followers was maintained through oral transmission. Only after many years was the Christian story recorded by more permanent means and in many different versions, only some of which later came to be included in what we now know as the Christian Bible.[4] Second, it was at that time impossible to assemble all the texts that might have composed a canon of Scripture in any one material vessel. Before the third or fourth centuries CE, copying of text into papyrus or parchment codices was rare, and the parchment or papyrus scrolls onto which most Scripture was transcribed could preserve texts of only limited length.[5]

The earliest Western medieval versions of the Old Testament depended on the Septuagint, a Greek translation of the Hebrew Bible with some additions that medieval commentators believed had resulted from the legendary miraculous inspiration of seventy or seventy-two translators in the third century BCE.[6] The Septuagint was most likely not copied in a single manuscript before the third or fourth century CE, however, and coexisted with other versions of the Old Testament in Greek.[7] Thus the translators of what is now known collectively as the *Vetus Latina*, or Old Latin translation of the Bible, had to rely on a variety of different manuscript sources, which they translated on an ad hoc basis.

By the late fourth century, however, the drawbacks of this piecemeal approach to the preservation and use of Scripture were perceived by many. At the same time that a definitive canon was being established, Jerome attempted to standardize the Latin Bible by translating a new version from Greek and Hebrew. The Bible that resulted eventually included all the books that would be accepted by the medieval Christian church, although not all were translated by Jerome himself, as he had rejected some books because they were not included in the Hebrew Bibles he consulted. In the high Middle Ages, this version of the Bible came to be known as the Vulgate. Despite the improvements made to the Bible text by Jerome's meticulous translation, the Vulgate Bible was not universally adopted until centuries after Jerome's death.

Jerome's translations appeared contemporaneously with the large-scale adoption of the vellum codex. The codex was a much more efficient and durable carrier of text than a papyrus roll and, in addition, was well suited to the way in which Christian Scripture was read. While cumbersome papyrus rotuli, or scrolls, were friable and needed to be unrolled before a reader could consult a discrete segment of text, a codex could be flipped open neatly at any given point—an arrangement suited to the early functions of parts of the Christian Bible within the liturgy and in scholarly circles.[8] Not until the seventh century does specific evidence appear that the various books of the Bible as we know it were read aloud in a given order, in the context of Christian ritual.[9] In the early medieval period, then, the Bible was most conveniently consulted as a set of codices, such as that described by Cassiodorus, a sixth-century scholar who endowed his own monastery, Vivarium, with one multivolume Bible and two single-volume Bibles, the earliest single-volume Latin Vulgate Bibles for which we have any sort of record.[10]

Medieval clerics, if asked, would have considered the Bible to be composed of the following components, often grouped roughly as follows:[11]

- The Pentateuch, or Five Books of Moses, also known to the Jews as the Torah: Genesis, Exodus, Leviticus, Numbers, and Deuteronomy. Written from the ninth to the fifth centuries BCE, these books tell the story of Creation and the earliest history of the Israelites from their captivity in Egypt to their journey to the Promised Land.
- The Historical Books, including Joshua, Judges, Ruth, the four books of Kings (known later as 1–2 Samuel and 1–2 Kings), and 1–2 Chronicles. Written from the ninth to the fourth centuries BCE, these books tell the continuing story of the Israelites, from their arrival in the Promised Land, through the establishment of the Jewish kingdoms, and finally the Babylonian captivity in the sixth century BCE and the return of the Jews from exile.
- The Great Prophets, Isaiah, Jeremiah, Ezekiel, their much later successor Daniel, and the twelve minor prophets. These sixteen books tell the sto-

ries of the lives and prophecies of individual prophets who lived between the eighth and second centuries BCE.

- The Psalter, a book of poems or hymns perhaps written for use in the first Temple, which was believed by medieval readers to have been written by King David and several assistants.

- Job, a poetic book written sometime between the fifth and second centuries BCE that seeks to justify the suffering of the innocent.

- The Wisdom Books: Proverbs, Ecclesiastes, Ecclesiasticus, the Wisdom of Solomon, and the Song of Solomon. This series of books, written between the fourth century BCE and the first century CE, seeks to explain the wisdom of God and advise God-fearing people on right actions. The Song of Solomon is a series of erotic poems written, not by Solomon, but centuries after his lifetime, perhaps in the third century BCE.

- The Apocryphal and Later Historical Books, including Ezra and Nehemiah, Tobit, Judith, Esther, and the two books of Maccabees. Written from the fifth century BCE to the first century CE, these books each tell the story of the Jews from the perspective of one storyteller or heroic individual. Most were not included in the Hebrew Bible.

- The Gospels: four books written, according to medieval belief, by four apostles, or early followers of Christ: Matthew, Mark, Luke, and John. Probably written between thirty and eighty years after the death of Jesus, these books record the life experiences of Jesus and his followers and explain the events central to Christian belief. The Gospels of Matthew, Mark, and Luke cover roughly the same material and are often termed the Synoptic Gospels. The Gospel of John is instead focused on the later part of Christ's life and his Passion, and the doctrines of the early Christians.

- The Acts: this book was also, according to tradition, written by the apostle Luke. Like the Gospels, it is a narrative that explains the early history of the Christian church and its leaders from the time of Christ's Ascension until St. Paul departed for Rome.

- Epistles: letters written in the first two centuries after the death of Jesus, from Sts. Paul, Peter, John, James, and Jude to various congregations, individuals, and cities. These letters explain Christian beliefs and practices as well as answers to the challenges faced by the early Church.

- Revelation: known to medieval readers as Apocalypse, written, according to medieval belief, by the apostle John, this book records the author's visions while on the island of Patmos in the Aegean Sea. The visions are a prediction of the events at the end of time, the second coming of Christ, the Resurrection of souls, and the Last Judgment, all described in allegorical terms.

References to biblical texts in this volume employ the Latin Vulgate because it was the single most common version in the medieval West.[12] The English translation cited is the Douay-Rheims version in the mid-eighteenth-century revision of Bishop Richard Challoner (1691–1781).[13] The Douay-Rheims translation, carried out in the sixteenth and seventeenth centuries by Roman Catholic scholars who had fled persecution in England during the Reformation and settled in the French cities of Rheims and Douai, is the most direct and literal English translation of the medieval Latin Bible available. The Challoner revision incorporates modernized spelling and verse divisions that render the text more intelligible to the modern reader. Those more accustomed to modern translations such as the New American Bible, the New Revised Standard Version, or the Twenty-First Century King James Bible, will find the syntax and vocabulary of the Douay-Rheims Bible obscure. Nonetheless, only the Douay-Rheims version preserves in English the sense that would have been known to most medieval readers of the Latin Bible, and thus it is the most appropriate resource for those studying the medieval Bible.[14]

In this volume we build on some great works of synthesis published in the middle decades of the twentieth century. Of these, the most familiar to English speakers are undoubtedly Beryl Smalley's *The Study of the Bible in the Middle Ages* (originally published in 1941) and Jean Leclercq's *The Love of Learning and the Desire for God: A Study of Monastic Culture* (original French edition published in 1957). Leclercq, a Benedictine monk, wrote from the standpoint of a practitioner of biblical reading and contemplation, treating the reception of Scripture in the framework of the monastic life. Smalley's survey of authors and schools led to a significant body of subsequent research and remains a fundamental resource today,[15] even though the field of biblical studies has changed radically in the nearly seven decades since *The Study of the Bible* first appeared. Smalley's introduction shows, for instance, that one of the major schools of medieval exegesis, the Augustinians of Saint Victor in Paris, was relatively little known in the mid twentieth century; in recent decades many of their commentaries have been newly edited and translated into various languages, including English.

A more detailed treatment of medieval biblical commentary can be found in Jesuit theologian Henri de Lubac's classic *Medieval Exegesis*,[16] a magisterial synthesis of Christian exegetical method up to the age of humanism. Organized both diachronically and thematically (around authors, senses of Scripture, and exegetical themes), *Medieval Exegesis* offers a vision of exegesis as a theological system—a conception of biblical hermeneutics that emanates from de Lubac's own vocation as a theologian.[17] In this regard, de Lubac contributed to the movements of reform and renewal that engaged many scholars within the Roman Catholic Church in the 1950s and 1960s.[18] As a study of approaches to the Bible (rather than a study of the Bible itself), *Medieval Exegesis* generally does not address the status of the biblical text in the Middle Ages, however. In particular, de Lubac did not take into account the influence on exegesis of the Bible's manuscript traditions, its role in the liturgy, or other forms of its oral transmission. By contrast, we emphasize the role of practice (whether in the form of performance or of manuscript production) in the shaping of biblical tradition. The chapters that follow explore the liturgical, exegetical, and pastoral expressions of the Bible in physical, textual, and aural forms and the way these shaped contemporary understanding of the Bible's contents and its place in Christian society.

We have aimed to convey some of the most essential aspects of the Bible as experienced in the Middle Ages. Readers may also wish to consult a reference work such as *The Cambridge History of the Bible*, vol. 2: *The West from the Fathers to the Reformation* (Cambridge: Cambridge University Press, 1969), which focuses on the text and transmission of the Bible (*The New Cambridge History of the Bible*, edited by E. Ann Matter and Richard Marsden, is forthcoming) or *Le Moyen Âge et la Bible*, ed. Pierre Riché and Guy Lobrichon, Bible de tous les temps 4 (Paris: Beauchesne, 1984).[19] The present volume can also be supplemented by examples of exegesis found in numerous editions and translations cited in the chapters by van Liere and Roest, as well as by studies that focus on particular genres, themes, or books of the Bible.[20] Specific treatment of some subjects is outside our purview. For information on the general field of biblical iconography, readers may turn to the standard reference work, Gertrud Schiller's *Iconography of Christian Art* (Greenwich, CT: New York Graphic Society, 1971).[21] We refer readers interested primarily in medieval Jewish exegesis to recent studies such as *Jewish Biblical Interpretation and Cultural Exchange: Comparative Exegesis in Context*, ed. Natalie B. Dohrmann and David Stern (Philadelphia: University of Pennsylvania Press, 2008).[22] The influence of Jewish scholars on Christian ones is addressed where relevant (see the chapters by van Liere and Francomano), but we have not attempted to do full justice to the contacts and encounters between the two traditions, which is a burgeoning scholarly field in its own right.[23]

## Notes

1. Karel van der Toorn, *Scribal Culture and the Making of the Hebrew Bible* (Cambridge: Harvard University Press, 2007).

2. A good impression of the density of references to books of the Tanakh in the Gospels can be gained from recent editions of the Douay-Rheims translation of the Vulgate, such as Tan Book Company's 1971 reprint. Footnotes at the base of every column in the Gospel texts function as cross-references to Old and New Testament passages. The fourth chapter of Matthew on the first temptation of Jesus, for instance, contains references to the books of Deuteronomy, Psalms, and Isaiah.

3. Christopher de Hamel, *The Book: A History of the Bible* (New York: Phaidon, 2001), pp. 40–63.

4. See ibid., pp. 298–329, on the earliest surviving biblical manuscript fragments and the many noncanonical contemporary religious texts. For a selection of those texts, see Montague R. James, *The Apocryphal New Testament* (Oxford: Clarendon, 1955).

5. See de Hamel, *The Book*, pp. 40–63; and Harry Y. Gamble, *Books and Readers in the Early Christian Church: A History of Early Christian Texts* (New Haven: Yale University Press, 1995), pp. 42–81, on the transition from scroll to codex; and pp. 203–41 on the development of Christian reading practice. Some of the earliest Bible fragments are reproduced in *In the Beginning: Bibles before the Year 1000*, ed. Michelle P. Brown (Washington, DC: Freer Gallery of Art and Arthur M. Sackler Gallery [Smithsonian Institution], 2006).

6. Karen J. Jobes and Moisés Silva, *Invitation to the Septuagint* (Grand Rapids, MI: Baker Academic, 2000). Additions to the Septuagint that were not part of the Hebrew Bible, or "Masoretic text," included the books of Tobit, Judith, Wisdom, Ecclesiasticus, 1–2 Maccabees, and Baruch.

7. Anthony Grafton and Megan Williams, *Christianity and the Transformation of the Book: Origen, Eusebius, and the Library of Caesarea* (Cambridge: Belknap, 2006), pp. 86–132.

8. Gamble, *Books and Readers*, pp. 42–81.

9. Diane J. Reilly, *The Art of Reform in Eleventh-Century Flanders: Gerard of Cambrai, Richard of Saint-Vanne and the Saint-Vaast Bible*, Studies in the History of Christian Traditions 128 (Leiden: Brill, 2006), p. 55. See also the reading instructions compiled by M. Andrieu, *Les Ordines romani du haut moyen âge*, 5 vols. (Louvain: Spicilegium Sacrum Lovaniense Bureaux, 1931–61), 2:480–526.

10. For a brief introduction to Cassiodorus's project, see Gamble, *Books and Readers*,

pp. 198–202; and Margaret T. Gibson, *The Bible in the Latin West*, The Medieval Book 1 (Notre Dame, IN: University of Notre Dame Press, 1993), pp. 3–4 and p. 24.

11. For general introductions to the origins of the biblical books, see *The New Interpreter's Dictionary of the Bible*, ed. George Arthur Buttrick, 3 vols. (Nashville: Abingdon, 2006); and, to the canon, Christopher de Hamel, *The Book: A History of the Bible* (New York: Phaidon, 2001), especially pp. 12–33 and pp. 298–329; and Jaroslav Pelikan, *Whose Bible Is It? A History of the Scriptures Through the Ages* (New York: Viking, 2005). For information on the grouping and ordering of medieval Bibles, see Samuel Berger, *Histoire de la Vulgate pendant les premiers siècles du moyen âge* (Paris: Hachette, 1893; repr. Hildesheim: Olms, 1976), appendixes 1 and 2.

12. *Biblia sacra iuxta vulgatam versionem*, ed. Robert Weber et al., 4th ed. (Stuttgart: Deutsche Bibelgesellschaft, 1994).

13. *The Holy Bible* (New York: Douay Bible House, 1941; repr. Fitzwilliam, NH: Loreto, 2004).

14. For the names of biblical personages and titles of biblical books referred to outside of quotations, we use the King James forms, because the Douay-Rheims versions are now so unfamiliar (for instance, it uses 1 Paralipomenon in place of the King James's 1 Chronicles) that using them might impede the reader's efforts to apply the information in these chapters to other contexts.

15. Beryl Smalley, *The Study of the Bible in the Middle Ages* (Oxford: Blackwell, 1941), with numerous later editions and reprints by the University of Notre Dame Press.

16. *Medieval Exegesis: The Four Senses of Scripture*, vol. 1: trans. Mark Sebanc, vol. 2: trans. E. M. Macierowski (Grand Rapids, MI: Eerdmans, 1998, 2000). Originally published as *Exégèse médiévale: Les quatre sens de l'écriture*, 4 vols. (Paris: Aubier, 1959–64). Equally valuable treatments, not yet translated into English, are Gilbert Dahan, *L'exégèse chrétienne de la Bible en Occident médiéval, XIIe-XIVe siècle* (Paris: Cerf, 1999); Ceslas Spicq, *Esquisse d'une histoire de l'exégèse latine au Moyen Âge*, Bibliothèque thomiste 26 (Paris: Vrin, 1944).

17. On de Lubac as a theologian, see Susan K. Wood, *Spiritual Exegesis and the Church in the Theology of Henri de Lubac* (London: Continuum, 1998).

18. Similarly, Jean Daniélou's *The Bible and the Liturgy* (Notre Dame, IN: University of Notre Dame Press, 1956), first published as *Bible et liturgie: La théologie biblique des sacrements et des fêtes d'après les Pères de l'Église* (Paris: Cerf, 1951), reflects the tenets of the Catholic liturgical movement in that period.

19. *Le Moyen Âge et la Bible* contains important surveys of the text of the Latin Bible and some aspects of its commentary traditions, while the second half is devoted to reception (quite broadly defined), surveying the role of Scripture not only in texts such as monastic rules and customaries, canon law, hagiography, sermons, and in the liturgy but also in images, politics, and social movements.

20. For instance, Andrew P. Scheil's *The Footsteps of Israel: Understanding Jews in Anglo-Saxon England* (Ann Arbor: University of Michigan Press, 2004) is an example of a close study of exegetical method in a specific context. Stephen Wailes's *Medieval Allegories of Jesus's Parables* (Berkeley: University of California Press, 1987) compiles and synthesizes commentary on the parables, thereby providing a useful panorama of medieval interpretation.

21. See also the original German version, *Ikonographie der christlichen Kunst* (Gütersloh: Mohn, 1966).

22. Recent volumes that treat both Jewish and Christian medieval exegesis include *Hebrew Bible/Old Testament: A History of Its Interpretation*, 1:2, *The Middle Ages*, ed. Magne Sæbø (Göttingen: Vandenhoeck and Ruprecht, 2000); *With Reverence for the Word: Medieval Scriptural Exegesis in Judaism, Christianity, and Islam*, ed. Jane Dammen McAuliffe, Barry D. Walfish, and Joseph W. Goering (Oxford: Oxford University Press, 2003). The later medieval period is also addressed in parts of *Hebrew Bible/Old Testament*, 2: *From the Renaissance to the Enlightenment* (2008).

23. See, for example, *Jews and Christians in Twelfth-Century Europe*, ed. Michael A. Signer and John van Engen (Notre Dame, IN: University of Notre Dame Press, 2001); Deeana Copeland Klepper, "Medieval Christian Use of Hebrew and Postbiblical Jewish Texts," in *The Insight of Unbelievers: Nicholas of Lyra and Christian Reading of Jewish Text in the Later Middle Ages* (Philadelphia: University of Pennsylvania Press, 2007), pp. 13–31.

# The Bible and the Liturgy

*Susan Boynton*

The Bible permeated the medieval Latin liturgy: biblical narratives and themes lay behind the fundamental structures of the liturgical year, and scriptural texts were ubiquitous in the form of chants and readings. On a more general level, biblical images and constructs influenced the thinking of the clerics performing the liturgy, shaping the role of the Bible in the new compositions produced during the Middle Ages.[1]

The diverse uses of the Bible in medieval Latin rites reflected the ideas associated with biblical texts in Christian exegesis, including allegorical and typological interpretation, and particularly Christological readings of the Old Testament. The juxtaposition of biblical texts in the liturgy, like the citation of authorities in a sermon, produced an implicitly exegetical structure. Singing and reading words from Scripture in combination and alternation with nonscriptural ones placed the biblical passages in new contexts, endowing them with multiple layers of meaning that were also articulated by exegetes. Thus the selection and combination of biblical texts in the chants and readings of the liturgy constitute a system of interpretation that parallels the readings of these same texts by patristic writers. The annual cycle of biblical readings at Mass both reflected a liturgical theology and provided the foundation for interpretations of feasts and seasons of the church year that were made manifest in the liturgical structures that grew up around them.

The two principal services celebrated each day were the Mass and the Divine Office. The Mass was the eucharistic service, understood as reenacting the ever-present, always-remembered sacrifice of Christ in the Last Supper. Mass was generally celebrated twice a day (early in the morning by a religious community alone, and once later in the morning in the presence of the lay congregation), although many additional Masses could be performed for specific purposes, such as special commemorations. The Divine Office comprised a series of eight separate prayer services distributed at regular intervals over the course of the day and night: Vespers in the late afternoon before dusk, Compline after dark and before retiring to bed, Matins in the middle of the night between midnight and dawn, Lauds around daybreak, Prime in the early morning followed by Terce later in the morning, Sext at midday, and None in the mid-afternoon. While the preparation for and administration of the Eucharist were the focus of the Mass, the hours of the Office were services in which the singing of psalms was the central component.

Medieval writers saw multiple levels of meaning in every element of the liturgy, frequently interpreting them in relation to the Bible. Allegorical interpretation characterizes two of the commentators best known today: Amalarius of Metz (ca. 775–ca. 850) and Guillaume Durand, the bishop of Mende (1230 or 1231–1296). Amalarius discusses the Old Testament precedents for the liturgical choir of singers, beginning with King David's establishment of priest musicians.[2] In his *Rationale* Durand (drawing upon earlier sources) correlates the hours of the Office with the different events in the life, death, and Resurrection of Christ and also with periods of biblical time beginning with the age of Adam.[3] Other writers on the liturgy likewise viewed it in biblical terms: in the twelfth century John Beleth and Honorius Augustodunensis interpreted the monastic office of Matins as illustrating the parable of the workers in the vineyard in Matthew 20.[4]

## Remembering the Bible

The medieval liturgy reenacted the events of the Bible in a recurring yet teleological progression: biblical and postbiblical events were memorialized in interlocking cycles and new commemorations were continuously added to the calendar. The typological dimensions of these events endowed the church year with further layers of temporality. Feasts related to the life of Christ and subsequent events form the underlying narrative framework. The liturgical year as a whole was composed of overlapping cycles of feasts; those of the Lord formed a cycle known as the *temporale* ("temporal" or proper of the time), which was complemented by the *sanctorale* ("sanctoral" or proper of saints), comprising essentially feasts of saints.[5] Most feasts of the *temporale* were moveable: their dates depended on the date of Easter Sunday in a given year, and the date of Easter was determined by the phases of the moon, following the earlier practice used to determine the date of the Jewish Passover. The feasts of the *temporale* that were related to Christmas, however, such as Epiphany and the Circumcision, were celebrated on the same day every year, just like Christmas. By contrast, the feasts in the *sanctorale* occurred on fixed dates.

The complex structure of the church year developed over a period of centuries. Commemorations of the beginning and end of Christ's life gradually developed into seasons of several weeks that anticipated and followed Christmas and Easter.[6] In the early Middle Ages, Advent, the period of four weeks preceding the Nativity of Christ on December 25, came to be defined as the beginning of the liturgical year.[7] The principal feasts in the weeks following Christmas commemorate events in Christ's childhood: the massacre of the male children at Bethlehem (Innocents' Day, December 28), the circumcision of the infant Jesus (January 1), the visit of the Magi (January 6), and the Presentation of Jesus in the Temple along with the Purification of Mary (February 2).[8] Soon thereafter, on Ash Wednesday, begins Lent, a period of penitence and fasting before Easter that commemorated the forty days Christ spent in the wilderness, which were understood typologically as the years of the Israelites' wandering in the desert. The Latin term for this period, *Quadragesima,* refers to the forty days; the first Sunday in Lent was called Quadragesima Sunday. The period of penitence actually began three weeks earlier, on Septuagesima Sunday (from the Latin for "on the seventieth day," even though technically it does not fall on the seventieth day before Easter).

The solemn anticipation of the Lenten fast culminated in Holy Week. The liturgy of each day in Holy Week represented and commented upon the Passion narratives in the Gospels, which were recited on Palm Sunday (Matthew), Monday (Mark), Tuesday (Luke), and Good Friday (John). While the recitation of the Passions was inherently dramatic, the biblical narrative came to life even more vividly through reenactments of the entry into Jerusalem in Palm Sunday processions and of the washing of the disciples' feet by Christ in the Holy Thursday Maundy (*mandatum*), which involved lay people as well as clergy and included details of ceremonial that were characteristic to each locality (for further discussion of the Maundy Thursday ritual, see Cochelin's chapter in this volume).[9] Holy Thursday (commemorating the institution of the Eucharist in the Last Supper) and Easter Sunday (celebrating the Resurrection) mark the boundaries of the paschal Triduum, the most ancient part of the liturgical year. After Easter, the fifty-day season of paschal time encompassed feasts commemorating biblical episodes that took place after Christ's earthly ministry: his Ascension into heaven and the apostles' reception of the Holy Spirit (Pentecost) on the fiftieth day. Numerous postbiblical feasts, including saints' days, were also part of the church calendar. The use of scriptural texts in the liturgy on these occasions generated a new layer of meaning by establishing or reinforcing a biblical typology for the life of the saint. In the case of a feast commemorating a nonbiblical event such as the Assumption of the Virgin Mary, the use of texts from the Song of Songs in the liturgy was an integral part of the exegetical context in which the doctrine of the Assumption was discussed and debated.[10]

## Living the Bible

The Bible was omnipresent in the daily routine of those observing monastic rules (see also Cochelin's chapter in this volume). Biblical texts and commentary on them were heard in the Mass, Divine Office, chapter, and refectory.[11] Of all the biblical texts that filled the lives of monks, the psalms were by far the most prominent.[12] The earliest form of the monastic office arose among the monks of the Egyptian desert, who attempted to follow the Pauline instruction to "pray without ceasing" (1 Thess. 5:17) by chanting psalms continuously for extended periods of time, achieving feats such as the recitation of all 150 psalms in a single night.[13] By the late fourth century, in part due to the influence of monasticism, the psalm had emerged as the central text of Christian liturgy and retained this preeminence throughout the formative period of the Western rites.[14]

The liturgical uses of the Psalter ranged from the excerpting of particular verses in chant texts to the chanting of psalms in their entirety, verse by verse. In every service entire psalms were sung to a simple recitation melody in alternation with antiphons, which are shorter chants with texts usually taken from the Psalms. The choice of a psalm for the antiphon text often reflected principles of allegorical interpretation.[15] In the early liturgy, antiphons may have been sung as a refrain in the course of a psalm performance, but in the Middle Ages they were sung before and after each psalm or group of psalms.[16]

The sixth-century Rule of Benedict prescribed a cycle that distributed the psalms so as to ensure the chanting of the entire Psalter in a week, and the psalms remained the centerpiece of the Divine Office.[17] Certain psalm verses were sung at the same time each day. The Night Office (Matins, called Nocturns in the rule) began with Psalm 50:17 chanted three times: "Lord, open my lips and my mouth shall proclaim your praise" (*Domine, labia mea aperies et os meum adnuntiabit laudem tuam*) followed by Psalm 3, and then Psalm 94, "Come, let us rejoice" (*Venite exultemus*) with an antiphon. After a nonscriptural hymn, six psalms were sung, each with its own antiphon. A short prose text known as a versicle was sung, followed by a blessing of the reader. Three readings were recited, each followed by the singing of a responsory, a lengthy and often ornate chant that could also be performed at Vespers.[18] These readings at Matins, known as lessons, could come from the Old Testament, the New Testament, or the church fathers. There followed six more psalms with six antiphons, a Pauline Epistle, a litany, and the Kyrie. On a Sunday or feast day, the number of lessons and responsories was increased to twelve. The series of psalms in groups of six always began on Sunday with Psalm 20.

The morning office of Lauds on Sundays and feast days began with Psalm 66, followed by Psalm 50 with a refrain, Psalms 117 and 62, an Old Testament canticle, Psalms 148–150, and a reading from Revelation (from a Pauline Epistle when it was neither a feast day nor a Sunday) followed by a short responsory. After a hymn and versicle were sung, and the *Benedictus* (the canticle with a text from Luke 1: 68–79) chanted with an antiphon, the litany, a prayer, and the concluding verse were recited. The third and fourth psalms were determined by the day of the week: Psalms 5 and 35 on Monday; 42 and 56 on Tuesday; 63 and 64 on Wednesday; 87 and 89 on Thursday; 75 and 91 on Friday; 142 on Saturday. After Lauds, the abbot was to recite the Lord's Prayer.

The briefer hours of Prime, Terce, Sext, and None all followed the same pattern, beginning with a verse from Psalms 69:2: "God, come to my assistance; Lord, make haste to help me" (*Deus in adiutorium meum intende, Domine ad adiuuandum me festina*), followed by a nonscriptural hymn.

TABLE 2.1    Outline of the Monastic Divine Office on a Sunday or Feast Day

*Matins*

Psalm 69:1
Psalm 50:1 (three times)
Psalm 3 (without antiphon)
Invitatory antiphon and Psalm 94
Hymn
First Nocturn:
Six psalms sung with six antiphons
Versicle and response, *Pater noster*, Absolution
Four lessons (often biblical) and responsories
Second Nocturn:
Six psalms sung with six antiphons
Versicle and response, *Pater noster*, Absolution
Four lessons and responsories
Third Nocturn:
Three variable canticles from the Old Testament, sung with
    one antiphon
Versicle and response, *Pater noster*, Absolution
Reading of a Gospel verse
Four lessons and responsories
*Te deum laudamus*
Gospel of the day
*Te decet laus*
*Kyrie, Pater noster*, preces
Collect

*Lauds*

Opening versicle: Psalm 69:1
Six psalms varying by day of week
Psalms 66 and 50
Old Testament canticle
Psalms 148–50
Chapter
Short responsory
Hymn
Versicle and response
Canticle (Luke 1:68–79) with antiphon
*Kyrie, Pater Noster*, Preces
Collect
*Benedicamus domino*

TABLE 2.1 *(continued)*

*Prime*

    Opening versicle: Psalm 69:1
    Hymn
    Psalms varying by day of week
    Chapter
    *Kyrie, Pater Noster*, Credo
    Preces
    *Pater noster*
    Confession, Absolution
    Preces
    Collect
    *Benedicamus domino*

*Terce, Sext, and None*

    Opening versicle: Psalm 69:1
    Psalms varying by day of week
    Chapter
    Versicle and response
    *Kyrie, Pater noster*, Preces
    Collect
    *Benedicamus domino*

*Vespers*

    Opening versicle: Psalm 69:1
    Psalms varying by day of week
    Chapter
    Hymn
    Versicle and response
    Canticle: Magnificat (Luke 1:46–55)
    *Kyrie, Pater noster*, preces
    Collect
    *Benedicamus domino*

*Compline*

    Versicle and response
    Psalm 69:1
    Psalms 4, 90 133
    Hymn
    Chapter

TABLE 2.1 *(continued)*

Versicle and response
*Kyrie, Pater noster, Credo*
Preces
Confession, absolution
Preces
Collect
*Benedicamus domino*

Three psalms were chanted, a short reading (often scriptural) was recited, and the office concluded with a sung versicle, the Kyrie, and a dismissal. The choice of psalms in these so-called Little Hours differed according to the day of the week. On Sundays they were devoted to singing the lengthy Psalm 118. On Mondays, Psalms 1, 2, and 6 were sung at Prime, while the other little hours divided up the remaining sections of Psalm 118. From Tuesday through Saturday, the three psalms at Prime were taken from the series 3–19 (omitting 4, which was sung at Compline, and dividing Psalms 9 and 17 into two parts each). Psalms 119–127, divided into consecutive groups of three, were sung at Terce, Sext, and None.

The office of Vespers consisted of four psalms, each with an antiphon, followed by a reading and responsory, a nonscriptural hymn, a versicle, the *Magnificat* (Luke 1:46–66), a litany, and the Lord's Prayer before the dismissal. During the week, the Vespers psalms were taken from Psalms 109–147 (with the omission of 117–127, 133, 142, and subdividing 138, 143, and 144). Compline was the final office of the day, to be sung before retiring to bed; it consisted of Psalms 4, 90, and 133, then a hymn, reading, versicle, Kyrie, blessing, and dismissal.[19]

In the Middle Ages, singing the Office became the primary occupation of monks. As the Benedictine Rule stated, "nothing is to come before the work of God" (*nihil operi Dei praeponatur*).[20] The constant citation of the psalms in the rule reflects a spirituality profoundly suffused with psalmody. Benedict's rationale for the number of offices to be celebrated daily comes from the psalms themselves; the verse "At midnight I arose to confess to you" (Ps. 118:62) is cited as an allusion to the Night Office, while "Seven times a day have I praised you" (Ps. 118:154) refers to the hours of the office celebrated during the day: Lauds, Prime, Terce, Sext, None, Vespers, and Compline.[21] Even the rule recognized that psalm verses provide guidelines for the ideal performance of the psalms: "We must always remember, therefore, what the Prophet says: *Serve the Lord with fear* [Ps. 2:11], and again, *Sing praise wisely* [Ps. 46:8], and *In the presence of the angels I will sing to you* [Ps. 137:1]. Let us consider, then, how we ought to behave in the presence of God and his angels, and let us stand to sing the psalms in such a way that our minds are in harmony with our voices."[22]

Beginning in the ninth century, in addition to the weekly cycle of psalms in the Office described by the Rule of Benedict, monks also sang groups of psalms with various commemorative functions. Several texts from the tenth and eleventh centuries describe these practices in detail. The "threefold prayer" (*trina oratio*) involved chanting all or some of the Penitential Psalms (6, 31, 37, 50, 101, 129, 142) in three groups, each group followed by a prayer. The *trina oratio* took place three times a day: before Matins, before Terce (in winter) or Prime (in summer), and after Compline. The Penitential Psalms were also recited after Prime and before the litany.[23] After the first *trina oratio* of the day, one recited the Gradual Psalms (*psalmi graduales*), which consisted of Psalms 119–133 in summer, and Psalms 119–150 in winter. The *psalmi familiares*, or Familiar Psalms, were recited after each hour of the monastic office with prayers on behalf of a monastery's patrons and benefactors, who, as friends and associates of the community, were understood to comprise a spiritual "extended family" (*familia*). The first psalm of each series was one of the seven Penitential Psalms, the second varied according to the hour, and the third and fourth were fixed.[24] Besides the *trina oratio*, Gradual Psalms, Penitential Psalms, and Familiar Psalms, there were the Special Psalms (*psalmi speciales*), to be recited on behalf of a monastery's benefactors and for the dead in general. The Special Psalms consisted of sixteen psalms to be chanted in groups daily, before Prime in summer, or between Matins and Lauds in winter. The first set of five psalms was for the king and all believers, friends, or associates (*familiares*), and almsgivers (Psalms 50, 53, 56, 66, 69); the second was a single psalm (Ps. 19) said for the king alone; the third group consisted of Psalms 5, 6, 114, 115, and 129, for all deceased believers; and the fourth group, said for all deceased monks and all faithful Christians, consisted of Psalms 22, 24, 25, 142, and 145.[25] Thus psalmody became a means of commemorating the deceased and including them in a symbolic community. These uses of the psalms are often associated with the Burgundian abbey of Cluny, founded in 910, which was renowned for elaborate liturgical practices that were transmitted to other monasteries both inside and outside its direct sphere of influence.[26] However, commemorative psalmody also forms part of the broader phenomenon of intercessory prayer in medieval monasticism.[27]

## Singing the Bible

As we have seen, the psalms were predominant among the chants of the medieval Latin liturgy with biblical texts. The psalm verses used in most chant texts of the early Middle Ages are taken from the early Latin translations, of which the oldest form a group collectively designated the Vetus Latina or "Old Latin" tradition. The branch of this tradition known as the Roman Psalter is the one most commonly used in early chant texts.[28] A third major Latin translation known as the Gallican Psalter is

TABLE 2.2   Outline of the Mass on a Sunday or Feast Day
(Outside Penitential Seasons)

Introit
*Kyrie eleison*
*Gloria in excelsis*
Collect
Epistle
Gradual
Alleluia
Sequence
Gospel
Creed
Offertory
Secret (prayer; also known as offertory prayer)
*Sursum corda*
Preface (prayer)
*Sanctus* and *Benedictus*
Canon of the Mass
*Pater noster*
*Pax domini*
*Agnus dei*
Communion
Postcommunion (prayer)
Dismissal

Jerome's second revision of an earlier Latin translation based on Origen's Greek Hexapla edition (which compared in six columns the Hebrew text, a transliteration of the Hebrew text in the Greek alphabet, three Greek translations, and Origen's own edition of the Septuagint version). Between the ninth and twelfth century, the Gallican Psalter gradually came to predominate in the chanting of entire psalms during the Divine Office, displacing the Roman Psalter (although the early chant texts taken from the Roman Psalter were retained).[29]

Many Mass chants were based on the psalms, and some create a commentary on the psalm text by altering its form so as to link it more explicitly to a liturgical occasion.[30] Texts that are appropriate to a specific liturgical occasion are known as propers (the introit, gradual, alleluia or tract, offertory, and communion).[31] The gradual was originally a responsorial psalm, sung by a soloist with responses by the congregation.[32] In some cases, the association of specific psalms to certain days can be traced back to late antiquity. Among early Christian writings, Augustine's sermons and psalm commentary (*Enarrationes in Psalmos*) provide particularly useful evidence for the singing of the gradual.[33] The Introit, a proper chant that accompanied the procession of the clergy at the beginning of Mass, consisted of an antiphon sung before and after a psalm.[34] The text of the antiphon itself could be taken from the Psalms as well as from other biblical books.

Some chant genres seem to reflect an intention to use psalm texts in sequence according to the church year. As James McKinnon has observed, this principle appears to some extent in the introits after Pentecost and is particularly evident in the cycle of communion chants for weekdays in Lent, whose texts are taken consecutively from Psalms 1–26, while those for the Sundays after Pentecost are set to texts from Psalms 1 to 118.[35]

Beginning in the ninth century, some chants of the Mass were expanded by the addition of tropes (interpolations of text, music, or both), creating a form of commentary on the scriptural text of the preexisting chant as well as on its liturgical occasion.[36] The offertory *Diffusa est gratia* for feasts of the Virgin Mary provides an instructive example of how a biblical text employed for a Mass chant conveys an allegorical interpretation (in this case a Marian reading of a psalm) that is enhanced by the addition of tropes. Offertories have two parts, the first being an antiphon, the second consisting of one or more verses (usually scriptural). In *Diffusa est gratia*, the text of the antiphon is from Ps. 44:3: "grace is poured abroad in thy lips; therefore hath God blessed thee forever" (*Diffusa est gratia in labiis tuis:*

*propterea benedixit te deus in aeternum et in saeculum seculi.*). The verse is from Psalm 44:2: "My heart hath uttered a good word; I speak my works to the king" (*Eructavit cor meum verbum bonum. Dico ego opera mea regi*). These texts were used in many different chants for feasts of the Virgin Mary and of virgin saints. The liturgical association of Psalm 44:3 with the Virgin Mary seems to have developed already in late antiquity; it is cited in an early Christian sermon for a Marian feast,[37] and Marian chants sung to this text formed part of the seventh-century Roman liturgy.[38] Other verses of Psalm 44 were also commonly used for the liturgical commemoration of Mary and of virgin saints.[39] Until the twelfth century, however, exegesis on Psalm 44 tended to emphasize a Christological reading of the psalm as celebrating the nuptials of Christ and the Church. Liturgical performance of verses from Psalm 44 on feasts of the Virgin gave the text a Marian connotation. In the tenth and eleventh centuries, newly composed trope texts that were transmitted with the offertory *Diffusa est gratia* enriched its symbolism with references to Mary's intact virginity and to her beauty "above the sons of men," echoing the first phrase of Psalm 44:3.[40] Thus the psalms were the foundation for the original chant text as well as for its later expansion.

Other books of the Old Testament were important sources for the responsories of the Divine Office. Many responsories have texts drawn from the same biblical book that was recited immediately before the responsory was sung.[41] For instance, on Septuagesima and Sexagesima Sundays, and throughout Lent, both the lessons and the responsories are taken from the book of Genesis.[42] In the summer, after Pentecost, the antiphons of Matins as well as the responsories were taken from the same Old Testament books that furnished the lessons.[43] Responsories composed in the eleventh and twelfth centuries sometimes reinterpreted texts from the Old Testament, even without quoting them literally. For instance, the liturgical use of Isaiah 11:1 influenced the texts of several new chants with nonscriptural texts, the best known being the responsory "Stirps Jesse" performed on feasts of the Virgin: "The stock of Jesse produced a rod, and the rod a flower, and on this flower rests the nourishing spirit. The rod is the virgin mother of God, and the flower is her son. And on this flower rests the nourishing spirit."[44] The text of the responsory offers a Christological interpretation of the root of Jesse in Isaiah 11:1 ("And a rod shall come forth from the root of Jesse, and a flower shall ascend from his root").[45] As Margot Fassler has shown, Christian commentators on Isaiah frequently conflated the flowering rod of Isaiah's prophecy with the blossoming rod of Aaron in Numbers 17. The allegorical reading that cast the rod as the Virgin Mary, and the flower it produced as Christ, became an important image in many chants sung on feasts of the Virgin Mary and during the Advent and Christmas seasons.[46] Several liturgical readings from Isaiah were also performed during Advent.[47] On these occasions, understood by Christian exegetes to signal the fulfillment of the prophecy of Isaiah, references to the text of Isaiah constituted a mode of interpretation that set forth the allegorical reading of the prophetic book through song.

In the medieval Divine Office, many biblical texts besides the Psalms were chanted to simple melodies, including canticles from the Old and New Testament. Other passages from the Old Testament, known as lesser canticles, were sung in the monastic office of Matins on Sundays and feast days in sets of three canticles that varied by occasion.[48] The office of Lauds included the *Benedictus* (Luke 1:68–79) as well as a lesser canticle from the Old Testament (a different one on every day of the week). Mary's words in the Annunciation narrative, the *Magnificat* (Luke 1:46–66), were sung at Vespers; the Song of Simeon (Luke 2:9–32), known by its incipit as the *Nunc dimittis*, was sung at Compline.

## Reciting the Bible

The readings at Mass and Matins were also chanted to a simple lection tone (a formulaic melody consisting principally of single repeated pitch), with somewhat more elaborate melodic formulas employed on major feasts.[49] The Mass in the Roman rite included a reading from the Pauline Epistles (or other biblical books) and one from the Gospels.[50] The yearly cycle of these readings was essentially in place by the eighth century.[51] On certain occasions the first reading at Mass was from the Old Testament or the Acts of the Apostles rather than from the Epistles.[52] The prophets were read on Epiphany and its octave, on all days in Lent except Sundays, on most days in Passion and Holy Weeks, and on the vigil and feast day of the Nativity of John the Baptist. The Acts of the Apostles were read to commemorate events that were described in the text, such as the stoning of Saint Stephen, the appearances of Christ to the apostles in Easter Week, the descent of the Holy Spirit on Pentecost, and the deeds of the apostles Peter and Paul.

Some Western Latin rites, such as that of Milan (which reflected ancient traditions entirely distinct from the Roman liturgy) had three readings at Mass, taken respectively from the Old Testament, the Epistles, and the Gospels.[53] At Rome itself, it is possible that a three-lesson system was employed until the seventh century, but this is not entirely clear from the extant sources.[54] During the Middle Ages, few Masses in the Roman rite had more than two scriptural lessons.[55]

The choice of Epistle at Mass reflected a continuous reading of the Bible and was therefore not always obviously relevant to the occasion. The Gospel reading at Mass, however, is often the key to the meaning of a feast or of a liturgical season, for it presents the basic theme around which the rest of the liturgy for that occasion was built.[56] The readings at Mass established typological connections between the Old and New Testaments. Lessons from Isaiah in the weeks from Advent through Epiphany presaged the coming of Christ; from Septuagesima through the Easter season, the readings presented the history of Israel as a prefiguration of salvation history.[57]

Scriptural lessons were also read during Matins. On Sundays and feast days in monasteries, Matins had twelve readings or lessons (*lectiones*) divided into groups of four, which, along with their accompanying chants, composed the subdivision known as a nocturn (for further discussion of the nocturns, see Reilly's chapter in this volume). Matins had only nine lessons on feast days in cathedrals and collegiate churches.[58] In monastic usage, the first four lessons were normally taken from the Bible, while those of the second nocturn were patristic or hagiographic in origin. The third nocturn began with the Gospel of the day's Mass, followed by a homily by a church father or pope. In practice, only the first sentence or two of the Gospel was actually read at Matins.

In the Roman rite, the scriptural lessons in the first nocturn of Matins had been organized into an annual cycle by the end of the seventh century; the earliest descriptions of it appear in two of the sets of liturgical prescriptions copied in the Frankish kingdom during the eighth century, now known collectively as the *Ordines romani*.[59] These documents outline an order of readings that became standard in the medieval Latin West. The Heptateuch was read from Septuagesima until the beginning of Holy Week,[60] when Jeremiah was read through Holy Saturday. From Easter until the Sunday after Pentecost the readings were taken from the Acts of the Apostles, the canonical Epistles, and Revelation. From the Sunday after Pentecost to the end of July, the lessons were taken from Kings and Proverbs. For the remainder of the fall and summer, the books were distributed by month. The book of Wisdom was read during August;

Job, Tobit, Judith, Esther, and Ezra during September; Maccabees in October; and in November, Ezekiel, Daniel, and the minor prophets. The seasonal pattern recommenced in Advent with readings from Isaiah. After Christmas, the Pauline Epistles furnished the readings until Septuagesima Sunday.[61] The lessons of Matins offered readers and listeners multiple approaches to the Bible in the form of scriptural readings in the first nocturn and exegesis in the second and third. Besides the longer scriptural readings of Matins, all the other offices of the liturgical day included the recitation of a short passage known as a *capitulum* (chapter). These texts were usually (although not always) taken from the Bible.[62]

## Representing the Bible

In addition to the liturgical chants and readings, the commemoration of biblical events was heightened by the performance of representational rituals (for more examples of performance of the Bible, see Cochelin's chapter in this volume). Although these ceremonies draw upon the liturgy and are often referred to as liturgical dramas, their liturgical functions and theatrical aspects remain a matter of debate.[63] They juxtapose diverse elements in a creative and thought-provoking manner, creating a new version of biblical events through an active process of interpretation that can be characterized as "performative exegesis." I have used this term elsewhere to describe a twelfth-century music drama representing the Massacre of the Holy Innocents that is profoundly shaped by exegesis on the narrative of the massacre in Matthew 2.[64] Themes of particular importance in the commentary tradition include the identification of the Innocents as the first martyrs (presaging the martyred souls who call out for vengeance in Revelation 4) and the eschatological interpretation of the Innocents as the 144,000 souls in Revelation 14 (adoring the Lamb of God at the end of time). However, the principal focus of commentary on Matthew 2 was the role of Rachel's lament there, which Matthew borrowed from Jeremiah 31:15 to illustrate the mourning of the mothers at Jerusalem. Exegetes linked Rachel's historical meaning as the wife of Jacob in Genesis 29 to her allegorical dimension as a figure of the Church (in opposition to Leah, Jacob's first wife, who was understood as the Synagogue). Commentators in the twelfth century showed heightened interest in the tropological or moral interpretation of Rachel's mourning. The music drama, identified in the manuscript as the *Ordo ad interfectio-*

*nem puerorum* (which can be translated approximately as "Service for the killing of the children"), incorporates all the themes of the commentary tradition as well as chants from the feast of the Innocents, the season of Advent, and the liturgy of Good Friday. The references to Advent evoke the Christological interpretations of the Innocents. These typologies literally would have come alive as boys sang words from the book of Revelation, identifying the Innocents with the 144,000 blessed, and the mourning Rachel sang an antiphon connecting her lament to that of Mary on Good Friday.[65] In performance, the *Ordo ad interfectionem puerorum* enacts and expands upon the exegetical tradition associated with the biblical narrative of the massacre.

Starting in the tenth century, nonscriptural musical dialogues enacting the visit of the three Maries to the sepulchre were performed within the Mass or Office in many churches on Easter Sunday.[66] These performances range from a brief dialogue between the women and the angel at the empty tomb, beginning with the question *Quem queritis?* ("Whom do you seek?") to lengthy multipart compositions.[67] Much has been written on the question of whether such dialogues are ritual, drama, or both; however one defines them, they bring the events of Easter into the ritual time of the present by representing the Gospel narrative in song.[68]

In the twelfth and thirteenth centuries the new genre of the Passion play emerged. Some early examples that essentially embellish the Passion narratives in the Gospels seem to have been associated with the services of Holy Week.[69] The so-called Benediktbeuern Passion Play, preserved in the thirteenth-century manuscript that also contains the corpus of Latin and Middle High German poetry known collectively as the *Carmina Burana* (or "songs of Beuron," after the Benedictine monastery in whose library the manuscript was discovered), begins with a Lenten responsory describing the entrance of Pontius Pilate and continues with dialogue based on the Gospel of Luke, followed by a series of chants for the procession on Palm Sunday.[70] Most of the remainder of the text is in newly composed Latin rhymed verse, with some vernacular speeches by Mary Magdalen, occasionally interrupted by brief passages from the Gospel narratives of the Passion and by chants with scriptural texts.

While most medieval liturgical dramas are based on the New Testament, some portray events from the Hebrew Bible, the most remarkable being the Play of Daniel (*Ludus Danielis*), which survives only in a manuscript copied at Beauvais in the early thirteenth century.[71] This remarkable work is surely the most colorful representation of a Bible story in medieval drama: its numerous characters sing in what were at that time modern styles of Latin song set to the rhymed rhythmic poetry of the period. The action takes place in exotic settings, such as the den of lions where Daniel is consigned to his fate until his rescue by Habakkuk. Margot Fassler has interpreted the play as a reformed version of a clerical festivity celebrated by the subdeacons on the Feast of Fools, representing Daniel as a role model for the subdeacons. The play is thus a performance both of Old Testament narrative and of clerical identity.[72]

Another liturgical drama based on the Old Testament is the twelfth-century Play of Adam, which depicts the Fall, the story of Cain and Abel, and a procession of prophets.[73] As Margot Fassler has shown, this work combines different levels of time in a richly symbolic juxtaposition of Old Testament, New Testament, and the liturgy. The combination of diverse liturgical sources in the play creates what she calls a "nonlinear sense of time, an 'all time,' wherein the beginning, the middle, and the end of human history can be viewed at once."[74] Two different periods in the church year are represented. In the first part of the play the choir sings responsories from Matins of Septuagesima and Sexagesima Sundays with texts from Genesis, articulating the episodes in the play depicting the story of the Fall and of Cain and Abel.[75] The Latin texts of the sung responsories frame the Anglo-Norman vernacular spoken by the characters. In the second part, the action shifts to the Old Testament prophets, whose prophecies in Latin are followed by vernacular glosses on them. The Latin prophecies are taken from a fifth-century sermon that was the source for the *ordo prophetarum*, a procession of prophets performed during the Christmas season.[76] Thus the Play of Adam fits into a broader tradition of performing prophetic texts. At the end of the play (which is incomplete), Isaiah engages in a debate on Christian doctrine with a character identified only as a Jew (*Judeus*), followed by a speech of King Nebuchadnezzar based on Daniel 3:24–25. By vividly recontextualizing events and characters through liturgical and scriptural texts in combination with newly composed dialogue, the Play of Adam brings the biblical narrative into the present.

In the Middle Ages, the words of the Bible were most often experienced through the chants and readings of the liturgy. Just as the written Bible was frequently accompanied by glosses and commentary, likewise the performance of Scripture was a form of interpretation: biblical texts were fragmented, altered, and combined with other texts in ways that reflected traditions of biblical hermeneutics. The ensuing juxtapositions in turn provoked new interpretations. The liturgy shaped the understanding of scriptural exegesis because it rendered audible, in real time, the relationships between the different parts of the Bible; even those few who used the Bible as a written book frequently heard and uttered its words in the context of worship services. Thus liturgical performance was the single most important factor influencing the reception of the Bible in the Middle Ages.

## Notes

1. For a brief general introduction to the history of the medieval Latin liturgy, see Michael S. Driscoll, "The Conversion of the Nations" and Timothy Thibodeau, "Western Christendom," in *The Oxford History of Christian Worship*, ed. Geoffrey Wainwright and Karen B. Westerfield Tucker (Oxford: Oxford University Press, 2006), pp. 175–215 and 216–53, respectively. Introductory essays on various aspects of the liturgy can be found in *The Liturgy of the Medieval Church*, ed. Thomas Heffernan and E. Ann Matter (Kalamazoo, MI: Medieval Institute, 2001).

2. *Liber officialis* 3.1, in Amalarius of Metz, *Amalarii episcopi opera liturgica omnia*, ed. Jean-Michel Hanssens, vol. 3, Studi e testi 140 (Vatican City: Biblioteca Apostolica Vaticana, 1950), pp. 265–69.

3. Guillaume Durand, *Guillelmi Duranti Rationale divinorum officiorum*, 5.6–9, ed. Anselme Davril and Timothy M. Thibodeau, CCCM 140A (Turnhout: Brepols, 1997), pp. 12–14 and 51–119. For the most recent study of Durand, see the introduction by Timothy M. Thibodeau to *The Rationale Divinorum Officiorum of William Durand of Mende: A New Translation of the Prologue and Book One*, trans. Timothy M. Thibodeau (New York: Columbia University Press, 2007), pp. xvii–xxv.

4. See Susan Boynton, "Work and Play in Sacred Music and Its Social Context, ca. 1050–1250," in *The Use and Abuse of Time in Christian History*, ed. Robert N. Swanson (Woodbridge: Blackwell, 2002), pp. 57–79, at 59–61.

5. For a basic introduction to the medieval church calendar, see John Harper, *The Forms and Orders of Western Liturgy from the Tenth to the Eighteenth Century: A Historical Introduction and Guide for Students and Musicians* (Oxford: Clarendon, 1991), pp. 45–57.

6. See Thomas J. Talley, *The Origins of the Liturgical Year*, 2d ed. (Collegeville, MN: Liturgical, 1991).

7. Margot Fassler, "Sermons, Sacramentaries, and Early Sources for the Office in the Latin West: The Example of Advent," in *The Divine Office in the Latin Middle Ages*, ed. Margot Fassler and Rebecca Baltzer (New York: Oxford University Press, 2000), pp. 5–47.

8. See Susan K. Roll, *Toward the Origins of Christmas* (Kampen: Kok Pharos, 1995).

9. For a case study, see Craig Wright, "The Palm Sunday Procession in Medieval Chartres," in *The Divine Office*, pp. 344–71.

10. Rachel Fulton, "'Quae est ista quae ascendit sicut aurora consurgens?' The Song of Songs as the *Historia* for the Office of the Assumption," *Mediaeval Studies* 60 (1998): 55–122.

11. On the readings of mass and office, see Aimé-Georges Martimort, *Les lectures liturgiques et leurs livres* (Turnhout: Brepols, 1992).

12. On the role of the Psalms in early monasticism, see James McKinnon, "The Book of Psalms, Monasticism, and the Western Liturgy," in *The Place of the Psalms in the Intellectual Culture of the Middle Ages*, ed. Nancy van Deusen (Albany: State University of New York Press, 1999), pp. 43–58.

13. See James McKinnon, "Desert Monasticism and the Later Fourth-Century Psalmodic Movement," *Music & Letters* 75 (1994): 505–21.

14. See Joseph Dyer, "The Desert, the City and Psalmody in the Late Fourth Century," in *Western Plainchant in the First Millennium: Studies in the Medieval Liturgy and its Music*, ed. Sean Gallagher et al. (Aldershot: Ashgate, 2003), pp. 11–43; Robert F. Taft, "Christian Liturgical Psalmody: Origins, Development, Decomposition, Collapse," in *Psalms in Community: Jewish and Christian Textual, Liturgical, and Artistic Traditions*, ed. Harold W. Attridge and Margot E. Fassler (Atlanta: Society of Biblical Literature, 2003), pp. 7–32. Many useful primary sources that show the importance of the Psalms in the fourth and fifth centuries are excerpted and translated in James McKinnon, *Music in Early Christian Literature* (Cambridge: Cambridge University Press, 1987).

15. Joseph Dyer, "The Psalms in Monastic Prayer," in *The Place of the Psalms*, pp. 59–90, at 75–76. For a case study of newly composed antiphons framing psalms, see Margot E. Fassler, "Hildegard and the Dawn Song of Lauds: An Introduction to Benedictine Psalmody," in *Psalms in Community*, pp. 215–39.

16. See Joseph Dyer, "Monastic Psalmody of the Middle Ages," *Revue bénédictine* 99 (1989): 41–74; and "The Singing of Psalms in the Early-Medieval Office," *Speculum* 64 (1989): 535–78.

17. See Robert Taft, *The Liturgy of the Hours in East and West: The Origin of the Divine Office and Its Meaning for Today* (Collegeville, MN: Liturgical, 1986; repr. 1993), pp. 134–40; Nathan Mitchell, "The Liturgical Code in the Rule of Benedict," in *RB 1980: The Rule of St. Benedict in Latin and English with Notes*, ed. Timothy Fry (Collegeville, MN: Liturgical, 1981), pp. 379–414, on chapters 9–18 of the rule (see *RB 1980*, pp. 202–15).

18. The responsories of Matins and Vespers are known as "great" or "prolix" responsories because of their length. Other hours of the Divine Office include the shorter and simpler genre called the brief responsory.

19. The Compline service in cathedral and collegiate churches included the Song of Simeon (*Nunc dimittis*, Luke 2:29–32) chanted in the manner of antiphonal psalmody, preceded and followed by an antiphon.

20. *Regula Benedicti* 43; *RB 1980*, pp. 242–43.

21. *Regula Benedicti* 16; *RB 1980*, pp. 210–11.

22. *Regula Benedicti* 19.3; *RB 1980*, pp. 216–17.

23. John Basil Lowder Tolhurst, *Introduction to the English Monastic Breviaries*, repr. ed. (Woodbridge: Boydell, 1993), p. 68, originally published in *The Monastic Breviary of Hyde Abbey, Winchester*, vol. 6 (London: Henry Bradshaw Society, 1942); see also Michael S. Driscoll, "The Seven Penitential Psalms: Their Designation and Usages from the Middle Ages Onwards," *Ecclesia orans* 17 (2000): 152–201.

24. Tolhurst, *Introduction,* p. 82.

25. Ibid., p. 72.

26. For the most recent discussion of Cluny and its liturgical influence, see Susan Boynton, *Shaping a Monastic Identity: Liturgy and History at the Imperial Abbey of Farfa, 1000–1125* (Ithaca: Cornell University Press, 2006), pp. 106–9, 112–15.

27. Susan Boynton, "Prayer as Performance in Eleventh- and Twelfth-Century Monastic Psalters," *Speculum* 82 (2007): 895–931.

28. Although scholars believed until fairly recently that the Roman Psalter was Jerome's revision of the Vetus Latina tradition (intended to make the Latin text correspond more closely to the Greek Septuagint translation), this attribution is now in doubt.

29. For a detailed discussion of this subject, see Joseph Dyer, "Latin Psalters, Old Roman and Gregorian Chants," *Kirchenmusikalisches Jahrbuch* 68 (1986): 11–30.

30. For an exemplary analysis of exegesis in the Easter introit, see William Flynn, *Medieval Music as Medieval Exegesis*, Studies in Liturgical Musicology 8 (Lanham, MD: Scarecrow, 1999), pp. 210–12.

31. While scriptural texts form the basis of many Mass propers, the *Sanctus* is the only one of the Ordinary chants of the Mass with a text based on the Bible (Isa. 6:3, Matt. 21:8, and Ps. 117:26). The chants of the Ordinary are the *Kyrie, Gloria, Agnus Dei*, and *Ite Missa Est*.

32. See Michel Huglo, "Le répons-graduel de la Messe: Évolution de la forme, permanence de la fonction," *Schweizerisches Jahrbuch für Musikwissenschaft,* n.f. 2 (1982): 53–77; James McKinnon, "The Fourth-Century Origin of the Gradual," *Early Music History* 7 (1987): 91–106.

33. See James McKinnon, *The Advent Project: The Later-Seventh-Century Creation of the Roman Mass Proper* (Berkeley: University of California Press, 2000), pp. 45–59; and "Liturgical Psalmody in the Sermons of St. Augustine: An Introduction," in *The Study of Medieval Chant: Paths and Bridges, East and West, in Honor of Kenneth Levy,* ed. Peter Jeffery (Woodbridge: Boydell, 2001), pp. 7–24.

34. On the early history of the Introit and its texts, see most recently McKinnon, *The Advent Project,* pp. 195–221.

35. Ibid., pp. 212–15, 326–55.

36. On the relationship between tropes and liturgical commentary, see Margot Fassler, "The Meaning of Entrance: Liturgical Commentaries and the Introit Tropes," in *Reflections on the Sacred: A Musicological Perspective*, ed. Paul Brain-

ard (New Haven: Yale Institute of Sacred Music, Worship, and the Arts, 1994), pp. 8–18.

37. Margot Fassler, "The First Marian Feast in Constantinople and Jerusalem: Chant Texts, Readings, and Homiletic Literature," in *The Study of Medieval Chant*, p. 63, notes that Chrysippus of Jerusalem (399–479) refers to Ps. 44:3 in a sermon for a feast of Mary celebrated on August 15 in Jerusalem.

38. See McKinnon, *The Advent Project*, pp. 182–87.

39. See Fassler, "The First Marian Feast"; Claire Maître, "Du culte marial à la célébration des vierges: À propos de la psalmodie de matines," in *Marie: Le culte de la vierge dans la société médiévale*, ed. Dominique Iogna-Prat, Éric Palazzo, and Daniel Russo (Paris: Beauchesne, 1996), pp. 44–65.

40. See the tropes on the offertory *Diffusa est gratia* in *The Feasts of the Blessed Virgin Mary*, ed. Ann-Katrin Johannson (Stockholm: Almqvist and Wiksell, 1998), pp. 149–53.

41. On Matins responsories, see David Hiley, *Western Plainchant: A Handbook* (Oxford: Oxford University Press, 1993), pp. 69–76. See also Bradford C. Maiani, "Readings and Responsories: The Eighth-Century Night Office Lectionary and the *Responsoria prolixa*," *Journal of Musicology* 16 (1998): 254–82.

42. Various configurations of the responsories from Septuagesima Sunday through the end of Lent can be seen in the manuscripts published synoptically by Réné-Jean Hesbert in *Corpus antiphonalium officii*, 6 vols. (Rome: Herder, 1963–79), 1:128–55 and 2:220–83 (hereafter *CAO*).

43. For examples, see *CAO* 1:382–93, 2:726–43.

44. *Stirps Iesse virgam produxit, virgaque florem, et super hunc florem requiescit Spiritus almus. Virga dei genitrix virgo est, flos filius eius. Et super hunc florem requiescit Spiritus almus.*

45. *Et egredietur uirga de radice Iesse et flos de radice eius ascendet et requiescit super eum spiritus domini.*

46. Margot Fassler, "Mary's Nativity, Fulbert of Chartres, and the *Stirps Jesse*: Liturgical Innovation circa 1000 and Its Afterlife," *Speculum* 75 (2000): 389–434.

47. For a summary of readings from Isaiah during Advent, see Flynn, *Medieval Music*, p. 111.

48. See Tolhurst, *Introduction*, 182–84; and Michael Korhammer, *Die monastischen Cantica im Mittelalter und ihre altenglischen Interlinearversionen* (Munich: Fink, 1976).

49. Examples of some tones can be found in Hiley, *Western Plainchant*, pp. 55–68.

50. For a detailed analysis of the mass readings in all the Latin liturgies, see Henri Leclercq, "Épîtres," and "Évangiles," in *Dictionnaire d'archéologie chrétienne et de liturgie*, vol. 5 (Paris: Letouzey and Ané, 1922), cols. 244–344 and 852–923, respectively.

51. For the structure of the early Roman mass lectionary, see Antoine Chavasse, *Les lectionnaires romains de la messe au VII et au VIII siècle: Sources et dérivés, 1–2* (Fri-

bourg: Éditions universitaires, 1993); Theodor Klauser, *Das Römische Capitulare evangeliorum* (Münster: Aschendorff, 1935).

52. During the four annual penitential periods known as Ember Days, the first reading at Mass was taken from one of the Old Testament books. On Ember Saturday in Lent, there were six of these readings before the Gospel. Although the rubrics in early sources identify this day as "sabbato in XII lectionibus," implying that there are twelve readings, they refer to the early practice of reading the lessons before the Gospel in both Latin and Greek.

53. On the Milanese lectionary, see most recently Patrizia Carmassi, *Libri liturgici e istituzioni ecclesiastiche a Milano in età medioevale: Studio sulla formazione del lezionario ambrosiano* (Münster: Aschendorff, 2001).

54. For a general introduction to lectionaries, see Cyrille Vogel, *Medieval Liturgy: An Introduction to the Sources*, ed. and trans. William G. Storey and Niels Krogh Rasmussen (Washington, DC: Pastoral, 1986), pp. 314–55.

55. The masses of Christmas and the Tuesday, Wednesday, and Friday of Holy Week had three lessons, as do Ember Wednesdays. See Aimé-Georges Martimort, "À propos du nombre des lectures à la messe," *Revue des sciences religieuses* 58 (1984): 42–51.

56. Fassler, "Sermons, Sacramentaries," p. 27.

57. Flynn, *Medieval Music*, pp. 110–13.

58. On the lessons of Matins, see Martimort, *Les lectures liturgiques*, pp. 71–102.

59. For the texts with introductions and commentary, see *Ordo romanus* 13A and 14 in *Les Ordines romani du haut moyen âge*, ed. Michel Andrieu, 5 vols. (Louvain: Spicilegium Sacrum Lovaniense Bureaux, 1931–61), 2:469–526 and 3:3–41.

60. The Heptateuch comprises the first seven books of the Hebrew Bible: Genesis, Exodus, Leviticus, Numbers, Deuteronomy, Joshua, and Judges.

61. A recent discussion of the scriptural lessons of Matins in monasteries during the central Middle Ages is Diane Reilly, "The Cluniac Giant Bible and the *Ordo librorum ad legendum*: A Reassessment of Monastic Bible Reading and Cluniac Customary Instructions," in *From Dead of Night to End of Day: The Medieval Cluniac Customs*, ed. Susan Boynton and Isabelle Cochelin (Turnhout: Brepols, 2005), pp. 163–89.

62. For editions of capitula, see Jean-Loup Lemaître, *Mourir à Saint-Martial: La commémoration des morts et les obituaires à Saint-Martial de Limoges du XIe au XIIIe siècle* (Paris: De Boccard, 1989), pp. 264–83; G. G. Meersseman, *Les capitules du diurnal de Saint-Denis (Cod. Verona Cap. LXXXVIII, saec. IX)*, Spicilegium Friburgense 30 (Fribourg: Éditions universitaires, 1986).

63. Nils Holger Petersen, "Liturgical Drama: New Approaches," in *Bilan et perspectives des études médiévales (1993–1998)*, ed. Jacqueline Hamesse, Textes et Etudes du Moyen Âge 22 (Turnhout: Brepols, 2004), pp. 625–44.

64. Susan Boynton, "Performative Exegesis in the Fleury *Interfectio puerorum*," *Viator: Medieval and Renaissance Studies* 29 (1998): 39–64.

65. Susan Boynton, "From the Lament of Rachel to the Lament of Mary: A Transformation in the History of Drama and Spirituality," in *Signs of Change: Transformations of Christian Traditions and Their Representation in the Arts, 1000–2000*, ed. Nicholas Bell, Claus Clüver, and Nils Holger Petersen (Amsterdam: Rodopi, 2004), pp. 319–40.

66. Clifford Flanigan, "The Liturgical Context of the *Quem queritis* Trope," *Comparative Drama* 8 (1974): 45–62; Timothy McGee, "The Liturgical Placements of the *Quem queritis* Dialogue," *Journal of the American Musicological Society* 29 (1976): 1–29.

67. Many of the texts are edited in *Lateinische Osterfeiern und Osterspiele*, ed. Walther Lipphardt, 9 vols. (New York: De Gruyter, 1975–90).

68. Clifford Flanigan, "Medieval Liturgy and the Arts: *Visitatio sepulchri* as Paradigm," in *Liturgy and the Arts in the Middle Ages: Studies in Honour of C. Clifford Flanigan*, ed. Eva Louise Lillie and Nils Holger Petersen (Copenhagen: Museum Tusculanum Press, 1996), pp. 9–35; Nils Holger Petersen, "The Representational Liturgy of the *Regularis concordia*," in *The White Mantle of Churches: Architecture, Liturgy, and Art Around the Millenium*, ed. Nigel Hiscock (Turnhout: Brepols, 2003), pp. 107–17.

69. What appears to be the earliest Passion play, preserved in a twelfth-century manuscript at the abbey of Monte Cassino, has no evident liturgical function. See Mario Inguanez, "Un dramma della Passione del secolo XII," *Miscellanea cassinese* 18 (1939): 7–55.

70. Munich, Bayerische Staatsbibliothek, clm 4660, fols. 107r–111r (greater Passion play), clm 4660a, fols. 3v–4v (*Ludus breuiter*). Text and translation in David Bevington, *Medieval Drama* (Boston: Houghton Mifflin, 1975), pp. 202–23. This manuscript contains plays representing the Resurrection and Christ's appearance to the apostles at Emmaeus (fols. 5r–7v).

71. London, BL Egerton MS 2615, fols. 95r–108r. For a transcription of the music with a facsimile of the manuscript, see *The Play of Daniel: Critical Essays*, ed. Dunbar Ogden (Kalamazoo, MI: Medieval Institute, 1996). The text is translated in Bevington, *Medieval Drama*, pp. 137–54.

72. Margot Fassler, "The Feast of Fools and *Danielis Ludus*: Popular Tradition in a Medieval Cathedral Play," in *Plainsong in the Age of Polyphony*, ed. Thomas Forrest Kelly (Cambridge: Cambridge University Press, 1992), pp. 65–99.

73. *Le Jeu d'Adam (Ordo representacionis Ade)*, ed. Willem Noomen (Paris: Champion, 1971); for an English translation see Bevington, *Medieval Drama*, pp. 81–121.

74. Margot Fassler, "Representations of Time in *Ordo representacionis Ade*," *Contexts: Style and Values in Medieval Art and Literature, Yale French Studies* special issue (1991): 97–113, 100.

75. The incipits of the responsories are *In principio creavit Deus* (Gen. 1:1, 27), *Formavit igitur Dominus* (Gen. 2:7), *Dixit Dominus ad Adam* (Gen. 2:17), *In sudore vultus tui* (Gen. 3:19,17), *Ecce Adam quasi unus* (Gen. 3:22), and *Ubi est Abel frater tuus* (Gen. 4:9–10) The full texts are edited by Hesbert, in *CAO*, 4:233, 186, 119–20, 235, 147, and 443.

76. See M. F. Vaughan, "The Prophets of the Anglo-Norman 'Adam,'" *Traditio* 39 (1983): 81–114. The Christmas play in the *Carmina Burana* manuscript (Munich, Bayerische Staatsbibliothek, clm 4660, fols. 107r–111r) also begins with a procession of prophets proclaiming their prophecies in rhymed Latin verse (text and English translation in Bevington, *Medieval Drama*, pp. 178–201).

# Early Medieval Bibles, Biblical Books, and the Monastic Liturgy in the Beneventan Region

*Richard Gyug*

One of the conceptual difficulties in considering early medieval Bibles is the tendency to confuse Bible and book, that is, the tendency to think of the Bible as something like the canonical one-volume Bible kindly provided by the Gideons in hotel night tables. While such expectations may have been reasonable from at least the thirteenth century when the one-volume "Paris" Bible became standard, this was not the case for the early Middle Ages, from which only a handful of one-volume Bibles (also known as pandects) survive. It is true that the first great Greek Bibles are pandects, the scriptorium at Wearmouth-Jarrow produced pandects such as the Codex Amiatinus in the seventh century, Alcuin's Carolingian Bibles were copied in single volumes, and the great deluxe Bibles of the eleventh and twelfth centuries were often written as individual or paired volumes, yet these are only a tiny fraction of the biblical books copied at the time.[1] Even if the concept of a fixed scriptural canon existed, biblical texts were much more likely to survive in copies of individual books or in small collections of biblical books, especially the Octateuch, Psalms, the books of Solomon, Prophets, the four Gospels, Epistles, and Acts with the Apocalypse.[2] When complete Bibles were copied, they may have been prepared in nine-volume sets like those described by Cassiodorus in the *Institutiones* or presented in the famous Ezra illustration of the Codex Amiatinus, in which an armarium (book cabinet) behind the author's portrait holds nine bound biblical codices stored flat on the shelves.[3]

The reasons for the arrangement and division of the biblical corpus into parts must be sought in the ways in which biblical books were read and used. In the early medieval West, most manuscripts were written in monastic scriptoria. It follows that most were intended for monastic uses, whether the devotional reading required by monastic rules or the celebration of the liturgy; biblical texts played a large part in both. Copies of early medieval biblical books are likely, therefore, to have been directed toward liturgical ends and are more fruitfully understood in such terms instead of as imperfect or proto-Bibles. Indeed, a closer look at the monastic manuscripts of one region, the Beneventan zone of southern Italy and Dalmatia (in which most manuscripts in the Beneventan script can be closely identified with monastic scriptoria and monastic practice), confirms that early medieval biblical books were produced in many forms, from excerpted passages in liturgical order to sequential biblical books that demonstrate liturgical use in their format or order. Most of these books were intended for use in the liturgy.

It is reasonable to expect that early medieval Bibles were ordered liturgically, and the manuscripts of the Beneventan region confirm the point.[4] The Beneventan script is a calligraphic book hand used in southern Italy and Dalmatia between the eighth and sixteenth centuries, although most items in the script come from the eleventh and twelfth centuries. Beneventan was a regional script with roots in the letter forms of early medieval scripts. When other regional scripts were supplanted in the Carolingian realms by the spread of reformed Caroline script in the eighth and ninth centuries, Beneventan continued to be used in southern Italy and Dalmatia. Only with the establishment of new religious orders such as the Mendicants and the spread of later Caroline and Gothic scripts did the monastic scriptoria of southern Italy and Dalmatia stop using Beneventan, although a few centers continued to do so for centuries.

## Liturgical Manuscripts in Beneventan Script

The Beneventan corpus has been well defined and intensively studied. E. A. Lowe[Loew]'s *The Beneventan Script*, published in 1914, constitutes a model study of a regional script. Lowe laid out the script's features and development and provided a handlist of the approximately six hundred known manuscripts written in this script. After the discovery of many additional items, *The Beneventan Script* was republished in 1980 in an edition revised by the late Virginia Brown. Thereafter, Brown regularly published new lists as further examples of the Beneventan script came to light—the corpus now consists of about two thousand manuscripts and fragments.[5] When Lowe wrote *The Beneventan Script*, palaeographers were particularly concerned with the establishment of classical texts, which are well represented in the Beneventan corpus by unique manuscripts of Varro's *De lingua latina*, Apuleius's *Metamorphoses*, and parts of the *Historiae* and *Annales* of Tacitus and the *Satires* of Juvenal, as well as significant witnesses to Seneca's *Dialogues* and works of Ovid and Cicero. Lowe recognized, however, that in its origins and use the Beneventan script was monastic. It is not surprising, therefore, that among the surviving works in Beneventan script, the majority (about 80 percent) are now known to be liturgical in function. The script's complex letter forms, graceful appearance, usually generous dimensions, and extreme regularity—even if it seems illegible to those unfamiliar with it—as well as the abundance of performance indications and elaborate punctuation reinforce the conclusion that Beneventan was intended for liturgical performance. For the celebration of the Mass, there survive over a hundred missals or fragments of missals, eight sacramentaries, thirty graduals, and nineteen evangelistaries, two gospel capitularies, one epistolary, and a combined Mass lectionary. For the Office, there are over fifty antiphonaries, twenty-four Psalters, almost twenty hymnaries, fifteen collectars or orationales, fifty breviaries or mixed Office books, chapter books, ordinals, and over a hundred collections of homilies or sermons. In addition, there are processionals, calendars, and twenty collections of ordines, including rituals and pontificals. Because Lowe was not primarily concerned with identifying liturgical texts specifically, there are also fifty-five items in his handlist labeled simply "liturgica."[6] Of particular concern here are the approximately two hundred Beneventan manuscripts and fragments containing biblical books, even excluding the Psalters, evangelistaries, and epistolaries. None of the biblical books is a complete Bible, and, as we shall see, many show signs of liturgical use.[7]

Several of the liturgical genres listed in the preceding paragraph are fundamentally biblical. In addition to the short biblical excerpts in graduals (proper chants of the Mass), extended scriptural passages were read during Mass as epistles or gospels. In practice, books of Epistles in canonical order or the four Gospels would have been difficult to use for the

Mass since the readings do not follow a canonical sequence; it was essential to have collections of readings arranged liturgically or guides and references to where a feast's readings could be found among the Epistles or Gospels. In the Latin West, the result was several general systems for providing Mass readings. One system was to list capitula, or chapter cues, which identified the order and location of epistle and gospel readings and with which readers could find the passages to be read in complete copies of Epistles or Gospels.[8] The same manuscripts often contain marginal indications of where readings begin and/or end, although similar marginal notes are found in many Epistle or Gospel books without guiding capitula. Some liturgist-scribes solved the practical problem of providing readings for the Mass by collecting the readings and arranging them in liturgical order, whether as epistolaries containing the excerpts from the Pauline and Catholic Epistles and Acts read during the Mass and arranged in the order of annual feasts, evangelistaries containing gospel pericopes, or, in some instances, Mass lectionaries containing both epistle and gospel readings.[9] Finally, missals include the epistles and gospel readings in a liturgical order along with the other proper parts for each feast. Although capitula begin to appear before epistolaries or evangelistaries, and missals were developed later, the systems were all used concurrently through much of the medieval period, as Theodor Klauser's study of reading systems shows (see table 3.1). This is especially the case with Gospel books, since deluxe volumes of Gospels were not easily replaced and are frequently marked with marginalia.

TABLE 3.1    Distribution of Systems of Mass Readings in Latin Manuscripts

| dates | marginal references | capitula for gospel readings | capitula for epistle readings | epistolaries/ evangelistaries |
|---|---|---|---|---|
| 700–99 | 2 | 2 | 1 | 1 |
| 800–99 | 2 | 140 | 1 | 14 |
| 900–99 | 2 | 96 | 1 | 30 |
| 1000–99 | 2 | 101 | 1 | 72 |
| 1100–99 | 2 | 63 | 1 | 91 |
| 1200–99 | 1 | 13 | 83 | 65 |
| 1300–99 | 1 | 6 | 53 | 45 |

From Theodor Klauser, *Das römische Capitulare evangeliorum* (Münster: Aschendorff, 1935).

The Beneventan corpus contains examples from each category, and a predominance of the mixed liturgical book (missals) not counted by Klauser (see table 3.2).

Although books of Epistles outnumber epistolaries, it is evident from the list in table 3.2 that Beneventan Gospels and Epistles were more frequently copied in excerpted, liturgical forms—evangelistaries or missals—than in whole Gospels or Epistles. Missals are the largest single category and the most evidently adapted to liturgical use. Evangelistaries are also well represented in the corpus.[10] There are fewer collections of the Gospels, but one of the four surviving manuscripts includes a list of Gospel capitula, which would have allowed it to be used in the liturgy.[11] It is unclear why there should be so many fewer epistolaries than evangelistaries, or why books of Epistles should outnumber epistolaries, the reverse of the case with Gospel books. Only one epistolary survives, and one Mass lectionary.[12] Nonetheless, among the thirteen manuscripts containing Epistle books, eight have indications of liturgical use, including musical notation in one case.[13]

## Scriptural Readings for the Divine Office

The Office or liturgy of the hours was even more dependent on biblical texts than the liturgy of the Mass. The foundation of the hours was the singing of psalms in continual repeated series; antiphons and responses were usually excerpted from biblical readings; and the Night Office (variously designated as Vigils or Matins), the most elaborate of the hours, included extended readings from books of the Bible, especially the books of the Christian canon of the Old Testament, in addition to readings from the church fathers and the lives of the saints. In the early Middle Ages, biblical books appear to have been read in *lectio continua* in the Night Office, meaning that each day's reading began where the previous day's reading had ended, as was the case with the psalms of the Office. Thus, for continuous reading of biblical passages at Matins and the repeated reading of the Psalms in sequence, unexcerpted biblical books would have sufficed. Such was indeed the case with the Psalms in Psalters, which are usually copied as a complete set. Even books of the Psalms show overt signs of liturgical use. Of the twenty-four Psalters in Beneventan script, for instance, ten are copied along with additional material used in

TABLE 3.2 Beneventan Manuscripts of Scriptural Readings for the Mass

| Dates | capitula for Gospel readings | Gospel books | books of Epistles | evangelistaries | epistolaries | Mass lectionaries | Missals* |
|---|---|---|---|---|---|---|---|
| 800–99 | | | I | | | | |
| 900–99 | | | 2 | | | | 4 |
| 1000–99 | 2 | I | 7 | 9 | | | 24 |
| 1100–99 | | 2 | 3 | 5 | | I | 41 |
| 1200–99 | | I | | 5 | I | | 28 |
| 1300–99 | | | | | | | 3 |
| 1400–9 | | | | | | | |
| 1500–99 | | | | | | | I |

In addition, manuscripts from Benevento or from the region of the Beneventan script use marginal annotations to indicate lections. Indeed, the three earliest biblical items from the region are not in Beneventan but have annotations indicating lessons, i.e., the uncial manuscripts Fulda, Hessische Landesbibliothek, Bonifatianus 1 (Gospels, Epistles of Paul, Acts, Catholic Epistles, and Apocalypse; sixth century); London, British Library, Additional ms 5463 (Gospels; mid-eighth century); and the half-uncial manuscript Split, Riznica Katedrale, Kaptolski Arhiv, D 621 (Gospels; early eighth century). For the Fulda and BL manuscripts, see Brown, "I libri della bibbia," pp. 285–86.

* For an early instance of arranging biblical readings in a liturgical order, see the eighth-century palimpsest uncial missal in Montecassino, Archivio dell'Abbazia, 271; the manuscript is studied by Antoine Chavasse, "Les fragments palimpsestes du Casinensis 271 (Sigle Z 6). A côté de l'Hadrianum et du Paduense, un collatéral, autrement remanié," *Archiv für Liturgiewissenschaft* 25 (1983): 9–33; and Virginia Brown, "Early Evidence for the Beneventan Missal: Palimpsest Texts (saec. X/XI) in Montecassino 271," *Mediaeval Studies* 60 (1998): 239–306.

the Office, an adaptation that moves Psalters in the direction taken by missals.[14]

While whole books would have been suited to continuous reading, by the seventh century (at the latest), only select passages were read instead of reading the entire text in order (although Office readings remained closer to *lectio continua* than the dispersed readings of the Mass). Moreover, the order of the books read at Matins was adapted to the season, so that, for instance, Isaiah's prophecies were read in Advent, Genesis was read on the Sundays in Lent, and the Catholic Epistles were read after Easter.[15] To read the right passage on the right day would have required biblical books marked in some usable manner or a collection of readings arranged in liturgical order. Beneventan manuscripts show exactly such adaptations.

Performance indications, including musical notation, were one such adaptation that would have suited the liturgy better than other ends. Thus, nine Beneventan manuscripts and fragments containing books of the Christian canon of the Old Testament were written with musical notation for the Lamentations of Jeremiah, which were to be sung in Holy Week.[16] Three of these manuscripts with noted Lamentations further indicate use through marginal annotations marking the beginning or end of Matins lections.[17] An additional eighteen manuscripts without original notation have marginal annotations marking the beginning or end of lections,[18] and eight of the manuscripts with annotations or original notation have added marginal or interlinear notation.[19]

Although twenty-seven items have performance indications (whether original or added), thirteen Beneventan manuscripts containing the Christian canon of the Old Testament and many more fragments do not have liturgical annotations or musical notation.[20] Nonetheless, one of the manuscripts without liturgical annotations, Benevento, Biblioteca Capitolare, 14, contains lives of the saints in addition to biblical books,[21] which suggests that it too may have been intended for liturgical use, as was also the case with Montecassino, Archivio dell'Abbazia (hereafter Montecassino) 211, which contained the Gospels and the Rule of Benedict, and with Montecassino 534 and Montecassino 552, which have liturgical annotations and additional sermons or passions.[22]

Another telling sign may be the order and selection of biblical books in Beneventan manuscripts without other indications of liturgical use. Thus, Rome, Biblioteca Vallicelliana, D 8, which does not have liturgical annotations, contains the Octateuch, 1 Samuel through Ecclesiasticus, Isaiah through Malachi, Baruch, Job, the Gospels, the Epistles of Paul, the letter to the Laodiceans, and Acts, but omits, for instance, the Psalms, Catholic Epistles, and the Apocalypse. Similarly, Montecassino 527, which does have liturgical annotations, contains Genesis, Exodus, 1–2 Samuel, 1–2 Kings, Proverbs, Job, Tobit, Judith, Esther, 1 Maccabees, Acts, James, 1–2 Peter, 1–3 John, Jude, Apocalypse, Romans, 1 Corinthians, and Hebrews, but omits the Psalms, prophets, several sapiential books, Gospels, and several Epistles. The rationale for such selections of books may lie in the liturgical order of reading at Matins. As noted, biblical passages were read at Matins in a seasonal, not canonical, order. Table 3.3 shows the earliest directions for such readings, and the adaptation of the order in Benevento:

TABLE 3.3    Biblical Readings at Matins

| Liturgical Seasons | Readings in Ordo romanus 13A (1st half of the eighth century)* | Readings in the Breviaries of Benevento† |
|---|---|---|
| Septuagesima–Lent | Genesis, Exodus, Leviticus, Numbers, Deuteronomy, Joshua, Judges, Ruth | Genesis, Exodus |
| Passion Sunday–Easter | Jeremiah, Lamentations | Jeremiah, Lamentations |
| Easter–Pentecost | Acts, Catholic Epistles, Apocalypse | Apocalypse, Catholic Epistles, Acts |
| After Pentecost | Samuel, Kings, Chronicles | 1 Samuel |
| August | Solomon (Proverbs, Ecclesiastes, Song of Solomon, Wisdom of Solomon, Ecclesiasticus) | Solomon (Proverbs, Ecclesiastes, Song of Solomon, Wisdom of Solomon, Ecclesiasticus) |
| September | Job, Tobit, Judith, Esther, Esdras | Job, Tobit, Judith, Esther |
| October | 1–2 Maccabees | 1–2 Maccabees |

TABLE 3.3 *(continued)*

| | | |
|---|---|---|
| November | Ezechiel, Daniel, Minor Prophets | Ezechiel, Daniel, Minor Prophets |
| December– Christmas | Isaiah | Isaiah |
| Saints of Christmas Week (Stephen, John the Evangelist, Innocents) | Acts, Apocalypse | Acts, Apocalypse |
| Epiphany | Isaiah | Isaiah |
| January– Septuagesima | Epistles of Paul | Epistles of Paul |

\* Andrieu, *Les Ordines romani*, 2:479–88.
† Mallet and Thibaut, *Les manuscrits*, 3:1301–8.

In table 3.4, the order of books in the Beneventan Bibles with books in a noncanonical order is compared with the order of lections at Matins:

TABLE 3.4   Comparison of the Order of Selected Beneventan Biblical Books with the Readings of Matins

| Liturgical Season | Readings in the Brevaries of Benevento | Montecassino 527 | Montecassino 552 | Vallicelliana D8 |
|---|---|---|---|---|
| Septuagesima– Lent | Genesis, Exodus | Genesis, Exodus | | Octateuch |
| Passion Sunday– Easter | Jeremiah, Lamentations | | | |
| After Easter | Apocalypse, Catholic Epistles, Acts | | Acts, Catholic Epistles, Apocalypse | |

TABLE 3.4 *(continued)*

| Liturgical Season | Readings in the Brevaries of Benevento | Montecassino 527 | Montecassino 552 | Vallicelliana D8 |
|---|---|---|---|---|
| After Pentecost | 1 Samuel | 1–2 Samuel | | 1–2 Samuel, 1–2 Kings |
| August | Solomon (Proverbs, Ecclesiastes, Song of Solomon, Wisdom of Solomon, Ecclesiasticus) | | | Solomon (Proverbs–Ecclesiasticus) |
| September | Job, Tobit, Judith, Esther | Job, Tobit, Judith, Esther | | |
| October | 1–2 Maccabees | 1 Maccabees | | |
| November | Ezechiel, Daniel, Minor Prophets | | | Isaiah–Malachi |
| December | Isaiah | | | |
| | | | | Baruch, Job Gospels |
| Saints of Christmas Week (Stephen, John the Evangelist, Innocents) | Acts, Apocalypse | | | |
| Epiphany | Isaiah | | | |

TABLE 3.4 *(continued)*

| Liturgical Season | Readings in the Brevaries of Benevento | Montecassino 527 | Montecassino 552 | Vallicelliana D8 |
|---|---|---|---|---|
| | | Acts, James, 1–2 Peter, 1–3 John, Jude, Apocalypse | | |
| January– Septuagesima | Epistles of Paul | Romans, 1 Corinthians, Hebrews | Epistles of Paul | Epistles of Paul |
| | | Solomon (Proverbs-Ecclesiasticus) Passions | | Laodiceans, Acts |

The Beneventan books present several solutions to the problem of how to provide readings for Matins. Montecassino 527 maintains a canonical order in the sequence of books, but selects books that would have been read for Matins while omitting those not read.[23] Montecassino 552 preserves selected books suitable for Matins lections after Easter and in August, with lessons and passions also suitable for the Office.[24] Finally, Vallicelliana D 8 is a biblical volume composed in five sections, four of which match seasonal readings: the Octateuch read in Septuagesima and Lent, Kings through Ecclesiasticus for the season post Pentecost, a series of prophets suited for Lent and November, and the Epistles of Paul with Acts, suited for the weeks after Epiphany and the weeks after Easter.[25]

Liturgical ends may also explain the division and grouping of biblical codices. Montecassino 527, Montecassino 552, and Vallicelliana D 8 could have supplied readings for several seasons, but most manuscripts contain fewer books and would have been suitable for shorter periods. In table 3.5, the surviving Beneventan biblical manuscripts are arranged by the season for which they could have supplied Matins readings. Although many of the manuscripts include books that would not have been read for Matins, and there are many variants, the books fall into several general groups:

TABLE 3.5   Beneventan Manuscripts Containing Biblical Books (Not Including Gospels or Psalters)

| | |
|---|---|
| A. Octateuchs or Pentateuchs with readings from Genesis and Exodus for Septuagesima-Lent | —**Benevento 68** ( . . . Gen.-Num. . . . )<br>—**Florence, Laurenziana, San Marco 738** (Gen.-Exod. . . . )<br>—**Montecassino 520** (Gen.-Ruth)<br>—**Montecassino 531** (Gen.-Judg. . . . )<br>—**Montecassino 534** (Gen.-Exod., Sermons for LXX–XL)<br>—**Montecassino 565** (Gen.-Ruth)<br>—Montecassino 583, pp. 1-336 (Gen.-Judg.)<br>—**Montecassino 759** (Gen.-Ruth . . . )<br>—**Montecassino 760** (Gen.-Ruth)<br>—**Naples VI AA 5** (Gen.-Ruth . . . )<br>—**Naples Vindob. lat. 10**, fols. 1–222 ( . . . Gen.-Judg.)<br>—Naples Vindob. lat. 10, fols. 223–29 ( . . . Judg. . . . )<br>—Vallicelliana A 15 + s. n. (Gen.-Deut. . . . ) |
| B. Books of Prophets with readings for Passion Sunday to Holy Week and/or November-December | *(a) Holy Week (Lamentations)*<br>—**Avezzano 50/T** ( . . . Lam. . . . )<br>—Bern, Ernst Boehlen Coll., 802 (Jer. . . . )<br>—**Vallicelliana R 32** ( . . . Lam. . . . )<br>—**Vallicelliana, ex S. Borr. Q I 4** ( . . . Lam. . . . )<br>—**BAV Ross. 297** ( . . . Lam. . . . )<br>*(b) Passion Sunday to Holy Week (Jeremiah, Lamentations) and November-December (Ezechiel, Daniel, Isaiah)*<br>—**Montecassino 535**, pp. 1–286 ( . . . Isa.-Mal.)<br>—**Montecassino 536** (Isa.-Dan. . . . )<br>—**Montecassino 543** (Isa.-Mal.)<br>—**Montecassino 571** (Isa.-Mal. . . . )<br>—**Montecassino 589** (Isa.-Zech. . . . )<br>—**Vallicelliana A 17** (Isa.-Mal.)<br>—**Vat. lat. 14726** (Isa.-Zech. . . . ) |

TABLE 3.5 *(continued)*

| | |
|---|---|
| C. Readings for the weeks after Easter and/or January to Septuagesima | *(a) Weeks after Easter (Acts, Catholic Epistles, Apocalypse )*<br>—**Berlin, DS, Hamilton 3** (Acts, Catholic Epistles, Apoc.)<br>—Cava 19 (Gospels, Apoc., 1 John)<br>—**Montecassino 521, pp. 1–48, 65–104** (Acts, Catholic Epistles, Apoc.)<br>—**Vallicelliana D 36** (Acts, Catholic Epistles, Apoc.)<br>*(b) Weeks after Easter (Acts, Catholic Epistles, Apocalypse) and January to Septuagesima (Epistles of Paul)*<br>—**Montecassino 349** (Acts, Catholic Epistles, Apoc., Epistles of Paul)<br>—Montecassino, Archivio Privato, 2 (Epistles of Paul, Catholic Epistles, Acts, Apoc.)<br>*(c) January to Septuagesima (Epistles of Paul)*<br>—**Paris, BNF, lat. 335, fols. 1–136** (Rom.-Titus 2: 8)<br>—**Montecassino 535, pp. 287–391** (Epistles of Paul)<br>—Paris, BNF, lat. 335, fols. 137–55 (Titus 2: 8-Heb.)<br>—Vienna, ÖN, 903 (1 Cor.-Heb.) |
| D. Readings for the weeks after Pentecost, August and/or September and October | *(a) Weeks after Pentecost (1–2 Sam., 1–2 Kings)*<br>—Montecassino 583, pp. 337–52 (2 Sam.-1 Kings)<br>—Vat. lat. 14728 (1–2 Sam., 1–2 Kings . . . )<br>*(b) Weeks after Pentecost (1–2 Samuel, 1–2 Kings) and August (Prov.–Ecclus.)*<br>—Benevento 14 (. . . 1 Sam.–Ecclus., vitae)<br>—**Montecassino 553** (1 Sam.–Ecclus.)<br>*(c) September–October (Job, Tobit, Judith, Esther, Maccabees)*<br>—Montecassino 521, pp. 433–64, 49–64 (1–2 Macc.)<br>—**Montecassino Comp. II** (Tob.-2 Macc.) |

TABLE 3.5 *(continued)*

|  | ***(d) Weeks after Pentecost (1–2 Sam., 1–2 Kings), August (Proverbs–Ecclesiasticus), and September and October (Job, Tobit, Judith, Esther, Maccabees)*** |
|---|---|
|  | —Vat. lat. 11978 (1 Sam.-2 Macc.) |
|  | —Montecassino 521, pp. 105–432 (1 Sam.-Esther) |
|  | —Montecassino 572 (1 Sam.-2 Macc.) |
| E. Mixed books | —**Montecassino Comp. I** (2 Cor.-Heb., Isa.-Hag.): suitable for January to Septuagesima and November-December |
|  | —**Montecassino 552** (Acts, Catholic Epistles, Apoc., Epistles of Paul, Prov.–Ecclus, Lections, Passions): suitable for the weeks after Easter, January to Septuagesima and August (see table 3.4) |
|  | —**Montecassino 527** (Gen., Exod., 1–2 Sam., Prov., Job, Tob., Jth., Esther, 1 Macc., Acts, James, 1–2 Pet., 1–3 John, Jude, Apoc., Rom., 1 Cor., Heb.): suitable for Septuagesima-Lent, the weeks after Pentecost, August, September, the weeks after Easter, and January to Septuagesima (see table 3.4) |
|  | —**Naples VI AA 3** ( . . . Tob.–2 Macc., Isa.–Zech. . . . ): suitable for September–October and November–December |
|  | —Vallicelliana D 8 (Octateuch, 1 Sam.-Ecclus., Prophets, Bar., Job, Gospels, Epistles of Paul, Laod., Acts): composed in sections suitable for Septuagesima and Lent, the season post Pentecost, November-December, and January to Septuagesima (see table 3.4) |

Manuscripts with musical notation or liturgical annotations are marked in **bold**; lacunae are shown with ellipses.

Table 3.5 shows that surviving books of the Christian canon of the Old Testament fall into three general groups, each with a number of variants: (A) the books of Genesis and Exodus, with or without the remaining books of the Octateuch, would have been suitable for Matins lections from Septuagesima through Lent; (B) the books of the Prophets could have been read in the Office in the two weeks before Easter and in Advent, i.e., November and December; and (D) the manuscripts with Kings, Wisdom, Judith, Esther, and Maccabees match the readings of the summer months, the season after Pentecost. With the addition of the books (C) containing Acts, the Catholic Epistles, the Apocalypse, and the Epistles of Paul, the sacristy would have had a shelf containing all the readings needed for Matins, and they would have been arranged in volumes roughly by season. With the addition of a Psalter—a genre with many examples in Beneventan script—the liturgical requirements of the Office would have been fully supported.[26]

Although Beneventan biblical manuscripts divide roughly into liturgical order, the group with prophets would have been used in two seasons— before Easter and in Advent—as could also have been the case for manuscripts with Acts, the Catholic Epistles, the Apocalypse, and the Epistles of Paul. All the manuscripts, however, contain biblical texts that would not have been read as part of the liturgy. They are, therefore, imperfect solutions to the problem of practice, rather than final liturgical adaptations in the same way evangelistaries or missals are. The variety of biblical solutions and their imperfections may reflect the possibility of multiple uses for the biblical volumes, perhaps indicating that parts of the Bible were meant to be read in their entirety in Lent for personal devotions. The greater continuity in Matins readings as compared to Mass lections may also have encouraged copyists to respect the integrity of the books or their order and grouping, as they seem to have done in the case of the prophetic books and the collections consisting of Acts, the Catholic Epistles, the Apocalypse, and the Epistles of Paul. Copyists were trying to accommodate two competing principles, one a received biblical order that would group, for instance, prophets with prophets or the Epistles of Paul with other books of the New Testament, the other the order of the liturgical seasons.

Beneventan copyists may have been thinking in terms of liturgical organization, but they also respected the concepts of a whole Bible and a biblical order. What is noteworthy, however, is that the Beneventan whole Bible, composed of multiple volumes, may not have corresponded to the Cassiodoran whole Bible, which likewise was composed of multiple volumes:

TABLE 3.6 The Cassiodoran and Beneventan Bibles

| Cassiodorus, Institutiones, I:1–9, 26 | Beneventan Bibles |
|---|---|
| 1. Octateuch | 1. Pentateuch or Octateuch |
| 2. Kings (1–2 Sam., 1–2 Kings, 1–2 Chron.) | 2. Kings + "Salomon" or Kings + "Hagiographorum" |
| 3. Prophets | 3. Prophets |
| 4. Psalter | 4. Psalter |
| 5. "Salomon" (Prov., Eccl., Song of Sol., Wisd. of Sol., Ecclus.) | (see no. 2) |
| 6. "Hagiographorum" (Job, Tobit, Esther, Judith, 1–2 Macc., 1–2 Esdras) | (see no. 2) |
| 7. Gospels | 5. Gospels |
| 8. Epistles | 6. Epistles of Paul |
| 9. Acts, Apocalypse | 7. Acts, Catholic Epistles, Apocalypse |

The organization of biblical books into liturgical groups can be seen also in medieval inventories from the region.[27] Six lists will be considered here. The earliest is the Commemoratorium of Theobald, prior of San Liberatore alla Maiella (1007–22) and later abbot of Montecassino (1022–35). Dating to 1019, the list contains works consistent with monastic practice: eighteen liturgical books, twenty-seven patristic or monastic books, three canonical collections, and thirteen biblical items, including commentaries.[28] The next list consists of the books commissioned by Desiderius while he was abbot (1058–87), which include several biblical works.[29] As Pope Victor III, Desiderius left an additional group of liturgical-biblical works to Montecassino on his death.[30] The third list is from a Cassinese dependency, Sant'Angelo in Formis, and dates to the twelfth century.[31] A list from the monastery of Santa Maria di Tremiti, also a Cassinese dependency, dated 1174–75 with thirteenth-century additions, has eleven biblical books in addition to other liturgical and monastic works.[32] From Benevento, there are two inventories. The first is a booklist from the monastery of San Pietro *extra muros* (located outside the walls of the city), added in the thirteenth century on a folio in an eighth-century book of the four gospels written in uncial and long kept in the Beneventan region. In addition to liturgical and patristic works, it contains four biblical books.[33] While the preceding lists have reflected the contents of a working monastery or sacristy or contemporary gifts, the second Beneventan list is an inventory of the volumes held in 1447 in the Biblioteca Capitolare of Benevento and provides a retrospective look at the range of books produced in the region. Among the books that the catalogue lists as written in Beneventan script (*litera longobarda*), one finds similar proportions of liturgical works to those now surviving in the corpus as a whole, as well as a number of biblical books.[34] (The term *litera longobarda*, literally "Lombard script," refers to the fact that Benevento was a Lombard duchy in the early Middle Ages.)

Taking into consideration only those books described as biblical (i.e., not including homiliaries, collections of vitae, sacramentaries, or books of directives), the following forms appear in the book lists:

TABLE 3.7  Beneventan Biblical Books in the Medieval Inventories of the Region

| Reconstructed Beneventan Biblical Set | Theobald, a. 1019 | Desiderian books and the legacy of Victor III | S. Angelo in Formis (twelfth century) | S. Maria di Tremiti 1174–75 | S. Pietro extra muros (twelfth century) | 1447 Benevento Catalogue |
|---|---|---|---|---|---|---|
| **Mass books** | | | | | | |
| Gospels | –Gospels –evangelistary | –Gospels (7 vols.) | –Gospels (3 vols.) | –evangelistaries (5 vols.) | | –Gospels |
| Epistles of Paul | –Epistles of Paul | –Epistles of Paul –epistolaries (2 vols.) | –Epistles of Paul | –Epistles of Paul (3 vols.) –epistolary | | –Epistles of Paul (2 vols.) |
| | –Gospels and Epistles of Paul | | –missals (2 vols.) | "libri comitis" (2 vols.; Mass lectionary?) | –missals (2 vols.) | |
| **Office books** | | | | | | |
| Gen.–Exod. (Pentateuch, Octateuch) | | | –Heptateuch | –Gen. | –Octateuch | –Gen. and homilies –Pentateuch (3 vols.) |
| Kings + "Salomon" or Kings + "Hagiographorum" | –Kings | –Paralipomenon (Chron.) | –Kings –"paravole Salomonis" | –Kings (2 vols.) –"Salomon" –Song of Sol. | –Kings | |

TABLE 3.7 (continued)

| Reconstructed Beneventan Biblical Set | Theobald, a. 1019 | Desiderian books and the legacy of Victor III | S. Angelo in Formis (twelfth century) | S. Maria di Tremiti, 1174–75 | S. Pietro extra muros (twelfth century) | 1447 Benevento Catalogue |
|---|---|---|---|---|---|---|
| | | | | –Job, Tobias, Judith, Esther and Macc. | | –Job, Tobias, Judith Esther, Esdras and Macc. (3 vols.) |
| Prophets | –Prophets | | –Prophets | –Prophets (2 vols.) | –Prophets | –Prophets<br>–Isa., Zac. and Lives of the Saints |
| Acts, Apocalypse, Catholic Epistles, and Epistles of Paul | –Acts | –Acts, Catholic Epistles and Apocalypse | –Acts | –Acts, Catholic Epistles, Apocalypse and Epistles of Paul | –Apocalypse | –Acts, Apocalypse and Catholic Epistles<br>–Apocalypse, Catholic Epistles, Epistles of Paul and Kings |
| Psalters | –Psalter | –Psalter | –Psalters (20 vols.) | –Psalters (19 vols.) | –Psalters (6 vols.) | –Psalter |

Although none of the lists corresponds exactly with the reconstructed seven-book biblical set, the library lists show many similar accommodations and, notably, no complete Bibles. The contents of at least one volume in the 1447 Benevento Inventory—the manuscript including the Apocalypse, the Catholic Epistles, Epistles of Paul, and Kings (for the weeks after Easter and Pentecost)—are best understood in a liturgical order, like the contents of the liturgically ordered volumes already considered (see tables 3.4 and 3.5, especially section E).

The lack of early medieval pandects (single-volume Bibles) and the fundamentally liturgical quality of early medieval biblical books have long been noted. Among manuscripts in the Beneventan script, which are shaped to a considerable degree by monastic concerns, the effects of such liturgical orientation took several forms, all of which confirm the practical emphasis of early medieval biblical copying. There were books adapted to liturgical uses (evangelistaries and epistolaries), others employed in their entirety for the liturgy (Psalters), and a series of manuscripts containing parts of the Christian canon of the Old Testament that are adapted (through notation, annotation, or ordering) for liturgical reading. While there appears to have been an understanding of a biblical canon and a biblical order, the exigencies of use and production led to a wide range of unexpected adaptations.

## Notes

A draft of this chapter was first presented as "Beneventan Bibles and the Liturgy" at The Bible and the Liturgy, Fourth Annual Symposium on "The Transmission of the Bible," Center for Medieval Studies (Fordham University); The Scriptorium: Center for Christian Antiquities; Department of Art and Archaeology (Princeton University); Index of Christian Art (Princeton University); and the Research Group for Manuscript Evidence; New York City, April 24, 1998. A full list of Beneventan biblical manuscripts and further analysis of their contents was subsequently published by Virginia Brown, "I libri della Bibbia nell'Italia meridionale longobarda," in *Forme e modelli della tradizione manoscritta della Bibbia*, ed. Paolo Cherubini (Vatican City: Scuola Vaticana di Paleografia, Diplomatica e Archivistica, 2005), pp. 281–307. The notes that follow will show my debt to Professor Brown's research and article, which together remain fundamental to the consideration of Beneventan Bibles. Finally, I presented a revised version of the paper, as "The Liturgical Arrangement of Monastic Bibles," at the conference "Performing and Presenting the Word: Medieval Bibles in Context," Columbia University and the Museum of Biblical Art, New York City, April 27,

2007. I would like to thank the organizer of the conference, Susan Boynton, and the editors of this volume, Susan Boynton and Diane Reilly, for the invitation to present the paper at the conference and publish it in this volume. Support for my research has been provided by a Faculty Fellowship from Fordham University and research grants from the Social Sciences and Humanities Research Council of Canada for the "Monumenta Liturgica Beneventana" project.

1. For the Carolingian, Greek, and Romanesque one-volume bibles, see Christopher de Hamel, *The Book: A History of the Bible* (New York: Phaidon, 2001), pp. 36–37, 50–52, 72–77; see also the survey of early medieval bibles in Michelle P. Brown, "Spreading the Word," in *In the Beginning: Bibles Before the Year 1000*, ed. Michelle P. Brown (Philadelphia: Freer Gallery of Art, Arthur M. Sackler Gallery, 2006), pp. 45–75.

2. de Hamel, *The Book*, p. 31. See also Brown, "I libri della Bibbia," p. 283 n. 7, citing Anscari Mundó, "'Bibliotheca.' Bible et lecture du Carême d'après saint Benoît," *Revue bénédictine* 60 (1950): 65–92, at 82, for references in the Rule of Benedict to the seven biblical books used in the liturgy.

3. Cassiodorus Senator, *Institutiones*, 1:1–9, 26. de Hamel, *The Book*, p. 32, notes that Cassiodorus described three sets of biblical books for Vivarium: the nine-volume Bible, the *Codex grandior* (a whole Bible, with the Christian canon of the Old Testament in Jerome's translation from Greek, not Hebrew), and a one-volume Bible, perhaps a Vulgate. See Brown, "I libri della Bibbia," p. 283 n. 6, citing Pierre Petitmengin, "Les plus anciens manuscrits de la Bible latine," in *Le monde latin antique et la Bible*, ed. Jacques Fontaine and C. Pietri (Paris: Beauchesne, 1985), pp. 89–123, at 94, for correspondences between early Bibles and the nine-volume Bible described by Cassiodorus.

4. As noted by, for instance, de Hamel, *The Book*, pp. 29–31; Richard Marsden, "'Ask What I Am Called': the Anglo-Saxons and Their Bibles," in *The Bible as Book: The Manuscript Tradition*, ed. John L. Sharpe III and Kimberly van Kampen (London: British Library, Oak Knoll, 1998), pp. 145–76, at 155–56.

5. E. A. Lowe [Loew], *The Beneventan Script. A History of the South Italian Minuscule*, ed. Virginia Brown, 2 vols., 2d ed. (Rome: Storia e Letteratura, 1980 [1914]). New items that were identified and discussed in E. A. Lowe, "A New List of Beneventan Manuscripts," in *Collectanea vaticana in honorem Anselmi M. Card. Albareda a Bibliotheca Apostolica edita* (Vatican City: Biblioteca Apostolica Vaticana, 1962), pp. 211–44, are incorporated in the second edition. On the script, see also E. A. Lowe, *Scriptura beneventana. Facsimiles of South Italian and Dalmatian Manuscripts from the Sixth to the Fourteenth Century*, 2 vols. (Oxford: Clarendon Press, 1929). For new items since the second edition of *The Beneventan Script* see the articles by Virginia Brown, "A Second New List of Beneventan Manuscripts (I)," *Mediaeval Studies* 40 (1978): 239–89; "A Second New List of Beneventan Manuscripts (II)," *Mediaeval Studies* 50 (1988): 584–625; "A Second New List of Beneventan Manuscripts (III)," *Mediaeval Studies* 56 (1994): 299–350; "A Second New List of Beneventan Manuscripts (IV)," *Mediaeval Studies* 61 (1999): 325–92; and "A Sec-

ond New List of Beneventan Manuscripts (V)," *Mediaeval Studies* 70 (2008): 275–355. An annual bibliography of references to manuscripts in the script has been published since 1993. See *BMB: Bibliografia dei manoscritti in scrittura beneventana* (Cassino: Dipartimento di Filologia e Storia and the Scuola di specializzazione per conservatori di archivistici e librari della civiltà medievale of the Università degli Studi di Cassino, 1993– ).

6. The list of manuscripts includes a number of overlapping genres and mixed books. Missals, for instance, typically include materials found separately in calendars, sacramentaries, graduals, and lectionaries. Moreover, manuscripts may contain elements of several genres. It is also worth noting that within each genre there could be many variants in the texts copied.

7. Approximately three quarters of the surviving biblical manuscripts exist as fragments. The approximately two hundred biblical manuscripts in Beneventan script include forty-eight complete manuscripts or extensive fragments (not including Psalters, evangelistaries, epistolaries, or books clearly intended for study). See Brown, "I libri della Bibbia," pp. 305–7, for a list of the forty-eight complete or extensive biblical manuscripts. Brown's list does not include volumes intended for study. Brown, ibid., p. 284 n. 10, cites, for instance, Rome, Biblioteca Casanatense, 1590, a twelfth-century copy of the Apocalypse and Iob with commentaries; and Rome, Biblioteca Vallicelliana, E 28 (1), a twelfth-century copy of the Epistles of Paul with glosses.

8. Capitula for the epistles and gospels could exist separately or in combination.

9. Epistolaries were the books of lectors and evangelistaries were the books of deacons. Mass lectionaries, like missals, may have been originally intended for smaller centers with fewer specialized celebrants or for private masses.

10. The nineteen Beneventan evangelistaries, including fragments, are listed by Brown, "I libri della Bibbia," pp. 290–91, especially 290 n. 20: Benevento, Biblioteca Capitolare, 31 (twelfth century); Berlin, Staatsbibliothek zu Berlin-Preussischer Kulturbesitz, Haus 2, Theol. lat. quart. 31 (twelfth century); Bisceglie, Archivio del Capitolo Cattedrale, s. n. (early eleventh century); Bitonto, Biblioteca comunale, A 45 + Stockholm, National-museum, 1614–1615 + Geneva, Bibliothèque Publique et Universitaire, Comites latentes 141 (early twelfth century); Montecassino, Archivio dell'Abbazia (hereafter Montecassino), 191, pp. 1–128 (third quarter of the eleventh century); Montecassino 229 (1071–87); Montecassino 424 (third quarter of the eleventh century); Oxford, Bodleian Library, Canon. bibl. lat. 61 (late eleventh century); Rab, Zupni ured, s.n. + Zagreb, Nacionalna i Sveučilišna Biblioteka, R 4.106 (thirteenth century); Rimini, Biblioteca Civica Gambalunga, Sezione chiusa, ms. 24 (late eleventh century); Rome, Biblioteca Angelica, 1439, fols. 1, 229 (twelfth century); Trogir, Riznica Katedrale, s. n. (thirteenth century, after 1228); Trogir, Riznica Katedrale, s. n. (after 1259); Vatican City, Biblioteca Apostolica Vaticana (hereafter BAV), Vat. lat. 5100 (thirteenth century); BAV, Vat. lat. 10644, fols. 28–31 (second half of the eleventh century); BAV, Borg. lat. 339 (after 1082); BAV, Ottob. lat. 296 (elev-

enth century); BAV, Ross. 297, fol. 6 (early thirteenth century); and Oslo/London, the Schøyen Collection, ms. 1680 (twelfth century).

11. For Beneventan Gospel books, see Brown, "I libri della Bibbia," p. 291 n. 22, listing Cava dei Tirreni, Archivio della Badia della SS. Trinità, 19 (calendar, Gospels, Apocalypse, I John, and Rule of Benedict; thirteenth century [after 1280], origin and provenance: Cava, and although the manuscript does not have liturgical indications, the parts could have liturgical roles); BAV, Vat. lat. 3741 (Gospels with a list of capitula for gospel readings, late eleventh century, provenance: Alatri); Montecassino 211 (Gospels, late eleventh or early twelfth century, origin: Montecassino, and this is a small deluxe volume without liturgical annotations and may have been intended for the private devotional use of Oderisius, abbot of Montecassino from 1087 to 1105); and Rome, Biblioteca Casanatense, 1101 (Gospels, twelfth century, origin: Puglia). de Hamel, *The Book*, pp. 29–30, notes that among early biblical manuscripts about half are Gospel books and many contain signs of use in the liturgy; de Hamel cites, for instance, Milan, Biblioteca Ambrosiana, C 39 inf. (sixth century, with seventh-century annotations) and Biblioteca Ambrosiana, I 61 sup. (seventh century, origin: Bobbio, with annotations indicating use into the late fourteenth century).

12. That is Trogir, Riznica Katedrale, s. n., fols. 1–78, in Beneventan, pp. 79–107 in Gothic script (epistolary, late thirteenth or early fourteenth century); and St. Petersburg, Biblioteka Rossiiskoi Akademii Nauk, F. no. 200, fols. 3r–64v (mass lectionary, twelfth century, provenance: Kotor).

13. For Beneventan manuscripts containing books of Epistles, see Brown, "I libri della Bibbia," pp. 305–7. Those with liturgical annotations are Berlin, Deutsche Staatsbibliothek, Hamilton 3 (Acts, Catholic Epistles, and Apoc.; twelfth century, origin and provenance: Benevento); Montecassino 349 (Acts, Catholic Epistles, Apoc., and Epistles of Paul; early eleventh century, provenance: Montecassino); Montecassino 521, pp. 1–48, 65–104 (Acts, Catholic Epistles, and Apoc.; early eleventh century, provenance: Albaneta); Montecassino 535, pp. 287–391 (Epistles of Paul, first half of the eleventh century, provenance: Albaneta, with both liturgical and musical annotations); Montecassino 552 (Acts, Catholic Epistles, Apoc., Epistles of Paul, Prov.-Ecclus., lections, passions; early eleventh century, provenance: Montecassino); Montecassino Comp. I (150 fragments; 2 Cor.-Heb., Isa.-Hag.; early eleventh century); Paris, Bibliothèque Nationale de France, MS Lat. 335, fols. 1–136 (Rom.-Titus 2: 8, eleventh century; also includes glosses); and Rome, Vallicelliana D 36 (Acts, Catholic Epistles, Apoc.; twelfth century). Manuscripts without indications of liturgical use are Matera, Archivio Diocesano, framm. 14–22, 58–61 (fragments of old and new testament books, eleventh century, provenance: Matera); Montecassino, Archivio Privato, 2 (Epistles of Paul, Catholic Epistles, Acts, Apoc.; late eleventh century, origin: Puglia, with glosses); Paris, Bibliothèque Nationale de France, MS Lat. 335, fols. 137–55 (Titus 2: 8–Heb., early tenth century, glossed; continues the ninth-century Epistles described previously in the present note, BNF, lat. 335, fols.

1–236); Vienna, Österreichische Nationalbibliothek, 903 (1 Cor.-Heb., early tenth century, with glosses); and Rome, Biblioteca Vallicelliana, E 28 (Rom.-Gal. 3: 29, twelfth century, with glosses; for this manuscript, see Brown, "I libri della Bibbia," p. 284 n. 10).

14. See Brown, "I libri della Bibbia," p. 283 n. 8, citing London, British Library, Additional MS 18859 (second half of the twelfth century, Montecassino); Los Angeles, J. Paul Getty Museum, Ludwig IX 1 (after 1153, Montecassino); Montecassino 559 (late eleventh or early twelfth century, Montecassino); Oxford, Bodleian Library, Douce 127 (late eleventh century, Sora); Paris, Bibliothèque Mazarine, 364 (after 1099–1105, Montecassino); Parma, Biblioteca Palatina, Palat. 315 (late eleventh century, Puglia); Pistoia, Biblioteca Comunale Forteguerriana, D. 296 (first half of the twelfth century); BAV, Vat. lat. 4928 (first half of the twelfth century, Benevento); and Vienna, Österreichische Nationalbibliothek, 1106 (twelfth century).

15. de Hamel, *The Book*, p. 29. The Rule of Benedict anticipates a selection of readings for Matins (chapter 9), although in Lent, the Rule may have required the entire Bible to have been read (chapter 68). See *La Règle de saint Benoît*, ed. Jean Neufville and trans. Adalbert de Vogüé, 2 vols. (Paris: Les Éditions du Cerf, 1971–72), 2:512 (chapter 9) and 2:602 (chapter 48); cited by Brown, "I libri della Bibbia," pp. 282–83, esp. nn. 4–5. For a liturgical order of readings, see *Ordo romanus* 13A in *Les Ordines romani du haut moyen âge*, ed. Michel Andrieu, 5 vols. (Louvain: Spicilegium Sacrum Lovaniense Bureaux, 1931–61), 2:479–88; the order of readings is presented in table 3.3.

16. Avezzano, Archivio diocesano dei Marsi, 50/T (fragment; Jer. 2: 15, 17–18; twelfth century); Rome, Biblioteca Vallicelliana, R 32, fols. 21–36, and s. n. (2 fols.; Lam. 3:41–61; late twelfth century); Rome, Biblioteca Vallicelliana, ex S. Borr. Q I 4 (Lam. 1:8–2:8; eleventh century); BAV, Rossianus 297, fols. 2–3 (Lam., late tenth or early eleventh century); and the following manuscripts listed by Brown, "I libri della Bibbia," pp. 293 and 305–7: Montecassino 589 (Isa.-Zech. [incomplete at the end], thirteenth century, provenance: Montecassino); Montecassino Comp. I (ca. 150 frags.; 2 Cor.-Heb., Isa.-Hag.; early eleventh century); Naples, Biblioteca Nazionale, VI AA 3 (Tob.-2 Macc., Isa.-Zech. [incomplete at the beginning and end]; twelfth century, provenance: Troia); Rome, Biblioteca Vallicelliana, A 17 (Isa.-Mal., twelfth century); BAV, Vat. lat. 14726 (Isa.-Zech. [incomplete at the end], second half of the eleventh century, provenance: Caiazzo).

17. That is, from the preceding note, Montecassino, Comp. I; Naples, BN, VI AA 3; and Vat. lat. 14726, which also has additional musical notation; see Brown, "I libri della Bibbia," pp. 305–7.

18. See Brown, "I libri della Bibbia," pp. 305–7, listing Benevento, Biblioteca Capitolare, 68 (Gen.-Num. [incomplete at beginning and end], late tenth or early eleventh century, provenance: Benevento); Florence, Biblioteca Medicea Laurenziana, San Marco 738 (Gen.-Exod. [incomplete at the end], eleventh century); Montecassino 520 (Gen.-Ruth, third quarter of the eleventh century, origin:

Montecassino); Montecassino 527 (Gen., Exod., 1–2 Sam., Prov., Job, Tob., Jth., Esther, 1 Macc., Acts, James, 1–2 Pet., 1–3 John, Jude, Apoc., Rom., 1 Cor., Heb.; late eleventh century, origin: Montecassino); Montecassino 531 (Gen.-Judg. [incomplete at the end], early eleventh century); Montecassino 534 (Gen.-Exod., Sermons for the period from Septuagesima to Quadragesima; third quarter of the eleventh century, origin: Montecassino); Montecassino 535, pp. 1–286 (Isa.-Mal. [incomplete at the beginning], first half of the eleventh century, provenance: Albaneta); Montecassino 536 (Isa.-Dan. [incomplete at the end], late eleventh century, origin: Montecassino); Montecassino 543 (Isa.-Mal., first half of the eleventh century, provenance: Cesamo, Montecassino); Montecassino 552 (Acts, Catholic Epistles, Apoc., Epistles of Paul, Prov.-Ecclus., Lections, Passiones; early eleventh century, provenance: Montecassino); Montecassino 553 (1 Sam.–Ecclus., early eleventh century, provenance: Montecassino); Montecassino 565 (Gen.-Ruth, twelfth century, origin: Montecassino); Montecassino 571 (Is.-Mal. [incomplete at the end], third quarter of the eleventh century, origin: Montecassino); Montecassino 759 (Gen.-Ruth [incomplete at the end], early eleventh century, provenance: Montecassino); Montecassino 760 (Gen.-Ruth, first half of the eleventh century, provenance: Cesamo, Montecassino); Montecassino Comp. II (ca. 80 fragments; Tob.–2 Macc., late eleventh or early twelfth century); Naples, Biblioteca Nazionale, VI AA 5 (Gen.-Ruth [incomplete at the end], late tenth or early eleventh century, provenance: Benevento); Naples, Biblioteca Nazionale, Vindob. lat. 10, fols. 1–222 (Gen.-Judg. 6:29 [incomplete at the beginning], twelfth century, origin and provenance: Benevento; provenance: Troia).

19. That is, from the preceding note, Florence, Biblioteca Medicea Laurenziana, San Marco 738; Montecassino 531; Montecassino 535, pp. 1–286; Montecassino 543; Montecassino 565; Montecassino 571; and Montecassino 760. See also Vat. lat. 14726, from nn. 16–17, this chapter, with added musical notation. All are cited in Brown, "I libri della Bibbia," pp. 305–7.

20. That is, from Brown, "I libri della Bibbia," pp. 305–7: Benevento, Biblioteca Capitolare, 14 (1 Sam.-Ecclus. [incomplete at the beginning], vitae sanctorum; late tenth or early eleventh century, origin: Benevento); Bern, Ernst Boehlen Coll., 802 (fragment; Jer., late ninth or early tenth century); Matera, Archivio Diocesano, framm. 14–22, 58–61 (incomplete sections from Old and New Testament, eleventh century, provenance: Matera); Montecassino 521, pp. 105–432 (1 Sam.-Esther, early eleventh century); Montecassino 521, pp. 433–64, 49–64 (1–2 Macc., early eleventh century); Montecassino 572 (1 Sam.-2 Macc., first half of the eleventh century, provenance: Montecassino); Montecassino 583, pp. 1–336 (Gen.-Judg., early eleventh century, provenance: Montecassino); Montecassino 583, pp. 337–52 (2 Sam.-1 Kings, early eleventh century); Naples, Biblioteca Nazionale, Vindob. lat. 10, fols. 223–29 (Judg. 5:14–18, 6, early eleventh century); Rome, Biblioteca Vallicelliana, A 15 + s. n. (Gen.-Deut. [incomplete at the end], thirteenth century, origin: Abruzzo); Rome, Biblioteca Vallicelliana, D 8 (Octa-

teuch, 1 Sam.-Ecclus., Prophets, Bar., Job, Gospels, Epistles of Paul, Laod., Acts; late twelfth century, provenance: possibly San Vincenzo al Volturno); BAV, Vat. lat. 11978 (1 Sam.-2 Macc., twelfth century); BAV, Vat. lat. 14728 (1–2 Sam., 1–2 Kings [incomplete at the end], second half of the eleventh century, provenance: Caiazzo).

21. In Benevento 14, fols. 133v–180v, the books of the Wisdom of Solomon and Ecclesiasticus are mixed without distinction; see Jean Mallet and André Thibaut, *Les manuscrits en écriture bénéventaine de la Bibliothèque capitulaire de Bénévent*, 3 vols. (Paris and Turnhout: Éditions du Centre National de la Recherche Scientifique, Brepols, 1984; 1997), 1:216–17.

22. See nn. 20-21, for Benevento 14, and n. 18 for Montecassino 534 and 552. Although suggestive, the addition of Lives of the Saints in Benevento 14 is not conclusive; the biblical books in the manuscript would have been read in the summer months, while the three vitae are for Peter of Alexandria, Barbara, and Nicolas, who were commemorated in November and December.

23. For Montecassino 527, see n. 18; and Brown, "I libri della Bibbia," p. 294 n. 28. Brown suggests that the manuscript may have been an intermediate stage in the development of an office lectionary.

24. For Montecassino 552, see nn. 18 and 22. Although Montecassino 552 omits the lessons from Kings for the season immediately after Pentecost, the readings may have been supplied from a separate book of Kings and Prophets like Montecassino 572 (1 Sam.-2 Macc.; see n. 20) or Vat. lat. 11978 (1 Sam.-2 Macc.; see n. 20).

25. For Vallicelliana D 8, see n. 20; and Brown, "I libri della Bibbia," p. 295, citing Virginia Brown, "Contenuti, funzione e origine della 'Bibbia di San Vincenzo al Volturno' (Roma, Biblioteca Vallicelliana, D 8)," *Nuovi annali della Scuola speciale per archivistici e bibliotecari* 18 (2004): 37–60, and arguing that the small scale of the volume and its numerous prefaces and corrections are signs that the volume was used for study and consultation, not liturgical presentations.

26. See de Hamel, *The Bible*, p. 31, for a description of a division of early Bibles into a similar grouping of seven books: the Octateuch, psalters, the books of Solomon, Prophets, the four gospels, Epistles, and Acts with the Apocalypse. See also Brown, "I libri della Bibbia," p. 283 n. 7, citing Mundó, "'Bibliotheca,'" p. 82, for references in the Rule of Benedict to seven biblical volumes.

27. On liturgical groups of manuscripts, see Brown, "I libri della Bibbia," pp. 302–3, citing the eleventh-century inventory of S. Maria dell'Albaneta, which includes gifts by the scribe Landus of "unum istoriarum continentem in se librum apokalipsis et actum apostolorum cum septem aepistole canonice" (i.e., Montecassino 521, pp. 105–432 [1 Sam.-Esther] + pp.1–48, 65–104 [Acts, Catholic Epistles, Apocalypse]) and "unum prophetarum continentem in se aepistulae pauli" (Montecassino 535, pp. 1–286 [ . . . Isa.–Mal.] + pp. 287–391 [Rom.-Hebr.]); these biblical books were seen as separate books forming part of a whole in a particular order. In their current configuration united with Montecassino 521,

pp. 433–64, 49–64 (1-2 Macc.), they would have provided readings for most of the liturgical year.

28. Commemoratorium of Theobald, after 1019 (San Liberatore alla Maiella), edited by Enrico Carusi, "Intorno al Commemoratorium dell'abate Teobaldo (a. 1019–1022)," *Bulletino dell'Istituto Storico Italiano* 47 (1932): 173–90, at 182–88. See also Lowe, *The Beneventan Script*, 1:79–80.

29. Chronicon casinense 3:63, in *Die Chronik von Montecassino/Chronica monasterii Casinensis*, ed. Hartmut Hoffmann, MGH Scriptores 34 (Hannover: Hahn, 1980), pp. 444–46. See also Lowe, *The Beneventan Script*, 1:81–82.

30. Chronicon casinense 3:74; *Die Chronik*, pp. 456–57.

31. In Montecassino 49 and Regesto 4, edited in *Catalogi bibliothecarum antiqui*, ed. Gustav Becker (Bonn: Cohen, 1885), 1:246–47, num. 120. See also Mauro Inguanez, *Regesto di S. Angelo in Formis* (Montecassino: Badia di Montecassino, 1925).

32. In BAV, Vat. lat. 10657, edited in *Codice diplomatico del monastero benedettino di S. Maria di Tremiti (1005–1237)*, ed. Armando Petrucci, 3 vols. (Rome: Istituto storico italiano per il medio evo, 1960), 3:369–71.

33. In London, British Library, Additional ms 5463, fol. 76v, edited by Sergio Mottironi, "La Chiesa di S. Pietro di Benevento e la sua biblioteca nel sec. xiii," in *Miscellanea di scritti vari in memoria di Alfonso Gallo* (Florence: Olschki, 1956), pp. 559–62, at 559–60. See also Theodor Gottlieb, *Über Mittelalterliche Bibliotheken* (Leipzig: Harrassowitz, 1890), p. 182, no. 529.

34. F. Luigi Theuli, "Inventario della Biblioteca del 1447," in Benevento, Biblioteca Capitolare, 451, fols. 1r–4v, edited by Richard Gyug, "Les bibliothèques du chapitre et de l'archevêque: Appendices," in *La cathédrale de Bénévent*, ed. Thomas Forrest Kelly (Ghent: Ludion, 1999), pp. 207–19, at 212–14. See also Alfredo Zazo, "L' 'Inventario dei libri antichi' della biblioteca capitolare di Benevento (sec. xv)," *Samnium* 8 (1935): 6–25; and Mallet and Thibaut, *Les manuscrits*, 1:105–7.

# When the Monks Were the Book

THE BIBLE AND MONASTICISM (6TH–11TH CENTURIES)

*Isabelle Cochelin*

From the early Middle Ages until the late eleventh century, monks embodied the Book. I argue here that monks of that period made the Bible alive for everyone to see and learn from. Later, monasticism changed, often privileging reason in its daily organization over tradition and biblical symbolism; concomitantly, in society at large, direct reliance on written texts including the Bible increased. Moreover, as lay people wanted to hear more of the content of the Bible, other members of the Church took a more visible role in the oral communication of its substance, but monks had long acted out and in some ways even incarnated the Bible.

## The Omnipresence of the Bible from the Monastic Walls to Monks' Daily Lives

The Bible gave meaning to and played an active role in every aspect of monks' lives from their childhood until old age, from the hour of their rising until they retired to sleep, season after season, so much so that, ideally, the thoughts, words, and actions of monks were rooted in Scriptures. The situation was different in the case of the secular clergy: the Bible was not so omnipresent in the lives of those in charge of the more technical aspects of the *cura animarum*, care for the souls of the rest of society (especially baptism, communion, confession, last rites, and—essentially after the eleventh century—matrimony). With the exception of the early ninth-century attempt to implement Chrodegang of Metz's rule for canons and the longer-lasting reform of some communities of canons in the late eleventh century (who henceforth became regular canons as they imitated the lives of monks, adopting the rule of Saint Augustine, living together, and following well-defined timetables), secular priests, whether canons or not, did not live a precisely scheduled life.[1] During most of their daily activities, they were left on their own and resided in private spaces. In contrast, the very regulated and secluded life of a monk had its sources, if not real then at least perceived, in the Bible. The Book was crucial to the process of transforming monks into earthly representatives of celestial inhabitants; the Bible was believed to be the essential means to reach this desired end.[2]

Fundamental to understanding the close connection between the Bible and the monastery is the perception that the monastic walls were impermeable and thus protected the monks from external influences. Hidden by the enclosure of the monastery, the monks lived (at least in theory) in complete isolation from the rest of the world. The organization of monasticism into orders dispersed over large territories only started in the late eleventh century.[3] Before that, the great majority of monks were attached to only one house, and theoretically lived forever behind its walls. The sources depicting the daily lives of the monks, primarily the rules and customaries, always focus on one house and its internal life;[4] their recommendations concerning the activities of the monks outside the monastery usually serve only to maintain an imaginary wall between the monastic travelers and the secular world, with the observance of specific liturgical duties and strict rules concerning eating and sleeping arrangements.[5] Ideally, within the enclosure, the monks were completely self-sufficient. From the Rule of the Master, written around 500, which inspired the Rule of Benedict of Nursia written a few decades later, to the minute description of the buildings of the second construction of Cluny in the "Book of the Path" (*Liber tramitis*) which details the customs of the Burgundian abbey around 1040, monastic sources occasionally underline the self-sufficiency of a house by proudly enumerating all the ways its buildings met the needs of the community.[6] The most famous example of this *topos* is given neither by a rule nor by a customary, but by a single large map (112 x 77 cm) that is the oldest surviving architectural drawing, designed around 820, and depicts an idealized version of the Swiss monastery of Saint Gall as a self-contained, self-sufficient space.[7] Because the monastery was conceived as a microcosm, theoretically impervious to external heterogeneous realities and possibilities, its own mode of construction and conceptualization had a profound impact. Central to this picture was the Bible.

In this ideally autonomous monastic place sheltered from the secular world, the Bible was everywhere. The founding of the monastic buildings themselves was sometimes explained by references to the Bible; according to the widely read Life of Saint Benedict by Pope Gregory the Great (d. 604), Benedict attracted so many followers in his eremitical dwelling of Subiaco that he founded twelve monasteries, each with twelve monks and a leader, thus imitating the most perfect of all communities, the one formed by Christ and his apostles.[8] The abbey of Menat in southwest France was created following Meneleus's dream under an oak tree, echoing Abraham's visions beside such trees and his dedication of an altar.[9] Duke William of Aquitaine justified his foundation of the abbey of Cluny in 910 on the basis of three biblical citations (Prov. 13:8, Luke 16:9, and Matt. 10:41), which proved, according to him, that the wealthy can be saved if they give to the poor and the just—in other words, to monks.[10] The ceremony of consecration of the building, as well as the celebration of the anniversary of this date, are almost exclusively constructed from biblical quotations, transforming the space both into a New Jerusalem (Rev. 21:2) and a gate to Heaven, a *porta caeli*, on the basis of Genesis 28:17.[11] In other words, year after year, the monastery was reinvented, with biblical pericopes at its core.

The Bible was also present visually inside the monastery, as it dominated the artistic landscape of the monks and their visitors. Scenes from the Book, mixed with stories of saints benefiting from a local cult, were either painted, carved, or sculpted on many walls of the monastery.[12] The examples from churches are numerous: for instance, the church of Saint Gall, under the abbot Hartmut (872–83) was covered with the story of the life of Christ. While many secular churches (whether simple chapels, basilicas, cathedrals, or parish churches) contained biblical art, monasteries (as the dwelling places of the monks) were also adorned with biblical scenes. Occasionally such depictions could be found in the dormitory, but more frequently in the cloister, where the monks read and rested. The chapter room, where they met to discuss all issues linked to the community and its goods, and the refectory too were covered with biblical scenes, maintaining the monks' constant visual contact with the Scriptures.[13] The chapter room of the abbey of Brauweiler, not far from Cologne, depicted among other themes Daniel with the lions and Job's sorrow, both mural paintings dating from the third quarter of the twelfth century. In the first third of the following century in the abbey of Lavaudieu in Auvergne, the same room was adorned with Christ in majesty surrounded by the symbols of the four Evangelists[14] and, in the female monastery of Sigena in Aragon, by the stories of Adam and Eve, and the Nativity.[15] The crucifix hung on the walls of many monastic refectories, but one could also have viewed scenes from Acts drawn in the late eleventh or twelfth century on the south wall of the refectory of Nonantola abbey, close to Modena in Italy. Between 1063 and 1071, a Pentecost scene was painted in the refectory at Montecassino, Benedict of Nursia's most famous monastery, south of Rome. The Last Judgment was represented in the eleventh-century refectory in Cluny.[16]

The Bible was also used as the most common referent to justify fundamental steps in the lives of monks, such as their taking the habit. The majority of Western monks and nuns up to the eleventh century were oblates.[17] This means that they entered the monastery as children, after weaning age and before reaching adulthood, some time between ages three and fourteen.[18] These boys or girls were given to a monastery by their parents for many possible reasons. The child may have been perceived as not fit to become a warrior or to beget children because of some physical or mental handicap, or the parents simply decided to privilege other heirs.[19] But the vitae of the saints reveal other justifications. The greatest act of love for God was offering one's child: Abraham's readiness to sacrifice Isaac had sealed his union with God (Gen. 22:1–19), and Samuel had been offered to the Temple after weaning age by his mother Hannah to serve the Lord (1 Sam. 1:24–28). These biblical images gave impetus to the medieval practice of oblation.[20] The great abbot Mayeul of Cluny preached to his oblates in the second half of the tenth century: "My whole sermon [is] now [addressed] to you, my children, who have been pushed away from the milk and taken away from the breasts; whom the water of baptism has transferred by the gift of the Holy Spirit to the new grace of adoption; who, at the example of Isaac, have been offered to God; who, from these same cradles, have sucked the nourishment of holy preaching with the milk of the flesh."[21]

In the Life of Abbot Stephen of Obazine, written in the second half of the twelfth century, its author tried to defend the institution of oblation practiced in the abbey of Obazine, but under attack since it had joined the Cistercian order. According to this anonymous monk, oblates were like angels whose simplicity and purity of innocence preserved them from any impurity of the exterior world, including sex, and therefore brought them closer to divine knowledge.[22] Having internalized biblical texts and symbolism from their infancy, these oblates were malleable clay on which the Bible could be forever impressed.

Specific sections of the Gospels were also quoted as the incentive that made adults choose the monastic life.[23] In the second half of the third century, a wealthy but orphaned young Egyptian, Antony, converted because, upon entering church one day with various biblical passages on his mind (Matt. 4:20 and 19:27; Acts 4:35–37), he heard Christ's famous answer to the young rich man: "If thou wilt be perfect, go sell what thou hast, and give it to the poor; and thou shalt have treasure in heaven" (Matt. 19:21). Antony followed this precept himself and gave his young sister as an oblate to a female community.[24] His Life, written soon after his death in the third quarter of the fourth century, was almost immediately translated into Latin and widely distributed in the West where it played an essential role in the dissemination of monasticism.[25] When Columbanus, the famous Irish hermit who enabled a new efflorescence of Western monasticism in the late sixth and early seventh century, was encouraged by a Merovingian king to settle in his kingdom, he explained his decision by quoting Christ's saying, "If any man will come after me, let him deny himself, and take up his cross daily, and follow me" (Luke 9:23).[26] For medieval people, the monastic life was the execution par excellence of this recommendation, as the denial of the self was at the heart of the monastic project, made possible primarily through utter obedience to the abbot and to the uses and customs of the monastery.[27] Monks never conceived conversion as a simple changing of habit or way of life, but, instead, as a radical shedding of the old man, internally and externally, to create a *novus homo* (Eph. 2:15 and 4:24).[28] *For* this new man and *in* this new man, the Bible had a central role to play.

After the new converts had cast off their old life, most of their activities related in some way or other to the Bible. It gave meaning to their conduct, and often their gestures were accompanied by silent or vocal recitation, reading or singing, of the biblical text. When the author of a monastic rule wanted to justify a specific practice, he normally referred to a biblical sentence. For instance, in order to explain the need to keep silent as often as possible, Benedict evoked Psalm 38:2–3 referring to the necessity of placing a guardian at one's mouth.[29] The intermingling of the Bible with the monastic life is particularly striking when connected with activities that we would not tend to associate with the Book. For example, silence was normally required during meals, and pious texts, regularly taken from the Bible, were read aloud for the benefit of the community. (For more information on refectory reading, see Reilly's chapter in this volume).[30] The goal was obviously to keep the minds of the monks focused on heaven and the narrow path leading to it, while they undertook a potentially distracting, self-indulgent, and carnal activity. Whenever Cluniac monks did manual work outside the cloister, which was not very often, they would sing psalms during most of the outing.[31] The best known rule for nuns, finished in 534 by Caesarius, Bishop of Arles, imposed the practice of listening to pious readings during meal times and manual activities, to be followed by ruminations on the word of God when the reading ended.[32]

The most prominent double anchoring of the Bible in the lives of the monks took place during study and liturgical activities, which occupied the greatest part of their waking hours. Not all monasteries were centers of learning, but all of them needed to teach reading and writing to their oblates. The apprenticeship of reading was based for the most part on the Psalter, which was the medieval reading primer.[33] Its use in reading instruction was not limited to the monasteries, but its importance for child monks was accentuated by the fact that they sang it daily in the Divine Office.[34] Learning to read required first and foremost the mastery of grammar. At the beginning of the ninth century the monk Smaragdus of Saint-Mihiel wrote a Latin grammar to replace Donatus's pagan grammatical treatises (the *Ars minor* and *Ars maior*) in order to focus all monastic knowledge in and around the Bible.[35] Smaragdus's grammar never became the standard text. However, no matter which pedagogical approach prevailed, the tasks of learning and understanding the Bible were the main activities in the *schola* (group or choir) of the oblates, running in parallel to the apprenticeship in the liturgy.

In certain periods in some monasteries, such as Saint Gall, Fulda (Germany), Wearmouth and Jarrow (England), St Germain d'Auxerre (Burgundy), or Fleury, studies went further than simply learning to read and write. Here they were devised on the same principle upheld by Cassiodorus in his Italian monastery of Vivarium in the middle of the sixth century (and also promoted before him by Augustine and shortly after him by Gregory the Great, two of the greatest Church fathers in the West who both started their ecclesiastical careers as monks). (For more discussion of early Biblical scholarship, see van Liere's chapter in this volume.) The seven liberal arts (grammar, rhetoric, and logic forming the *trivium*, and arithmetic, geometry, music, and astronomy constituting the *quadrivium*) were all devised with one main goal: a deeper understanding of the Bible.[36] This concept had been well summed up by the monk Haimo of Auxerre in the ninth century when he claimed that the Scriptures were the queen of arts (*domina artium*).[37]

One privileged occasion for study in medieval monasteries was the two hours per day (three during Lent and more on Sundays) reserved by Benedict for the spiritual reading known as *lectio divina*. During that time, monks would read books of their choice; however, most often these texts concerned the Bible directly or indirectly. Chapter 48 of the Benedictine Rule demanded that codices from the *bibliotheca* be distributed during Lent for the *lectio divina*.[38] By *bibliotheca*, Benedict was possibly referring to the nine books that constituted the Bible in his day, which meant that the monks' study time during the weeks preceding Easter centered on Scripture even more than usual.[39] However, Benedict's meaning of *bibliotheca* in the Rule was later lost, and by Carolingian times chapter 48 was interpreted as referring to any book from the library, including some pagan ones.[40] Even considering this evolution, the Bible still occupied the central and privileged place in monastic readings, as illustrated by the list of books given in the *Liber tramitis*.[41] The majority of books distributed (thirty-three of a total of sixty-four), were sections of the Bible (four) or commentaries on the Bible (twenty-nine).[42] In contrast, surviving lists of books from parish churches contain essentially liturgical books and almost never parts of the Bible, except for the occasional Psalter.[43]

The exegetical texts consulted and copied so often were approached by monks of the early and central Middle Ages with a specific frame of mind.[44] Whenever members of the secular clergy studied the Bible and its commentaries in cathedral schools, they usually had some further end in mind, such as preparing sermons for the laity or debating problematic issues (*quaestiones*) with other scholars; they meant to grasp the text and make it their own, before presenting it in front of an audience.[45] Monks, however, aspired not to learning but to spirituality;[46] they wanted to immerse themselves in the text, making themselves the text rather than making the text their own, in order to elevate themselves in the contemplation and imitation of God and those who dwelt in heaven.[47] This approach to study and to the Bible was linked to the conception of Scripture in the period prior to the twelfth century: its literal meaning was considered to be of secondary importance.[48] For instance, reading the Song of Songs, medieval monks did not see an erotic poem celebrating intimacy between a man and a woman, but rather an inspirational text for contemplation.[49] As Henri de Lubac has demonstrated, Scripture was perceived as a sky of profound height, an unfathomable abyss, an immense sea for voyaging on with billowing sails to infinitude, an ocean of mysteries.[50] Besides this allegorical and anagogical reading of the Bible, essential for contemplation,[51] the monks of the early and central Middle Ages also privileged moral interpretation to facilitate their own external and inner transformation through imitation. The Bible was the monks' guidebook for living the most perfect life, while the monks in turn were the guides of perfect living for society at large.[52]

Benedict of Nursia had balanced the daily lives of the monks between manual labor, *lectio divina,* and the liturgy, the latter occupying some four hours per day. But, increasingly, the tendency was to privilege the liturgy to the detriment of manual work. By the time Cluny was considered the most admirable monastery of Europe in the eleventh century, eight hours a day were normally devoted to liturgy.[53] (For more on the Mass and Office, see Boynton's chapter in this volume.) Of these eight hours, the celebration of Mass occupied only a small portion. At least until the late eleventh century, the principal and most time-consuming occupation of the monks was praising God during the *opus Dei*, the Divine Office. This activity of corporate prayer, transforming monks into terrestrial images of the celestial troops of angels singing unceasing praises to the Lord in Heaven, was based primarily on the Psalter, in its organization as well as its content.[54] It consisted mainly of eight services (Matins, Lauds, Prime, Terce, Sext, None, Vespers, and Compline) reflecting the words of Psalm 118:62, 164, quoted in chapter 16 of the Benedictine Rule: "I arose in the middle of the night to give thanks to thee" and "seven times a day, I praised thee."[55] At the time of Benedict, the 150 psalms were sung during the *opus Dei* in their entirety once a week, but, by the eleventh century, the Cluniacs sang all of them daily. Antiphons and collects were added, but these were also mostly taken from the Bible. The final result was such that "the texts of the liturgy [were] chiefly made up of extracts from the Bible, collected and arranged in such a way as to make of them a poem of inexhaustible meaning and profundity."[56]

All in all, the omnipresence of the Bible in the daily life of monks was such that they generally knew it by heart—if not all, at least the Psalter—and their utterances were suffused with biblical reminiscences.[57] In his 1140s collection of miracles, Peter the Venerable paints a striking portrait of the perfect monk: among other characteristics, Peter stresses that one should be a direct imitation of Benedict, whose "mouth is unceasingly ruminating on the divine words."[58] The Bible was so often voiced by the monks that one cannot help wonder whether the continual correlations made in monastic writings between past, present, and future events and biblical passages were only rhetorical devices, used to give more power to their assertions, or rather the normal consequence of their habit of seeing, hearing, feeling, tasting, and understanding the world through the lens of the Book.[59]

## The Monastic Life as a Living Bible

Monks also lived out the Bible through more unusual liturgical and paraliturgical activities. In front of the laity again and again throughout the year, the monks acted out—at least symbolically, if not realistically—various scenes from the Bible, especially from the New Testament.[60] They performed numerous processions covered with ash during Lent, to illustrate the forty days Christ spent in the desert as well as the approach of his death, and one yearly procession with palms on Palm Sunday, to mark the entrance of Christ in Jerusalem before his arrest, when he was received by a joyful crowd. In all processions for which we have a list of the objects displayed, the Bible or parts of the Bible also occupied an important place.[61]

The celebration of Easter is especially telling. The Resurrection of Christ was made visible inside the monastic churches by a striking opposition between darkness and light, silence and music. According to an unlocalized and undated early customary fragment, the monks bathed on Holy Saturday.[62] At the same time, the church was decorated. According to later customaries, this meant that the church was first washed, then tapestries were hung, coverings were placed on the choir seats, and newly washed cloths were laid on the altars.[63] The lay population was called to church by the striking of a *tabula* (board) instead of the usual bell (*signa*), as Christ was not yet resurrected.[64] The rituals that followed were thus performed under the gaze of the laity. The presence of lay people at Mass is rarely evoked in customaries; therefore, their mention on Holy Saturday, at least in some customaries, suggests that their attendance was essential to the dynamic of the ceremony. The *Regularis concordia* ("Monastic Agreement," hereafter referred to as *RC*), written in England around 973 under the aegis of King Edgar, insists on the didactic significance of the public rituals surrounding Easter:

> This manner of arousing religious compunction was, I think, devised by Catholic men for the purpose of setting forth clearly both the terror of the darkness which, at our Lord's Passion, struck the tripartite world with unwonted fear, and the consolation of that apostolic preaching which revealed to the whole world Christ obedient to His Father even unto death for the salvation of the human race. Therefore it seemed good to us to insert these things so that if there be any to whose devotion they are pleasing, they may find therein the means of instructing those who are ignorant of this matter.[65]

As specialists of the liturgy have demonstrated, however, the main reason for these rituals was not so much to educate the population as to enable the laity and the monks to relive the events that had taken place in the first century.[66] In order to do so, monks made themselves into biblical figures and their church into Jerusalem.[67]

In this newly refurbished church where newly washed and dressed monks celebrated, a new light was produced. The church had been left dark on Good Friday, with altars bare to mark the death of Christ.[68] After the singing of the ninth hour on Holy Saturday, one of the higher officials blessed the new light, which was produced by striking a special stone.[69] In some monasteries, the ritual was performed three days in a row, concluding on Holy Saturday when the blessing was read by someone of higher hierarchical rank than his two predecessors, symbolizing the rekindling of the Spirit at three different times on earth, twice at the time of the Old Testament and once at the time of the New Testament.[70] From this new fire, a first candle was lit, the paschal candle, representing the new light that is Christ; then two lit candles were placed on either side of the altar (also a symbol of Christ), centering the attention of the congregation upon it.[71] Later, the other candles were also lit, the whole choir sang *Kyrie eleison*, and the bells were rung.[72] This magnificence of cleanliness, cloth, light, and sound represented the Resurrection of Christ and the dawn of a new era. Prior to the explosion of radiance and music, the words *in prin-*

*cipio* ("in the beginning"), pronounced to begin a reading from Genesis, served to reiterate the same message, as did any baptisms of newly born children that were performed.[73]

The monks did not stop at these dramatic yet relatively static effects; they also acted out biblical scenes. Before Matins in the night between Saturday and Sunday, the cross was raised and replaced in its usual position to vividly illustrate the Resurrection of Christ. The sudaries, which symbolized the material that covered Jesus in his tomb, were left at some sort of sepulchre until "the visit."[74] At least since the early tenth century (but probably much earlier), most monasteries sang the discovery of the empty tomb by the three Marys and their simultaneous encounter with an angel. First the question of the angel(s) was sung, "Whom do you seek in the sepulchre, O followers of Christ" (giving the name to this Easter dialogue: *Quem quaeritis*), and then the answer, "Jesus of Nazareth, who was crucified, O heavenly dweller."[75] This dialogue, based on Mark 16, Matthew 28, and Luke 24, was often accompanied by a symbolic visit to the sepulchre (*Visitatio sepulchri*) where the empty sudaries illustrated the Resurrection.[76] All in all, by a multiplicity of signs, the monks embodied the Resurrection of Christ for themselves and the laity. Through such representational practices, every participant was able to visualize and, even more, live out the New Testament stories and their prefigurations in the Old Testament.[77]

During this particular event, the *populus* (congregation) was only invited to observe passively. On other occasions, the laity was directly incorporated into the biblical representation performed by the monks, thus making more vivid for medieval society the possible identification of the monks with the Bible. While ideally the medieval monks should not leave their enclosure to wander into the world except for urgent necessities, the world was allowed to come and visit them because of a specific biblical pericope. Medieval monasteries had dwellings outside the enclosure to receive passersby and the sick; this tradition of hospitality and care was directly based on the sayings of Christ: "I was hungry and you gave me to eat; I was thirsty and you gave me to drink; I was a stranger and you took me in" (Matt. 25:35; Benedictine Rule 53:1).[78] Until the late eleventh century, in a world where European cities were still few in number and very small in size, monasteries provided the main hotels and hospices for society. Ulrich of Zell claims, for instance, that in a given year seventeen thousand poor had been fed by the Cluniacs.[79] The enormous number is better understood through a comparison: around the same period (the last quarter of the eleventh century), one of the most important cities of England, Norwich, numbered between seven and eight thousand inhabitants![80]

The best illustration of the occasional participation of the secular world in the monks' embodiment of the Bible is to be found in the multiple monastic interpretations of the ceremony of the washing of feet.[81] According to John 13:4–17, it was during the Last Supper that the Son of God, who had become human to save humanity, lowered himself in front of his apostles to wash their feet and demanded that they continue to perform this action later among themselves. Because of this divine command, the ritual is called the *mandatum* (literally "command") and the day on which it takes place Maundy Thursday. In its oldest form in the West, each member of the community was asked to serve one week in turn in the kitchen and the refectory. Either everyday or at the end of the shift, the whole group of weekly servants washed the feet of the whole community (*RB* 35.9).[82] In obeying Jesus's instruction to the apostles to perform this action for one another, the monks came to represent the apostles themselves. In some of the oldest customaries, a second version of this ritual can be found. Asked by the noble Theodoric at the end of the eighth century about the customs of the abbey of Montecassino, Abbot Theodomar explained that on Maundy Thursday, after the first part of the meal had been eaten, all the monks left table to have their feet washed by the abbot, and then the monks returned to the refectory to finish eating.[83] In this second version, most details of the original scene were copied, including the date in the yearly calendar. Therefore the abbot was impersonating Christ, and the monks the apostles. In some later customaries, one learns that the *mandatum* on Maundy Thursday was not performed by the abbot alone but that he was helped by some other monks, often taken from the ranks of the *priores* (monks with seniority based on their long residence in the monastery).[84] However, the monks were also asked by the Benedictine Rule to wash the feet of their visitors: thus the poor and travelers were received as Christ-like figures (*RB* 53.13–15).[85] While this latter monastic ritual progressively disappeared through the Middle Ages, another version of the practice became customary in most monasteries, at least during the ninth century if not earlier.[86] On Maundy Thursday, two ceremonial washings of feet took place, one internal—the abbot and some other brothers washed the feet of all the community; the other external—the monks washed the feet of the poor.[87] Moreover, at some monasteries at least by the late tenth century, the whole community took turns in groups of two or three and performed a small *mandatum* with a similar number of poor people daily, all year long or for part of the year.[88] Assigned roles were therefore regularly exchanged: monks personified Christ, the apostles, and the simple believers receiving Christ in turn. The biblical scene and Christ's commandment were thus made alive for the monks and the laity.[89]

Theoretically, monks aspired to act out the Bible everywhere and always. The representations of the monks in the early and central Middle Ages rarely depicted straightforward scenes from the Old or New Testament. Their images were both simpler—playing extensively on contrasts between darkness, silence, and dirtiness, on one side, and light, music, and cleanliness, on the other—and more complex: for instance, the resurrected Christ was represented through a multiplicity of symbolic gestures performed in different places (such as at the main altar and the sepulchre) during the Easter Vigil and on Easter Day. The fact that monks impersonated all the characters is striking: they were not only to be identified with Christ and the apostles when performing the *mandatum* between themselves or, more generally, when celebrating the Eucharist; they were also the Jerusalemites acclaiming Jesus's arrival in the procession on Palm Sunday, and they (at least in theory) received the sick and travelers as Christlike figures visiting their dwellings. In other words, the monks embodied the whole Bible, moving ceaselessly back and forth between all its parts, making it alive and current. Their life was anchored, guided, and given meaning by the Bible.

From the late eleventh century onward, the dynamic relationship between the laity, the secular Church, and monasteries started to evolve quite drastically, and so did their mutual interconnection with the Bible. The knowledge of and desire for close proximity with Scripture became far more diffused.[90] Literacy increased and the laity asked more frequently for translations of the Bible, as illustrated by the history of the Waldensian heresy, whose main protagonist had the Bible translated into Provençal.[91] By cause or consequence, from the twelfth century on, the Church began implementing an important program to improve the education of its secular clergy; unlike the Carolingian ecclesiastical reform, which had been launched primarily by the stronger figures of the Carolingian family and declined with the weakening of its power, the twelfth-century development was not short-lived. The papacy promoted the importance of parish priests reading and knowing the Bible.[92] By the early thirteenth century, new religious orders were founded, especially the Dominicans and the Franciscans, whose primary task was to preach to the population and hence to discuss the Bible. Therefore the laity increasingly received its main glimpses of the Bible's messages through priests' homilies and preachers' sermons, if not by its own means.[93] In addition, the monks, now mainly adult converts who therefore sometimes had a heavy conscience to expiate, gave more room in their writings to the topics of penance and suffering than had their angelic predecessors, who had striven to build paradisiacal dwellings on earth on the basis of biblical references.[94]

## Notes

I thank Susan Boynton, Joe Goering, Irene Kabala, Jacques Ménard, Matthew Ponesse, and Diane Reilly for commenting on this chapter; however, any remaining mistakes are mine. Many thanks also to Jennifer Harris and Greti Dinkova-Bruun for initially asking me to write on the topic.

1. Mayke de Jong, "Carolingian Monasticism: The Power of Prayer," in *The New Cambridge Medieval History*, vol. 2: *c. 700–c. 900*, ed. Rosamond McKitterick (Cambridge: Cambridge University Press, 1995), pp. 622–53, at 627–29. On the rule(s) of Chrodegang of Metz, see Jerome Bertram, *The Chrodegang Rules: The Rules for the Common Life of the Secular Clergy from the Eighth and Ninth Centuries: Critical Texts with Translation and Commentary* (Aldershot: Ashgate, 2005). The best known of the new orders regrouping regular canons was the Premonstratensian order. See Jörg Oberste, *Visitation und Ordensorganisation: Formen sozialer Normierung, Kontrolle, und Kommunikation bei Cisterziensern, Prämonstratensern und Cluniazensern: 12.–frühes 14. Jahrhundert* (Münster: LIT, 1996). On the contrast between the monks and secular canons, see Michel Parisse, "Être moine ou chanoine à la fin du IXe siècle," in *Au cloître et dans le monde: Femmes, hommes, et sociétés (IXe–XVe siècles)*, ed. Patrick Henriet and Anne-Marie Legras (Paris: Presses de l'Université de Paris-Sorbonne, 2000), pp. 91–101.

2. Texts illustrating the belief in the monastic process of total transformation and preparation for the next life are numerous. Benedict of Nursia concludes the prologue of his *Rule* explaining that the monastic life prepares the individual to become coregent in Christ's kingdom; see the Rule of Benedict (hereafter *RB*), prologue, paragraph 50, in *RB 1980: The Rule of St. Benedict in Latin and English with Notes*, ed. and trans. Timothy Fry (Collegeville, MN: Liturgical, 1981), pp. 166–67. In his *Life of Antony*, Athanasius of Alexandria claims that becoming a monk means reproducing the life of the celestial city on earth. Athanasius of Alexandria, *Vie d'Antoine*, ed. and trans. G. J. M. Bartelink, SC 400 (Paris: Cerf, 1994) chapter 14, pp. 174–5; English translation of the Latin translation by Evagrius of Antioch in *Early Christian Lives*, trans. Caroline White (London: Penguin, 1998).

3. Cécile Caby, "De l'abbaye à l'ordre: Écriture des origines et institutionnalisation des expériences monastiques, XIe–XIIe siècle," *Mélanges de l'École française de Rome* 115 (2003): 235–67; Gert Melville, "Cluny après 'Cluny': Le treizième siècle, un champ de recherches," *Francia* 17 (1990): 91–124; Oberste, *Visitation und Ordensorganisation;* and Sharon Farmer, *Communities of Saint Martin: Legend and Ritual in Medieval Tours* (Ithaca: Cornell University Press, 1991), pp. 127–50.

4. On the rules produced in Latin between 400 and 700, see Adalbert de Vogüé, *Les règles monastiques anciennes (400–700)* (Turnhout: Brepols, 1985). On customs and customaries, see Anselme Davril, "Coutumiers directifs et coutumiers descriptifs d'Ulrich à Bernard de Cluny"; and Isabelle Cochelin, "Évolution des coutumiers monastiques dessinée à partir de l'étude de Bernard," in *From Dead of Night to End of Day: The Medieval Customs of Cluny; Du coeur de la nuit à la fin du jour: Les coutumes clunisiennes au Moyen Âge*, ed. Susan Boynton and Isabelle Cochelin (Brepols: Turnhout, 2005), pp. 23–28 and 29–66, respectively.

5. See among others *RB* 7.62–63, 50–51, and 67; *RB 1980*, pp. 198–201.

6. *Regula magistri* 95.17–18; *La règle du maître*, ed. and trans. Adalbert de Vogüé, SC 106 (Paris: Cerf, 1964), p. 446; English translation in *The Rule of the Master*, trans. Luke Eberle (Kalamazoo: Cistercian, 1977). *Liber tramitis aeui Odilonis abbatis*, ed. Peter Dinter, CCM 10 (Siegburg: Franz Schmitt, 1980), pp. 204–6.

7. Walter Horn and Ernest Born, *The Plan of St-Gall: A Study of the Architecture and Economy of, and Life in, a Paradigmatic Carolingian Monastery* (Berkeley: University of California Press, 1982). For another reading of this plan, see Richard E. Sullivan, "What Was Carolingian Monasticism? The Plan of St Gall and the History of Monasticism," in *After Rome's Fall: Narrators and Sources of Early Medieval History, Essays presented to Walter Goffart*, ed. Alexander Callander Murray (Toronto: University of Toronto Press, 1998), pp. 251–87.

8. Gregory the Great, *Dialogues: Tome 2, Livres I–III*, ed. Adalbert de Vogüé, trans. Paul Antin, SC 260 (Paris: Cerf, 1979), 2.3.14, p. 150. For an English translation see *Early Christian Lives*, p. 172.

9. Amy Remensnyder, *Remembering Kings Past: Monastic Foundation Legends in Medieval Southern France* (Ithaca: Cornell University Press, 1996), pp. 52–53.

10. *Les plus anciens documents originaux de l'abbaye de Cluny*, ed. Harmut Atsma and Jean Vezin with Sébastien Barret (Turnhout: Brepols, 1997), #4, 1:33–42. English translation in *Readings in Medieval History*, trans. Patrick Geary, 2d ed. (Peterborough, ON: Broadview, 1997), pp. 304–6.

11. Remensnyder, *Remembering Kings Past*, p. 50; Jennifer A. Harris, "Building Heaven on Earth: Cluny as *locus sanctissimus* in the Eleventh Century," in *From Dead of Night*, pp. 131–51; Dominique Iogna-Prat, "Lieu de culte et exégèse liturgique à l'époque carolingienne," in *The Study of the Bible in the Carolingian Era*, ed. Celia Chazelle and Burton Van Name Edwards (Turnhout: Brepols, 2003), pp. 215–44, at 224–31; *Mises en scène et mémoires de la consécration de l'église dans l'Occident médiéval*, ed. Didier Méhu (Turnhout: Brepols, 2007).

12. Occasionally, the shape of the building itself was influenced by biblical texts. For instance, the cloister of the monks of Canterbury "had the hallowed dimen-

sions of the heavenly Jerusalem—144 feet square (Rev. 21:16–17), cubits having been read to mean feet"; see Wolfgang Braunfels, *Monasteries of Western Europe: The Architecture of the Orders*, trans. Alastair Laing (London: Thames and Hudson, 1972), p. 164.

13.    I thank Irene Kabala for her suggestions on this subject.

14.    This image is not directly taken from the Bible, but its elements lead the spectator to Holy Scripture where it represents the four beasts of the Apocalypse surrounding the lamb (i.e., Christ; see Rev. 4:6–7 and Rev. 5:6), and, more significantly, these four are read as the symbols of the four Evangelists.

15.    Otto Demus, *Romanische Wandmalerei*, photographs by Max and Albert Hirmer (Munich: Hirmer, 1992), plates 84–85, and figures 149 and 181–83.

16.    Irene Kabala, "Medieval Decorated Refectories in France, Italy, and England until 1250," 2 vols. (Ph.D. diss., Johns Hopkins University, 2001), 2:309–39. See also Hélène Toubert, *Un art dirigé: Réforme grégorienne et iconographie* (Paris: Cerf, 1990); and Braunfels, *Monasteries*, pp. 136–38 and 145–47.

17.    *Oblatus* (in the masculine, *oblata* in the feminine) is the past participle of the verb *offero*, to offer. When oblates may have started to become preponderant in monasteries is a fundamental question that requires more research. On oblation during the Carolingian period, see Mayke de Jong, *In Samuel's Image: Child Oblation in the Early Medieval West* (Leiden: Brill, 1996); and "Carolingian Monasticism," pp. 640–49. On the decline of oblation from the late eleventh century onward, see Nora Berend, "La subversion invisible: La disparition de l'oblation irrévocable des enfants dans le droit canon," *Médiévales* 26 (1994): 123–36; and Isabelle Cochelin, "Enfants, jeunes, et vieux au monastère: La perception du cycle de vie dans les sources clunisiennes (909–1156)" (Ph.D. diss., Université de Montréal, 1996), pp. 215–28.

18.    On the monastic conception of the life cycle, see Isabelle Cochelin, "Introduction: Pre-Thirteenth-Century Definitions of the Lifecycle," in *Medieval Lifecycles: Continuity and Change*, ed. Isabelle Cochelin and Karen Smyth (Turnhout: Brepols, forthcoming). On medieval childhood in general, see Nicholas Orme, *Medieval Children* (New Haven: Yale University Press, 2001).

19.    The most violent attack on oblation is to be found in the introduction to the third Cluniac customary, written by Ulrich of Zell c. 1080; see Ulrich of Zell, *Consuetudines antiquiores cluniacenses*, PL 149:643–779, at 636. English translation in *From Dead of Night*, p. 335.

20.    For other biblical images used to justify oblation, see de Jong, *In Samuel's Image*, pp. 156–63.

21.    "Totus mihi nunc ad uos sermo, o pueri, qui segregati estis a lacte, appulsi ab uberibus, quos unda baptismatis per donum sancti spiritus in nouam transtulit adoptionis gratiam, qui ad exemplum Isaac deo oblati estis, qui ab ipsis cunabilis potum sanctae predicationis suxistis cum lacte carnis," in Dominique Iogna-Prat, *Agni immaculati: Recherches sur les sources hagiographiques relatives à Saint Maïeul de Cluny (954–994)* (Paris: Cerf, 1988), p. 291.

22. *Vie de Saint Étienne d'Obazine*, ed. and trans. Michel Aubrun (Clermont-Ferrand: Institut d'Études du Massif Central, 1970), pp. 170–73.

23. Marie-Christine Chartier, "Présence de la Bible dans les règles et coutumiers," in *Le Moyen Âge et la Bible*, ed. Pierre Riché and Guy Lobrichon (Paris: Beauchesne, 1984), 305–25, at 305; and Paul Tombeur, "*Audire* dans le thème hagiographique de la conversion," *Latomus* 24 (1965): 159–65. I thank Pascal Boulhol for this last reference.

24. Athanasius, *Vie d'Antoine*, ch. 2–3.

25. Adalbert de Vogüé, *Histoire littéraire du mouvement monastique dans l'antiquité*, vol. 1: *Le monachisme latin: De la mort d'Antoine à la fin du séjour de Jérome à Rome* (356–385) (Paris: Cerf, 1991), pp. 17–22.

26. Jonas of Bobbio, *Ionae vitae sanctorum Columbani, Vedastis, Iohannis*, ed. Bruno Krusch, MGH, Scriptores rerum Germanicarum 37 (Hannover: Hahn, 1905), 1.1.6, p. 163; and *Vita di Columbano e dei suoi discepoli*, ed. Inos Biffi and Aldo Granata (Milan: Jaca, 2001), 1.1.6, p. 42. English translation in Jonas of Bobbio, *Life of St. Columban*, ed. Dana Carleton Munro (Felinfach: Llanerch, 1993). On this source, see Albrecht Diem, "Monks, Kings, and the Transformation of Sanctity," *Speculum* 82 (2007): 521–59.

27. The European monasteries used the numerous rules written between 400 and 700 relatively freely at least until the eighth century and the beginning of the Carolingian reform. See de Vogüé, *Les règles monastiques*.

28. On the early medieval monks as a "sacred gender," see Lynda Coon, "'What Is the Word If not Semen?' Priestly Bodies in Carolingian Exegesis," in *Gender in the Early Medieval World: East and West, 300–900*, ed. Leslie Brubaker and Julia M. H. Smith (Cambridge: Cambridge University Press, 2004), pp. 278–300.

29. Also *RB*, prologue, paragraph 17; *RB* 1980, pp. 160–61. On the multiple references to the Bible in the Benedictine Rule, see Jean Gribomont, "La règle et la bible," in *San Benedetto nel suo tempo: Atti del 70 Congresso internazionale di Studi sull'alto medioevo*, 2 vols. (Spoleto: Centro italiano di studi'alto medievo, 1982), 1:355–89.

30. Diane Reilly, "The Cluniac Giant Bible and the Ordo librorum ad legendum: A Reassessment of Monastic Bible Reading and Cluniac Customary Instructions," in *From Dead of Night*, pp. 163–89.

31. See, for instance, *Liber tramitis*, pp. 200–1.

32. Caesarius of Arles, *Œuvres monastiques*, vol. 1, SC 345 (Paris: Cerf, 1988), pp. 192, 194, 196 (paragraphs 18, 20, and 22). English translation in *The Rule for Nuns of Saint Cæsarius of Arles: A Translation with a Critical Introduction*, ed. and trans. Maria Caritas McCarthy (Washington, DC: Catholic University of America Press, 1960), pp. 175–77.

33. Malcolm Parkes, "Reading, Copying and Interpreting a Text in the Early Middle Ages," in *A History of Reading in the West*, ed. Guglielmo Cavallo and Roger Chartier, trans. Lydia G. Cochrane (Amherst: University of Massachusetts Press, 1999), pp. 90–102.

34. The intensive use of the Psalter in medieval monasteries for didactic, contemplative, and liturgical purposes led to the production of glossed Psalters, with marginal explanations usually taken from the church fathers. See Margaret Gibson, "Carolingian Glossed Psalters," in *The Early Medieval Bible: Its Production, Decoration, and Use,* ed. Richard Gameson (Cambridge: Cambridge University Press, 1994), pp. 78–100.

35. Smaragdus of San Mihiel, *Liber in partibus Donati,* ed. Bengt Löfstedt, Louis Holtz, and Adele Kibre, CCCM 68 (Turnhout: Brepols, 1986); Jean Leclercq, *The Love of Learning and the Desire for God: A Study of Monastic Culture,* trans. Catharine Misrahi, 3d ed. (New York: Fordham University Press, 1982), pp. 44–46; and Matthew Ponesse, "Learning in the Carolingian Court: Compilation and Innovation in the Writings of Abbot Smaragdus of St Mihiel" (Ph.D. diss., University of Toronto, 2004). On the education of oblates at Cluny, see Susan Boynton and Isabelle Cochelin, "The Sociomusical Role of Child Oblates at the Abbey of Cluny in the Eleventh Century," in *Musical Childhoods and the Cultures of Youth,* ed. Susan Boynton and Roe-Min Kok (Middletown, CT: Wesleyan University Press, 2006), pp. 3–24; and Isabelle Cochelin, "Besides the Book: Using the Body to Mould the Mind. Cluny in the Tenth and Eleventh Centuries," in *Medieval Monastic Education,* ed. George Ferzoco and Carolyn Muessig (London: Leicester University Press, 2001), pp. 21–34.

36. See Giulio d'Onofrio, "Il rinascere della Christianitas (secoli vi–viii)," in *Storia della teologia nel medioevo,* vol. 1: *I princìpi,* ed. Giulio d'Onofrio (Casale Monferrato: Piemme, 1996), pp. 37–60, at 37.

37. Haimo of Auxerre, *Historiae sacrae epitome,* l.6.3, PL 118:851A, as cited by Henri de Lubac, *Exégèse médiévale: Les quatre sens de l'écriture,* vol. 1: *Théologie* (Paris: Aubier, 1959), p. 80.

38. *RB* 48.14–16; *RB* 1980, pp. 150–51.

39. Anscari Mundó, "'Bibliotheca.' Bible et lecture du Carême d'après Saint Benoît," *Revue bénédictine* 60 (1950): 65–92, at 80–82. I thank Michel Huglo for this reference.

40. Ibid., pp. 65–92; and Benjamin Victor, "Aux origines de la bibliothèque monastique: la distribution du Carême," *Scriptorium* 50 (1996): 247–53.

41. *Liber tramitis,* pp. xlv, 190, 261–64.

42. André Wilmart, "Le convent et la bibliothèque de Cluny vers le milieu du XIe siècle," *Revue Mabillon* 11 (1921): 89–124.

43. Donald Bullough, "The Carolingian Liturgical Experience," in *Continuity and Change in Christian Worship,* ed. Robert N. Swanson, Studies in Church History 35 (Woodbridge, Suffolk: Boydell, 1999), pp. 29–64, at 44–49.

44. On the history of exegesis, see Guy Lobrichon, "L'exégèse biblique—Histoire d'un genre littéraire (VIIe–XIIIe siècle)," in *Le Moyen Âge et la Bible,* pp. 55–70; and the essays in this book by Frans van Liere and Bert Roest.

45. See C. Stephen Jaeger, *The Envy of Angels: Cathedral Schools and Social Ideals in Medieval Europe, 950–1200* (Philadelphia: University of Pennsylvania Press, 1994);

and Carolyn Walker Bynum, "The Spirituality of Regular Canons in the Twelfth Century," in *Jesus as Mother: Studies in the Spirituality of the High Middle Ages,* ed. Carolyn Walker Bynum (Berkeley: University of California Press, 1982), pp. 22–58.

46. As Leclercq recounted of Bernard of Clairvaux, the teaching of Holy Scripture should be "oriented not toward teaching but toward spirituality"; Leclercq, *Love of Learning,* p. 5.

47. *RB* 73.3 (*RB* 1980, pp. 294–97); and Jacques Dubois, "Comment les moines du moyen âge chantaient et goûtaient les Saintes Écritures," in *Le Moyen Âge et la Bible,* pp. 261–98, at 261. See also Smaragdus of San Mihiel on the regenerative power of the singing and reciting of the Psalms, which transforms an individual from a penitent to a perfected soul (preface to the *Expositio psalmorum,* PL 129:1024AB, partially quoted in Ponesse, "Learning in the Carolingian Court," p. 124).

48. On literal versus tropological, allegorical, and anagogical readings of the Bible in the period prior to the twelfth century, see Beryl Smalley, *The Study of the Bible in the Middle Ages,* rev. ed. (Oxford: Basil Blackwell, 1983), pp. vii–viii; and Lobrichon, "L'exégèse biblique," p. 63. See also van Liere's chapter in this volume.

49. Leclercq, *Love of Learning,* pp. 84–86. On other medieval readings of the Song of Songs, see Rachel Fulton, "'Quae est ista quae ascendit sicut aurora consurgens?' The Song of Songs as the Historia for the Office of the Assumption," *Mediaeval Studies* 60 (1998): 55–122.

50. De Lubac, *Exégèse médiévale,* 1:119–20; John J. Contreni, "Carolingian Biblical Culture," in *Iohannes Scottus Eriugena: The Bible and Hermeneutics,* ed. Gerd Van Riel, Carlos Steel, and James McEvoy, Proceedings of the Ninth International Colloquium of the Society for the Promotion of Eriugenian Studies, held at Leuven and Louvain-la-Neuve, June 7–10, 1995 (Louvain: Leuven University Press, 1996), pp. 1–23, at 13; and Édouard Jeauneau, "Artifex Scriptura," in *Iohannes Scottus Eriugena,* pp. 351–65, at 357–58.

51. Leclercq, *Love of Learning,* p. 117; and de Jong, "Carolingian Monasticism," p. 637.

52. Leclercq, *Love of Learning,* pp. 79–80. The fundamental concept of monks as exempla for good living can be found in various parts of the rule for nuns by Caesarius of Arles. See William E. Klingshirn, *Caesarius of Arles: The Making of a Christian Community in Late Antique Gaul* (Cambridge: Cambridge University Press, 1994), pp. 117 and 122. It is also presented as evidence in Charlemagne, *Encyclica de litteris colendis,* ed. G. H. Pertz, in *MGH Leges,* vol. 1 (Hannover: Hahn, 1835), p. 53; for an English translation, see *The Reign of Charlemagne: Documents on Carolingian Government and Administration,* ed. H. R. Loyn and J. Percival (London: Arnold, 1975), pp. 63–64.

53. See the extremely detailed Cluniac daily timetable reconstituted by Candida Elvert, "Das Kluniazensische Horarium im 10./11. Jahrhundert," in *Clavis voluminum CCM 7/1–3,* ed. Candida Elvert, CCM 7.4 (Siegburg: Franz Schmitt, 1986), 1–7.

54. Leclercq, *Love of Learning*, pp. 57–58; and John Harper, *The Forms and Orders of Western Liturgy from the Tenth to the Eighteenth Century: A Historical Introduction and Guide for Students and Musicians* (Oxford: Clarendon, 1991), pp. 18–19 and 74.

55. Adalbert de Vogüé, *The Rule of Saint Benedict: A Doctrinal and Spiritual Commentary*, trans. John Baptist Hasbrouck (Kalamazoo, MI: Cistercian, 1983), pp. 239–50; Robert F. Taft, *The Liturgy of the Hours in East and West: The Origin of the Divine Office and Its Meaning for Today* (Collegeville, MN: Liturgical, 1986; repr. 1993); and Patrick Henriet, *La parole et la prière au moyen âge: Le verbe efficace dans l'hagiographie monastique des XIe et XIIe siècles* (Brussels: Université DeBoeck, 2000), pp. 31–35.

56. Jean Leclercq, "The Exposition and Exegesis of the Scripture, 2: From Gregory the Great to Saint Bernard," in *The Cambridge History of the Bible*, vol. 2: *The West from the Fathers to the Reformation*, ed. G. W. H. Lampe (Cambridge: University Press, 1969), pp. 183–97, at 189; and Dubois, "Comment les moines," pp. 278–88.

57. Dubois, "Comment les moines," pp. 264–70 and 298, where he illustrates the medieval monks' great mastery of the Bible through monastic games (*ioca monachorum*).

58. Peter the Venerable, *De miraculis libri duo*, ed. D. Bouthillier, CCCM 83 (Turnhout: Brepols, 1988), 1.20 (p. 61); and Dubois, "Comment les moines," p. 262.

59. See Dubois "Comment les moines," p. 262 and 288–97; and Leclercq, *Love of Learning*, pp. 73–77.

60. See Bullough, "The Carolingian Liturgical Experience," pp. 51 and 54.

61. The *Liber tramitis* is one of the best sources for the types of objects displayed during a monastic procession: see, for instance, pp. 23, 68, 108, 115, 151, and 242.

62. André Wilmart, "Le samedi-saint monastique," *Revue bénédictine* 34 (1922): 159–63, at 160–62; Mary Alfred Schroll, *Benedictine Monasticism as Reflected in the Warnefrid-Hildemar Commentaries on the Rule* (New York: Columbia University Press, 1941), pp. 37–39; Anselme Davril and Éric Palazzo, *La vie des moines au temps des grandes abbayes* (Paris: Hachette, 2000), p. 111; and Gerd Zimmermann, *Ordensleben und Lebensstandard: Die Cura corporis in den Ordensvorschriften des abendländischen Hochmittelalters* (Münster: Aschendorff, 1973), pp. 124–26. Following a long period of uncleanliness, especially during Lent, this Easter bath symbolized also the renewal by baptism associated by Paul with Christ's death and Resurrection (Rom. 6:1–5 and Col. 2:12). I thank Jacques Ménard for pointing out this biblical symbolism to me.

63. See Ulrich of Zell, *Consuetudines*, PL 149: 663a and 661c; the church was thoroughly washed two days earlier, on Thursday. See also *Regularis concordia anglicae nationis*, ed. Thomas Symons and Sigrid Spath, in CCM 7.3 (hereafter *RC*), p. 111.5–8; English translation in *Regularis Concordia Anglicae nationis monachorum sanctimonialiumque: The Monastic Agreement of the Monks and Nuns of the English Nation*, trans. Thomas Symons (hereafter *RCE*) (London: Thomas Nelson, 1953), p. 39; and *Ælfric's Letter to the Monks of Eynsham* (hereafter *Ælfric*), ed. and trans.

Christopher A. Jones, Cambridge Studies in Anglo-Saxon England 24 (Cambridge: Cambridge University Press, 1998), pp. 126–27.

64. André Wilmart, "Le samedi-saint," p. 160.

65. RC, p. 109.14; RCE, p. 37.

66. J. P. van Dijk, "The Bible in Liturgical Use," in The Cambridge History of the Bible, 2:220–52, at 221–22.

67. Nils Holger Petersen, "The Representational Liturgy of the Regularis Concordia," in The White Mantle of Churches: Architecture, Liturgy, and Art Around the Millennium, ed. Nigel Hiscock (Turnhout: Brepols, 2003), pp. 107–17, at 113–14.

68. Ælfric, p. 187; and RC, p. 109n.

69. RC, 113.1 (RCE, p. 39), refers to a flint.

70. Ælfric, pp. 190–91. Also RC, 113:2–5 (RCE, p. 39), CA, 77:13–19, Ulrich of Zell, Consuetudines, PL 149: 659a.

71. As interpreted by Amalarius of Metz, Liber officialis, in Amalarii episcopi opera liturgica omnia, vol. 2, ed. Jean-Michel Hanssens, Studi e testi (Biblioteca apostolica vaticana) 139 (Vatican City: Biblioteca apostolica vaticana, 1948), l.1.12 (p. 90) and 20 (p. 121).

72. Wilmart, "Le samedi-saint," p. 161n.

73. Ibid., p. 161, #12–13. On baptisms of newborn babies in monasteries on that day, see also Ælfric, p. 135.

74. Wilmart, "Le samedi-saint," p. 162, #24–25 and 28.

75. C. Clifford Flanigan, "Medieval Liturgy and the Arts: Visitatio sepulchri as a Paradigm," in Liturgy and the Arts in the Middle Ages: Studies in Honour of C. Clifford Flanigan, ed. Eva Louise Lillie and Nils Holger Petersen (Copenhagen: Museum Tusculanum Press, 1996), pp. 9–35, at 13.

76. See especially C. Clifford Flanigan, "Medieval Latin Music-Drama," in The Theatre of Medieval Europe: New Research in Early Drama, ed. Eckehard Simon (Cambridge: Cambridge University Press, 1991), pp. 21–41.

77. I thank Nils Holger Petersen for pointing out to me the inappropriateness of the term dramatization for the mimetic activities of the monks, as we cannot conceive of them today as actors playing out a part; Petersen, "The Representational Liturgy," pp. 111–12.

78. Adalbert de Vogüé, La règle de Saint Benoît, vol. 6: Commentaire historique et critique (parts 7–9 and index), SC 186 (Paris: Cerf, 1971), pp. 1256–79; RB 1980, pp. 254–57.

79. Ulrich of Zell, Consuetudines, PL 149: 753bc.

80. Bärbel Brodt, "Norwich," in Lexikon des Mittelalters, vol. 6 (Munich: Artemis and Winkler, 1993), col. 1270.

81. Thomas Schäfer, Die Fusswaschung im monastischen Brauchtum und in der lateinischen Liturgie (Beuron in Hohenzollern: Beuroner Kunstverlag, 1956); Georg Richter, Die Fußwaschung im Johannesevangelium, Biblische Untersuchungen 1 (Regensburg: Friedrich Pustet, 1967), pp. 64–71; Philippe Rouillard, "Lavement des

pieds," in *Catholicisme: Hier, aujourd'hui, demain,* vol. 7 (Paris: Letouzey and Ané, 1975), pp. 92–97; and Eliana Magnani, "Le pauvre, le Christ et le moine: la correspondance de rôles et les cérémonies du mandatum à travers les coutumiers clunisiens du XIe siècle," in *Les clercs, les fidèles et les saints en Bourgogne médiévale,* ed. Vincent Tabbagh (Dijon: EUD, 2005), pp. 11–26.

82. Only a few of the ancient rules compared by Benedict of Aniane discussed the mandatum; see *Benedicti Anianensis concordia regularum,* ed. Pierre Bonnerue, CCCM 168A (Turnhout: Brepols, 1999), p. 370, line 51 and p. 375, line 190; and *Concordia regularum,* ed. Pierre Bonnerue, CCCM 168 (Turnhout: Brepols, 1999), pp. 46–53. However, the council of Aix-la-Chapelle (Aachen) led by the same Benedict of Aniane testified that it was regularly performed in Carolingian monasteries. See "Synodi primae aquisgranensis decreta authentica (816)" and "Synodi secundae aquisgranensis decreta authentica (817)," ed. Josef Semmler, in *Initia consuetudinis Benedictinae, Consuetudines saeculi octavi et noni,* ed. Kassius Hallinger, CCM 1 (Siegburg: Franz Schmitt, 1963), p. 463, lines 5–8 and 463n.

83. Theodemar, "Theodomari abbatis Casinensis epistula ad Theodoricum gloriosum (778–797)," ed. J. Winandy and Kassius Hallinger, in *Initia consuetudinis Benedictinae,* p. 130, line 14.

84. For instance *Ælfric,* 131:41; and Ulrich of Zell, *Consuetudines,* PL 149: 660bc.

85. This ceremonial reception of guests already existed in pagan antiquity. See Schäfer, *Die Fusswaschung,* p. 20; and Rouillard, "Lavement des pieds," col. 92–93.

86. Schäfer, *Die Fusswaschung,* p. 34; and Rouillard, "Lavement des pieds," col. 96.

87. "Regula sancti Benedicti abbatis Anianensis," p. 535, lines 21–23, and "Legislationis monasticae Aquisgranensis collectio Sancti Martialis Lemovicensis (ante 850)," ed. Josef Semmler, in *Initia consuetudinis Benedictinae,* p. 558, lines 15 and 18; *RC,* p. 112 (*RCE,* p. 39); *Ælfric,* p. 129, line 36; "Redactio sancti Emmerammi dicta Einsidlensis," ed. Maria Wegener and Candida Elvert, in *Consuetudinum saeculi X/XI/XII monumenta non-Cluniacensia,* ed. Kassius Hallinger, CCM 7.3 (Siegburg: Franz Schmitt, 1984), p. 226, line 52.

88. *RC,* p. 138, line 94 (*RCE,* p. 61); *Ælfric,* p. 141, line 62; *Consuetudines floriacenses antiquiores,* ed. Anselme Davril and Lin Donnat, in *Consuetudinum saeculi X/XI/XII momumenta,* p. 21, line 4; "Redactio vallumbrosiana saec. XII (V)," ed. Nicola Vasaturo, in *Consuetudines Cluniacensium antiquiores cum redactionibus derivatis,* ed. Kassius Hallinger, CCM 7.2 (Siegburg: Franz Schmitt, 1983), p. 345, line 17 and p. 346, line 2.

89. Magnani, "Le pauvre."

90. Various new orders from the twelfth century onward based their mode of life on the Bible more than previous orders had done; Chartier, "Présence," p. 317, evoking the rule of Grandmont and the first rule of Francis. But the emphasis was now less on rumination and contemplation of the whole Bible and more on the *vita apostolica,* the imitation of the life of the apostles.

91. Paolo Chiesa, "Le traduzioni," in *La Bibbia nel medioevo,* pp. 15–27.

92. *The Register of Eudes of Rouen,* ed. Jeremiah F. O'Sullivan, trans. Sydney M. Brown (New York: Columbia University Press, 1964).

93. R. E. McLaughlin, "The Word Eclipsed? Preaching in the Early Middle Ages," *Traditio* 46 (1991): 77–122, at 77–87, 106, and 112.

94. John Van Engen, "The 'Crisis of Cenobitism' Reconsidered: Benedictine Monasticism in the Years 1050–1150," *Speculum* 61 (1986): 269–304; and Giles Constable, *The Reformation of the Twelfth Century* (Cambridge: Cambridge University Press, 1996). The change was neither sudden nor definitive nor on all fronts; Bernard of Clairvaux has some beautiful pages on the soul rising to heaven to share a cubiculum with Christ, and Leclercq gives him the place of honor among nonscholastic, monastic theologians; Leclercq, *Love of Learning,* pp. 4–6, 55–56, and 79.

# The Bible and the Meaning of History in the Middle Ages

*Jennifer A. Harris*

H istory is the confluence of time and place: historical events are necessarily located both temporally and spatially. But what is time? Augustine, the fifth-century bishop of Hippo (354–430), is well known for his answer: "Provided that no one asks me, I know."[1] Despite Augustine's perplexity, he expended enormous effort in his reflections on time, which he described as "the vehicle of sin and tragedy as well as the medium of redemption."[2] For Augustine, the problem of time was resolved in part by the redemption possible in time or, more precisely, in history as the temporal narrative of God's saving actions toward humanity. In this essay, I examine how the Bible and its narrative of salvation came to shape the meaning of history and the nature of some history writing in the Middle Ages. The Bible provided medieval theologians and historians with a trustworthy narrative founded in creation, tracing all human societies back to their common ancestors, Adam and Eve. The Bible also provided models for historical development and visions of events yet to come.

Christian historiography emerged over the first five centuries of the church. The genre developed from two competing visions of history, both of which were rooted in the Bible. The first was universal and embodied a sense of progress by means of the *translatio imperii*, the transmission of secular power from one kingdom to another. It found its biblical source in Daniel's dream (Daniel 4) and was most effectively addressed by Paulus Orosius. The second employs the biblical narrative as a whole, reflecting divine administration over all history, yet focusing on the sacred history of God's work in Israel and the church. This second vision was embraced by Augustine of Hippo. Both models influenced historical thinking and writing in the high Middle Ages. As this study demonstrates, medieval Europe never fully abandoned its debt to the Bible as the anchor of historical unity: the Bible was essential for understanding the past, present, and future in the medieval period.

## Historia: The Meaning of History

Beryl Smalley observed that medieval historians inherited their literary genres and models from the classical world and their content, scope, and purpose from the Bible and its Christian interpreters.[3] The scope and content of the Bible was seen as the narrative of salvation. The idea of salvation history was already present in the Hellenized Jewish context from which Christianity emerged. In the centuries preceding the Christian movement, the foundational importance of history was reflected in the collecting and arranging of the Bible itself. The experience of the Babylonian exile in the seventh century BCE was a catalyst for Hebrew historians to craft a narrative of God's providential care for Israel, resulting eventually in the Hebrew Bible we know today.[4]

Christian adoption of biblical ideas about salvation history may seem, in retrospect, quite natural; however, the Greco-Roman intellectual environment of the early church exerted enormous ideological pressure on the burgeoning community. For this culture, history was less about salvation and more about temporal matters.[5] The Greek term *historia* signified inquiry in general or, more specifically, the record of human happenings, especially recent past and contemporary political and martial events and their import for the future.[6] Of primary interest were heroic examples from the past rather than the shape and direction of the story itself.[7] Greek philosophical sensibilities demanded rational explanations for events; Herodotus and Thucydides—who created the norms of classical historiography—complied. The conclusion of reasonable inquiry into

events was that the gods play a part in human events but do not determine its ultimate direction and meaning. Later Hellenistic historians
maintained this prohibition on providence.

Late-antique Latin historians were more likely to discuss the place of
fortune in the shape of human events.[8] Thus Roman historiography mediated between ancient Greek and Christian perspectives. Still, Roman history writing concentrated on the considerable political and military
exploits of the Roman Republic and the Empire. This form of classical
historical writing continued until the collapse of the western Empire in
the fifth century.[9]

## Universal and Ecclesiastical Historiography

Before the conversion of the emperor Constantine, literary activity, in
the context of a small and illicit Christian movement, was focused on protecting the memory of the earliest community and its most heroic members. Brian Croke and Allana Emmett suggest that during the formative
period from the third to the fifth century CE, the writing of history was
transformed from classical models into Christian idioms.[10] The result was
a conflation of contemporary military and political events with a providential view of history itself.

The "father" of Christian historiography is Eusebius of Caesarea (263–
339). Eusebius began his *Chronicles* (c. 300) in the period of persecution
that preceded the conversion of Constantine and the gradual Christian-
ization of Rome.[11] The *Chronicles* provided a singular, synchronized view of
secular and biblical events. While Eusebius was immersed in classical ideas
of history writing (for example, using the chronological customs of imperial reigns and Olympiads), his work was also innovative, notably in his
construction of a narrative that included the whole known world.[12] Eusebius took the birth of Abraham as his temporal point of departure, dividing history into six periods: 1. from Adam to the flood, 2. from the flood to
Abraham, 3. from Abraham—when history proper begins—to Moses, 4.
from Moses to the construction of Solomon's Temple, 5. from the first
Temple to the Second Temple, and 6. from the Second Temple to the ministry of Jesus.[13] Through his chronological scheme, he demonstrated the
antiquity of biblical history and the sovereignty of God over all history.

Eusebius's *Chronicles*, as transmitted in Jerome's Latin translation, was
hugely influential during the Middle Ages.[14] Jerome (c. 342–420) contin-

ued beyond Eusebius's *terminus* of 303 CE into his own age (c. 378), reworking the Eusebian text to include the decisive beginning of history with creation (rather than the birth of Abraham and the calling of Israel). In pressing back to the foundation of history, Jerome included the history of the Gentiles (descended from Japtheth, son of Noah), which was "the actual or inherited experience of most Christian readers" at the time.[15] Jerome's work was consciously broader than previous histories, and he "explicitly accented God's hand as the force behind the sweep of world empires."[16]

Eusebius is better known for his ecclesiastical history. His *Historia ecclesiastica* (c. 325) focused on the events of the church since the life of Christ and assumed the providential structure of history delimited in the *Chronicles*.[17] In its ten books Eusebius constructed the first systematic history of the church, a work that had an enormous impact on the writing of history. In particular, it forged a historical identity for the Christian community as it emerged from a period of marginalization to take its place at the helm of the Empire.[18] This was no small deed: the history of Rome provided a universal sense of identity for all citizens, which was routinely traced back to the legendary foundations of the Eternal City. The fourth-century Christian church needed a new narrative of collective identity that maintained continuity between the pre-Constantinian community of martyrs and the postconversion established church. This story was shaped in the universal chronographies of the third century, and completed in the creation of ecclesiastical history in the fourth.

The techniques of universal historiography developed quickly beyond the bare account of the earlier chronographies. In the fifth century, on the heels of transalpine invasions into Rome, Paulus Orosius (d. 419) compiled his *Historiarum adversum paganos libri VII* (*Seven Books of History Against the Pagans*).[19] Orosius, a Spanish priest, was Augustine's protégé and composed the work at his mentor's request, c. 416–17. His work, in one scholar's words, was the first real attempt at a world history using documentary sources and presenting an argument for the meaning of history.[20] In it Orosius narrated the calamities of history surrounding the conversion of Rome to Christianity. Like Jerome, the Spaniard was not afraid to equate the progress of worldly empires with the progress of God's activity in history, a different view from that held by his mentor Augustine.[21] Orosius popularized the political interpretation of the four kingdoms in Daniel's vision of four beasts (Daniel 7).[22] This model of historical development, known as *translatio imperii* (or "transfer of rule"), remained influential throughout the Middle Ages.[23] Orosius interpreted Daniel's vision as decisively foretelling the continuity of Rome (the fourth and final kingdom) until the end of history, and he placed this teleological observation at the heart of his historiography.[24] Orosius's use of the "four kingdoms" brought history writing into the realm of eschatology.[25]

What was most enduring in Orosius's work was the "alliance of spiritual faith and secular state."[26] His idea of secularized providential history dominated medieval universal and national histories in the period after the transformation of governance in Europe following the demise of the empire.[27] Many medieval libraries included a copy of Orosius's work.[28] His text was translated into Old English by Alfred the Great,[29] and Otto of Freising acknowledged his debt to Orosius at the outset of his *Chronicon*.

Universal historiography allowed the newly established church to insert itself into a model of history shaped by the Bible and the Roman Empire. The vision of Daniel linked biblical sensibilities to imperial realities. The idiom of universal history thus became a distinctly Christian one. While different from biblical sacred history, universal histories are nevertheless an indication of the importance of the Bible in shaping a Christian sense of history. It is to the sense of a "sacred history" that I now turn.

## The Bible and Sacred History

When the Roman Empire embraced Christianity in the fourth century, the possibility of reading contemporary events through the lens of biblical prophecy was tempting. By 392, when the emperor Theodosius I established Christianity as the religion of the empire, a giddy sense of historical fulfillment appeared in the work of such diverse authors as Augustine and Prudentius (348–c. 410).[30] Yet soon after the transformation of the Roman Empire into a Christian one, Augustine reflected anew upon the events of salvation as expressed in the Bible and found there no approbation of the empire. He asserted that sacred history subsisted in the biblical story alone, without recourse to secular events. His historical theology suggested that the dynamic story of divine promise could not easily be tied to contemporary events.[31] Augustine, therefore, problematized Christian universal historiography.

Nevertheless, Augustine was aware of the importance of history and wrote about its meaning for the Christian dispensation.[32] One can trace a development in his thought from his conversion to his greatest work on the theology of history, *De civitate Dei*, composed in the 420s.[33] Augustine moves from belief in the interconnection between sacred and secular realms to his final works in which history is clearly divided into two spheres. Only the sacred sphere, the narrative of salvation in the Bible, merited exposition; it alone bore traces of God's salvatory acts. Secular history, by contrast, was an account of the vale of tears in human affairs and was unworthy of notice.

Earlier I noted the significance of history writing for the collective memory and identity of the new Christian movement. Similarly, immediately after the empire's conversion to Christianity, few Romans would have been familiar with either the Jewish or the Christian vision of history. A model of historical pedagogy that placed the biblical story at the disposal of a new generation of Christians was needed.[34] Inculcating the Christian sense of history was accomplished through catechesis, instruction for initiates to the faith.[35] In his treatise on catechism, *De catechizandis rudibus* (*On the catechizing of the uninstructed*, composed c. 400), Augustine offered such an introductory course in the Christian faith, using the scheme of history as his foundation.[36] The six ages of Augustine's narrative comprised the biblical story of salvation. God's sole governance of history was the point of the scheme, and Augustine rejected human potential to influence its timing or outcome.

In his catechesis, Augustine gathered a coherent biblical narrative from creation in Genesis to the new creation in Revelation. He divided the story of sacred history into six ages, which correlated to the six days of creation and the six ages of humanity. Augustine adapted Eusebius's periodization of history, but reduced the number of pre-Christian ages to five and matched them to the genealogical generations found in the first chapter of Matthew's Gospel: from Adam to Noah, from Noah to Abraham, from Abraham to David, from David to the exile in Babylon, from exile to the advent of Jesus. The sixth (and, for Augustine, the present) age began with the Incarnation, and comprised the entire history of the church, including events yet to come.[37] This present age, he noted, will cease with the second coming and Last Judgment, marking also the conclusion of the concurrent seventh age (which parallels the whole history of the world since Abel as the age of rest for the righteous) and the beginning of the eighth age, or eternity. The influence of this educational program may be found throughout the Middle Ages.[38]

Along with its view of the two cities (one of God, the other of the devil), the catechetical treatise quickly became the foundation for Augustine's magisterial theology of history, as articulated in the *De civitate Dei* (*On the City of God*, c. 410–27 CE).[39] One significant difference between these two works is their political context: the former was written during the triumphant years of the Theodosian establishment, when Augustine and others conceived the Christian empire as fulfilling prophecy and taking Christianity to the ends of the earth; the latter was written after the sack of Rome and the collapse of the Roman imperial project.[40] The gap between them transformed an optimistic view of history into a politically neutral historiography that more fully embraced the blessings and curses meted out in God's providence.[41]

## Biblical Historiography in the Middle Ages

The arrival of the Germanic peoples into Roman Europe reinforced the biblical frame of history in the minds of its narrators, whether in the form of the four kingdoms or the six ages of the world. An example of early medieval biblical historiography, written on the heels of the barbarian incursions into Europe, is the *Decem libri historiarum* (*Ten Books of the Histories*), commonly called the *Historia francorum* (*History of the Franks*), by Gregory, bishop of Tours and historian of sixth-century Gaul (c. 538–93/4).[42] Gregory was the first historian since Orosius to compose a history in the western Roman world, yet Gregory used a biblical model of history.[43]

Gregory's first book sketched out the history of the world from creation to the death of Martin of Tours in 397. He opened with a statement of faith, drawn from the Nicene Creed, and stated his purpose: to recount the years since creation, in order to allay fears about the imminent rise of the Antichrist. Gregory adopted an Augustinian calm in the face of such fears. No one can know the hour when Antichrist will come, yet knowledge of history can aid in preparation for his arrival.[44] After introducing this eschatological theme, however, Gregory paid little heed to such concerns; instead, his historiography focused on memory and identity, which he adapted to his context. What is striking about Gregory's construction of the past is his lack of belief in development within the biblical narrative. Goffart observes that "although Gregory's times, like all others, obviously moved between Creation and Final Judgment, the world he portrayed might as well have been indeterminate or timeless."[45] Instead, as the remainder of Gregory's narrative demonstrates, all history is subordinated to the purpose of moral instruction, which after all is the purpose of telling the story of the Franks. The moral purpose of history also pervades the sensibility of Gregory's namesake, Pope Gregory I. The pope's worldview was at once more and less biblical than Augustine's. Pope Gregory, who lived two hundred years after Augustine in a society utterly shaped according to the biblical vision, could not conceive the Augustinian separation of the secular realm from the inherently Christian one.[46] The pope's eschatological sensitivity also set him at odds with Augustine's cautions. In one particularly apocalyptic sermon, Gregory drew parallels between recent, catastrophic events in Rome and the prophecy of the end found in Luke's Gospel.[47] By the sixth century, for a now fully Christianized society, history had become transparent, the sixth age filled with meaningful events to be interpreted within a biblical sense of history.

The popularization of dynamic biblical historiography began in earnest in the work of seventh-century Spanish encyclopedist, Isidore of Seville (c. 560–636). In book 5 of his *Etymologies,* Isidore included a brief world chronicle. Using Eusebius's *Chronicles* (translated and updated by Jerome) with the addition of the pre-Abrahamic ages and Augustine's six ages of the world, the Spanish bishop's chronicle collapsed the distinction between biblical or sacred and secular historical narratives.[48] In this work Isidore created the "first world chronicle dated according to the *annus mundi,*"[49] meaning the Jewish and Christian measure of historical time beginning with the creation of the world. This was a constant system in Christian historiography until the eleventh century, when the *annus Domini* system ("year of the Lord"), proposed by Dionysius Exiguus (c. 535) and popularized by Bede (c. 735),[50] came to dominate.[51] The work of the Venerable Bede brought the genre of universal history into the mainstream of Christian historiography. (On biblical commentaries by these same authors, see van Liere's chapter in this volume.)

The Venerable Bede of Jarrow (673–735), an eighth-century Northumbrian monk, is best known for his *Historia ecclesiastica gentis Anglorum* (*Ecclesiastical History of the English People,* c. 731), his mature work on the conversion of the English.[52] Yet even more germane is Bede's computistical work, *De temporum ratione* (*On the Reckoning of Time,* c. 725).[53] This work about "measuring time and constructing a Christian calendar" also includes a world chronicle. By including a chronicle in the *computus,* Bede expressed the link between theological notions of time and historiography. His writings demonstrate that *all* time is governed "by the *ratio* of

Divine providence."[54] Bede's *computus* was read both in insular society and on the Continent, and formed the basis of Easter tables throughout the Western church well beyond the end of the Middle Ages.[55]

The momentum of biblical historiography, both the progressive Orosian and the providential Augustinian models, increased during the cultural renewal at the Carolingian court in the eighth and ninth centuries. Rosamond McKitterick notes that scholars of the Carolingian era were particularly interested in reading and copying history books, which served "as an enabling mechanism in the expression of an elite memory and identity."[56] She stresses that "the books read and produced in the Frankish centres indicate the formation of a sense of the past—biblical, Roman and Christian—to which the Franks collectively belonged and which they inherited."[57] Chief among these texts are a number of history books, including those of Josephus, Orosius, Eusebius, Isidore, Bede, and Gregory of Tours.[58] Nearly all Carolingian monastic libraries contained copies of these works, which formed the basis of original historical works composed in the period.

One vehicle by which Carolingian identity was most clearly fixed in the biblical narrative was the *translatio imperii*, meaning in this context the movement of providential rule from East to West. Carolingian authors who used it were pleased to identify their realm with the Roman Empire.[59] The universality of such a view of the past is disputed by modern scholars, most notably Lawrence Nees.[60] He argues that Carolingian thought did not so much affirm pagan antiquity as rejoice in the great authority of the past, in particular the biblical vision of history described by Augustine.

Frankish kings were particularly fascinated by biblical history. Mayke de Jong has argued that this interest stemmed from the appropriation of the Augustinian distinction between sacred and secular history.[61] Nees too offers a fascinating study of the subversion of the Orosian model in such important material remains at the throne of Charles the Bald (c. 860).[62] Yet the Orosian model of *translatio imperii* was also present in Carolingian historiography, collapsing Augustine's distinction by situating secular rulers within a biblical frame. This biblical emphasis may be observed directly in the outpouring of commentaries on Old Testament books and indirectly in history writing informed by the sacred narrative, such as Frechulf of Lisieux's *Chronicle*, or by the theory of empire denoted in Daniel's vision and repeated in numerous Carolingian annals.

The Carolingian self-image as an elect people ruled by a biblical king was but a dream. By the ninth century the model of society was, by and large, the "church of the nations" (*ecclesia gentium*) in which "patristic rhetoric about the universal church was harnessed to the cause of Carolingian empire,"[63] that is, a hierarchical vision of a divine society ruled by God's appointed king. Although not the literal deployment of Old Testament social models, this ecclesiastical empire was nevertheless rooted in the biblical historiography that preceded it. Such an identity depended on the construction of common ancestry in the biblical historiography of the early church and early Middle Ages.[64]

## The Twelfth Century and the Renewal of History

The end of Carolingian rule ushered in a lengthy period without substantial history writing. Biblical models of historiography eventually reasserted their authority, however.[65] With the rise of the Ottonian dynasty in Germany and the Capetian monarchy in France in the late tenth century, new forms of governance and social order arose. The population began to concentrate in towns and cities. Urban revival expanded opportunities for education and study. Cathedral schools were established to teach the liberal arts, and in cities such as Paris and Bologna the schools became a driving force within the community.[66] In this context of civic restoration, new and renewed models of history writing grappled with enormous changes in social organization. As before, the Bible provided most of the prevalent historiographical idioms.[67]

The Bible provided the narrative for a shared sense of the past and a means for understanding present events in its light.[68] As in late antiquity, the sense of continuity between past and present was cultivated in the medieval period in the use of anachronism (depiction of things in the wrong temporal setting) and anatopism (depiction of things in the wrong geographical place) in art and architecture.[69] This grasping toward an idea of unity of history in Christian art arguably reached its apex in the twelfth century. Anachronistic depictions of biblical scenes routinely portrayed their subjects in contemporary dress, facilitating identity between those within the image and those outside it.[70] Even the built physical environment of the high Middle Ages bespoke the continuation of past time into the present.[71]

The twelfth century was, therefore, endowed with a rich sense of history, biblically rooted. The explosion of history writing in the monasteries, courts, and schools of the twelfth century reflected this sense.[72] A well-known example of this relationship between Bible and historiography was the *Historia scholastica* (c. 1150), written by Peter Comestor (d. c. 1179). As one of the three key textbooks for the medieval schools (along with Gratian's *Concordia discordantium canonum* (*Concordance of Discordant Canons*) on canon law and Peter Lombard's four books of theological *Sententiae*), Comestor's *Historia* was an essential component of higher education.[73] His collocation of biblical history was not, however, an effort to further historiography so much as a renewed presentation of the doctrines of the church via their biblical origins, not unlike Augustine's catechesis.

One of the features to note in Peter's text is his insertion of *incidentiae* ("occurrences"), that is, events in secular history that took place concurrently with the story within the biblical narrative. For example, when Ahialon was judge over Israel, Peter notes, Paris seized Helen, thus beginning the Trojan War.[74]

Comestor's *Historia* is just one twelfth-century intersection between the Bible and history writing. Historical writers of this age composed chronicles, annals, saints' lives, and autobiography; most of the examples appeal to the Bible frequently. History writing in the eleventh and twelfth centuries, like that of earlier ages, developed in accordance with the needs of the time.[75] Chief among these needs was to address observable change within history. The present age, often described as the sixth age or the old age of the world, was, by the twelfth century, one of tremendous social and institutional change. In both Augustine's theology of history and the theory of *translatio imperii*, the present age was the final age, which permitted no significant development.[76] The very existence of change demanded explanation within the overall meaning of history. Whereas Augustine articulated a pessimistic sense of present historical unfolding, his successors in the twelfth century, such as Hugh of St. Victor and Anselm of Havelberg, were more optimistic.[77]

Hugh of St. Victor (d. 1141) was not a historian per se, yet his theological vision of restoration was rooted in the development of history: from the Fall, through an age of natural law, to the age of God's law and, finally, to the age of grace since the Incarnation.[78] Hugh's ideas about the meaning of history and its progression evince a sense of historical development unparalleled among his contemporaries. As Southern notes, the stages of history are laid out in Hugh's theological compendium, *De sacramentis fidei Christianae* (*On the Sacraments of the Christian Faith*), in which the biblical narrative serves as an organizing principle for his theological system.[79] Smalley calls Hugh's *summa* "a manual for the use of students of Arts and theology in the form of a universal chronicle."[80] This teaching tool was consciously modeled, Southern argues, on the human quest for knowledge, to overcome limitations imposed after the fall. The shape of the work points to the paradoxical conjunction of *uchronia*—the timelessness of Christian doctrine and truth—and the chronology Hugh believed essential to theology. The first half of this work concerns creation and fall, the second half restoration.[81]

Hugh also presented his scheme for the historical succession of events in the second part of his *Didascalicon*, his guide to the liberal arts. History, he says, provides the events from which theology develops doctrine and is thus fundamental to the theological enterprise.[82] Moreover, the working out of the divine plan in history permits change and development. Hugh, and few others, saw the need to account for historical change as an implication of the transference of divine election from people in the East to the West for sacred (as opposed to secular) history.[83] He believed that change, indeed positive development, was occurring in the sixth age of the world. But Hugh's vision of historical development was not well received by some of his contemporaries; Peter Abelard even questioned its orthodoxy.[84]

For Anselm of Havelberg (d. 1155), change in the present was most clearly manifest in the rise of new forms of religious life and the debates among the orders that ensued. Anselm, like Hugh, was an Augustinian canon, a new form of ordered religious life that emerged with the rise of cities in the later eleventh century. In the first of his *Dialogi*, Anselm argued for the possibility of innovation within the present as an expression of the work of the Holy Spirit.[85] This interest in divine activity in history invited Anselm to posit a Trinitarian view of history. Fellow German monk-theologian Rupert of Deutz (c. 1075–1129) also suggested that the shape of history is patterned on the Triune God.[86] But it was Joachim of Fiore (c. 1132–1202), the Calabrian abbot and prophet, who invested the tripartite shape of history with its greatest significance: as a key to understanding prophecy and the future.[87]

Indeed, Joachim's interest in a prophetic reading of biblical history is the major contribution to medieval historiography in the twelfth century. Of course, the future never disappeared entirely from the medieval imagination. The Carolingian court received a Latin translation of the *Pseudo-Methodius*, an eschatological text that popularized the legend of the last emperor who would participate in end-time events prior to the rise of the Antichrist.[88] Just before the turn of the first millennium, Adso of Montier-en-Der (d. 992) wrote of the eschatological narrative in a letter to Queen Gerberga (c. 950) called the *Libellus de ortu et tempore Anti-christi* (*Essay on the Birth and Time of the Antichrist*). It recounts the legends of the end times found in the Bible and in popular culture.[89] Adso was concerned to show the queen that the Antichrist had, in fact, not yet risen.[90] The effect of his work appears, however, to have fueled the antici-pation of the end times.[91]

In his *Chronica sive historia de duabus civitatibus* (*Chronicle or History of Two Cities*), Otto of Freising composed a universal history, which included reflections on the end of the world.[92] Most important among Otto's ancient and contemporary sources was Orosius, who supplied the tempo-ral scheme of the four monarchies. Otto's discussion of the history of sal-vation in the *Chronicon* mirrors a periodization peculiar to twelfth-century historiography: the tripartite division between time before the law (*ante legem*), time under the law (*sub lege*), and the period under grace (*sub gratia*). Otto superimposed this plan on the six ages of Augustine and the four monarchies of Orosius. Despite his proximity to the imperial throne, Otto's assessment of the current state of affairs, while permitting a robust sense of the *translatio imperii* into Germany from the Franks, was less than positive. He suggested that the disarray of the present age was testimony of the decline of the final age toward its ordained end. Otto's eighth book explicates the age of the Antichrist, which he felt would arrive very soon.[93]

The most dramatic appropriation of prophecy into the sense of history was the work of Joachim of Fiore (d. 1202) on the three *status* or ages of the world.[94] For him the key to understanding history was to see the seven seals of revelation manifest in both the Old and New Testaments. Joachim believed that the biblical dispensations, expressed in the old and the new laws, were parallel and could be read in concordance in order to reveal the true meaning of history.[95] The shape of the historical narrative was reflected in the personages of the Triune God: the period before the Incarnation he called the "Age of the Father"; with the Incarnation began the "Age of the Son." This second age continued into Joachim's own day, but soon, he believed, the third age of the Holy Spirit would begin.[96] The third age could be forecast in light of the previous two. The arrival of the third age would be characterized by the holiness of its spiritual men fol-lowing upon the arrival of a new Elias and the emergence of the first Anti-christ. The defeat of the Antichrist would presage the true beginning of the third age (see Roest's chapter in this volume).

Joachim's reputation as a visionary spread far. Shortly after his death, however, his formulation of the Trinity was tested at the Fourth Lateran Council and found heterodox. This rebuke did not slake the thirst for meaning in history, and Joachim's prophesies continued to inspire an enthusiastic following.[97] The life of Francis of Assisi and his mendicant followers suggested, to some, the fulfillment of the first sign of the third *status*; the emergence of Emperor Frederick II also invited comparison to the emergent figure of the Antichrist. But any direct imposition of Joachim's time frame onto contemporary events was ultimately frustrated by the events themselves.[98]

The twelfth century also witnessed the incursion of Western European Christians into Islamic Spain, the Slavic territories, and the Levant. The historiography of these conquests had no precedent and hence developed its own idiom.[99] While the localized narratives of campaign and conquest avoided most overt references to the larger story of salvation, comparisons between contemporary and biblical events abound. For example, in his *Chronicle of the Slavs* (c. 1167/68 and 1172), Helmond, a priest of Bosau in Germany, wrote of the German invaders resembling the children of Israel taking possession of the Promised Land.[100] Nowhere is this clearer than in the crusader chronicles. From the earliest eyewitness account, the *Gesta Francorum* (*Deeds of the Franks*), written c. 1099, to the later reflections by "professional" historians such as William of Tyre, the deeds of the Crusaders were frequently given meaning by means of biblical analogies. The Norman Anonymous, the author of the *Gesta Francorum*, begins his tale with the Council of Clermont, at which Pope Urban II proclaimed the effort to repossess the Holy Sepulchre.[101] The soldiers who fall in this endeavor are portrayed as martyrs, filling up the number prophesied in Revelation 6. In his *Dei gesta per Francos* (*The Deeds of God through the Franks*, c. 1108–11), Guibert de Nogent recounts Urban's sermon using the Maccabees as the prime example of martyrdom, suggesting that the Crusaders are like the earlier defenders of the Jerusalem Temple.[102] Baldric, bishop of Dol, the twelfth-century chronicler, likened the crusaders to the "children of Israel, who were led out of Egypt."[103]

The needs of twelfth-century readers were varied. Social and political changes, including the expansion of Europe overseas, the assimilation of new peoples from the East, the variety of religious vocations beyond the traditional Benedictine monastery, and the rise of cities, all required explanation. Historians wrestled with these events. I should note that novelty in the twelfth century was as unwelcome as it was in the third. Tradition remained the driving force of order. For instance, the new religious orders invariably appealed to ancient traditions: the canons to Augustine's community of priests in fifth-century Hippo, the Cistercians to the original austerity of the Benedictine Rule. Even the expansion of Europe was painted as the recollection of the traditional boundaries of Christendom, a deliverance of the holy places from infidel oversight. Nevertheless, the sheer volume of change inspired the reinterpretation of the enduring historical models. Such adjustment allowed for development even within a static age.

Change was a theme that propelled the meaning of history and the practice of history writing in Christian antiquity and the Middle Ages. Whether it was the conversion of Constantine, the renewal of the empire under Charlemagne, or the rise of cities and new forms of religious life, historians had to grapple with the meaning of change within a worldview conditioned to esteem stability and continuity. We have seen how Christian historiography developed in response to changing social and political conditions. On the one hand, the sequence of events was seen to flow *sub specie aeternitatis* (literally "under the aspect of eternity," implying universal truth), giving eternal and divine approbation to particular and mundane matters. Yet the experience of temporality was never overlooked in order to leap from the visible to the invisible. As the *series narrationis* ("order of narrative") of sacred and secular history piled change upon change, efforts to reconcile the two were strained. But the Bible provided enough of a thread to keep the two together, its providential thrust unifying the particulars of history under the eternal administration of God.

## Notes

1. "Quid est ergo tempus? Si nemo ex me quaerat, scio," *Confessionum libri XIII*, 11.14.17, ed. Luc Verheijen, CCSL 27 (Turnhout: Brepols, 1981), p. 202; for an English translation see *Confessions*, trans. Henry Chadwick (Oxford: Oxford University Press, 1991), p. 230.

2. Robert A. Markus, *Saeculum: History and Society in the Theology of Saint Augustine*, rev. ed. (Cambridge: Cambridge University Press, 1988), p. 10.

3. Beryl Smalley, *Historians in the Middle Ages* (London: Thames and Hudson, 1974), p. 13.

4. Arnaldo Momigliano, *The Classical Foundations of Modern Historiography* (Berkeley: University of California Press, 1990), p. 19. Robert L. P. Milburn, *Early Christian Interpretations of History*, Bampton Lectures of 1952 (London: Adam

and Charles Black, 1954), p. 1, discusses the moral purpose of history writing in both classical and Jewish historiography.

5. Though problematic for its positivism, Robin G. Collingwood, *The Idea of History*, rev. ed. (Oxford: Clarendon, 1993), pp. 14–45, remains a useful discussion of classical history writing.

6. Lloyd G. Patterson discusses these ideas in *God and History in Early Christian Thought* (London: Adam and Charles Black, 1967), pp. 13–26.

7. Patterson, *God and History*, pp. 15–21; Momigliano, *Classical Foundations*, p. 18.

8. Patterson, *God and History*, pp. 21–27; Momigliano, *Classical Foundations*, pp. 103–31.

9. Arnaldo Momigliano, "Pagan and Christian Historiography in the Fourth Century A.D.," in *The Conflict Between Paganism and Christianity in the Fourth Century*, ed. Arnaldo Momigliano (Oxford: Clarendon, 1963), pp. 79–99, at 80–81.

10. Brian Croke and Allana M. Emmett, "Historiography in Late Antiquity: An Overview," in *History and Historians in Late Antiquity*, ed. Brian Croke and Allana M. Emmett (Sydney: Pergamon, 1983), pp. 1–13, at 1; and Smalley, *Historians*, p. 13.

11. Eusebius of Caesarea, *Eusebi chronicorum canonum*, vol. 2 of *Eusebi chronicorum libri duo*, ed. Alfred Schöne (Berlin, 1873; repr. Dublin: Weidmann, 1967).

12. Indrikis Sterns, *The Greater Medieval Historians* (Washington, DC: Catholic University Press of America, 1981), p. 9.

13. Momigliano, "Pagan and Christian Historiography," p. 84, suggests that Eusebius used the "era of Abraham" to avoid the pitfalls of dating from the first chapters of Genesis.

14. Jerome, *Chronicon*, in *Eusebius Werke*, vol. 7: *Die Chronik des Hieronymus*, ed. Rudolf Helm (Berlin: Akademie-Verlag, 1956); English translation, *A Translation of Jerome's Chronicon with Historical Commentary*, trans. Malcolm D. Donaldson (Lewiston: Mellen University Press, 1996). See the discussion of Jerome's Eusebius in Alden A. Mosshamer, *The Chronicle of Eusebius and Greek Chronographic Tradition* (Lewisburg, PA: Bucknell University Press, 1979), pp. 37–73.

15. Michael I. Allen, "Universal History 300–1000: Origins and Western Developments," in *Historiography in the Middle Ages*, ed. Deborah Mauskopf Deliyannis (Leiden: Brill, 2003), pp. 17–42, at 24.

16. Ibid., p. 26.

17. See the critical edition of the Greek text with a Latin facing-page translation, *Eusebius Werke*, vol. 2: *Die Kirchengeschichte*, ed. Edward Schwartz and Theodor Mommsen, 2 vols. (Leipzig: Hinrichs'sche Buchhandlung, 1903–8). References are from the English translation, *The History of the Church from Christ to Constantine*, trans. Geoffrey A. Williams (London: Penguin, 1965).

18. Momigliano, "Pagan and Christian Historiography," p. 83.

19. The standard Latin edition, *Historiarum adversum paganos libri VII*, ed. Karl Zangemeister, CSEL 5 (Vienna: Gerold, 1889), has been supplemented by *Histoires (contre les païens)*, ed. and trans. Marie Pierre Arnaud-Lindet, 3 vols. (Paris: Belles Lettres, 1990–91).

20. Milburn, *Early Christian Interpretations*, p. 92.

21. Jerome understood change in history, but his sense of the present was rather gloomy. See, for example, the preface to his *Vita Malchi*, PL 23:55, in which he refers to present "dregs." See Walter Goffart, *The Narrators of Barbarian History (AD 550–800): Jordanes, Gregory of Tours, Bede, and Paul the Deacon* (Princeton: Princeton University Press, 1988), p. 227.

22. Paulus Orosius, *Historiarum adversum paganos*, 2:1–2; English translation, *The Seven Books of History Against the Pagans*, trans. Roy J. Deferrari (Washington, DC: Catholic University of America Press, 1964), pp. 81–85. See the discussion of this text in its original context in John Joseph Collins, *The Apocalyptic Imagination: An Introduction to Jewish Apocalyptic Literature*, Rev. ed. The Biblical Resource Series (Grand Rapids, MI: Eerdmans, 1998), pp. 78–92.

23. The standard study of the doctrine of *translatio imperii* remains Werner Goez, *Translatio imperii: Ein Beitrag zur Geschichte des Geschichtsdenkens und der politischen Theorien im Mittelalter und in der frühen Neuzeit* (Tübingen: Mohr, 1958). More recently, see the discussion of John G. A. Pocock, *Barbarism and Religion*, vol. 3: *The First Decline and Fall* (Cambridge: Cambridge University Press, 1999), pp. 98–107.

24. On the vision of the four beasts, see Jerome, *Commentariorum in Danielem*, 2:7, ed. F. Glorie, CCSL 75A (Turnhout: Brepols, 1964), pp. 837–50. Sulpicius Severus, *Chronicorum libri*, 2:3.5–7, ed. Karl Halm, CSEL 1 (Vienna: Geroldi, 1866), 58–59; Martin Haeusler, *Das Ende der Geschichte in der mittelalterlichen Weltchronistik* (Cologne: Böhlau Verlag, 1980), pp. 17–19.

25. Markus, *Saeculum*, p. 1.

26. Allen, "Universal History," p. 28.

27. Smalley, *Historians*, pp. 53–56, discusses the impact of the conflation of secular and sacred historical idioms on the narration of barbarian history in the sixth to the ninth centuries.

28. Rosamond McKitterick, *History and Memory in the Carolingian World* (Cambridge: Cambridge University Press, 2004), pp. 186–217, notes the presence of Orosius in the libraries of important Carolingian monasteries, Lorsch and St. Amand.

29. *The Old English Orosius*, ed. Janet Bately, Early English Texts Society 6 (Oxford: Oxford University Press, 1980).

30. Markus, *Saeculum*, pp. 23–41, discusses the period at the end of the fourth century.

31. The idea of the two cities is, of course, laid out in *The City of God*, but Augustine began to reflect on it in his catechetical treatise.

32. Sterns, *Greater Medieval Historians*, pp. 14–26, provides a helpful and brief summary of Augustine's historical ideas.

33. Markus, *Saeculum*, pp. 34–44, discusses Augustine's changing views of history in the post-400 period.

34. Momigliano, "Pagan and Christian Historiography," pp. 82–87, brilliantly explores the need for a new historical education in the fourth century.

35. William Harmless, *Augustine and the Catechumenate* (Collegeville, MN: Liturgical, 1995).

36. Augustine of Hippo, *De catechizandis rudibus*, ed. I. B. Bauer, CCSL 46 (Turn-hout: Brepols, 1969), pp. 115–78; Harmless, *Augustine*, p. 127.

37. Augustine, *De catechizandis rudibus* 22:39–40, pp. 163–65. Eusebius began the Christian era (his seventh period) in his *Chronicle* with the public ministry of Jesus, rather than the Incarnation.

38. Harmless, *Augustine*, p. 108, discusses this influence. See also Jean-Paul Bouhot, "Alcuin et le 'De catechizandis rudibus' de saint Augustin," *Recherches augustiniennes* 15 (1980): 176–240 (noted by Harmless).

39. Augustine of Hippo, *Concerning the City of God Against the Pagans*, trans. Henry Bettenson (London: Penguin, 1984; hereafter cited as *City of God*).

40. John O'Meara, "Introduction," in *City of God*, p. xv, n. 2, notes that the books on history (part 4, books 15–22) were composed in 427.

41. Jocelyn N. Hillgarth, "L'Influence de la *Cité de Dieu* de saint Augustin au Haut Moyen Age," *Sacris Erudiri* 28 (1985): 5–34, sketches the influence of this work on later medieval thought. He notes the particular importance of Augustine's vision in the ninth century.

42. Gregory of Tours, *Historiarum libri X*, ed. Bruno Krusch and Wilhelm Levison, 2d ed., MGH Scriptores rerum Merovingicarum 1, pt. 1 (Hanover: Hahn, 1965); English translation by Lewis Thorpe, *The History of the Franks* (London: Penguin, 1974). Regarding the title of the work, see Goffart, *Narrators*, p. 107.

43. Goffart, *Narrators*, p. 169.

44. Gregory of Tours, *History of the Franks*, p. 68.

45. Goffart, *Narrators*, p. 204.

46. Robert A. Markus, *Gregory the Great and His World* (Cambridge: Cambridge University Press, 1997), p. 39.

47. Gregory the Great, *Homiliae XL in evangelia*, 1.1.1, 5, ed. Raymond Etaix, CCSL 141 (Turnhout: Brepols, 1999), pp. 5, 9. See Markus, *Gregory the Great*, p. 50.

48. Allen, "Universal History," p. 33.

49. Faith Wallis, "Commentary," in *Bede: The Reckoning of Time*, trans. Faith Wallis (Liverpool: Liverpool University Press, 1999), p. 357.

50. Dionysius Exiguus, *Libellus de cyclo magno paschae*, PL 67:483–508. See Georges Declercq, *Anno Domini: The Origins of the Christian Era* (Turnhout: Brepols, 2000), pp. 97–147.

51. Daniel P. McCarthy, "The Emergence of *Anno Domini*," in *Time and Eternity: The Medieval Discourse*, ed. Gerhard Jaritz and Gerson Moreno-Riaño (Turnhout: Brepols, 2003), pp. 31–53.

52. Bede the Venerable, *Bede's Ecclesiastical History of the English People*, ed. Bertram Colgrave and Roger A. B. Mynors, Oxford Medieval Texts (Oxford: Oxford University Press, 1969). See Robert A. Markus, *Bede and the Tradition of Ecclesiastical Historiography*, Jarrow Lecture 1975 (Newcastle-upon-Tyne: Bealls, 1976).

53. Bede the Venerable, *De temporum ratione*, ed. Charles W. Jones, CCSL 123b (Turnhout: Brepols, 1967). See also the canonical tables in Bede the Venerable, *De temporibus*, ed. Charles W. Jones, CCSL 123c (Turnhout: Brepols, 1980).

54. Wallis, "Commentary," p. lxix.

55. See the discussion in McKitterick, *History and Memory*, pp. 92–97.

56. McKitterick, *History and Memory*, p. 7.

57. Ibid., p. 8.

58. Ibid., p. 139–49.

59. Janet Coleman, *A History of Political Thought: From the Middle Ages to the Renaissance* (Oxford: Blackwell, 2000), pp. 18–19, describes the effect of the coronation of Charlemagne as renewing "Golden Rome." She points out that this notion of renewal informed the Ottonian dynasty as well, where one finds *renovatio imperii Romanorum* on the imperial seal.

60. Lawrence Nees, *A Tainted Mantle: Hercules and the Classical Tradition in the Carolingian Court* (Philadelphia: University of Pennsylvania Press, 1991).

61. Mayke de Jong, "The Empire as *Ecclesia*: Hrabanus Maurus as biblical *historia* for rulers," in *Uses of the Past in the Early Middle Ages*, ed. Yitzhak Hen and Matthew Innes (Cambridge: Cambridge University Press, 2000), pp. 191–226, at 197–99.

62. Nees, *Tainted Mantle*, pp. 154–55.

63. Mayke De Jong, "Introduction—Rethinking Early Medieval Christianity: A View from the Netherlands" *Early Medieval Europe* 7 (1998): 261–75, at 273.

64. McKitterick, *History and Memory*, p. 14, notes that for the first time the written histories in the Carolingian era were also concerned to forge a common past with distant Rome and Troy. For example, the *Liber historiae francorum* (c. 727) explicitly rejects the common ancestry of the Franks with the Bible (as constructed by Gregory of Tours), by selecting the descendants of Troy as the original Franks.

65. Peter Classen, "*Res Gestae*, Universal History, Apocalypse: Visions of Past and Future," in *Renaissance and Renewal in the Twelfth Century*, ed. Robert L. Benson and Giles Constable with Carol D. Lanham (Cambridge: Harvard University Press, 1982; repr. Toronto: University of Toronto Press and the Medieval Academy of America, 1991), pp. 387–417, at 398–99.

66. John W. Baldwin, *The Scholastic Culture of the Middle Ages, 1000–1300* (Prospect Heights, IL.: Waveland, 1997 [1971]), pp. 35–58.

67. The exception that proves this rule is the civil service histories, noted by Smalley, *Historians*, ch. 8.

68. Matthew Innes, "Introduction: Using the Past, Interpreting the Present, Influencing the Future," in *Uses of the Past*, pp. 1–8.

69. Giles Constable, "A Living Past: The Historical Environment of the Middle Ages," *Harvard Library Bulletin*, n.s. 1 (1990): 49–70.

70. Aron Gurevich, *Categories of Medieval Culture*, trans. G. L. Campbell (London: Routledge and Kegan Paul, 1985), pp. 126–30, notes that anachronism was "an inseparable feature of medieval historiography."

71. Constable, "Living Past," p. 62, suggests that Renaissance sensibilities began to mark the separation of the present and past within history.

72. Classen, "*Res gestae*," p. 387, notes the rapid increase in the production of historiography in the twelfth century.

73. PL 198 contains the complete text of the *Historia scholastica*. A critical edition is now available for the book of Genesis: Petrus Comestor, *Historia scholastica: Liber Genesis*, ed. Agneta Sylwan, CCCM 191 (Turnhout: Brepols, 2005).

74. Judges 14, *incidentia*; PL 198:1285.

75. Giles Constable, "Past and Present in the Eleventh and Twelfth Centuries: Perceptions of Time and Change," in *L'Europa dei secoli XI et XII fra novità e tradizione: Sviluppi di una cultura* (Milan: Università cattolica del Sacro Cuore, 1989), pp. 135–70, at 141.

76. Timothy Reuter, "Past, Present, and No Future in the Twelfth-Century *Regnum Teutonicum*," in *The Perception of the Past in Twelfth-Century Europe*, ed. Paul Magdalino (London: Hambledon, 1992), pp. 15–36.

77. Smalley, *Historians*, pp. 97–98.

78. Richard Southern, "Aspects of the European Historical Tradition 2: Hugh of Saint Victor and the Idea of Historical Development," in *History and Historians: Selected Papers by R. W. Southern*, ed. Robert J. Bartlett (Oxford: Blackwell, 2004), pp. 30–47, at 38.

79. Southern, "Aspects 2," pp. 35–37. See *Hugh of Saint Victor on the Sacraments of the Christian Faith (De sacramentis)*, 1.1.3, 1.3.3., 1.8.3, 11, trans. Roy Deferrari (Cambridge: Mediaeval Academy of America, 1951), pp. 8–9, 42–43, 143, 148–49, and passim.

80. Smalley, *Historians*, p. 98.

81. Marie-Dominique Chenu, "Theology and the New Awareness of History," in *Nature, Man, and Society in the Twelfth Century*, trans. Jerome Taylor and Lester K. Little, Medieval Academy Reprints for Teaching (Toronto: University of Toronto Press, 1997 [1985]), pp. 162–99, at 180, suggests that Hugh understood the "the correspondence between the succession of the days of creation and the stages in the redemptive restoration in biblical chronology: *sex dies* equaled *sex aetates.*"

82. Hugh of St. Victor, *The Didascalicon of Hugh of St. Victor: A Medieval Guide to the Arts*, trans. Jerome Taylor, Records of Western Civilization 64 (New York: Columbia University Press, 1961), pt. 2, bks. 4 and 5; cited in Chenu, "Theology," pp. 164–65.

83. *Hugh of Saint Victor on the Sacraments*, 8; cited by Chenu, "Theology," p. 172. See also Hugh of St. Victor, *De arca Noe morali: Libellus de formatione arche,* 4.9, ed. Patrick Sicard, CCCM 176 (Turnhout: Brepols, 2001), pp. 111–17.

84. Southern, "Aspects 2," p. 40.

85. Chenu, "Theology," p. 174.

86. Rupert of Deutz, *De Trinitate et operibus eius,* ed. Hrabanus Haacke, CCCM 21–24 (Turnhout: Brepols, 1971–73). Noted in Chenu, "Theology," p. 191.

87. Constable, "Past and Present," p. 140, argues persuasively that these and other contemporary theologians "contributed more to the development of historical thought in the twelfth century than even the greatest annalists and chroniclers."

88. Marjorie Reeves, *The Influence of Prophecy in the Later Middle Ages: A Study in Joachism* (Oxford: Clarendon, 1969), p. 300.

89. Bernard McGinn, "Introduction" to Adso's letter, in *Apocalyptic Spirituality* (New York: Paulist, 1979), p. 86. Critical edition: *De ortu et tempore Antichristi,* ed. Daniel Verhelst, CCCM 45 (Turnhout: Brepols, 1976).

90. Daniel Verhelst, "Adso of Montier-en-Der and the Fear of the Year 1000," in *The*

*Apocalyptic Year 1000: Religious Expectation and Social Change, 950–1050,* ed. Richard Landes (Oxford: Oxford University Press, 2003), pp. 81–92, at 83.

91. McGinn, "Introduction," p. 88, notes seven subsequent revisions to Adso's letter in the eleventh and twelfth centuries, some circulating under the names of important authors, including Augustine.

92. Chistopher Mierow, "Introduction," in *The Two Cities by Otto, Bishop of Freising,* trans. Christopher Mierow (New York: Columbia University Press, 1928; repr. New York: Octagon, 1966), pp. 4–5; Critical edition: *Chronik: Die Geschichte der Zwei Staaten,* ed. Adolph Schmitt and Walther Lammers (Berlin: Rütten and Loening, 1960).

93. Joseph de Ghellinck, *L'Essor de la littérature latine au XIIe siècle,* 2d ed. (Brussels: Desclée de Brouwer, 1955), p. 328.

94. Richard W. Southern, "Aspects of the European Historical Tradition 3: History as Prophecy," in *History and Historians,* pp. 48–56.

95. While Joachim composed an exposition of the symbols in the Book of Revelation, his examination of the shape of history is found in his *Liber concordia novi ac veteri testamenti,* ed. E. Randolph Daniel (Philadelphia: American Philosophical Society, 1983). See the discussion of the figurae in Marjorie Reeves and Beatrice Hirsch-Reich, *The Figurae of Joachim of Fiore* (Oxford: Oxford University Press, 1972).

96. This is a vastly oversimplified account of Joachim's view of history. For a more detailed discussion, see Reeves, *Influence of Prophecy,* pp. 16–27.

97. Southern, "Aspects 3," p. 64, notes that Joachim's vision of prophecy in history remained current until the end of the seventeenth century, and cites the work of Sir Isaac Newton as "the last great scientific mind in European history to accept biblical prophecy as a source for the detailed study of historical facts."

98. Robert E. Lerner, *The Feast of Saint Abraham: Medieval Millenarians and the Jews* (Philadelphia: University of Pennsylvania Press, 2001).

99. Smalley, *Historians,* p. 122.

100. Ibid., p. 127.

101. *Gesta francorum et aliorum Hierosolymitanorum,* ed. Heinrich Hagenmeyer (Heidelberg: C. Winter, 1890).

102. *Dei gesta per Francos,* 2, ed. Robert B.C. Huygens, CCCM 127a (Turnhout: Brepols, 1996), pp. 112–13; English translation in *The First Crusade: "The Chronicle of Fulcher of Chartres" and Other Source Materials,* 2d ed., ed. Edward Peters, Middle Ages series (Philadelphia: University of Pennsylvania Press, 1998), p. 34. Penny Cole, *The Preaching of the Crusades* (Cambridge: Mediaeval Academy of America, 1991), pp. 27–29, discusses Guibert's report of the sermon, citing the influence of Hrabanus Maurus's *Commentaria in Libros Machabeorum,* PL 109:1125–1256.

103. See *The First Crusade,* p. 31.

# Lectern Bibles and Liturgical Reform in the Central Middle Ages

*Diane J. Reilly*

L avishly decorated and distinctively large, lectern Bibles appeared in monasteries and houses of regular canons usually in the wake of the reform of a foundation's common life. From the late eighth century through the twelfth, monasteries and canonries marked their commitment to reform by either producing a lectern Bible of their own or commissioning one from a respected scriptorium elsewhere.[1] The amount of decoration frequently added to these manuscripts marks them as perhaps the most significant investment a monastery made in its infrastructure, beyond buildings and liturgical implements. A two- or three-volume large-format Bible could have consumed the hides of hundreds of cattle, in addition to the thousands of hours of labor invested over the course of many years to copy and decorate each volume. Significantly, the only other manuscripts on which similar amounts of decoration were lavished were either liturgical books, such as Gospel books, Psalters and benedictionals, sacramentaries and lectionaries, or the vitae of monastic patron saints. Strikingly diverse in decorative program, ordering, and apparatus, lectern Bibles nonetheless shared many traits that indicate their intended function: to undergird the reformed liturgy of the hours that was the backbone of regular life. These Bibles, expensive and time-consuming to produce, functioned as symbols of the renewed vigor of communal worship and signal the continued centrality of the Bible text to monastic and canonical observance.

Monasteries and houses of regular canons would always have possessed Bibles, or parts of the Bible, in various forms used for different tasks.[2] Several component parts of the Bible were used constantly in the performance of the Mass and the Office, and thus every house of monks or regular canons would have owned copies of these books (on the Bible in the Mass and Office, see Boynton's chapter in this volume). Copies of the four Gospels and lectionaries, containing Gospel lections in the order in which they were read over the course of the church year, were essential tools for worship, and every foundation would have owned at least one. Numerous examples of Gospel books and lectionaries, both decorated and undecorated, survive from across Western Europe and testify to their almost constant use. The Psalter was read in its entirely by observant monks every week, as prescribed in the Rule of Saint Benedict.[3] While experienced monks doubtless sang the songs from memory, novices and oblates may have learned the Psalms from a manuscript copy.

The status of other biblical manuscripts in monasteries and canonries is more nebulous. While the Benedictine Rule had also indicated that daily reading was the goal of the monks (especially during Lent) and prescribed that books were to be assigned from the library for this task, Benedict did not specify the contents of the reading.[4] Thus it was left to the authors of later monastic customaries to define the appropriate reading material for this labor.[5] In addition to the homilies, commentaries, vitae, and other spiritual texts that were assigned by the abbot, prior, or librarian, books of the Bible could have been included in this edifying reading program. Any humble codex containing a biblical text could have served this purpose, however, and one would not expect to find much physical evidence of this function in the manuscripts themselves. Other Bible manuscripts were more obviously didactic in format. Glossed versions of the Psalter and other Scripture survive from monastic contexts, signaling their use in schools for oblates and novices, and perhaps during the private *lectio divina* of more senior monks.[6] Manuscripts of the entire Bible with relatively small dimensions, small script, encyclopedic collections of prologues, and many annotations may have served as reference works[7] or as exemplars for scribes,[8] though it is difficult to visualize the resulting product, whether it was a larger, more lavish single-volume "pandect" Bible or a smaller version of one of its component parts, such as a book of Major Prophets, that may have been appropriate for private study.

In fact, aside from instructions included in a Biblical manuscript itself, the size of a Bible or Bible part is probably the characteristic most indicative of its intended function. Scriptural manuscripts produced in the scriptoria of monasteries and houses of canons during the central Middle Ages can be divided into two main formats: smaller volumes generally under thirty-five centimeters tall, and except for the Psalter and Gospels, usually less lavishly produced; and the typically more splendid larger volumes between thirty-five and sixty centimeters tall.[9] For the most part, scripture codices within the larger set of dimensions are pandects or multivolume Bibles, usually with fewer than fifty lines of script per folio, engendering an easily read text block. Though great numbers of these survive to the present day, they were, in reality, an uncommon class of manuscript—expensive to produce, difficult to transport, and limited in their function. Their appearance signals a new or renewed purpose for Bible reading in religious communities.

The most famous of medieval large-format Bibles, the illustrated Bibles produced by the Carolingian scriptoria of Saint Martin in Tours, in Reims, and elsewhere, first established the connection between the size of a Bible and its function.[10] These manuscripts, transcribed in the newly invented, highly legible Caroline minuscule script, are among the largest Bibles ever made. While some have lavish decorative programs of full-page miniatures whose iconography is both educative and political in nature, such as the Moutier-Grandval Bible,[11] the First Bible of Charles the Bald (both from Tours),[12] or the Bible of San Paolo fuori le mura, probably from Reims,[13] in others the scribes concentrated their efforts on producing a carefully written and ornamented text with large illuminated initials.[14] A representative example is the so-called Rorigo Bible, now Paris, Bibliothèque nationale de France, Lat. MS 3.[15] This single-volume Bible was copied at Tours around 835 and given by Count Rorigo to the abbey of Saint-Maur-de-Glanfeuil in Anjou, then later transferred to the abbey of Saint-Maur-de-Fossés, perhaps when Odo of Glanfeuil became its abbot in the later ninth century. The Rorigo Bible has 409 folios of two-column, 51- or 52-line text, with an apparatus of rubrics, running titles or incipits in silver or gold on purple grounds, and is decorated throughout with thirty-nine painted initials and a full complement of canon tables, (fig. 6.1, fol. 183v, Osee). At 49.5 centimeters tall and 38 centimeters wide when closed, this is a quintessential lectern volume.

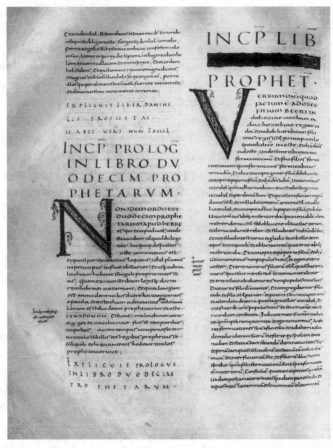

6.1. Paris, Bibliothèque nationale de France, lat. 3, fol. 183v, Osee. *Bibliothèque nationale de France.*

The sudden appearance of large-format Bibles in the middle of the ninth century coincided with a fervor of ecclesiastical reform, first assayed by Pepin, furthered by Charlemagne, and later propagated by his heir, Louis the Pious, and Louis's clerical advisers.[16] Scholars agree that the most lavishly decorated Bibles first functioned as gifts from powerful lay and religious leaders to rulers and the most influential religious foundations and were intended to solidify strategic relationships.[17] After the initial gift, however, such showpieces and the other more humble Bible manuscripts produced in this period were probably used to support the renewed liturgical life of their proprietary foundations, whether houses of Benedictine monks or regular canons.[18] While dozens of Bibles were produced for export by the canons of St. Martin in Tours, many other foundations redacted new Bibles for themselves rather than waiting to receive one from a patron.[19] In some instances, codicological characteristics of the Bible volumes themselves point to their anticipated role as choir manuscripts, intended to provide lections for the Night Office. Redundant books, such as the Gospels or Psalter, could be written in script of a reduced size or omitted altogether.[20] The Biblical books were on occasion reordered to accord with the cycle of readings for Matins.[21] Most large-format Carolingian Bibles were equipped with running titles, a distinct hierarchy of script, and a clear Caroline minuscule with few abbreviations and wide line spacing,[22] all of which would have enabled the assigned reader to vocalize the text clearly and without error in a darkened choir.

No explicit statements, either in the Bible manuscripts themselves or in other contemporary documentation, explain their utilization during a renewed Night Office. Instead, links between the production of these large-format Bibles and their reform context are more tangential. The goal articulated by Charlemagne and his advisers in calling for a new edition of the Bible text was to facilitate the best practices in schools, monasteries, and cathedrals,[23] and to allow for theological questions to be answered correctly.[24] Alcuin, one of the clerics who committed himself to producing such an edited text, however, stated more plainly in one of the volumes itself that it was intended to be read in the choir of a church. "Whosoever as a reader in church reads in the sacred body of this book the high words of God distinguishing the meanings, titles, cola and commata with his voice, let him say with his mouth as he knows the accent sounds."[25] Most scholars now believe that reading—whether in the church during Mass or Office or in the privacy of the monk's cell—was still predominantly an oral exercise in the ninth century, lending some ambiguity to Alcuin's prayer.[26] Pronunciation marks that sometimes littered the pages of these works could have been employed for the *praelectio*, or practice session, as lection readers prepared to read aloud in church, or to instruct oblates and novices in the correct understanding of the text, rather than for liturgical reading itself.[27] Yet the daily life of monks and regular canons was reformed according to a court mandate at the same time that Pepin, Charlemagne, and his followers demanded corrected texts. Clues in the directions for reform themselves hint that these two initiatives were intended to complement each other.

Church reform under the Carolingians included a push to impose the Benedictine Rule on monastic houses and to regularize the life of cathedral canons, including an effort to reinvigorate the Divine Office.[28] The three leading lights of this movement were Benedict of Aniane (c. 751–821),[29] who compiled a concordance of all the monastic rules available in the early ninth century, Chrodegang of Metz (c. 712–66),[30] who wrote a rule for regular canons, and Amalarius of Metz (c. 775–c. 850),[31] who attempted to amplify the Benedictine Rule for application in Carolingian houses. All three men emphasized the importance of psalmody and reading during the Night Office. Benedict of Aniane, for instance, enlarged on Benedict of Nursia's brief instructions for the Night Office with quotes from John Cassian's *Institutions*, Cassian's *Rule*, the *Rule of the Master*, Isidore's *De ecclesiasticis officiis*, and the Rule of Saint Columbanus, among others.[32] Amalarius wrote in a discussion of the first Nocturn, "We have laboured, we have given alms, as the apostles taught; we have fasted, we have obtained food by our own hands. What now ought we to do? Go to the theatre? To worldly entertainments? No, brother, but to what? Sit still, and I will show you something even more delightful. Let there be the reading of a lesson; there you will find apt matter in abundance from which to nourish your soul. Therein you will taste how flavourful and sweet is our creator, a sweetness than which there is no greater."[33] Other surviving liturgical instructions, including many new copies of the *ordo librorum* (a list of the Biblical reading cycle as adapted for the Night Office), also indicate that reformers were attempting to foster a renewed enthusiasm for reading from the Bible, reading that had formed part of the Night Office since late antiquity.[34]  In fact, one of the Carolingian Bibles created to accommodate the Night Office reading cycle, Reims, Bibliothèque Municipale, MS 1, includes an *ordo librorum* penned by its original scribe, providing our only direct evidence that this type of Bible was sometimes copied with this function in mind.

It has long been assumed that there was a wide gulf between the assessed goals of Church reformers (to enhance the spiritual observance of monks or canons) and efforts to restore and even expand the program of prayers, psalms, antiphons, versicles, and readings, all either memorized or read from a preexisting text. (On the details of the Night Office, see Susan Boynton's "The Bible and the Liturgy" in this volume.)[35] Because the components of Office worship were not spontaneous but rather repetitive and difficult to learn, modern scholars have not considered them able to inspire the "authentic" spirituality that should, apparently, have sprung from interiorized meditation facilitated by the *lectio divina*: private, solitary reading of inspirational texts.[36] On the contrary, however, as John Cassian, and later, Benedict, had originally pointed out, reading of

Scriptures was a mechanism for, not an impediment to, lifting the mind and spirit to God. (See also Cochelin's chapter in this volume.)[37] To Benedict, nothing about the Divine Office was to be considered merely mechanical or habitual. In chapter 19 of the Benedictine Rule, "How the Office Should Be Performed," he instructed,

> We believe that the divine presence is everywhere, and that in every place the eyes of the Lord are watching the good and the wicked. But beyond the least doubt, we should believe this to be especially true when we celebrate the Divine Office. . . . Let us consider, then, how we ought to behave in the presence of God and his angels, and let us stand to sing the psalms in such a way that our minds are in harmony with our voices

and, quoting Psalm 47, "Sing praise wisely."[38] Monastic reformers attempted to invest the Office with its original fervor and purpose by restoring its original length and complexity, not by simplifying it or degrading its importance to monastic life. In addition to designing more detailed rules and explanations of liturgy, such as those by Amalarius and Chrodegang, reformers sought to provide the material tools for this renewed choir worship in the form of books, including lectern Bibles like those produced at Tours and in scriptoria throughout the Carolingian Empire.[39]

While this circumstantial evidence suggests that Carolingian Bibles ultimately fulfilled a liturgical function associated with church reform, the surviving contemporary texts and descriptions give clear evidence only that they were sometimes originally intended to serve as gifts or reference volumes and were read aloud in the church. In contrast, the evidence for the intended function of eleventh- and twelfth-century lectern-sized Bibles is unequivocal. The dozens, perhaps hundreds of Bibles that were manufactured in monasteries throughout Europe beginning at the end of the tenth century are firmly linked to monastic reform. Moreover, while only a few of the Bibles produced by the Carolingians were lavishly decorated, the eleventh- and twelfth-century "Giant" Bibles as a class are replete with picture cycles as well as directions on how the Bibles themselves were to be used.

Beginning in the second half of the tenth century, waves of monastic reform again swept over Europe. Unlike the Carolingian reformers who had preceded them, these later churchmen acted less according to the directives of secular rulers than at the behest of their spiritual guides,

including the pope in Rome. Monastic reformers such as William of Vol-
piano, Richard of Saint-Vanne, and Lanfranc of Bec caused many preexisting Benedictine monasteries to be reorganized, both internally, in terms of
their liturgy, finances, and leadership, and externally, in their relationships
with other foundations.[40] In the case of new orders like the Cistercians,
Premonstratensians, and Carthusians, reformers also founded new monasteries and canonries.[41] Each of these foundations, whether newly
reformed or newly founded, received a Bible, usually lectern-sized, and
often outfitted with a complement of illustrations and decorated initials.[42]
Although the Bibles differed markedly from each other, their apparently
simultaneous appearance in monasteries and houses of canons throughout
Europe indicates that they answered a more widespread need to reinvigorate nocturn reading during the Night Office and to expand Bible reading
into other contexts as well.

There were many ways in which less conscientious monks and canons
could prune the Night Office, allowing more time for what they lacked
most: sleep. The easiest way, however, was to truncate scripture readings.
In particularly egregious cases, the lector might only read the first sentence of a passage—the sentence that might have been inserted into a
breviary to help the reader find the full passage in his source text.
Remarkably, monastic reformers of all stripes seemed to regard the Night
Office as a key component of their reforms. Giant Bibles were produced
by traditional Benedictines, Cluniacs, Cistercians, and Augustinian canons, including the Premonstratensians. Even the Carthusians, an order of
hermits who celebrated much of the Office in their individual cells, gathered to celebrate the Night Office in their oratory. The scriptorium of the
Grande Chartreuse produced at least three Giant Bibles to provide the
lections for the nocturns.[43] Hints of how important this reading was to
monks and canons surface in many contexts. Reformers explained how
often the monks were to read the Bibles, though they seldom referred to
the manuscripts themselves. Ælfric, an early eleventh-century English
reformer, explained in an epistle to the monks of his abbey, Eynsham, that
"in the course of the year, the entire canon [of the Bible] ought to be read
in church, but because we are lazy and slothful servants, we read in the
refectory whatever we do not cover in church."[44] The redactor of the Cluniac *Liber Tramitis* explained, "The book of Genesis is to be read at the
Night Office for so long a time until it is finished; and thereafter the others which after that remain, as much in the refectory as in the church, so
that they may be completed at the beginning of the fast on [Ash] Wednes-

day."[45] Over time the instructions found in monastic customaries for how to divide the contents of the Bible between the seasons and the services grew ever more detailed and explicit, until discrete parts of each book and its companion commentaries and sermons were sometimes assigned to specific days and nights in the church calendar.[46]

Now that they were routinely reading from an immense and heavy Bible manuscript, the monks had to find a way to move it from the choir, where it was read at night, to the refectory, where it was read during the day. Monastic customaries gave detailed instructions about who was to carry it and who should help. The monks were also to make sure no part of the text was skipped when the manuscript was transferred from one reader to another, as each reader was instructed to indicate the starting point of the next lection to the reader who was to take his place at the next service or meal.[47] These eleventh and twelfth-century Giant Bibles were also typically embellished with marginalia (most often Roman numerals counting from one to eight or twelve) that divided each biblical book into lections of an appropriate length.

As in the case of the Carolingian Bibles that had preceded them, the Romanesque Bibles were, for the most part, produced piecemeal to suit the needs of each individual foundation, contributing to their great diversity in contents and appearance. (On the contrasting model provided by the production of Italian Giant Bibles, see Yawn's chapter in this volume.) After centuries of copying, each monastery's scriptorium usually possessed a motley collection of Bible parts that could vary dramatically from those possessed by other nearby institutions. Rather than one standardized exemplar being distributed from a reforming center, each monastery, heeding the call to reform its approach to reading the Scriptures, refurbished an old Bible or assembled its own unique Bible from the separate volumes in its own collection or pieces borrowed from other houses.[48] As had been true of the Carolingian Bibles, the resulting Romanesque Bibles exhibited great variations in ordering, chapter divisions, chapter titles, incipits, and even contents. At least a half-dozen northern French Bibles did not include the Gospels or the Psalter because these were copied in separate liturgical books. Other Bibles could include extra, noncanonical books. A series of Bibles from the Archdiocese of Reims was ordered according to the cycle of choir readings rather than the roughly chronological order in which the Bible was more customarily arranged.[49]

We can tell that these houses preferred their own, homegrown, idiosyncratic Bibles over corrected, more authoritative texts because even as much as a century later, when the same monasteries typically copied new and more lavishly decorated Bibles, they tended to use their old flawed Bibles as textual models.[50] Typical is the series of events that happened at Christ Church, Canterbury: Lanfranc of Bec was invited to reform the house by William the Conqueror in the wake of the Norman Conquest. Lanfranc and his followers apparently directed that the late tenth-century Bible he found there, London, BL Royal MS I.E.VII–VIII, be adapted and used, as it was for almost the next century.[51] Finally, in the middle of the twelfth century, their old pre-Conquest Bible text was copied into a new volume, the Dover Bible (Cambridge, Corpus Christi College MS 3–4), which they decorated with a complement of lavish miniatures and initials.[52] These bear almost no resemblance to the decoration found in their old Bible, however. The monks may have expressed their local identity through their attachment to their homegrown version of the Bible text. On the other hand, the Bible itself, which we think of today as more of a fixed text, may have then been considered more mutable and subject to personal and institutional preference.

The decorative programs of these dozens of Bibles show equal variety. Some subjects were popular in many scriptoria: the first illustration of a large-format Bible is typically found before the book of Genesis and frequently depicts the creation of the world or the creation of Adam and Eve, such as in the late-eleventh-century Flemish Alardus Bible from the Benedictine monastery of Saint Amand-des-Eaux (fig. 6.2, Valenciennes, Bibliothèque municipale MS 9, fol. 5v). The *Sponsus* and *Sponsa*, or heavenly bridegroom and bride, are a common illustration for the Song of Songs, as in MS 10, fol. 113 from the same Bible (fig. 6.3).[53] But, more often than not, the programs of miniatures and initials are heterogeneous, even arbitrary. While the size and style of a Bible's decorative components were dictated by the customs of a monastery's scriptorium, the choice of which parts of a Bible to illustrate and how to render the texts into images may have been dictated instead by how the Bible functioned as well as the pressing concerns within a monastery at the time its leadership decided to invest in the production of a new Giant Bible.

Why, when they could have more easily distributed collections of small volumes around the monastery for the purpose, did the monks insist on using large, cumbersome, and expensively decorated Bibles? Certainly when reading at night and by candlelight, the large, evenly spaced script of a Giant Bible eased the burden of the reader, who had to sing the text according to a memorized tone pattern (see also Boynton's chapter in this

6.2. Valenciennes, Bibliothèque municipale, 9, fol. 5v, Genesis. *By permission of the Biblio-thèque Municipale, Valenciennes.*

volume). But miniatures do nothing to make the text more plain. Instead, they expand on and interpret the text, often adding a commentary that makes the meaning relevant to the time and place where the Bible was created.

For instance, the Floreffe Bible, a twelfth-century Bible illuminated for the Premonstratensian canons of Floreffe in present-day Belgium, is introduced by a pair of elaborate frontispiece illustrations showing motifs and narratives drawn from the biblical books of Job through Revelation (London, BL Additional MS 17737, fols. 3v and 4r, figs. 6.4 and 6.5).[54] The

6.3. Valenciennes, Bibliothèque municipale, 9, fol. 113, Song of Songs. *By permission of the Bibliothèque Municipale, Valenciennes.*

complex assemblages that make up each miniature may be read independently as allegories of the active (fol. 3v) or contemplative (fol. 4r) lifestyles through which the Holy Spirit furthered the process of salvation. They can also be read in concert as a historical continuum of past, present, and future Christian history, from Job through the Epiphany, or as a combination of three exegetical interpretations of the composite texts of this volume, corresponding to the three senses of Scripture—historical, allegorical, and moral—as explained by Gregory the Great in his *Moralia in Job*.[55] The way in which the artist or designer chose to depict these themes was dictated by the situation of the Premonstratensian regular canons, who saw their own lives as a valuable blend of both active and contemplative vocations, in contrast to traditional Benedictine monasticism, which favored the contemplative life. The highly educated Premonstratensians would have recognized the references in the paintings drawn from such sources as Augustine's *Tractatus in Evangelium Joannis*, which interpreted the ap-pearance of the apostles Peter and John, whom the author has switched from their usual placement, as an allegory for action and contemplation.[56]

6.4. London, British Library Add. 17737, fol. 3v. *Copyright British Library Board. All Rights Reserved.*

A historiated initial in the Bible of Stephen Harding (Dijon, Bibliothèque municipale MS 15, fol. 56v, fig. 6.6), illuminated in the first decades after the foundation of Cîteaux, similarly builds on the biblical text to address contemporary doctrinal issues.[57] While the beginning of the Gospel of John was typically illuminated with an evangelist portrait (and sometimes with the evangelist's symbol, an eagle), in this case a seated man has been clothed in the white habit of the Cistercians, while the

6.5. London, British Library Add. 17737, fol. 4r. *Copyright British Library Board. All Rights Reserved.*

eagle perches on his head, talons piercing the putative monk's mouth, ear, and eye. The monk holds a scroll inscribed with a statement of Arian belief, *Arrius. Erat aliquando quando non erat* ("Arius. There was a time when He was not") repudiated at the Council of Nicaea in 325, while the eagle who assaults him holds the first words of the Gospel of John, *Iohannes. In principio erat verbum et verbum erat apud Deum* ("John. In the beginning was the Word and the Word was with God").[58] These words from John were frequently quoted in literature intended to argue against the Arian heresy, including Augustine's *Tractatus in Evangelium Iohannis* (*Tractates on the Gospel of John*) which was copied at Cîteaux in the same campaign), his *De Trinitate* (*On the Trinity*, which was copied there near the same time), his *Contra Arianos* (*Against the Arians*), and Ambrose's *De fide orthodoxa contra Arianos* (*On the Orthodox Faith Against the Arians*).[59]

The eagle attacks the heretic's organs of sight, hearing, and speech, thus interrupting the perception and transmission of the heresy. By the twelfth century, mutilation of the speech organ was a common punishment for blasphemy and the theme was frequently depicted in Burgundian sculpture contemporary to the Cîteaux manuscript's illustrations.[60] Moreover, while Arianism had long since disappeared as a doctrinal threat

6.6. Dijon, Bibliothèque municipale 15, fol. 56v. *By permission of the Bibliothèque Municipale, Dijon.*

by the time this Bible was illuminated, other heresies were then flourishing in northern Europe, and contemporary crusaders for orthodoxy typically painted these new heresies with broad strokes, comparing them to the early Christian heresies with which they were familiar from patristic literature.[61] The threat of heresy was thus here juxtaposed with its solution, an argument based on the meaning of the biblical text itself.

It could also be argued that the decorations and imagery added to the Giant Bibles of the eleventh and twelfth centuries were designed to facilitate recall of the texts by the readers, both the monks responsible for reading the lections during the meals and Night Office and the listeners who would have glimpsed the embellishments to these gigantic lectern volumes as they stood open. Particularly in the case of Bible miniatures that depicted the text in a more straightforward, less interpretive way, the pictures aided in the memorization, and thus the internalization, of the text.[62]

Along with the tituli, rubrics, and decorative initials that subdivided the text and marked it into manageable blocks, the images that appeared at the beginning of some books could provide a summary or synopsis of the most important events in that text. Unlike the Psalter, which was memorized by observant monks through their weekly chanting of all 150 Psalms in the course of the Office, the majority of the Bible was read only once a year and thus remained relatively unfamiliar. While child oblates were undoubtedly more familiar with rarely read sections of the Old Testament and may have heard and read them a dozen times by the time they reached adulthood,[63] adult novices may have never before encountered some biblical books.[64] Nonetheless, reformed monks were expected to learn the texts so that they could benefit from them spiritually, a point emphasized by theological writers of the period.[65] For the majority of eleventh- and twelfth-century monks, the most consistent exposure to the text of the whole Bible was during the Night Office, when it was read from a lectern copy.

Sermons potentially written to accompany the Bible readings in the Night Office hint that the monks were supposed to listen to and absorb the biblical text in preparation for listening to the sermon to follow as a two-stage learning process. Gilbert of Hoyland, in his *Sermones in Canticum*, exhorted the monks not only to maintain discipline of the body during the Office but also to concentrate on the meaning of the words.[66] In his seventh sermon on the Song of Songs, Bernard of Clairvaux spoke eloquently on the subject of the Night Office, chastising monks whose sleepiness rendered them unable to participate in this joyous celebration in communion with the denizens of the heavenly kingdom.[67]

Not every edifying biblical manuscript in a monastery was outfitted with the elaborate complement of full-page illustrations, historiated initials, and decorated letters that are found in Giant Bibles, however. The attention lavished on these Giant Bibles contributed to their function as didactic tools, but also signals their status as symbols of reform, as had been the case in the Carolingian era before. As the foundational text of religious life, the Bible encapsulated all that a monk or regular canon should embody. Producing a luxurious new version of the text ultimately contributed to the reinvigoration of that life, both in word and in deed.

## Notes

1. Walter Cahn, *Romanesque Bible Illumination* (Ithaca: Cornell University Press, 1982); Marilena Maniaci and Giulia Orofino, *Le Bibbie atlantiche: Il libro delle Scritture tra monumentalità e rappresentazione* (Milano: Centro Tibaldi; Rome, Ministero per i beni culturali e ambientali, 2000); and Herbert L. Kessler, *The Illustrated Bibles from Tours*, Studies in Manuscript Illumination 7 (Princeton: Princeton University Press, 1977).

2. Margaret T. Gibson, *The Bible in the Latin West*, Medieval Book 1 (Notre Dame, IN: University of Notre Dame Press, 1993).

3. *Rule of Benedict* (hereafter *RB*) 9, 17, 18; text and English translation in *RB 1980: The Rule of St. Benedict in Latin and English with Notes*, ed. and trans. Timothy Fry (Collegeville, MN: Liturgical, 1981), pp. 202–5, 210–15.

4. *RB*, 49; *RB 1980*, pp. 252–53.

5. Anscari Mundo, "'Bibliotheca.' Bible et lecture du Carême d'après Saint Benoît," *Revue bénédictine* 60 (1950): 65–92.

6. Margaret Gibson, "Carolingian Glossed Psalters," in *The Early Medieval Bible: Its Production, Decoration and Use*, ed. Richard Gameson (Cambridge: Cambridge University Press, 1994), pp. 78–100.

7. Lawrence Nees, "Problems of Form and Function in Early Medieval Illustrated Bibles from Northwest Europe," in *Imaging the Early Medieval Bible*, ed. John Williams (University Park: Pennsylvania State University Press, 1999), pp. 121–77, at 125–41.

8. Virginia Brown, "Contenuti, funzione et origine della 'Bibbia di San Vincenzo al Volturno,' (Roma, Biblioteca Vallicelliana, D8)," *Nuovi annali della Scuola Speciale per Archivisti e Bibliotecari* 18 (2004): 37–60, at 55.

9. Richard Marsden, "The Old Testament in Late Anglo-Saxon England: Preliminary Observations on the Textual Evidence," in *The Early Medieval Bible*, pp. 101–24, at 104.

10. Rosamond McKitterick, "Carolingian Bible Production: the Tours anomaly," in *The Early Medieval Bible*, pp. 63–77, at 67–70.

11. London, British Library Add. MS 10546; Kessler, *The Illustrated Bibles*.

12. Paris, Bibliothèque Nationale de France MS Lat. 1; Paul E. Dutton and Herbert L. Kessler, *The Poetry and Paintings of the First Bible of Charles the Bald* (Ann Arbor: University of Michigan Press, 1997).

13. Abbazia di S. Paolo fuori le mura. See Joachim Gaehde, "The Touronian Sources of the Bible of San Paolo fuori le mura," *Frühmittelalterliche Studien* 5 (1971): 359–400.

14. Wilhelm Koehler, *Die karolingischen Miniaturen*, vol. 1: *Die Schule von Tours*, 6 vols. (Berlin: Deutscher Verlag für Kunstwissenschaft, 1930–99).

15. *Catalogue général des manuscrits latins*, 8 vols. (Paris: Bibliothèque nationale, 1939– ), 1:2–3; and Koehler, *Die karolingischen Miniaturen*, 1:381–82.

16. Bonifatius Fischer, "Bibeltext und Bibelreform unter Karl dem Grossen," in *Karl der Grosse: Lebenswerk und Nachleben,* 4 vols., ed. Wolfgang Braunfels, vol. 2: *Das geistige Leben*, ed. Bernhard Bischoff (Dusseldorf: L. Schwann 1965–67), pp. 156–216, at 156.

17. Christopher de Hamel, *The Book: A History of the Bible* (New York: Phaidon, 2001), pp. 37–38; and Nees, "Problems of Form and Function," pp. 133–41.

18. David Ganz, "Mass Production of Early Medieval Manuscripts: The Carolingian Bibles from Tours," in *The Early Medieval Bible*, pp. 53–62, at 59. For a fuller discussion, see Diane J. Reilly, *The Art of Reform in Eleventh-Century Flanders: Gerard of Cambrai, Richard of Saint-Vanne and the Saint-Vaast Bible*, Studies in the History of Christian Traditions 128 (Leiden: Brill, 2006), pp. 49–53.

19. Fischer, "Bibeltext und Bibelreform," pp. 162–216.

20. Ganz, "Mass production," p. 59; and Fischer, "Bibeltext und Bibelreform," p. 186.

21. Fischer, "Bibeltext und Bibelreform," pp. 191, 196, and 212–14.

22. McKitterick, "Carolingian Bible Production," p. 75.

23. *Admonitio generalis*, ed. Alfred Boretius, in *MGH. Leges*, 5 vols. (Hanover: Hahn, 1883), 1: *Capitularia regum Francorum*, pp. 52–62, at 60, ll. 2–7.

24. *Opus Caroli regis contra synodum (Libri Carolini)*, ed. Ann Freeman, in *Monumenta Germaniae Historica. Concilia* II, supp. 1 (Hanover: Hahn, 1998), pp. 165–66.

25. Ganz, "Mass Production," pp. 55–56; and *Monumenta Germaniae Historica, Poetae Latini aevi Karolini*, ed. Ernst Dümmler and trans. David Ganz, 4 vols. (Berlin: Weidmann, 1881–1923), 1:285.

26. Paul Saenger, *Space Between Words: The Origins of Silent Reading* (Stanford: Stanford University Press, 1997), pp. 4, 21, 39.

27. Saenger, *Space Between Words,* pp. 55–91.

28. Rosamond McKitterick, *The Frankish Church and the Carolingian Reforms, 789–895* (London: Royal Historical Society, 1977), pp. 122–23.

29. Benedict of Aniane, *Benedicti Anianensis Concordia Regularum*, ed. Pierre Bonnerue, 2 vols., CCCM 168 (Turnhout: Brepols, 1999), 1:32.

30. Martin A. Claussen, *The Reform of the Carolingian Church: Chrodegang of Metz and the* Regula canonicorum *in the Eighth Century* (Cambridge: Cambridge University Press, 2004).On the Night Office, from a longer rule that drew on Chrodegang's *Regula Canonicorum* distributed after the Aachen synod of 816, see Jerome Bertram, *The Chrodegang Rules: The Rules for the Common Life of the Secular Clergy from the Eighth and Ninth Centuries: Critical Texts with Translations and Commentary* (Aldershot: Ashgate, 2005), pp. 242–44.

31. Both his *Liber officialis* and his *Liber antiphonarii* address the Night Office in detail. Amalarius of Metz, *Amalarii episcopi opera liturgica omnia*, ed. Jean-Michel Hanssens, 3 vols., Studi e testi (Biblioteca apostolica vaticana) 138–40 (Vatican City: Biblioteca apostolica vaticana, 1948–50), 1:138–140; 2:442–80, and 3:13–15 on Bible reading in the Night Office.

32. *Benedicti Anianensis Concordia Regularum*, pp. 173–87.

33. Christopher A. Jones, *A Lost Work by Amalarius of Metz: Interpolations in Salisbury, Cathedral Library, MS 154* (London: Henry Bradshaw Society, 2001), p. 257.

34. Gérard Moyse, "Monachisme et réglementation monastique en Gaule avant Benoît d'Aniane," in *Sous la règle de saint Benoît. Structures monastiques et sociétés en France du moyen âge à l'époque moderne*, Centre de recherches d'histoire et de philologie 5, Hautes etudes médiévales et modernes 47 (Geneva: Droz, 1982), pp. 8–9; and Cyrille Vogel, "Les échanges liturgiques entre Rome et les pays francs jusqu'à l'époque de Charlemagne," in *Le chiese nei regni dell'Europa occidentale e i loro rapporti con Roma sino all'800*, Settimane di studio del Centro italiano di studi sull'alto Medioevo 7 (Spoleto: Presso la sede del Centro, 1960), pp. 218–57.

35. R. W. Southern, *Western Society and the Church in the Middle Ages*, Pelican History of the Church 2 (Harmondsworth: Penguin, 1970), p. 231.

36. Rachel Fulton, "Praying with Anselm at Admont: A Meditation on Practice," *Speculum* 81 (2006): 700–33, at 702–5.

37. Ibid., p. 710. On the use of Holy Scriptures for correcting a monk's behavior, see *RB* 28; *RB* 1980, pp. 224–25; on the weekly reader's task (without specific information on the text to be read), see *RB* 38, *RB* 1980, pp. 236–37. See also John Cassian, *The Conferences*, trans. Colm Luibheid (New York: Paulist, 1985), "First Conference, On the Goal of the Monk," p. 41, chapter 7: "For this we must practice the reading of the Scripture, together with all the other virtuous activities, and we do so to trap and to hold our hearts free of the harm of every dangerous passion and in order to rise step by step to the high point of love."

38. *RB* 19:1–7, *RB* 1980, pp. 214–17.

39. Similarly, Charlemagne requested in the *Epistola Generalis* that Paul the Deacon compose a new Homiliary in two volumes, covering the cycle of homiletic reading for the year, to be distributed throughout his realm. A homily was a standard component of the third Nocturn during Matins. See Vogel, "Les échanges liturgiques," pp. 289–92, and note 302.

40. On the spread of tenth and eleventh century reform initiatives, see John Nightingale, *Monasteries and Patrons in the Gorze Reform: Lotharingia c. 850–1000* (Ox-

ford: Clarendon, 2001); Josef Semmler, "Das Erbe der karolingischen Klosterreform im 10. Jahrhundert," in *Monastische Reformen im 9. und 10. Jahrhundert*, ed. Raymund Kottje and Helmut Maurer (Sigmaringen: Jan Thorbecke, 1989), pp. 29–78; Kassius Hallinger, *Gorze-Kluny: Studien zu den monastischen Lebensformen und Gegensätzen im Hochmittelalter*, Studia Anselmiana 22–23 (Rome: "Orbis catholicus," Herder, 1950–51); Barbara H. Rosenwein, *Rhinoceros Bound: Cluny in the Tenth Century* (Philadelphia: University of Pennsylvania Press, 1982); and Neithard Bulst, *Untersuchungen zu den Klosterreformen Wilhelms von Dijon (962–1031)*, Pariser historische Studien 11 (Bonn: Ludwig Röhrscheid, 1973).

41. Martha G. Newman, *The Boundaries of Charity: Cistercian Culture and Ecclesiastical Reform* (Stanford: Stanford University Press, 1996); *San Bruno di Colonia: un eremita tra Oriente e Occidente*, ed. Pietro De Leo, Soveria Mannelli [Catanzaro]: Rubbettino, 2004); and Giles Constable, *The Reformation of the Twelfth Century* (Cambridge: Cambridge University Press, 1996).

42. Cahn, *Romanesque Bible Illustration*; Peter Brieger, "Bible Illustration and the Gregorian Reform," in *Studies in Church History* 2 (1965): 154–64; and de Hamel, *The Book*, pp. 64–91.

43. Grenoble, Bibliothèque municipale MSS 16–18 [1, 3, 8], late eleventh or early twelfth century, which may predate the foundation, MSS 12–15, late twelfth century, MS 384, and MS 28, early thirteenth century. See Walter Cahn, *Romanesque Manuscripts: The Twelfth Century*, 2 vols. (London: Harvey Miller, 1996), 2:58–60; and *Romanesque Bible Illustration*, pp. 271–72.

44. "Epistula ad monachos Egneshamnenes directa," ed. Hadrian Nocent, in *Consuetudinum saeculi X/XI/XII monumenta non-Cluniacensia*, ed. Kassius Hallinger, CCM VII/3 (Siegburg: Franz Schmitt, 1984), p. 184. For an English translation see *Ælfric's Letter to the Monks of Eynsham*, ed. and trans. Christopher A. Jones, Cambridge Studies in Anglo-Saxon England 24 (Cambridge: Cambridge University Press, 1998).

45. *Liber tramitis aevi Odilonis abbatis*, ed. Peter Dinter, CCM 10 (Siegburg: Franz Schmitt, 1980), p. 48.

46. Diane J. Reilly, "The Cluniac Giant Bible and the Ordo librorum ad legendum: A Reassessment of Monastic Bible Reading and Cluniac Customary Instructions," in *From Dead of Night to End of Day: The Medieval Customs of Cluny; Du coeur de la nuit à la fin du jour: les coutumes clunisiennes au moyen âge*, ed. Susan Boynton and Isabelle Cochelin (Turnhout: Brepols, 2005), pp. 163–89, at 174–75.

47. Ibid., pp. 175–76.

48. Diane J. Reilly, "French Romanesque Giant Bibles and Their English Relatives: Blood Relatives or Adopted Children?" *Scriptorium* 56 (2002): 294–311; and Reilly, "The Cluniac Giant Bible," pp. 163–89.

49. Reilly, *The Art of Reform*, pp. 66–93.

50. Reilly, "French Romanesque Giant Bibles," pp. 310–11.

51. Mary P. Richards, *Texts and Their Traditions in the Medieval Library of Rochester Cathedral Priory* (Philadelphia: American Philosophical Society, 1988), p. 64.

52. C. R. Dodwell, *The Canterbury School of Illumination, 1066–1200* (Cambridge: Cambridge University Press, 1954), p. 48–59; and Richards, *Texts and their Traditions,* p. 83.

53. Cahn, *Romanesque Bible Illustration,* p. 283.

54. Anne-Marie Bouché, "Anomaly and Enigma in Romanesque Art," in *The Mind's Eye: Art and Theological Argument in the Middle Ages,* ed. Jeffrey Hamburger and Anne-Marie Bouché (Princeton: Princeton University Press, 2006), pp. 306–35.

55. Ibid., pp. 313–17.

56. Ibid., p. 315.

57. Walter Cahn, "A Defense of the Trinity in the Cîteaux Bible," *Marsyas* 11 (1962–1964): 58–62.

58. Yolanta Załuska, *L'Enluminure et le scriptorium de Cîteaux au XIIe siècle* (Cîteaux: Commentarii cistercienses, 1989), pp. 195–96.

59. Cahn, "A Defense," p. 59; and Zaluska, *L'Enluminure,* pp. 206–7, 225–26.

60. Cahn, "A Defense," p. 62.

61. Robert I. Moore, *The Formation of a Persecuting Society: Power and Deviance in Western Europe, 950–1250* (New York: Blackwell, 1987), pp. 68–72.

62. Mary J. Carruthers, *The Book of Memory: A Study of Memory in Medieval Culture,* Cambridge Studies in Medieval Literature 10 (Cambridge: Cambridge University Press, 1990), pp. 221–24.

63. Susan Boynton, "Training for the Liturgy as a Form of Monastic Education," in *Medieval Monastic Education,* ed. George Ferzoco and Carolyn Muessig (London: Leicester University Press, 2000), pp. 7–20, at 8–16.

64. By the twelfth century some new monastic orders refused outright to accept child oblates, meaning all their novices would have been adults. See Joseph. H. Lynch, "The Cistercians and Underage Novices," *Cîteaux: commentarii cistercienses* 24 (1973): 283–97.

65. On Bernard of Clairvaux, see Brian Stock, *The Implications of Literacy: Written Language and Models of Interpretation in the Eleventh and Twelfth Centuries* (Princeton: Princeton University Press, 1983), pp. 403–10.

66. Gilbert of Hoyland, *Sermones in Canticum Salomonis* 23.3, *Sermons on the Song of Songs,* trans. Lawrence C. Braceland, 3 vols., Cistercian Fathers Series, 14, 20, 26 (Kalamazoo, MI: Cistercian, 1978–79), 20:287; also PL 184:120.

67. Bernard of Clairvaux, *Sermons sur le Cantique I* (Oeuvres Complètes 10), SC 414 (Paris: Cerf, 1996), p. 163.

# The Italian Giant Bibles

*Lila Yawn*

I n October of 1168 a widow named Mattilda Veckii donated a
hundred *solidi* to the church and monastery of S. Vito in Pisa.[1]
It was a considerable sum, roughly enough to buy thirty-three
*librae* of honey or more than a hundred of pepper—a Pisan *libra* equaled
about three-quarters of a U.S. pound.[2] A hundred solidi might also have
purchased twenty-five casks of wine or a Saracen slave, but Mattilda had
her sights set on a different item: a custom-made Bible for the religious
community at the heart of her riverside neighborhood.[3] Since the 1150s,
the Pisan commune, then one of the great trading powers of the Mediterranean, had established an important guard station of the customs office
there and enclosed S. Vito and the surrounding settlement within the
city's new walls.[4]

Mattilda's contribution was what today we might call seed capital, an
initial, stimulating investment earmarked for the purchase of parchment.
It paid for 240 sheets.[5] A first requisite for the crafting of medieval manuscripts, parchment consists of cleaned, stretched, split, and smoothed
animal skins—in Italy usually those of sheep or goats were used.[6] By the
twelfth century, state-of-the-art Bibles had such expansive pages that one

whole animal hide sufficed to make only two contiguous leaves, or folios, each with a front and a back for writing. (On Giant Bibles generally, see Reilly's chapter in this volume).[7] The Bible crafted for S. Vito would eventually require at least 428 skins, far more than the widow's generous gift could finance.[8]

Five dozen neighbors, including three bakers, two fishermen, a smith, a mason's wife, and twelve other women, chipped in with smaller contributions, more than tripling the available funds. Burnettus the smith gave 25 solidi, his son Vullanus 21, and Guido de Classo another 10. Signorellus donated for the welfare of his wife's soul, Soperkia for her husband, Guido Certanus for his mother-in-law, and Berta for her own sake. The only clergyman among the donors, a priest named Gregorius, contributed five solidi for the good of a cousin, while another benefactor, probably Benfaita, offered six *denarii* (one-half *solidus*) for the benefit of "a certain dead youth from Elba."[9] In the end, the townsfolk accumulated just over 313 solidi, enough to buy the required parchment with cash left over.[10]

Their contributions did not suffice to pay the craftsmen, however. Albertus of Volterra and at least one other professional scribe copied out the prefaces, indexes, and Bible texts, and an illuminator named Adalbertus enlivened them with ornate initials, all in return for payment. Andreas and Caloiannes were also paid, the former "on account of a letter," or perhaps letters, probably illuminated ones, and the latter for an unspecified contribution.[11] All told, the artisans garnered more than 446 solidi, with a certain Master Vivianus alone collecting over 300.[12] In addition to his calligraphic work, Vivianus likely oversaw the labor of the others and perhaps procured the requisite inks, pigments, and precious metals. He also earned the monks' trust. Contemporary charters from S. Vito name a "Master Vivianus, scribe" who in 1171 witnessed several transactions concerning the monastery's estates and even acted once as its agent, accepting a donation of land on its behalf.[13] After that date, Vivianus disappears from the monastery's records, having perhaps moved on to some other artistic venture.

Between the donors and craftsmen stood one additional, crucial group: the priests and monks of S. Vito, the Bible's future owners, who served as paymasters and administrators and probably also as cofinanciers, supplementing the donated funds out of the monastery's income. A priest named Gerardus acted as general manager, collecting money, purchasing parchment, disbursing cash to the scribes, and keeping careful records, which he transcribed into the Bible. We have his exacting inscription to thank for the rich information that survives about the project.[14] Payments to the illuminators passed through the hands of the monastic chamberlain and prior, a sign that the Bible's decorators probably did their work inside the monastery. The priest Gregorius, on the other hand, received a handsome payment from Gerardus when he "brought back the quaternions," meaning the packets, or gatherings, of folded, nested sheets of parchment that would later be bound together to form the Bible.[15] Perhaps Gregorius had corrected the scribes' work against textual models housed in another religious institution.[16] Since the craftsmen received their wages individually from Gerardus or the monks, they were likely independent contractors assembled for the endeavor rather than members of a stable workshop. Furthermore, with the exception of Gregorius, all appear to have been laymen.[17] In the final tally, between materials and labor, expenses for the undertaking totaled at least 759 solidi and 10 denarii. This amounted to nearly two-thirds of the purchase price of a house, garden, and vineyard in Borgo San Vito that Guido Certanus and his wife, Aldigarda, would sell in 1181, about a decade after the Bible's completion.[18]

Now commonly called the Calci Bible after the Carthusian monastery that acquired it in the fourteenth century, the manuscript that Mattilda and her neighbors subsidized is clearly no ordinary book.[19] Bound in four imposing volumes, its pages measure 22 x 15 inches (560 x 385 mm), as high as those of the *New York Times* (22 inches) and a little wider (the *Times* recently reduced its page width from 13.5 to 12 inches).[20] Tucking the Bible under an arm on the way home from the newsstand would be taxing, however. The weight of the lightest volume can be estimated at about 20.5 pounds (9.3 kg), and that of all four together at more than 95 pounds (c. 43 kg).[21]

Like great treasure chests for words, these prodigious codices shelter a rich array of prologues, prefaces, and biblical books as well as chapter summaries, or *capitula*, which encapsulate the content of each book in a series of brief, numbered synopses. Penned in ample lettering, the volumes seem thoughtfully planned for use during the Night Office, when a monk charged with reading aloud to the community would have had only a lamp or candle to illuminate the page. Where a new book or an important preface begins, the normal minuscule script—that is, the main, lowercase writing—erupts into opulence, providing a showy place-finding cue. Tall, curvilinear characters in red and in black announce the new text—declaring, for example, that "The Prophet Joel Begins"—and spell out its opening line, apart from the first letter, which dwarfs the others in

7.1. Pisa, Museo Nazionale di San Matteo, deposito provvisorio (Bibbia di Calci), vol. 4, fol. 7r (detail): incipit and late geometrical initial (Book of Joel). *Pisa, Museo Nazionale di San Matteo, deposito provvisorio (Bibbia di Calci), vol. IV, fol. 7r (AFSPI. n. 44520 su concessione del Ministero dei Beni e le Attività Culturali/Soprintendenza Pisa, Prot. 542 del 4 Mar. 2009).*

size and extravagance. Bordered in gold, the largest, most ornate letters frequently frame their own luxuriant fantasy worlds, with vine-rich jungles cascading from the mouths and ears of satyrs and other creatures or sprouting spontaneously from the letter or its interior. Elsewhere, a prophet or apostle peers out as if from a window, offering a foretaste of the coming text on a minutely inscribed scroll.[22]

## The Giant Bible Family

Though remarkably rich and imposing, the Calci Bible constitutes only one late example of a large and important genre of manuscript whose roots extend deep into the previous century. More than a hundred such

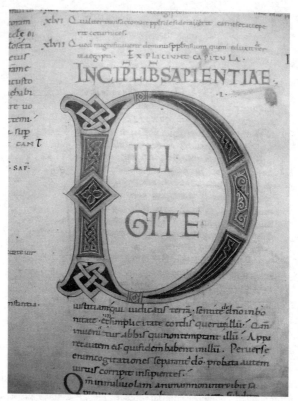

7.2. Admont, Stiftsbibliothek, Cod. D, fol. 46r (detail): incipit and early geometrical initial (Book of Wisdom). *By permission of the Stiftsbibliothek Admont.*

Italian Giant Bibles—also called Atlantic Bibles, or *Bibbie atlantiche* in Italian, after their oversize, atlaslike format—survive in whole or in part, and most predate 1168.[23] Most, furthermore, are bound in one or two volumes, rather than in four, and many are fragmentary or incomplete. Yet nearly all resemble Mattilda's codices in important ways: in folio size and script; in the selection of prefaces and prologues; in the tidy page layouts, which normally have two columns per page, though in Psalms there are sometimes three; and in the predominance of the distinctive "geometrical" initials (figs. 7.1–7.2), which together with titanic size constitute the group's most recognizable hallmark. Edward Garrison coined the term *geometrical* in the 1950s to describe these ornamented initials, which consist of multiple panels, usually long rectangles filled with stylized leaves or interlaced filaments in red, dark green, blue, or lavender and set end to

7.3. Parma, Biblioteca Palatina, Palat. 386, fol. 165v (detail): miniature of the prophet Obadiah and full-shaft initial. *Su concessione del Ministero per i Beni e le Attività Culturali.*

end to form the letter.[24] Yellow or gold bands frame the panels, twisting into elaborate knots at one or more of the letter's extremities. Most Italian Giant Bibles also contain initials of the "full-shaft" variety, in which one or two adjacent, parallel colored strips compose the letter and act as trellises for meandering vines. Birds, fish, and other animals occasionally round out the decorative repertoire, their bodies or body parts forming all or part of an initial or inhabiting its spaces.[25]

As figure 7.3 shows, Bibbie atlantiche sometimes also feature illustrations of persons and events from the Bible. Frequently, a prophet, king, queen, or apostle sits or stands alongside an initial or inside or above it, introducing and commenting upon the ensuing text, sometimes in surprising ways.[26] A Bible in Parma, for example, shows Ezekiel clasping an object of an unexpected sort—not the parabolic or rectangular scroll, or rotulus, held by other prophets in the manuscript (fig. 7.3), but rather a clublike protuberance, apparently a large erection, swelling from the prophet's groin (fig. 7.4).[27] This unusual image seems to offer an imaginative interpretation of Ezekiel 3:3, "And he said to me: Son of man, thy belly shall eat, and thy bowels shall be filled with this book which I give thee."[28]

7.4. Parma, Biblioteca Palatina, Palat. 386, fol. 141r (detail): miniature of the prophet Ezekiel and geometrical initial. *Su concessione del Ministero per i Beni e le Attività Culturali.*

7.5. Rome, Biblioteca Angelica, 1273, fol. 5v: miniature of the creation and fall. *Rome, Biblioteca Angelica, Ms. 1273, fol. 5v, su concessione del Ministero per i Beni e le Attività Culturali. Unauthorized reproduction prohibited.*

Selected narrative themes crop up repeatedly. King David writes or strums a harp accompanied by musicians or dancers at the head of Psalms in several lavish examples, including the Edili Bible, which was once owned by Florence Cathedral; the Bible of S. Cecilia in Trastevere in Rome; and the Pantheon Bible, formerly at S. Maria ad Martyres in the Roman Pantheon.[29] Other miniatures show, inter alia, Elijah riding to

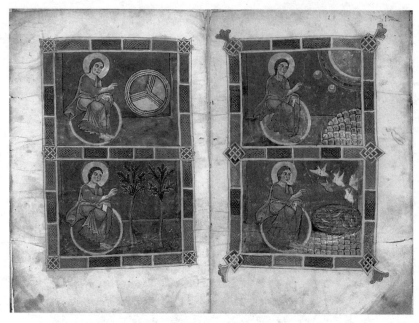

7.6. Perugia, Biblioteca Comunale Augusta, L. 59, fols. IV–2r: miniature of the creation of the dry land and plants (*left*) and heavenly bodies, birds and fish (*right*). *Biblioteca comunale Augusta, Perugia. All rights reserved.*

heaven in a chariot (Edili, Pantheon, Parma); Samson breaking the lion's jaw (Edili, Parma); Judas Maccabeus and his men battling the Seleucids (Edili, Pantheon, Parma); and Judith decapitating Holofernes, an event illustrated in at least seven Bibbie atlantiche, sometimes with vivid displays of gore.[30]

No fewer than thirteen examples include prominent creation miniatures, and in ten the narrative sequence derives from prestigious models: frescoes that once decorated the naves of Rome's apostolic basilicas, St. Peter's on the Vatican hill and St. Paul's Outside the Walls.[31] The creation scenes in these late antique mural cycles focused principally upon the second of the two main biblical creation stories, the Jahwist account (Gen. 2:4–3:24), in which the Creator creates Adam from the earth, forms Eve from Adam's rib, and later has the two cast out of the Garden of Eden for eating from the Tree of Knowledge. The Genesis miniature of a Bible in the Biblioteca Angelica in Rome shows this "apostolic" creation narrative at its fullest (fig. 7.5), starting with a frontal view of the Creator in the heavens and ending with the expulsion and toil. Other manuscripts show only part of the apostolic sequence—the Riccardiana Bible, for example,

7.7. Vatican City, Biblioteca Apostolica Vaticana, Pal. lat. 3, fol. 5r: miniature of the separation of light and darkness (*top*) and the creation and/or blessing of the first man and woman (*bottom*). *Vatican City, Biblioteca Apostolica Vaticana, Pal. lat. 3, fol. 5r, copyright Biblioteca Apostolica Vaticana.*

has only the first three scenes.[32] Miniatures in several other Bibbie atlantiche concentrate upon an entirely different creation story, the first, or Priestly, account (Gen. 1:1–2:3), in which God calls the universe into being over the course of six days, ending with the creation of mankind, male and female, in his own image. A Giant Bible in Perugia (Biblioteca Augusta, Ms. L.59, hereafter "Perugia L. 59") dedicates four full-page miniatures to this story—two are shown in figure 7.6—while an appealingly homespun painting in the Füssen, or Palatine, Bible (fig. 7.7) seems to emphasize its beginning and culminating events: the separation of light and darkness and the Creator's blessing of the first man and woman on the sixth day.[33]

## Forebears

No two Italian Giant Bibles are identical. Nevertheless, an unaccustomed observer opening contemporary specimens to corresponding text pages risks a momentary sensation of double vision, an effect made all the more remarkable by the physical norms for Bibles when the Bibbie atlantiche first appeared on the scene. Biblical manuscripts from early medieval Europe and eleventh-century Italian monastic workshops typically contain one or a few books of the biblical canon or at most a well-defined segment, such as the Pentateuch or Prophets.[34] (On these early medieval Bible parts, see Gyug's chapter in this volume.) This fragmentation meant that full Bibles, where they existed, normally encompassed multiple, often heterogeneous volumes. The use of such librarylike *bibliothecae* survived into the early high Middle Ages. A twelfth-century inventory from S. Eutizio in Valcastoriana in eastern Umbria lists separate codices of Genesis, Isaiah, Samuel and Kings, Wisdom, Job, Ezekiel, Psalms, and Revelation.[35] Completed in 1017 by Stephanus, a monk of S. Salvatore ad Isola, near Monteriggioni in central Tuscany, a playfully decorated book of the Prophets may once have belonged to such a collection.[36] Relatively small (310 x 225 mm), it concludes with a colophon explaining that Stephanus completed it when he was in his twenties.[37]

Such subdivided, agglomerated precedents must have made the integrated format, monumental dimensions, and consistent graphic and decorative systems of the Bibbie atlantiche seem strikingly innovative. To the well-informed eleventh-century observer, however, they may also have appeared venerably retrospective, given that full Old and New Testaments in one volume (called pandect Bibles) had survived in limited numbers from distinguished early medieval workshops. In the ninth century, under Alcuin of York (died 804) and his successors, the scriptoria of Tours had produced a steady stream of such manuscripts. While usually smaller than the Italian giants, members of this Carolingian manuscript family furnished the basic pattern for their geometrical initials, served as a major source for their texts, and inspired the multiregister miniatures (fig. 7.5) that decorate the most elaborate examples.[38] Perhaps written at Reims around 870, one illustrated manuscript of the Tours variety, the Bible of S. Paolo fuori le mura, was in central Italy in the eleventh century, when a scribe, probably working in southern Tuscany, copied its prologue at the beginning of an Italian Giant Bible.[39]

Early medieval Bibles from Tours and related scriptoria were by no means the only models. Textual variants—meaning characteristic phrasings, errors, omissions, additions, and the like—that were typical of Bibles from Tours frequently appear in the Bibbie atlantiche alongside variants from other early strains of the Latin Vulgate Bible, especially those associated with Italy and Spain.[40] Unillustrated and smaller than their cousins from Tours, the elegant Bibles created under Theodulf (d. 821), bishop of Orleans and an important member of Charlemagne's court school, sometimes served as a special point of reference.[41] Like Stephanus of Isola, the scribes of two important illustrated Bibbie atlantiche, the Edili Bible and Perugia L.59, copied several prefaces to the Prophets from a Theodulf Bible closely related to the ninth-century Bible of Saint-Germain-des-Prés.[42] The redactors of several Tuscan Bibbie atlantiche, including the Edili Bible, also drew upon Theodulfian exemplars for their chapter summaries to books of the Octateuch.[43]

Composed by Bede (d. 735), these distinctive chapter summaries, or capitula, had originally appeared with slightly different readings in at least one, and perhaps three, very large Bibles made during the late 600s or early 700s in northern England at the monasteries of Wearmouth and Jarrow, where Bede resided.[44] By the era of the Bibbie atlantiche, the grandest of the three, the Codex Amiatinus, had found its way to S. Salvatore of Monte Amiata, an abbey located in southern Tuscany, about 42 miles (68 km) southeast of Isola, just off the Via Francigena, the main north-south road to Rome, and approximately the same distance southwest of Perugia. At Monte Amiata the manuscript's classicizing illustrations, 1,030 elegantly written folios, and more than 75 pounds (34 kg) of heft clearly made an impression.[45] Bonizo, a monk and scribe of Monte Amiata, adapted parts of its dedicatory text for his introduction and conclusion to the first part of a massive codex of St. Gregory's *Moralia in Iob* made in the abbey's scriptorium, while an anonymous painter copied one of its illustrations, a portrait of the prophet Ezra, in another large volume containing works by Origen, Augustine, Bede, and others (fig. 7.8, Perugia, Biblioteca Capitolare, Cod. 3, hereafter "Perugia 3").[46]

Although no Bibbie atlantiche display any such clear, direct imitation of the Codex Amiatinus, the oversize exegetical manuscripts—that is, biblical commentaries—crafted at Monte Amiata in the eleventh century belong to a large class of books that typically accompanied Giant Bibles in monastic and cathedral libraries, sometimes as gifts of the same

7.8. Perugia, Biblioteca Capitolare, 3, fol. 353v: miniature of the prophet
Ezra. *By permission of the Biblioteca Capitolare, Perugia.*

donors.[47] The important book collection presented to the cathedral of
Troia in Apulia by Bishop Gulielmus II (1107–42) includes significant
examples presumably made in or near Rome.[48] Whether Monte Amiata's
scriptorium produced Giant Bibles is uncertain. However, a fragmentary
eleventh-century Old Testament in the Biblioteca Casanatense (Cod.
470, hereafter "Casanatense 470") once belonged to the abbey and seems
to have been made there or nearby.[49] It has no geometrical initials but
includes Bede's capitula with Theodulfian variants as well as a fancy initial
inhabited by a dog in royal blue and chocolate brown, colors richly
favored in Bonizo's *Moralia in Iob*.[50] The areas of each page ruled for
text—that is, the manuscript's writing blocks (c. 386 x 240 mm)—are
smallish with respect to those of most other Bibbie atlantiche, but
approximate those of the Codex Amiatinus (360–75 x 260 mm) and come
even closer to those of Perugia L.59 and of an eleventh-century manuscript of Augustine's *Enarrationes in Psalmos* in the Perugia Capitular
library.[51] With nearly identical writing areas (c. 400 x c. 240 mm), the two
Perugian manuscripts probably came from the same milieu or originated
as a matched set.[52]

## Patrons and Scribes

Apart from Gerardus, individuals who financed and crafted Bibbie atlantiche left behind little direct information about themselves and their
activities of book production. Made a century or more before the Calci
volumes, Perugia L.59 shows us its sponsors, a man and woman dressed in
the finery of wealthy laypeople offering gifts to a sainted hermit, bishop,
and apostle (fig. 7.9).[53] No names are provided. However, the bishop may
be Herculanus, Perugia's patron saint, whose remains were transferred to
the city's cathedral in the tenth century.[54]

A somewhat later manuscript in the Biblioteca Casanatense (Cod. 722,
hereafter "Casanatense 722") names some of its sponsors in informal notes
scrawled across the bottoms of pages.[55] The entries are ambiguous, but
suggest that the people involved, who included a certain Zicarus Marti-
nus and Petrus of Albona, his brother, and their wives, had participated in
something akin to a modern buy-a-brick campaign in which each family
or individual figuratively "built," "wrote," or "composed" a portion of the

7.9. Perugia, Biblioteca Comunale Augusta, L. 59, fols. 2v–3r: miniature of the creation of the
land animals and of Eve (*left*) and donors presenting gifts to saints (*right*). *Biblioteca comunale
Augusta, Perugia. All rights reserved.*

volume by paying for its materials and workmanship.[56] Three anonymous scribes wrote the manuscript, assisted by an illuminator who botched several initials, painting, for example, an ostentatious *H* where the text calls for an *F*.[57]

The scribe of another Giant Bible, Corbolinus, was more precise and forthcoming. Upon completing a richly decorated volume in 1140, he recorded the date in a self-referential inscription, or colophon, along with his name, his native city (Pistoia), and some of the rewards that he hoped for in return for the work, mainly prayers for his salvation from future readers.[58] Since he calls himself only a "scribe" (*scriptor*) and not a monk or priest, Corbolinus may well have been a layman who volunteered his services with an eye to spiritual rather than monetary gain. A pastiche written in shifting and sometimes flawed poetic meters and prose, his colophon is partly adapted from an earlier one written by Cantarus, scribe of an exegetical manuscript in Pistoia.[59]

In 1146, brother Atto of S. Croce of Fonte Avellana, a hermitage in the Apennines northeast of Gubbio, penned a rhymed inscription in another *Bibbia atlantica*.[60] Unlike Corbolinus, Atto left the circumstances of his involvement in the manuscript's creation vague. The art historian Knut Berg concluded that Atto had ordered the book from a professional scribe and funded it with help from Savinus, prior of Fonte Avellana (1143–59), whom the poem mentions. However, one could also infer that both men had participated in crafting the Bible, an idea that Berg rejected since the volume differs visibly from books definitely made at Fonte Avellana.[61] The inscription provides one additional detail in the form of an arithmetical brainteaser: the codex was made, it tells us, in the "thousand-sixth year" plus "a decade twice, thrice, and nine times over"—in short, in 1146.[62]

Medieval inventories and inscriptions added to Bibles at their points of arrival name additional donors but no scribes. King Henry IV of Germany gave an Italian Giant Bible to the monastery of St. Aurelius at Hirsau, near Stuttgart, at some moment before his imperial coronation in 1084. In the same period, a closely related Bible went to St. Magnus at Füssen in Bavaria courtesy of another layman, a certain Odalricus, who described himself in a dedicatory note as "known to highest princes."[63] In the same period, the cathedrals of Geneva and Sion received Bibbie atlantiche from their respective shepherds, Archbishop Frederick (c. 1032–c. 1073) and Bishop Ermenfried (1055–c. 1088), while the Abbey of Admont was given an Italian Giant Bible by its founder, Archbishop Gebhard of Salzburg (1060–88).[64]

## Rome and the Reform

The involvement of these three eminent churchmen tallies nicely with a near-consensus among current scholars that the earliest Bibbie atlantiche, and indeed much of the group, originated in Rome and its environs in concert with the ambitious reform of religious and clerical life promoted by the popes and their allies starting in the mid eleventh century, building upon earlier transalpine trends. What had begun in the late 1040s as a joint effort between church and empire to eradicate clerical marriage (nicolaitism) and the sale of church offices (simony) rapidly blossomed into a broader campaign to reform the communal life of monks and priests and to secure the church's freedom from lay control. Giant Bibles constituted important equipment for the project, offering complete texts for the yearly cycle of biblical readings during the Night Office and in the refectory—many Bibbie atlantiche are inscribed with lists or rubrics specifying when each text was to be read over the course of the year.[65] Bibles were also consummate symbols of church authority, another important theme of the reform. Beginning with Stephen IX (1057–58), popes and their supporters insisted ever more forcefully upon the church's liberty to choose and confirm its leaders without the customary intervention of the German kings and emperors. Tensions spiraled out of control under Pope Gregory VII (1073–85), who excommunicated Henry IV and released Henry's subjects from their fealty. Henry in return attempted to compel Gregory to resign and in 1084 occupied Rome, setting up an antipope in his place.[66]

Today most specialists believe that the production of Giant Bibles in Italy began in Rome around 1050 as a service to the emerging reform. Opinions differ concerning where the first examples were crafted—whether in one large workshop or in a more scattered fashion in imitation of a church-approved prototype. However, most agree that the finished Bibles typically went to cathedrals, monasteries, and churches in Italy and abroad as gifts of reform advocates seeking to revitalize religious life in their home territories while inspiring loyalty to the papacy and its policies.[67] If this idea is correct, then the Bibbie atlantiche were a Roman invention, which soon spread to other parts of Italy, resulting in local productions that never fully abandoned the Roman blueprint.

The seeds of this hypothesis lie in the textual studies of Carlo Vercellone, who in the 1860s noted that some of the Pantheon Bible's most unusual textual variants also appear in biblical quotations in the letters of

St. Peter Damian (d. 1072), an early and important advocate of the reform.[68] Starting in 1912, Pietro Toesca published art-historical arguments
in favor of a central Italian, and especially Umbro-Roman, origin for the
group, citing stylistic similarities between early Giant Bible miniatures
and wall paintings in Rome, Latium, and southern Umbria.[69] Edward Garrison reaffirmed Toesca's findings in the 1950s and posited that Rome had
been the genre's birthplace. Rome's immense prestige as the capital of
Latin Christendom made it one of the great hubs of book production and
diffusion in Europe, Garrison reasoned, as well as a center for the invention of new fashions in calligraphic ornament, including the geometrical
initial.[70] Garrison's prodigious, thousand-page *Studies in the History of
Mediaeval Italian Painting* (1953–62) canonized this idea and, with it, Vercellone's Rome hypothesis, which few have subsequently challenged.

## Tuscany and Umbria

Not all evidence points to Rome, however, particularly in the field of paleography. The scribes of the Bibbie atlantiche wrote in a distinctive script
whose use is not attested in any identifiable Roman scriptorium. Its early
medieval progenitor, Caroline minuscule, the ancestor of the typeface
printed on this page, had emerged as a book hand in the late eighth and
ninth centuries in association with the Carolingian *renovatio* in northern
Europe and soon spread to other areas, including northern and central
Italy.[71] By the late 900s, scribes in Rome and neighboring areas had developed their own distinctive regional variant, a charming writing whose
flattened, rhomboid characters tend to embrace one another along the
tops and bottoms and to lean jauntily to the right as if to help the reader
along.[72]

　　This brings us to the crux of the puzzle, for Italian Giant Bible scribes
did not write in this *romanesca* script, as we might expect in Rome and
its environs, but rather in a more generic Caroline minuscule—sometimes called "reformed" Caroline—found in only a few other kinds of
books, mainly oversize volumes containing biblical commentaries.[73]
Reformed Caroline letters are generally rounder, heavier in construction,
and more constant in size than their romanesca counterparts. They also
sit more perpendicular to the baseline and lack the limblike horizontal
connectors that sometimes bind romanesca characters together like
dancers in a chorus line.

Paola Supino Martini's extensive research into the history and diffusion of the romanesca script documented the existence of multiple romanesca writing workshops associated with specific religious institutions in and around Rome. Supino Martini found no evidence, however, that Roman scriptoria specialized in reformed Caroline minuscule, apart from the hypothetically Roman Giant Bibles and related exegetical manuscripts. Even for St. John Lateran, Rome's cathedral, where she conjectured a Giant Bible prototype had been approved or perhaps even produced, no clear traces of the practice of reformed Caroline minuscule survive.[74]

Non-romanesca variants of Caroline minuscule appear to have been common in Tuscany and northern Umbria, however, and some books made there—for example, Perugia 3, with its Ezra portrait copied from the Codex Amiatinus—contain writing strikingly similar to the scripts of eleventh-century Giant Bibles. Michael Gorman has recently suggested that the earliest Bibbie atlantiche originated not in Rome but rather at Monte Amiata. Not only did the abbey own the Codex Amiatinus, a compelling inspiration for anyone wishing to endow new Bibles with a physical dignity consonant with their content; its scriptorium also seems to have specialized in producing oversize manuscripts in a period when such tomes were rare.[75]

Significantly, a codex that may be the oldest surviving central-Italian Bibbia atlantica, a fragmentary Old Testament in the Sessorian collection of Rome's National Library, shares an unusually large number of textual variants with the Codex Amiatinus in Genesis, Exodus, and especially Leviticus. Its unusual chapter summaries for Exodus and Leviticus, furthermore, confirm that its makers also copied from another, rare model, now apparently lost, that was later used by the scribes of the Edili Bible and of Perugia L.59.[76] Only one other early Bibbia atlantica has capitula copied from this exemplar, an unillustrated giant Old Testament in the abbey of S. Pietro, just outside Perugia's city walls (fig. 7.10).[77] The writing blocks of the Sessorian Bible vary in size (340–86 x 226–55 mm) but generally resemble those of the Codex Amiatinus, while its scripts and initials, which recall the decorations of Stephanus's *Prophets* of 1017, confirm that it was a primitive experiment in Giant Bible production carried out before the norms of decoration and size had been established.[78]

This precocious example and its textual relatives, two of which (Edili; Perugia L.59) also drew—as previously noted—upon a Theodulf Bible that Stephanus seems to have consulted, suggest that at least one cradle of

7.10. Rome, Biblioteca Nazionale Centrale, Sessor. 9, fol. 21v: text page, with chapter summaries and initial. *With permission of the Biblioteca Nazionale Centrale, Rome. Unauthorized reproduction prohibited.*

Giant Bible production lay well to the north of Rome, in the broad swath of central Italy bordered to the southwest by Monte Amiata, to the north by Isola, Siena, and Arezzo, and to the east by Perugia and Fonte Avellana, where Peter Damian, protagonist of Vercellone's Rome hypothesis, spent much of his adult life, in between his many travels.[79] The region was rich in monasteries and cathedrals. It also experienced a religious renewal that anticipated the broader Roman reform movement by several decades. By 1009, Bishop Helmpertus of Arezzo had reorganized his cathedral clergy into a community of canons living together according to a rule.[80] Cathedral canonries were also founded at Perugia (1001–24), Città di Castello (c. 1020), Assisi (1029), and Gubbio (by c. 1047), probably with encouragement from St. Romuald of Ravenna (died c. 1027) and his disciples.[81] In 1022 Romuald was briefly assigned charge of Monte Amiata by the emperor, Henry II, and soon afterward established new communities of hermits and monks at Camaldoli and Sitria in the dioceses of Arezzo and Perugia. Sitria lies very close to Fonte Avellana, where Romuald's biographer and countryman, Peter Damian, would become prior in 1043.[82]

Material renewal accompanied this spiritual renascence. Imposing new cathedrals were built at Assisi (c. 1029) and Arezzo (1014–33), the latter modeled upon S. Vitale in Ravenna.[83] Abbot Winizo erected a grand new abbey church at Monte Amiata. Eighteen bishops and cardinals attended its consecration in 1035.[84] At the time, the abbey was also building its book collection and helping other monasteries and churches in the region to do the same by lending manuscripts at a distance, almost certainly for copying.[85] Peter Damian obtained many books for his monks, although not necessarily from Monte Amiata, including full texts of the Old and New Testaments, which he corrected himself, "if hastily," he later wrote, "and thus not precisely."[86]

## Professionals

If the region's new and revitalized religious houses clearly created a demand for books before 1050 and provided some inspirations and models for early Bibbie atlantiche, the scribes and painters who produced the manuscripts are rather more mysterious. Codices written in scripts very similar to reformed Caroline minuscule were copied from exemplars owned by the area's monasteries, most notably S. Salvatore of Monte Amiata.[87] However, local monastic calligraphers who signed their works—in short, the only scribes we can be certain were monks—wrote in more personal hands, even when transcribing biblical and exegetical texts. Stephanus of Isola's broad, buoyant writing is a case in point. So is Bonizo's whimsical calligraphy, with its tendency to transform below-the-line elements, especially the descenders of *f* and *g*, into baroque spirals or the heads of flamingolike birds.[88]

These monastic scribes also had distinctive working habits. In the Amiatine *Moralia in Iob*, Bonizo copied no fewer than 488 consecutive, folio-size pages before a second monk, Petrus, took over to pen the remaining 612.[89] Such solitary calligraphic marathons were atypical of Giant Bible scribes, who normally worked in larger ensembles carefully orchestrated for efficiency. Comparatively brief textual segments, such as the Minor Prophets or Samuel and Kings, were divvied up between individual copyists or small groups for writing out in self-contained packets, clusters of sequential gatherings that would later compose the finished manuscript. With this system, the S. Cecilia Bible was penned by at least seven scribes, the Todi Bible by eight, the Palatine Bible by eleven, and the Pantheon Bible by no fewer than twenty-one, excluding rubricators and illuminators. Furthermore, there seems to have been little or no duplication of personnel, meaning no single scribe or miniaturist who worked on more than one of the four Bibles.[90] Where artisans participated in multiple Giant Bible projects, they tended to do so in changing combinations. Perugia L.59 and the Parma Bible, for example, were written by different scribes but have creation miniatures by the same, talented painter. On the contrary, the Hirsau and Palatine Bibles shared at least two scribes but were illustrated by different miniaturists, albeit miniaturists working in similar styles and from the same or nearly identical models.[91]

Subtly different writing habits confirm that Giant Bible scribes learned their minuscule in different milieus. The calligraphers of Bibles whose texts or decorations suggest that they came from Tuscany or northern Umbria, for example, frequently fused *r* and *i* in a stylish, slashing ligature (i.e., a merger of adjacent letters) also typical of manuscripts from Monte Amiata but absent in most other Bibbie atlantiche, including the S. Cecilia, Todi, and Palatine manuscripts.[92] Of the Pantheon Bible's nearly two dozen scribes, only one used this ligature, a flamboyant master whose most unusual trademarks—broad, flat-topped ligatures of other letters; a cruciform abbreviation of *-us*; an occasional extra loop in the tail of *g*—resemble those of a notary and doctor of law from Arezzo named Aritius (active 1068–95).[93] Eleventh-century Aretine notaries were avantgarde in their adaptation of Caroline minuscule for the drafting of documents, although the question of whether any moonlighted as Giant Bible scribes, supervised their work, or learned their letters from the same masters requires further study.[94]

In the late 900s, the future Pope Sylvester II, Gerbert d'Aurillac, observed that in Italy scribes were available for hire both in the cities and in the countryside, and scattered references indicate that the employment of professionals, including laymen, for the copying and ornamenting of religious books was not a new phenomenon when Gerardus called

Vivianus and his coworkers to S. Vito in 1168.[95] Given the large and apparently mobile work force involved in crafting the early Bibbie atlantiche,
as well the streamlined methods, fluid collaborations, subtly diverse writing habits, and habitual anonymity of their scribes, it seems likely that
many early examples were created in more or less the same fashion as the
Calci Bible—that is, by professional artisans hired for the purpose by religious institutions in need of books, by churchmen or lay benefactors
wishing to donate Bibles locally or abroad, or by some combination of the
two.

## Patrons and Imagery

Illustrations in Bibbie atlantiche sometimes appear to provide coded
information about their sponsors. A creation miniature imitating the
frescoes of St. Peter's Basilica and St. Paul's Outside the Walls, for example, may have expressed the papal sympathies or affiliations of a Bible's
commissioning patrons. For knowledgeable medieval observers, such
images must have resonated with papal authority, mimicking, as they
did, paintings located near the tombs of the two apostles to Rome, one of
them the first pope, and portraying the original sin, which made mankind
utterly dependent upon salvation available only through the Church.[96]

Given the frequency of such pictures in early Bibbie atlantiche and the
prestige of their models, the choice of a different creation narrative,
focused upon the Priestly account, was probably both deliberate and
meaningful. The illustrations of Perugia L. 59 show the six days sequen-
tially (fig. 7.6), with one element borrowed from the Jahwist story: a final
vignette of Eve emerging from Adam's side (fig. 7.9). This depiction of the
first man and woman before the Creator in their primordial state of
bodily union seems to underline the sanctity and indissolubility of the
marriage of the two donors—it exactly faces their double portrait. In the
book of Matthew, Jesus invokes the creation stories in his prohibition of
divorce, with special attention to the creation of both male and female
and the physical union of husband and wife, concluding with the admonition, "What therefore God hath joined together, let no man put asunder"
(Matt. 19:4–6). A document of 994 from Pietralata in the territory of Volterra commemorates the *Morgengab*, or morning gift, that a husband made
to his wife on the morning after the consummation of their marriage

under the Longobard law (still widely observed in tenth- and eleventh-century Tuscany) and begins by referring to this passage and to the creation of Eve from Adam's rib.[97]

To eleventh-century viewers, the creation miniature of the Palatine Bible (fig. 7.7) may have evoked a related directive, the divine command to procreate. The miniature reduces the six days to their first and last events: the separation of light and darkness (Gen. 1:3–5) and the creation and/or blessing of the first man and woman, whom the Creator instructs to "increase and multiply, and fill the earth, and subdue it" (Gen. 1:26–28).

7.11. Munich, Staatsbibliothek, Clm 13001, fol. 92v: page with miniature of Esther and inscription commemorating Henry IV's gift of the Bible. *Bayerische Staatsbibliothek München Clm 13001, fol. 92v. By permission of the Bayerische Staatsbibliothek.*

While medieval observers might well have interpreted this command to fertility in figurative terms, a miniature evoking it nevertheless seems a curious choice for the visual summing up of Genesis in a manuscript intended for monks, particularly during the antinicolaitist campaigns of the reform. (The most influential patristic interpreter of Genesis, St. Augustine, ultimately concluded that the passage referred to sexual reproduction.)[98] In his dedicatory inscription, the Palatine Bible's donor, Oldaricus, refers repeatedly to his family and descendents, a sign that he perhaps considered the production of children an especially meaningful theme.[99] However, whether he commissioned the Bible and had a say in its decoration remains an open question. His inscription says only that he "acquired" and donated the Bible to St. Magnus after a devastating fire.[100]

The close relationship between the Palatine Bible and the Bibbia atlantica that King Henry IV donated in the same period to the monastery of Hirsau invites us to imagine one other possible reason for the alternative iconography—that is, a desire on the patron's part to minimize allusions to the Roman apostolic basilicas, with their powerful papal associations.[101] Whether Henry's Bible had a creation miniature similar to that of the Palatine Bible we can only speculate, for the codex now lacks its opening books, including Genesis. However, several of its surviving illustrations seem designed to affirm the sacred character of royal authority, including Henry's own. Three of the manuscript's most imposing pictures show biblical sovereigns, David, Solomon, and Esther, each wearing a crown and a holding a rotulus or codex, emblems of their dual dignity as both earthly rulers and intermediaries between God and man.[102]

Henry's presence permeates the volume. Latin inscriptions added in red in an eleventh-century hand at or near the start of each book of the Bible commemorate his gift: "King Henry IV gave this book to St. Aurelius" (fig. 7.11).[103] Often abbreviated, these marginal rubrics seem to have been intended as cues to the monk-lectors of Hirsau to recall Henry's gift aloud before each new phase in the yearly cycle of biblical readings, a practice that would have made his generosity to the monastery a constant memory in the shared devotional experience of the monks. Though written only once, and so perhaps less frequently read, the inscription penned nearly a century later by Gerardus in the Giant Bible begun with Mattilda Veckii's hundred solidi may have had a similar, if less politically charged function, encouraging the monks of S. Vito to recall, periodically and in perpetuity, the widows, bakers, fishermen, and other twelfth-century

Pisans who bettered their hopes for salvation by subsidizing a fittingly grand copy of the most sacred of all books.

## Notes

1. Pisa, Museo Nazionale di San Matteo, Bibbia di Calci, IV, fol. 230r (marked 231); Knut Berg, *Studies in Tuscan Twelfth-Century Illumination* (Oslo: Universitetsforlaget, 1968), pp. 151–57, 205–6, 226–27. My knowledge of the inscription comes from Berg's transcription corrected against a photograph of fol. 230r.

2. Walter Cahn, *Romanesque Bible Illumination* (Ithaca: Cornell University Press, 1982), pp. 224–26; Bernardo Maragone, *Gli Annales Pisani di Bernardo Maragone*, ed. Michele Lupo Gentile (Bologna: Zanichelli, 1930–36), p. 60; Giovanni Scriba, *Il cartolare di Giovanni Scriba*, ed. Mario Chiaudano and Mattia Moresco, 2 vols. (Rome: R. Istituto Storico Italiano per il Medio Evo, 1935), 1:426; Mario Chiaudano, "La Moneta di Genova nel secolo XII," in *Studi in onore di Armando Sapori*, 2 vols. (Milan: Istituto Editoriale Cisalpino, 1957), 1:189–214, at 200–1; Cinzio Violante, *Economia società istituzioni a Pisa nel Medioevo* (Bari: Dedalo, 1980), p. 214.

3. Maragone, *Annales*, p. 60; Giovanni Scriba, *Il cartolare*, 1:283–84, 423.

4. Gabriella Garzella, *Pisa com'era: topografia e insediamento dall'impianto tardoantico alla città murata del secolo XII* (Naples: GISEM/Liguori, 1990), pp. 165, 173.

5. Berg, *Studies*, p. 226.

6. Marilena Maniaci, "La struttura delle Bibbie atlantiche," in *Le Bibbie Atlantiche. Il libro delle Scritture tra monumentalità e rappresentazione*, ed. Marilena Maniaci and Giulia Orofino (Milan: Centro Tibaldi, 2000), pp. 47–60, at 49.

7. Maniaci, "La struttura," p. 49.

8. Berg, *Studies*, pp. 224–25.

9. "*Pro quodam iuvene de ilba mortuo*" (Bibbia di Calci, IV, fol. 230r [photograph]).

10. Cf. Christopher de Hamel, *The Book: A History of the Bible* (New York: Phaidon, 2001), p. 91, whose calculations differ.

11. Berg, *Studies*, p. 227.

12. Vivianus received "fifteen pounds and more" ("*libras XV et amplius*") (Berg, *Studies*, p. 227). One pound (*libra*) equaled twenty solidi. See Maria Luisa Ceccarelli Lemut, "L'uso della moneta nei documenti pisani dei secoli XI e XII," in *Studi sugli strumenti di scambio a Pisa nel medioevo*, ed. G. Garzella, M. L. Ceccarelli Lemut, and B. Casini (Pisa: Pacini, 1979), pp. 47–121, at 52–53.

13. "*Magistrum Vivianum scriptorem.*" Maria Luigia Orlandi, *Carte dell'archivio della Certosa di Calci (1151–1200)* (Ospedaletto, Pisa: Pacini, 2002), pp. 90–93, 95–99.

14. Transcribed in Berg, *Studies*, pp. 226–27.

15. "*Quando reduxit quaternos.*" Ibid., p. 227.

16. de Hamel, *The Book*, p. 91.

17. Berg, *Studies*, pp. 205–6; Cahn, *Romanesque Bible Illumination*, pp. 224–26.

18. Orlandi, *Carte*, pp. 203–5.

19. Antonia d'Aniello, "55. Pisa, Museo nazionale di San Matteo, deposito provvisorio (Bibbia di Calci)," in *Le Bibbie Atlantiche*, pp. 303–10, at 305.

20. d'Aniello, "55. Pisa," p. 303; "New York Times to Cut Size 5 Percent; Keller Says Paper Better Off Smaller," *New York Observer*, http://www.observer.com/node/32911 (accessed July 17, 2006).

21. Calculated via comparison with Perugia, Biblioteca Comunale Augusta Ms. L. 59 (hereafter "Perugia L. 59"), which has 253 leaves of slightly smaller dimensions (535 x 355 mm) and weighs approximately 11 kg.

22. Berg, *Studies*, figs. 249–68.

23. For catalogs, see *Le Bibbie Atlantiche*, pp. 107–323; Edward Garrison, *Studies in the History of Mediaeval Italian Painting*, 4 vols. (Florence: "L'Impronta," 1953–62), passim; and Berg, *Studies*, pp. 223–326.

24. Garrison, *Studies*, 1:20–32, 43–67; 2:47–69.

25. Ibid.

26. On prophet portraits as visual prologues, see Robert Timothy Chasson, "Prophetic Imagery and Lections at Passiontide: The Jeremiah Illustrations in a Tuscan Romanesque Bible," *Gesta* 42 (2003): 89–114.

27. Parma, Biblioteca Palatina, Palat. 386 (hereafter "Parma"), fol. 141r.

28. *The Holy Bible* (New York: Douay Bible House, 1941; repr. Fitzwilliam, NH: Loreto, 2004), p. 792. All subsequent biblical quotations are from this edition.

29. Florence, Biblioteca Medicea Laurenziana (hereafter BML), Edili 125–26 (hereafter "Edili"), and in particular Edili 126: fol. 12v; Biblioteca Apostolica Vaticana (hereafter BAV), Barb. Lat. 587, fol. 194r (hereafter "S. Cecilia"); BAV, Vat. lat. 12958, fol. 186v (hereafter "Pantheon").

30. *Le Bibbie Atlantiche*, pp. 114, 120–21, 126–28, 144–46, 158, 262–64, 271–76. Judith illustrations appear in Edili; Pantheon; Parma; S. Cecilia; the Hirsau Bible (Munich, Bayerische Staatsbibliothek, Clm 13001, hereafter "Clm 13001"); the Palatine Bible, from Füssen ( BAV, Pal. lat. 3–5, hereafter "Pal. lat. 3–5"); and a Bible formerly in Todi (BAV, Vat. lat. 10405, hereafter "Todi").

31. On the miniatures, see Garrison, *Studies*, 4:201–10; for the frescoes, Herbert Kessler, "*Caput et Speculum Omnium Ecclesiarum*: Old St. Peter's and Church Decoration in Medieval Latium," in *Italian Church Decoration of the Middle Ages and Early Renaissance*, ed. William Tronzo (Bologna: Nuova Alfa, 1989), pp. 119–46. Like the Angelica Bible (Rome, Biblioteca Angelica, Ms. 1273), the Pantheon, Parma, S. Cecilia, and Todi Bibles illustrate the "apostolic" version of the Creation and Fall in full. In the S. Cecilia Bible, the miniature is a twelfth-century replacement. The following Bibles abbreviate the sequence to three or more scenes: Edili 125; Cividale, Museo Archeologico Nazionale, Biblioteca Capitolare, I; Florence, Biblioteca Riccardiana, 221 (hereafter "Riccardiana 221"); Genoa, Biblioteca Civica Berio, Sezione di conservazione e raccolta locale, m.r. Cf. 3.7; and Toledo, Archivo Capitular, Ms. 3.

32. Riccardiana, 221 fol. 4r; *Le Bibbie Atlantiche*, pp. 260–62.

33. Perugia L.59, fols. 1r–2v; Pal. lat. 3, fol. 5r. Montalcino, Archivio Comunale, Fondi diversi 1, fol. 5v, also shows the Six Days. See Marie-Louise Thèrel, "Remarques sur une illustration du livre de la Genèse dans la Bible de Montalcino," *Revue d'Histoire des Textes* 12 (1972): 231–38.

34. Paola Supino Martini, *Roma e l'area grafica romanesca (secoli X–XII)* (Alessandria: Edizioni dell'Orso, 1987), pp. 27–29.

35. Paola Supino Martini, "La scrittura delle Scritture (sec. XI–XII)," *Scrittura e civiltà* 12 (1988): 101–18, at 103–8.

36. Siena, Biblioteca Comunale degli Intronati, F.III.3.

37. *"Ego frater Stephanus . . . scripsi hunc librum . . . circa \*\*\*\*\* atque xx^{mum} annum aetatis meae"* (Siena, F.III.3, fol. 186v; Berg, *Studies*, p. 320).

38. On the Bibles from Tours, see David Ganz, "Mass Production of Early Medieval Manuscripts: The Carolingian Bibles from Tours," in *The Early Medieval Bible: Its Production, Decoration, and Use*, ed. Richard Gameson (Cambridge: Cambridge University Press, 1994), pp. 53–62.

39. On the S. Paolo Bible, see Joachim E. Gaehde, "The Bible of San Paolo fuori le mura in Rome: Its Date and Its Relation to Charles the Bald," *Gesta* 5 (1966): 9–21. BAV, Barb. Lat. 588, fol. 1r, begins with a copy of its prologue. Cf. Berg, *Studies*, pp. 23–28, 312–13.

40. Guy Lobrichon, "Riforma ecclesiastica e testo della Bibbia," in *Le Bibbie Atlantiche*, pp. 15–23, at 19–22.

41. On the Theodulf Bibles, see Léopold Delisle, *Les Bibles de Théodulfe* (Paris: A. Champion, 1879); and Lawrence Nees, "Problems of Form and Function in Early Medieval Illustrated Bibles from Northwest Europe," in *Imaging the Early Medieval Bible*, ed. John Williams (University Park: Pennsylvania State University Press, 1999), pp. 121–77, at 125–31.

42. Paris, Bibliothèque Nationale de France, Ms. lat. 11937; Lila Yawn-Bonghi, "The Illustrated Giant Bible of Perugia (Biblioteca Augusta, Ms. L.59). A Manuscript and Its Creators in Eleventh-Century Central Italy," (Ph.D. diss., University of North Carolina, Chapel Hill, 2004), pp. 125–33, 305–7.

43. Robert Timothy Chasson, "The Earliest Illustrated Tuscan Bible (Edili 125/126)," (Ph.D. diss., University of California, Berkeley, 1979), pp. 127–29, 357–65, 369–82.

44. Paul Meyvaert, "Bede's *capitula lectionum* for the Old and New Testaments," *Revue bénédictine* 105 (1995): 348–80, at 366–72.

45. Florence, BML, Amiat. 1; Michael Gorman, "Manuscript Books at Monte Amiata in the Eleventh Century," *Scriptorium* 56 (2002): 225–93, at 254–55, 261; Nees, "Problems," pp. 148–74.

46. BAV, Barb. Lat. 573, fols. IV and 244v; Gorman, "Manuscript Books," esp. pp. 254, 267. Perugia, Biblioteca Capitolare, Ms. 3, fol. 353v. On the contents and origins of Ms. 3, see Gorman, "Manuscript Books," pp. 263–64; Leonardo Magionami, *I manoscritti del capitolo di San Lorenzo di Perugia* (Rome: Jouvence, 2006), p. 33; and

Antonin Caleca, *La Miniatura in Umbria. I—La Biblioteca Capitolare di Perugia* (Florence: Marchi and Bertolli, 1969), pp. 35–53, 140–46.

47. Gorman, "Manuscript Books," esp. pp. 243–74, discusses the Amiatine manuscripts.

48. Gabriella Braga, "I manoscritti del vescovo Guglielmo II: significato di una scoperta," in *Le Bibbie Atlantiche*, pp. 87–90.

49. Rome, Biblioteca Casanatense, Cod. 470.

50. Casanatense 470, fol. 1r. On the manuscript's provenance and *capitula*, see Chasson, "The Earliest Illustrated Tuscan Bible," p. 128; on the palette of Bonizo's manuscript and others from Monte Amiata, see Gorman, "Manuscript Books," p. 254.

51. Perugia, Biblioteca Capitolare, Ms. 42.

52. Gorman, "Manuscript Books," p. 256, provides measurements for the Codex Amiatinus and Perugia 42.

53. On the Bible's date, see Yawn-Bonghi, "The Illustrated Giant Bible," pp. 274–75; and Ayres, "An Italian Romanesque Manuscript of Hrabanus Maurus's 'De Laudibus Sanctae Crucis' and the Gregorian Reform," *Dumbarton Oaks Papers* 41 (1987): 13–27.

54. Lila Yawn, "Perugia, Biblioteca comunale Augusta, L.59 (pt. 2)," in *Le Bibbie Atlantiche*, pp. 172–73; Emore Paoli, "Agiografia e culto dei santi a Perugia tra alto e basso medioevo," in *La Chiesa di Perugia nel primo millennio*, ed. Attilio Bartoli Langeli and Enrico Menestò (Spoleto: Fondazione Centro Italiano di Studi sull'Alto Medioevo, 2005), pp. 41–84, at 63–65, esp. n. 114.

55. Rome, Biblioteca Casanatense, Cod. 722.

56. " . . . hedificauerunt quaternum istum . . ."; " . . . quaternum scripsit . . ."; " . . . quaternum ex suis rebus componere . . ." (Casanatense 722, fols. 121r, 129r, 137r). Cf. Lucinia Speciale, "57. Roma, Biblioteca Casanatense, Casanat. 722 (+ Casanat. 723 = seconda Bibbia della Casanatense)," in *Le Bibbie Atlantiche*, pp. 312–15, who interprets the inscriptions differently.

57. Casanatense 722, fol. 1v; Speciale, "57. Roma," p. 315.

58. Florence, BML, Conv. Soppr. 630, fol. 324v, transcribed in Berg, *Studies*, p. 260.

59. Pistoia, Archivio Capitolare, Cod. 116, fol. 258v, transcribed in Garrison, *Studies*, 3:132 n. 2.

60. BAV, Vat. lat. 4216, fol. 294v; Berg, *Studies*, pp. 175–78, p. 315.

61. Berg, *Studies*, pp. 175–78, 207–8.

62. "*Temporis annus sextus millenus bis ter noviesque decenus*" (Vat. lat. 4216, fol. 294v; Berg, *Studies*, p. 315).

63. "*Odalricus summis principibus notus*" (Garrison, *Studies*, 1:10).

64. Garrison, *Studies*, 1:10–17. On the evidence for Ermenfried's donation see Larry Ayres, "Le Bibbie Atlantiche. Dalla Riforma alla diffusione in Europa," in *Le Bibbie Atlantiche*, pp. 27–37, at p. 31.

65. Examples: BAV, Barb. lat. 588, fol. 1r; Parma, Palat. 386, fol. 3v; Milan, Biblioteca

Ambrosiana, Ms. B. 47 inf., fol. 4r; and Casanatense 722, fol. 287v. See also Diane J. Reilly, "French Romanesque Giant Bibles and Their English Relatives: Blood Relatives or Adopted Children?" *Scriptorium* 56 (2002): 294–311, esp. 300–1; and Ayres, "Le Bibbie Atlantiche," pp. 27–28.

66. Hanna Vollrath, "The Western Empire Under the Salians," and Giovanni Tabacco, "Northern and Central Italy in the Eleventh Century," in *The New Cambridge Medieval History* vol. 4, c. 1024–c. 1198, ed. David Luscombe and Jonathan Riley-Smith (Cambridge: Cambridge University Press, 2004), pp. 38–69, at 46–65, and 72–93, at 83–87, respectively.

67. See especially the introductory essays in *Le Bibbie Atlantiche*.

68. *Variae Lectiones Vulgatae Latinae Bibliorum editionis*, ed. Carlo Vercellone, 2 vols., (Rome, 1860–64), 1:lxxxvii; see also 1:xix, xci; 2:xviii–xx. Cf. Larry Ayres, "Le Bibbie Atlantiche," p. 27.

69. Pietro Toesca, *La pittura e la miniatura nella Lombardia dai più antichi monumenti alla metà del quattrocento* (Milano: Ulrico Hoepli, 1912), pp. 78–79; and "Miniature romane dei secoli XI e XII: Bibbie miniate," *Rivista del Reale Istituto d'Archeologia e Storia dell'arte* 1 (1929): 69–96.

70. Garrison, *Studies*, 1:24–28.

71. Bernhard Bischoff, *Latin Palaeography*, trans. Dáibhí ó Cróinín and David Ganz (Cambridge: Cambridge University Press, 1990), pp. 112–27.

72. Supino Martini, *Roma*, esp. pp. 21–46.

73. Supino Martini, "La scrittura," pp. 101–8; Supino Martini, *Roma*, pp. 25–33; Bischoff, *Latin Palaeography*, pp. 125–26; Garrison, *Studies*, 1:37–41. Supino Martini found only one Giant Bible partly written in *romanesca*: Città del Vaticano BAV, Archivio di San Pietro A. 1 (Supino Martini, *Roma*, pp. 27–29, esp. p. 28 n. 14).

74. Supino Martini, *Roma*, passim, esp. pp. 27, 46–56; Supino Martini, "La scrittura," pp. 101–8; and Paola Supino Martini, "Origine e diffusione delle Bibbie atlantiche," in *Le Bibbie Atlantiche*, pp. 39–43, at 41–42.

75. Gorman, "Manuscript Books," pp. 243–78. See also Magionami, *I manoscritti*, pp. 13–14.

76. Rome, Biblioteca Nazionale Centrale, Sessor. 9, fols. 21v, 38v–39r. On the Amiatine variants, see D. J. Chapman, "The Families of Vulgate mss in the Pentateuch," *Revue bénédictine* 37 (1925): 21–45.

77. Perugia, Archivio di S. Pietro, Cod. 1; Yawn-Bonghi, "The Illustrated Giant Bible," pp. 115–25, 291–93; Chasson, "The Earliest Illustrated Tuscan Bible," pp. 131a–32.

78. Cf. Berg, *Studies*, pp. 60, 310.

79. Owen J. Blum, *St. Peter Damian: His Teaching on the Spiritual Life* (Washington, DC: Catholic University of America Press, 1947), pp. 5–35.

80. Giovanni Tabacco, "Canoniche aretine," in *La Vita commune del Clero nei secoli XI e XII. Atti della Settimana di studio: Mendola, settembre, 1959*, 2 vols. (Milan: So-

cietà Editrice Vita e Pensiero, 1962), 2:245–46; Ubaldo Pasqui, *Documenti per la storia della città di Arezzo nel medio evo*, 3 vols. (Florence: G. P. Viesseux, 1899–1937), 1:129.

81. Ugolino Nicolini, "La Vita commune del clero a Perugia nei secoli XI e XII," in *La Vita comune del clero*, 2:260–63; Giovanni Miccoli, "Pier Damiani e la vita commune del clero," in *La Vita commune del Clero*, 1:186–219.

82. Giovanni Tabacco, "Romualdo" (pt. 1), in *Bibliotheca Sanctorum*, ed. Istituto Giovanni XXIII della Pontificia Università Lateranense, 12 vols. (Rome: Città Nuova Editrice, 1961–2000), 11:366–75; Blum, *St. Peter Damian*, p. 9.

83. Elvio Lunghi, *Il Museo della Cattedrale di San Rufino ad Assisi* (Assisi: Accademia Properziana del Subasio, 1987), p. 19; Guglielmo De Angelis d'Ossat, "Il 'Duomo Vecchio' di Arezzo," *Palladio* 22 (1978): 7–46, at 7.

84. Gorman, "Manuscript Books," p. 225.

85. Ibid., pp. 243–47.

86. *"licet cursim ac per hoc non exacte."* Peter Damian, *Petri Damiani Epistulae/Pier Damiani Lettere*, ed. K. Reindel, G. I. Gargano, and N. D'Acunto, 4 vols. (Rome: Città Nuova, 2000–5). See also Ayres, "Le Bibbie Atlantiche," p. 27.

87. Gorman, "Manuscript Books," pp. 263–69.

88. Barb. Lat. 573, fols. 27v, 181v, and passim.

89. Barb. Lat. 573, passim; Gorman, "Manuscript Books," pp. 254–55.

90. I drew these conclusions from a direct, page-by-page study of the manuscripts.

91. Garrison, *Studies*, 2:132 and 140.

92. For examples of the ligature in manuscripts from Monte Amiata, see Città del Vaticano BAV, Barb. lat. 572, 573, 581, 582, 679. Gorman, "Manuscript Books," pp. 253–57, discusses the provenance of these volumes.

93. On Aritius, see Giovanna Nicolaj, "Alle origini della minuscola notarile italiana e dei suoi caratteri storici," *Scrittura e civiltà* 10 (1986): 49–82, esp. p. 67 and tav. 9.

94. On Aretine notaries generally, see Nicolaj, "Alle origini," pp. 49–50.

95. Berg, *Studies*, pp. 205–20; Gerbert d'Aurillac, *Lettres de Gerbert (983–997)*, ed. Julien Havet (Paris, 1889), pp. 117–18.

96. On uses of the Bible in polemical literature of the period, see Jean Leclercq, "Usage et abus de la Bible au temps de la réforme grégorienne," *The Bible and Medieval Culture*, ed. Willem Lourdaux and Daniel Verhelst (Louvain: Leuven University Press, 1979), pp. 89–108.

97. Paolo Cammarosano, *Abbadia a Isola. Un monastero toscano nell'età romanica* (Castelfiorentino: Società Storica della Valdelsa, 1993), pp. 174–75.

98. Jeremy Cohen, *"Be Fertile and Increase, Fill the Earth and Master It": The Ancient and Medieval Career of a Biblical Text* (Ithaca: Cornell University Press, 1989), pp. 221–70.

99. On the inscription, see Lucinia Speciale, "4. Città del Vaticano, Biblioteca Apostolica Vaticana, Vat. Pal. lat. 3-4-5 (Bibbia Palatina)." In *Le Bibbie Atlantiche*, pp. 120–26, at 126.

100. *"Acquisivi librum."* Garrison, *Studies*, 1:10–11.

101. On similarities in the illustrations in the Hirsau and Palatine Bibles, see Garrison, *Studies*, 2:132 and 140.

102. For an alternative interpretation, see Larry Ayres, "The Bible of Henry IV and an Italian Romanesque Pandect in Florence," in *Studien zur mittelalterlichen Kunst 800–1250: Festschrift für Florentine Mütherich zum 70. Geburtstag*, ed. Katharina Bierbrauer, Peter K. Klein, and Willibald Sauerländer (Munich: Prestel, 1985), pp. 157–66.

103. *"HEINRICUS IIII REX DEDIT HUNC LIBRUM SANCTO AURELIO"* (Clm 13011, passim.)

# Biblical Exegesis Through the Twelfth Century

*Frans van Liere*

This chapter provides an overview of the most important trends and developments in biblical exegesis from the early Middle Ages through the twelfth century.[1] As the most widely read text within Christendom, the Bible was also the one with the most plentiful commentary tradition. But one must remember that "the Bible" was still a fluid concept during this period. The canon, that is, the books now regarded as part of Sacred Scripture, was not yet firmly established, in part because the full text of what is today considered the Bible was rarely found within a single volume. Such single volumes, when they did exist, were called pandects. But most "Bibles" were in fact only partial Bibles, often single biblical volumes containing only the Gospels, the Psalms, the Pentateuch, the Prophets, or the Epistles of Paul.[2] (For further discussion of early biblical codices, see Gyug's chapter in this volume.) As a result, some biblical books were more widely available and also more widely read and commented upon than others. Ample commentaries survive on the Pentateuch or the Pauline Epistles, for example, while commentaries on the (apocryphal) books of III–IV Ezra or Baruch are relatively rare. Social and spiritual contexts also determined which books received the most commentary. Although the Song of Songs is rarely read or preached in today's churches, within the monastic circles of the high Middle Ages it was one of the books on which the most commentaries were written because it was read not as erotic love poetry but as an allegory of Christ's love for the human soul.[3] The Pentateuch and Gospels outlined the history of Christian salvation and were frequently read during the liturgical year; the Pauline Epistles were seen as a primer in doctrinal theology; and the Psalms and biblical canticles were widely read and sung in the monastic liturgy. All these books, then, were among those most frequently commented upon in the early and high Middle Ages.

## Monastic Education and Exegesis

As the main text read in early medieval monasteries, the Bible served as the basis of the medieval educational system. In the turbulent sixth century, when Italy was the scene of a protracted struggle between the Byzantine Empire and the Ostrogothic and later Lombard rulers of Italy, education became increasingly located in monastic communities rather than public grammar or rhetoric schools. This trend was followed elsewhere in Western Europe, especially in the British Isles, where monks from Rome had established missionary outposts in the kingdoms ruled by the still pagan Anglo-Saxons. In these monasteries, the Bible was read as an exercise in spiritual formation; this slow form of reading, often referred to as the *lectio divina*, was supposed to bring the soul closer to God. (For more discussion of monastic spiritual reading, see Cochelin's chapter in this volume.) Monasteries also needed texts to guide monks in their spiritual formation, and the production of these texts became a standard aspect of monastic labor. The result was a transformation of the late antique conception of the monastery from an ascetic refuge, a place in the "wilderness" away from the world, to a school and a scriptorium, a place where biblical texts were read, studied, preserved, and reproduced.[4]

One such community was the monastery of Vivarium, founded by the former Roman nobleman and senator Cassiodorus (d. ca. 585). Cassiodorus, together with Pope Agapitus, had made plans in 530 to found a Christian school to counter the secular academies of Rome. This academy eventually took shape not in Rome but in Cassiodorus's country estate in southern Italy where he founded a monastery in 554. In his

*Institutiones,* Cassiodorus not only outlines the canon of Scripture and the basic writings of the church fathers that were useful for a life of monastic study but also delineates the basic rules of grammar and spelling necessary for monks dedicated to the copying and study of the Bible.[5] Thus the study, reproduction, and explanation of Scripture became specifically associated with the monastic vocation, and the monastery became the place to pursue education as a lifelong vocation. No longer was education designed to prepare one for a life of public civic duty; monastic pedagogy in the early Middle Ages emphasized the perfection of morals and the achievement of wisdom as private virtues, based on close study of Scripture. Job, the patient wise man, trusting in God in the face of great adversity, was seen as the epitome of this new ideal of monastic wisdom. No wonder, then, that the future Pope Gregory the Great (d. 604) chose to preach a series of sermons on the book of Job for the Latin monastic community in Constantinople. His *Moralia in Job* became a "best seller" in the Western European Middle Ages.[6]

## The Senses of Scripture: Medieval Hermeneutics

The hermeneutics of scriptural exegesis employed in early medieval biblical commentaries were largely inherited from the patristic period. On the one hand, there was a practical, philological approach to Scripture, with a keen interest in biblical *realia*—the persons, places, and events in the Bible. This historical approach sought to explain the literal sense of the text in order to make it more comprehensible for the reader who, after all, lived in different cultural surroundings than those in which the Bible texts had been composed. But besides the historical or literal sense of Scripture, there was the notion that the text was in its entirety a great code containing a deeper, hidden meaning: the mystery of salvation through Jesus Christ, which could in principle be detected even in those passages that did not seem to address salvation history overtly. The Western church fathers, such as Augustine, Gregory the Great, and even a more philologically adept scholar like Jerome (whose commentaries became foundational for medieval approaches to Scripture), shared the assumption that the spiritual sense of the Bible was its hidden yet true meaning, only perceptible to those who were initiated into the mysteries of faith. At the same time, these mysteries could lead to a moral application in daily life. Thus a system of interpretation developed that perceived multiple levels of meaning in Scripture, broadly divided into the literal or historical level, the allegorical level (sometimes subdivided into allegory and anagogy, a form of allegory that referred specifically to the afterlife), and the moral application (also called the tropological level).[7]

The first level of interpretation, the literal interpretation of Scripture, commonly meant paraphrasing the text and interpolating into it short explications to make clear its overt meaning (*sensus*). The exegete could provide a short grammatical analysis of the text, suggest alternative forms of punctuation, or even provide alternative readings. But, most commonly, this type of exegesis explained the historical context of the biblical text, identified biblical persons, provided some geographical background, and provided explanations of the customs of the past necessary to understand the text on a basic level. The moral or tropological interpretation of Scripture was also relatively straightforward. It emphasized the moral actions that were implied in the story and outlined which elements in the biblical passage the reader or listener should try to imitate and which ones to avoid.

The allegorical interpretation of Scripture is probably the type with which modern students are least familiar. Christian allegorical interpretation of the Bible originated in the earliest days of Christianity, when it was a common way of reading texts that were authoritative but difficult to comprehend. Homer's epics were commonly allegorized in the Hellenistic world by scholars who insisted that behind the crude anthropomorphic descriptions of the ancient gods a higher and deeper truth lay hidden. Likewise, the Jewish philosopher Philo of Alexandria advocated an allegorical approach to most of the Hebrew Bible.[8] Midrash, the common Jewish exegetical practice of the time, dealt with Scripture in a similar way; the aim of this type of exegesis was to make the story relevant to the contemporary situation in a process of creative reinterpretation, rather than to provide an explanation of its original historical setting. Just as Hellenistic readers were challenged by the "otherness" of the Homeric epics, Christians faced a similar challenge in their approach to the Old Testament. It was considered a sacred text, but at the same time it was also intrinsically connected to Judaism, a religion from which Christianity had come to disassociate itself. While some heretics wanted to do away with the Old Testament altogether, believing that the God who created heaven and earth was not the same as the Father of Jesus Christ, orthodox Christians continued to feel a strong sense of historical continuity between their own community of believers and the Israel of the Old Testament. To emphasize their differences from Judaism, however, they also maintained that the "old Israel," the Jews, had been superseded by the "new Israel," the Christian Church. This argument, with its polemic against Judaism, was continuously read into the text of the Old Testament, which was thus allegorically reinterpreted in light of Christian beliefs. The images of the Old Testament story were understood to foreshadow the New Testament mysteries. We can see traces of this method of interpretation in the New Testament itself when, for instance, Jesus compares his death and Resurrection to Jonah in the whale (Matt. 12:40) and likewise compares his crucifixion to Moses holding up the brazen serpent in the desert (John 3:14).

Typical of this approach to exegesis was its sensitivity to imagery and the sense that these images (called types) represented a blueprint for God's plan of salvation. They recurred throughout history and found their fulfillment in the mystery of salvation through Christ. Thus the historical figures of Samuel, David, and Solomon could all prefigure Christ. Modern scholars have sometimes called this connection between figures in the Old and New Testaments typology, while they generally reserved the term *allegory* for the line-by-line spiritual interpretation of the biblical narrative. Medieval exegetes, however, did not make such a distinction: they used terms like *type, spiritual meaning,* and *allegory* interchangeably in their characterizations of this kind of exegesis.

Illustrations of these three approaches to reading Scripture can be found in the way that various medieval exegetes explained 2 Samuel 11, the story of David's adultery with Bathsheba. A good example of literal exegesis can be found in Andrew of St. Victor's commentary on Samuel, written around the middle of the twelfth century. In his explanation, Andrew is not particularly concerned with the theological or even the moral implications of this story. Only two points attract his attention: in the commentary on 2 Samuel 11:1, "at the time when kings go forth to war," he explains that this was usually in the time of harvest. And at 2 Samuel 11:4, "She came in to him and he slept with her, and presently she was purified from her uncleanness," Andrew explores in considerable detail what this purification of Bathsheba's uncleanness meant. It could be that she took a bath to cleanse herself from (menstrual) impurity, but it is more likely that the text intends to say that she conceived, because "pregnant women do not menstruate, because nature is keeping that blood inside, to feed the newly conceived fetus," says Andrew, in line with the medical theory of his time.[9]

Writing a few centuries before Andrew, Angelomus of Luxeuil had given the following allegorical interpretation of the same passage: David, walking on the roof of his palace, signifies Christ. He sees a beautiful woman, Bathsheba, washing herself, which stands for the church of the Gentiles, who is washing herself in the waters of baptism. She was previously wedded to Uria, who stands for the devil, but Christ's power killed him, so that the church could become Christ's new bride. To a modern reader, this interpretation may seem to invert the original intention of the text, but this was a commonplace occurrence among medieval exegetes. Much of Angelomus's exegesis depended on the interpretation of the names mentioned in the text (Bathsheba, for instance, allegedly meant "seventh well," which signified the seven gifts of the Holy Spirit, bestowed on the church) or the symbolic meaning given to seemingly insignificant details. David walking "on the sun-roof of his house," for instance, was a reference to Christ because it reminded the medieval exegete of the Christological prophecy in Psalm 18:6: "He hath set his tabernacle in the sun, and He, as a bridegroom coming out of his bride chamber, hath rejoiced."[10]

Angelomus's contemporary, Hrabanus Maurus, gives a good example of the story's moral or tropological explanation. He warns the reader that the above-cited allegory should not divert the reader's attention from the moral implications of the passage. Hrabanus explains that Scripture tells us about the sins of great men, such as David and Peter, so that the ruin of the great can serve as a warning for the common people. "Let no one be proud of his own state on account of David's fall, and also, let no one despair about his own downfall, on account of David's restoration." According to Hrabanus, then, the Bible thus warns us against sin by the example of David's adultery, but it also admonishes us to penitence, by the example of David's subsequent remorse and repentance.[11]

Some scholars have wanted to see two distinct exegetical traditions in ancient Christianity: one more prone to allegorization—the Alexandrine tradition, mainly represented by the Church father Origen and one more literal—the Antiochene tradition, represented by the Church fathers Chrysostom and Theodore of Mopsuestia.[12] But it was the allegorical approach that set the tone for the exposition of Scripture in monasteries during the following centuries. Allegorical interpretation, essentially a form of monastic meditation, was also frequently used in medieval sermons. For the medieval reader, it was a given that God intended Christians to meditate on these texts, reading them over and over both in the liturgy and for personal devotion. Monks, according to Bernard of Clairvaux, were like ruminant animals: they chewed and chewed on Sacred Scripture to extract its spiritual nourishment. Thus God spoke to them through the Bible. But the dangers of an excessively free rumination on Scripture were all too clear as well: some readers found interpretations that, according to certain church authorities, led them away from, rather than towards, sound Christian doctrine. Therefore medieval authors stayed anxiously within the boundaries of tradition as defined by the church fathers, whom they believed were inspired by the Holy Spirit.

## The Early Middle Ages

In the early Middle Ages in Visigothic Spain, scholars like Isidore of Seville (d. 636) built upon the patristic tradition while providing a number of additional allegorical interpretations of biblical passages that would become standard fare throughout the Middle Ages.[13] Also in this period, numerous commentaries and Bible glosses were produced in early medieval monastic centers of learning such as Canterbury, Saint Gall, Werden, Bobbio, and Reichenau. Some scholars have associated these texts specifically with "Irish" monasticism, and, indeed, many of the monastic centers that produced them were founded by Irish missionaries who had traveled to the Continent. While a few of these glosses and commentaries may have been composed in Ireland (or more likely by Irish scholars living in continental monastic settlements), in many cases the connection to Ireland is tenuous.[14] Most commentaries constitute typical school texts; many of them are anonymous (although some of them were later attributed to Bede or Isidore of Seville), and many take the form of short glosses on the biblical text. They are often characterized by a certain curiosity about the historical circumstances of the biblical narrative and they show a keen interest in biblical *realia*, leading some scholars to characterize them as "Antiochene."[15] Some even betray the influence of Greek patristic authors, such as Theodore of Mopsuestia. A few can be traced back to the scholarly activity of Archbishop Theodore (d. 690), a Greek, and his companion Hadrian, whose arrival in Canterbury in the seventh century marked the beginning of a rich tradition of learning in the British isles, which eventually culminated in the work of the Venerable Bede (d. 735).[16] A native of Northumbria who lived his entire life in the monastery of Jarrow, Bede certainly stands out as the most learned mind of the eighth century. He wrote numerous biblical commentaries, as well as works that explain biblical chronology, computation, and world history.[17] His exegetical activity shows that around the turn of the eighth century, Northumbria had become a major center for education and housed a well-equipped library of patristic and biblical books. Barely a century later, this thriving center of biblical learning was gone, a victim of raids by Viking plunderers from the North.

If before the eighth century the picture is fragmentary and incomplete, the ninth century on the Continent witnessed a flourishing of schools and scholarly activity and a proliferation of biblical commentaries, many of them associated with monasteries such as Fulda, Auxerre, and Saint Gall. The recovery and conservation of the patristic heritage was an important theme in the revival of biblical studies during what scholars have come to call the "Carolingian Renaissance." Much of the resurgence in schools and schooling can be credited to royal initiative. In his *Admonitio generalis* of 789, Charlemagne admonished his bishops to establish schools to study sacred literature and to take great care that the copies of their Bibles should be well corrected.[18] (On this initiative, see also Reilly's chapter in this volume.) Likewise, in his capitulary *De litteris colendis*, Charlemagne encouraged monks to "devote their efforts to the study of literature and to the teaching of it," because he perceived that "their lack of knowledge of writing might be matched by a more serious lack of wisdom in the understanding of Scripture."[19]

Charlemagne himself took the initiative for many of these educational reforms by attracting to his court a number of outstanding scholars who often subsequently became abbots of influential monasteries in the Frankish realm. One such scholar was Alcuin of York, who was reared and educated at the school of York Minster and joined Charlemagne's court in the 780s.[20] Later in life he was made abbot of the monastery of Tours, where he oversaw the copying of a few large Bibles, one of which was sent to Charlemagne as a present on the occasion of his coronation as emperor in 800. Throughout the ninth century, until its decline after attacks by the Vikings, the abbey of Tours continued to be an important center of Bible production. The number of Bibles produced here made the so-called Touronian Bible text the basis for many subsequent copies, so much that some scholars have tried to see Alcuin's Bible as the officially propagated, corrected text of the Carolingian Empire. Today most scholars no longer believe that Charlemagne's directive had a direct impact on the surge in Bible manuscript production in the ninth century, even though it did reflect the spirit of reform that was expressed in the *Admonitio generalis.*[21]

Another important figure from Charlemagne's circle was Theodulf of Orleans (d. 760). Of Spanish Visigothic descent, Theodulf made a career as court theologian, and he was an important influence behind the so-called *Libri Carolini,* works of theological polemic directed against the Byzantine Church.[22] Theodulf eventually became abbot of Micy near Orleans, where he oversaw the production of a corrected Bible text. Though not as widespread as the Tours Bibles, the quality of the text he produced is often seen as better: for his understanding of the Hebrew text he relied on the scholarship of a converted Jew from southern France who helped him iron out textual difficulties by comparing the Latin version to the Hebrew. Many other monastic centers used Theodulf's text to correct the errors in their own texts.[23] Still its influence seems to have been limited; only a few copies of Theodulf's Bible are extant today. Nevertheless, both the Tours and Theodulf Bible texts were important for establishing a unified Bible text of Jerome's translation for liturgical and scholarly use in medieval Christendom, and their versions would be the basis for many subsequent copies of the Latin Bible made in the later Middle Ages.[24]

A more significant flourishing of monastic biblical commentary took place during the reign of Charlemagne's successors, Louis the Pious and Charles the Bald, when cracks started to appear in the political unity of Charlemagne's empire. Much of the effort remained concentrated on the preservation and presentation of the patristic heritage, however, and those who look for great originality in these Carolingian commentaries will be disappointed. The aim of the Carolingian commentators was primarily educational: to make the patristic heritage accessible to clergy and monastics by inventorying and classifying the diverse patristic commentaries, sermons, homilies, treatises, histories, and handbooks and transforming them into consistent, running commentaries on almost the entire Bible. Among these exegetes, Claudius of Turin (d. 827), Haimo of Auxerre (d. 855), Paschasius Radbertus (d. 865), Johannes Scottus Eriugena (d. 877), and Hrabanus Maurus (d. 856) stand out.[25] The last, abbot of Fulda, was perhaps the greatest biblical exegete in this period. He systematically assembled commentaries on almost the entire Bible by collecting exegetical opinions of the church fathers. He can also be considered the father of the footnote: Hrabanus often listed the original authors of the exegetical excerpts by means of indexing signs: A for Augustine, G for Gregory the great, and so on. In this way, he created a new genre of Bible commentary, which would have enormous influence on the formation of the twelfth-century *Glossa ordinaria* ("Ordinary Gloss").[26] Of a similar stature is the work of Haimo of Auxerre, which has only recently begun to be uncovered. Due to the anonymous character of many of these early medieval biblical commentaries, much of Haimo's work has been misattributed, and the monk from Auxerre was often confused with his namesake Haimo of Halberstadt. Some of his other works were misattributed to his colleague Remigius of Auxerre (d. 908), who was also a prolific biblical scholar. Under Haimo, and later Remigius, Auxerre grew into a center of biblical study, tracing its origins back to Irish roots, in the person of the monk Muretach, the teacher of Remigius.[27]

In the eighth and ninth centuries, persistent Viking and Saracen raids in Western Europe often targeted monasteries with devastating effects that must have contributed to the general decline of monasticism in the tenth century. The level of both Latin learning and biblical studies suffered considerably, and in the tenth and eleventh centuries relatively few Bible commentaries were composed. Some attempted to use the vernacular as a means of promoting the study of the Bible. King Alfred the Great (d. 899) tried to make his court into a center of intellectual revival that stimulated study not in Latin, as was usually the case, but in the vernacular. His example set the tone for a tradition of vernacular education that would be quite unique in Europe. Much of this intellectual activity in the vernacular has been associated with Ælfric of Eynsham (d. 1009), who, as a Benedictine monk in tenth-century Winchester and later Cerne Abbas, came under the influence of the monastic reform of bishops Ethelwold and Dunstan. During the last years of his life, as abbot of the Benedictine abbey of Eynsham near Oxford, Ælfric worked on an Old English translation of Genesis at the request of his lay patron Æðelwærd. This text eventually served as the basis for a translation that was completed by the beginning of the eleventh century, known as the Old English Hexateuch. (For more information on this translation, see Marsden's chapter in this volume.) But Ælfric envisaged a larger program of vernacular education based on both biblical exegesis and catechetical instruction. In addition to his translation of the Old Testament, he translated into Old English a large collection of homilies as well as Alcuin's commentary on Genesis.[28] On the Continent we also find the occasional use of the vernacular for biblical commentaries in the tenth century. For instance, Williram, the abbot of Ebersberg (d. 1084), wrote a commentary on the Song of Songs that includes a translation into Old High German of the biblical text along with a bilingual commentary.[29] In the long run, however, Latin remained the principal language of learning, and the role of vernacular languages in biblical studies was limited.

## The Twelfth Century

Whatever the reason for the decline in biblical studies in the tenth century,[30] their revival in the late eleventh and twelfth centuries shifted the social setting of medieval learning and education. Cities grew considerably in this period, and the city's cathedral, as the main church and center of ecclesiastical administration, became the best place to be schooled. For a short while, until cathedral schools outgrew their cathedral setting and grew into the first universities, they attracted many outsiders who took advantage of the education that was offered there free of charge. Especially popular were those subjects that prepared one for a life of public service, either in royal or ecclesiastical courts, both of which were expanding in this period.[31] It was often in these schools that the main exegetical works of this period were composed. In the long run, this development changed the character of biblical exegesis. It was transformed from a monastic method of spiritual reading into a discipline whose main aim was to strengthen church doctrine, legislation, and preaching.

Schools at monasteries and abbeys, such as Bec, Fleury, and Liège, continued to play important roles in the early stages of this intellectual renewal. In Bec the glosses of Lanfranc of Pavia (d. 1089) on the Pauline Epistles would have considerable influence on the formation of the later *Glossa ordinaria*.[32] In Liège Rupert, later abbot of Deutz (d. 1129), wrote a lengthy commentary on the entire Bible entitled *On the Trinity and Its Works,* in which he interpreted biblical history as a gradual unfolding of the three persons of the Trinity: Father, Son, and Holy Ghost.[33] This text proved to be an inspiration for the later work of the Calabrian abbot

Joachim of Fiore (d. 1202), whose commentary on the Apocalypse influenced later medieval apocalyptic movements.[34] (See Roest's chapter in this volume.)

The best example of the flourishing of twelfth-century monastic learning was perhaps the abbey of Saint Victor near Paris. Founded in 1108 by William of Champeaux, it developed into a prestigious center of spiritual learning with outstanding masters such as Hugh (d. 1142), Richard (d. 1173), and Andrew of St. Victor (d. 1175) teaching and writing biblical commentaries that were widely read beyond the monastery walls. Andrew's commentaries, for instance, were frequently used by Peter Comestor (d. 1178) in his *Historia scholastica,* which would become the standard exegetical handbook for much of the later Middle Ages.[35] The greatest exegetical accomplishment of the twelfth-century cathedral schools was the compilation of patristic and Carolingian exegesis into a gloss on the entire Bible, the *Glossa ordinaria.* This type of commentary provided edited excerpts of patristic exegesis, written in the margins and between the lines of the biblical text. It was unique in that it combined the two prevalent formats of biblical commentary at the time: a marginal commentary surrounding the central biblical text and interlinear glosses featuring short explications. Until the mid twentieth century, scholars assumed that the origin of the *Glossa ordinaria* was Carolingian, because of its heavy reliance on Carolingian authors such as Hrabanus Maurus and Haimo of Auxerre.[36] But the compilation of the *Glossa* is more correctly attributed to Anselm of Laon (d. 1117), who by the beginning of the twelfth century had already built a reputation for biblical exegesis that attracted great scholars such as Peter Abelard (who, incidentally, would be greatly disappointed by the critical skills of this master).[37] Anselm was assisted by his brother Ralph of Laon (d. 1133), who continued to work on glossing biblical books after the former's death. They were probably the authors of the gloss on the Gospels and Romans, while Gilbert of Auxerre (d. 1134, also nicknamed "the Universal") was the probable author of the gloss on Lamentations, the Twelve Prophets, and possibly Samuel and Kings.

It is not clear when the *Glossa ordinaria* received its final redaction, and there are strong indications that it was not conceived, or indeed produced, as one complete book; individual Bible books were glossed at different dates, by different authors, and probably in different places. The gloss on Psalms, for instance, went through no fewer than three successive redactions, by Anselm of Laon, Gilbert of Poitiers (d. 1154), and Peter Lombard (d. 1160).[38] From the 1130s through the 1150s, Paris (possibly the collegiate abbey of Saint Victor) became a major center for the copying of these glossed Bibles. Many of the early manuscripts of the *Glossa ordinaria* from the 1130s and 1150s originated in the abbey of Saint Victor, and there are indications that exegetes there, such as Andrew of St. Victor and Peter Comestor, relied on it for much of their access to patristic exegesis. It is unlikely that any of the glosses were composed there, however.[39]

## The School of Saint Victor

At the same time that the *Glossa ordinaria* was being composed, blind reliance on patristic authority was coming under closer scrutiny in the emerging schools of the twelfth century. Peter Abelard (d. 1142), in his *Sic et Non*, led a frontal attack on the uncritical use of patristic quotations to solve theological problems. With the rise of a more critical attitude toward authoritative texts, scriptural interpretation needed a more sound theoretical foundation as well.

Hugh of St. Victor offered one solution in his introduction to the study of the liberal arts, the *Didascalicon*, which is based on the theory of signification presented by Augustine in his *De doctrina christiana* and *De magistro*. For Hugh (following Augustine), God speaks to people in two ways: through his Word (Scripture in its overt meaning) and, on a secondary level, through the created world (through things, facts, and deeds).[40] Or, in the words of Alan of Lille (d. 1203), the whole world could be seen as a book, written by God's hand.[41] The Bible was not only the word of God but also the record of God's deeds in history, and it therefore had a double meaning: the words had an overt meaning, but they also signified the higher reality of salvation history, which had its culmination in salvation through Jesus Christ. (On this conceptualization of history, see Harris's chapter in this volume.) This way of reading the Bible was more than just free allegorization; one needed a good basic comprehension of historical facts through literal exegesis before one could apprehend the spiritual dimension of Scripture. Allegorization could never contradict the historical sense of salvation history narrated in the Bible. Hugh saw the literal, historical meaning of the text as the foundation on which one could erect the building of faith. Allegory, which established Christian doctrine, formed its walls, and moral behavior was its exterior covering.

Hugh's methodology gave the study of literal interpretation a new impetus. We can see his influence not only in the writing of Andrew of St. Victor but also in exegetes who either had direct ties to the abbey of Saint Victor, such as Peter Comestor (d. 1179) and Herbert of Bosham (d. after 1189) or, indirectly, in the schools of the Parisian Dominicans and Franciscans, such as Hugh of St. Cher (d. 1263) and Nicholas of Lyra (d. 1349), who continued the trend of scholarly biblical studies with an emphasis on literal sense that Hugh had started. (On mendicant exegesis, see Roest's chapter in this volume.)

When it comes to biblical exegesis, Andrew of St. Victor was perhaps Hugh's most original student.[42] Andrew left a fairly limited oeuvre, including commentaries on the Old Testament alone. These works are interesting not so much for what they say as for what they do not say. Andrew dedicated himself almost entirely to a reading of Scripture in its literal sense, restricting himself to literary and historical comments on the biblical text while eschewing allegorization and doctrinal interpretation. He identified figures of speech, gave geographical or historical explanations, and inserted brief explanations into the biblical text, introduced by expressions like *that is* or *infer*. In other cases he paraphrased the whole passage, weaving words of the biblical text into his own paraphrase.

Andrew's exegetical technique can best be characterized as "close reading," and it stands in sharp contrast to the allegorical exegesis that was much more common in his time, practiced by, among others, Hugh's other student, Richard of St. Victor.[43] In the long run, however, Andrew's commentaries were not as influential as those of Peter Comestor, who wrote the *Historia scholastica*, a running commentary on almost the entire Bible according to its literal sense. Comestor relied on both the *Glossa ordinaria* and on Andrew's commentaries to produce this doctrinally sound literal commentary.[44] The *Historia*, although never as popular as the *Sentences* of Peter Lombard, almost immediately became the standard textbook for teaching Sacred Scripture.

## Christian Hebrew Scholarship

For his literal commentaries, Andrew made frequent use of Jewish sources. On this point, he was greatly indebted to the school of Jewish exegesis that had become prominent in Northern France by the twelfth century. Many Jewish commentaries on the biblical text provided either legal guidelines on matters of ritual conduct or moral edification in the form of homiletic commentaries. The earliest Jewish biblical commentaries, dating from late antiquity and the early Middle Ages, were called *midrashim*. These commentaries were often associative and allegorical, and they explained the text by providing a narrative that expanded the biblical text. As already mentioned, they tried to make the story relevant to the contemporary situation rather than to provide an explanation in its original historical context. In the eleventh and twelfth centuries, however, Jewish exegesis in northern France took a distinctive turn away from this more associative exegesis (called *derash*), and, starting with the commentaries of Rabbi Solomon b. Isaac of Troyes (Rashi, d. 1105), exegetes increasingly emphasized the "simple," that is, more literal and direct, meaning of scripture, the *peshat*. Rashi's example was followed by a number of northern French exegetes, such as his son-in-law R. Solomon b. Meir (Rashbam, d. 1174), Joseph Kara (d. 1170), Eliezer of Beaugency (12th c.), and Rabbi David Kimhi (Radak, d. 1235). The rise of Hebrew philology, exemplified by the Spanish/Southern French commentator Abraham Ibn Ezra (d. 1164), may have influenced this *peshat* exegesis as well. The *peshat* tradition may have originated as a polemic against the Christian allegorical interpretation of the Old Testament, which often had a distinctly anti-Judaic flavor. But, ironically, this more textual form of exegesis had considerable influence on Christian exegetes of its time such as Andrew of St. Victor and Herbert of Bosham.[45]

Andrew of St. Victor was not the only one engaged in textual scholarship in the twelfth century. For instance, Stephen Harding, abbot of Cîteaux in the first quarter of the twelfth century, led an impressive effort to produce a reliable Vulgate text for use in the Cistercian order. The results are preserved in the multivolume Bible of Cîteaux, now in the Bibliothèque municipale of Dijon.[46] One of the most accomplished textual critics of the century was the Cistercian Nicholas Maniacoria, who lived in the middle of the century in Rome. Nicholas wrote a critical treatise on the correction of the Bible text and produced a list of corrections to the text of the Hebrew Psalter.[47] All these scholars set a new standard of textual scholarship that became the basis for the textual criticism of the Bible as it was practiced, for instance, by the Dominicans at the convent of Saint Jacques in Paris in the thirteenth century.[48] Still, this burgeoning biblical philology had surprisingly little influence on the text of the Bible.

Textual criticism of the Bible was more often a learned discourse among commentators than a catalyst for new versions of biblical texts, because at this time the Bible was copied increasingly by professional scribes who were unaware of biblical scholarship.

## The Biblical-Moral School

Most biblical scholarship in the twelfth century had a practical purpose: it was employed in the pastoral training of clerics. The ecclesiastical reform movement, which profoundly influenced and altered ideas about the role and function of the church in society from the eleventh century onward, had stressed the pastoral responsibilities of the clergy, especially preaching and confession. As a result, cathedral schools and, later, the nascent universities began to offer a more practical form of training for men embarking on ecclesiastical careers. Concurrently, biblical exegetes began to emphasize the doctrinal and moral implications of Scripture over the more meditative spiritual exegesis that had been characteristic of the monastic tradition. We can see this development represented in the works of schoolmen like Peter the Chanter (d. 1197), Alexander Neckham (d. 1217), and Stephen Langton (d. 1228), all scholars who were not only active as exegetes but also as clerics and bishops. They were representative of what has been dubbed the biblical-moral school.[49] Most of their biblical exegesis took the form of sermons, but many of them also wrote commentaries and created biblical reference tools that offered students materials they could immediately apply in crafting sermons. Concordances, for instance, made it possible to look up biblical passages quickly, and metrical poems listing key words for each chapter of the Bible were intended to be memorized so that students could quickly locate biblical topics from memory. Collections of distinctions listed biblical keywords, each accompanied by three or more allegorical and moral applications and the relevant biblical verse. For instance, Peter the Chanter's *Distinctiones,* or *Summa Abel,* was essentially a huge database of potential minisermons.[50] It became possible to look up keywords in the biblical text quickly because of a standardized chapter division for the Vulgate text that emerged by the late twelfth century. The creation of this system of chapter divisions has often been ascribed to Cardinal Stephen Langton (d. 1228), a Parisian scholar who later became archbishop of Canterbury. Recently, scholars have pointed out that this "Langtonian" chapter division actually predates Langton.[51] In the thirteenth century, Dominican scholars divided the existing chapters into even shorter sections, each designated by a letter, from A to D, or A to E, depending on the length of the chapter.[52] These commentaries and lexical tools provided basic training in biblical scholarship for those who would become leaders in the church.

By the end of the twelfth century, the study of the Bible had been transformed from a mainly meditative practice for monks into a scholarly discipline in the service of a life of ecclesiastical administration and preaching. This would set the tone for the practice of biblical exegesis at the universities in the subsequent centuries, when the field was dominated by the two mendicant orders, the Franciscans and the Dominicans, founded at the beginning of the thirteenth century. Even though their exegesis still emphasized an allegorical reading of the Bible and therefore owed a great debt to the church fathers (now mainly read through the mediation of the *Glossa ordinaria*, which would become a standard reference work in subsequent centuries), some of the attitudes toward the text that had appeared in the twelfth century continued to dominate biblical scholarship of the thirteenth and fourteenth centuries. The hermeneutic developments of the later Middle Ages that culminated in the Renaissance and Reformation all had their roots in the twelfth century. The primacy given to the literal sense of Scripture (as exemplified by Peter Comestor's *Historia scholastica*), the growth of textual criticism, the emphasis on the investigation of the Hebrew text of the Bible that we find in Nicholas Maniacoria and Andrew of St. Victor, and the emphasis on doctrine and morals that we find among the later twelfth-century "masters of the sacred page" all attest to the twelfth century's lasting contributions to exegetical method.[53]

## Notes

1.  The best introductions to this subject are still Ceslas Spicq, *Esquisse d'une histoire de l'exégèse latine au Moyen Âge*, Bibliothèque thomiste 26 (Paris: J. Vrin, 1944); and Beryl Smalley, *The Study of the Bible in the Middle Ages* (Oxford: Blackwell, 1952; 1983). A catalogue of commentaries in translation, *Medieval Christian Biblical Exegesis in English Translation*, compiled by Jonathan Hall, can be found online at http://purl.oclc.org/net/jonhall/transbib.html.

2.  *Le Moyen Âge et la Bible*, ed. Pierre Riché and Guy Lobrichon, Bible de tous les temps 4 (Paris: Beauchesne, 1984), pp. 31–54.

3. E. Ann Matter, *The Voice of My Beloved: The Song of Songs in Western Medieval Christianity* (Philadelphia: University of Pennsylvania Press, 1990).

4. Peter Brown, *The Rise of Western Christendom: Triumph and Diversity, A.D. 200–1000*, The Making of Europe (Oxford: Blackwell, 2003), pp. 196–98, 232–47; Robert Austin Markus, *The End of Ancient Christianity* (Cambridge: Cambridge University Press, 1998; Canto, 1999), pp. 191–97.

5. Cassiodorus Senator, *Institutions of Divine and Secular Learning* and *On the soul*, trans. James W. Halporn and Mark Vessey, Translated Texts for Historians 42 (Liverpool: Liverpool University Press, 2004).

6. Gregory the Great, *Morals on the Book of Job*, trans. James Bliss, Library of Fathers of the Holy Catholic Church, 18, 21, 23, 31 (Oxford: J. H. Parker, 1844–50).

7. Some medieval authors distinguished three senses of Scriptures, others four. On these various hermeneutical systems, see especially Henri de Lubac, *Exégèse médiévale. les quatre sens de l'écriture*, vol. 1: *Théologie* (Paris: Aubier, 1959), pp. 129–69.

8. Jean Pépin, *La tradition de l'allégorie de Philon d'Alexandrie à Dante. Études historiques* (Paris: Études Augustiniennes, 1987), pp. 7–40.

9. Andreas de Sancto Victore, *Expositio hystorica in librum Regum*, ed. Frans van Liere, CCCM 53A (Turnhout: Brepols, 1996), p. 77. Translation in Andrew of St. Victor, *Commentary on Samuel and Kings*, trans. Frans van Liere, TEAMS Commentary Series (Kalamazoo: Medieval Institute, 2009).

10. Angelomus Luxoviensis, *Enarrationes in Libros Regum*, PL 115:362D–363A.

11. Hrabanus Maurus, *Commentaria in Libros IV Regum*, PL 109:99AB.

12. Frances Young, "Alexandrian and Antiochene Exegesis," in *A History of Biblical Interpretation*, vol. 1: *The Ancient Period*, ed. Alan J. Hauser and Duane F. Watson (Grand Rapids: Eerdmans, 2003), pp. 334–54.

13. Dominique Poirel, "Un manuel de l'exégèse spirituelle au service des prédicateurs: les Allegoriae d'Isidore de Séville," *Recherches Augustiniennes* 33 (2003): 95–107.

14. Bernhard Bischoff, "Wendepunkte in der Geschichte der lateinischen Exegese im Mittelalter," *Sacris erudiri* 6 (1954): 189–281; repr. in Bischoff, *Mittelalterliche Studien. Ausgewählte Aufsätze zur Schriftkunde und Literaturgeschichte* (Stuttgart: Hiersemann, 1966), 1:205–73; Michael Murray Gorman, "The Myth of Hiberno-Latin Exegesis," *Revue bénédictine* 110 (2000): 42–85; Dáibhí O Cróinín, "Bischoff's Wendepunkte Fifty Years On," *Revue bénédictine* 110 (2000): 204–37.

15. M. L. W. Laistner, "Antiochene Exegesis in Western Europe during the Middle Ages," *Harvard Theological Review* 40 (1947): 19–31.

16. *Biblical Commentaries from the Canterbury School of Theodore and Hadrian*, ed. Bernhard Bischoff and Michael Lapidge, Cambridge Studies in Anglo-Saxon England 10 (Cambridge: Cambridge University Press, 1994).

17. Bede, *On the Temple*, trans. Seán Connolly and Jennifer O'Reilly, Translated Texts for Historians 21 (Liverpool: Liverpool University Press, 1995); Bede, *A Biblical Miscellany*, trans. W. Trent Foley and Arthur G. Holder, Translated Texts for

Historians 28 (Liverpool: Liverpool University Press, 1999); Bede, *The Reckoning of Time*, trans. Faith Wallis, Translated Texts for Historians 29 (Liverpool: Liverpool University Press, 1999); Bede, *On Ezra and Nehemiah*, trans. Scott DeGregorio, Translated Texts for Historians 47 (Liverpool: Liverpool University Press, 2006); Bede, *On Genesis*, trans. Calvin B. Kendall, Translated Texts for Historians 48 (Liverpool: Liverpool University Press, 2008).

18. Elisabeth Magnou-Nortier, "L'Admonitio generalis': étude critique," in *Jornades internacionals d'estudi sobre el Bisbe Feliu d'Urgel. Crònica i estudis. La Seu d'Urgell, 28–30 de setembre de 1999*, Studia, Textus, Subsidia 9 (Barcelona: Facultat de Teología de Catalunya, 2000), pp. 195–242.

19. *Admonitio generalis*, vol. 1: *Capitularia regum Francorum,* ed. Alfred Boretius and Victor Krause, MGH Leges (Hannover: Hahn, 1883; repr. 1960), no. 29, p. 78. An English translation is available online in Paul Halsall's *Medieval Sourcebook*: http://www.fordham.edu/halsall/source/carol-baugulf.html.

20. Donald A. Bullough, *Alcuin: Achievement and Reputation*, Education and Society in the Middle Ages and Renaissance 16 (Leiden: Brill, 2004), pp. 127–472. ·

21. Bonifatius Fischer, *Die Alkuin-Bibel*, Aus der Geschichte der lateinischen Bibel 1 (Freiburg im Breisgau: Herder, 1972; orig. *Die Bibel von Moutier-Grandval: British Museum Codex Add. 10546*. Bern: Verein Schweizerischer Lithographiebestizer, 1969); Rosamond McKitterick, "Carolingian Bible Production: The Tours Anomaly," in *The Early Medieval Bible: Its Production, Decoration, and Use*, ed. Richard Gameson (Cambridge: Cambridge University Press, 1994), pp. 63–77.

22. On Theodulf and the Libri Carolini, see Ann Freeman, *Theodulf of Orleans: Charlemagne's Spokesman Against the Second Council of Nicaea* (Aldershot: Ashgate, 2003).

23. David Ganz, "Mass Production of Early Medieval Manuscripts: The Carolingian Bibles from Tours," in *The Early Medieval Bible*, pp. 53–62.

24. Michelle P. Brown, "Predicando con la penna: il contributo insulare alla trasmissione dei testi sacri dal VI al IX secolo," in *Forme e modelli della tradizione manoscritta della Bibbia*, ed. Paolo Cherubini, Littera Antiqua 13 (Vatican City: Scuola Vaticana di Paleografia, Diplomatica e Archivistica, 2005), pp. 61–108.

25. *The Study of the Bible in the Carolingian Era*, ed. Celia Chazelle and Burton Van Name Edwards, Medieval Church Studies 3 (Turnhout: Brepols, 2003); John J. Contreni, "The Biblical Glosses of Haimo of Auxerre and John Scottus Eriugena," *Speculum* 51 (1976): 411–34. Very few of these commentaries have been translated into English, with the exception of Haimo of Auxerre, *Commentary on the Book of Jonah*, trans. Deborah Everhart, TEAMS Commentary Series (Kalamazoo: Medieval Institute, 1993); and Haimo of Auxerre, *Second Thessalonians: Two Early Medieval Apocalyptic Commentaries*, trans. Steven R. Cartwright and Kevin L. Hughes, TEAMS Commentary Series (Kalamazoo: Medieval Institute, 2001).

26. Johann Baptist Hablitzel, *Hrabanus Maurus. Ein Beitrag zur Geschichte der mittelalterlichen Exegese*, Biblische Studien 11/3 (Freiburg im Breisgau: Herder, 1906);

*Hrabanus Maurus und seine Schule. Festschrift der Hrabanus-Maurus-Schule 1980*, ed. Winfried Böhne (Fulda, 1980).

27. *Études d'exégèse carolingienne: Études autour d'Haymon d'Auxerre. Atelier de recherches, 25–26 avril 2005, Centre d'Études médiévales d'Auxerre*, ed. Sumi Shimahara, Collection Haut Moyen Âge 4 (Turnhout: Brepols, 2007).

28. *The Old English version of the Heptateuch. Ælfric's Treatise on the Old and New Testament and His Preface to Genesis*, ed. Samuel John Crawford, Early English Text Society, o.s. 160 (London: Early English Text Society, 1922), reprinted with the text of two additional manuscripts edited by William Lisle et al., *The Old English Version of the Heptateuch. Ælfric's Treatise on the Old and New Testament and his Preface to Genesis* (London: Early English Text Society, 1969); *Ælfric's Anglo-Saxon Version of* Alcuini Interrogationes Sigeuulfi Presbyteri in Genesin, ed. George Edwin MacLean (Halle: Karras, 1883).

29. Williram Ebersbergensis, *Die älteste Überlieferung von Willirams Kommentar des Hohen Liedes. Edition, Übersetzung, Glossar*, ed. Rudolf Schüzeichel, Birgit Meineke, and Dieter Kannenberg, Studien zum althochdeutschen 39 (Göttingen: Vandenhoeck and Ruprecht, 2001).

30. Beryl Smalley suggests that, rather than "the moralizing effect of war and Viking invasion," it was a shift in interest towards liturgy at the expense of study that caused the decline. Smalley, *Study of the Bible*, pp. 44–45.

31. On cathedral schools, see C. Stephen Jaeger, *The Envy of Angels: Cathedral Schools and Social Ideals in Medieval Europe 950–1200* (Philadelphia: University of Pennsylvania Press, 1994).

32. Ann Collins, *Teacher in Faith and Virtue: Lanfranc of Bec's Commentary on Saint Paul*, Commentaria: Sacred Texts and Their Commentaries, Jewish, Christian, and Islamic 1 (Leiden: Brill, 2007).

33. John H. Van Engen, *Rupert of Deutz*, Publications of the UCLA Center for Medieval and Renaissance Studies (Berkeley: University of California Press, 1983).

34. Gioacchino da Fiore, *Introduzione all'Apocalisse*, ed. Kurt-Victor Selge, trans. Gian Luca Potestà, Centro internazionale di studi gioachimiti S Giovanni in Fiore, Opere di Gioacchino da Fiore: testi e strumenti 6 (Rome: Viella, 1995); Marjorie E. Reeves, *The Influence of Prophecy in the Later Middle Ages: A Study in Joachimism* (Oxford: Clarendon Press, 1969).

35. Smalley, *Study of the Bible*, pp. 83–195; Grover A. Zinn, "History and Interpretation: 'Hebrew Truth,' Judaism, and the Victorine Exegetical Tradition," in *Jews and Christians: Exploring the Past, Present, and Future*, ed. James H. Charlesworth, Shared Ground Among Jews and Christians: A Series of Explorations 1 (New York: Crossroad, 1990), pp. 100–22.

36. On the myth of the Gloss's Carolingian origins, as well as its refutation, see the introduction by Karlfried Froehlich to *Biblia latina cum glossa ordinaria*. Facsimile Reprint of the editio princeps Adolph Rusch of Strassburg 1480/81, ed. Karlfried Froehlich and Margaret T. Gibson, 4 vols. (Turnhout: Brepols, 1992).

37. Peter Abelard, *The Letters of Abelard and Heloise*, trans. Betty Radice (London: Penguin Books, 1974), pp. 62–64.

38. Beryl Smalley, "Gilbertus Universalis, Bishop of London (1128–34), and the Problem of the 'Glossa Ordinaria,'" *Recherches de Théologie ancienne et médiévale* 7 (1935): 235–62; and Beryl Smalley, "Gilbertus Universalis, Bishop of London (1128–34), and the Problem of the 'Glossa Ordinaria,'" *Recherches de Théologie ancienne et médiévale* 8 (1936): 24–60. A translation of the gloss on Song of Songs is available in *The* Glossa ordinaria *on the Song of Songs*, trans. Mary Dove, TEAMS Commentary Series (Kalamazoo: Medieval Institute, 2004). A translation of the gloss on the first book of Lamentations is available in Gilbertus Universalis, *Glossa ordinaria in Lamentationes Ieremie prophete; prothemata et liber I*, ed. Alexander Andrée, Studia Latina Stockholmiensia 52 (Stockholm: Almqvist and Wiksell International, 2005). For the latest and most complete study on the *Glossa ordinaria*, see Lesley Smith, *The* Glossa ordinaria: *The Making of a Medieval Bible Commentary*, Commentaria: Sacred Texts and Their Commentaries, Jewish, Christian, and Islamic 3 (Leiden: Brill, 2009).

39. Frans van Liere, "Andrew of St. Victor and the Gloss on Samuel and Kings," in *Media Latinitas: A Collection of Essays to Mark the Occasion of the Retirement of L. J. Engels*, ed. Renée I. A. Nip and Hans van Dijk, Instrumenta Patristica 28 (Steenbrugge and Turnhout: Brepols, 1995), pp. 249–53; Margaret T. Gibson, "The Twelfth-Century Glossed Bible," in *Papers Presented to the Tenth International Conference on Patristic Studies Held in Oxford 1987*, ed. Elizabeth A. Livingstone, Studia Patristica 23 (Leuven: Peeters, 1989), pp. 232–44; Christopher de Hamel, *Glossed Books of the Bible and the Origins of the Paris Booktrade* (Woodbridge: Brewer, 1984).

40. Hugh of St. Victor, *The Didascalicon of Hugh of St. Victor: A Medieval Guide to the Arts*, trans. Jerome Taylor, Records of Western Civilization 64 (New York: Columbia University Press, 1961), pp. 120–22; Gillian R. Evans, "Hugh of St Victor on History and the Meaning of Things," *Studia Monastica* 25 (1983): 223–34.

41. Alan of Lille, *De incarnatione Christi*, PL 210:579A.

42. Beryl Smalley, "Andrew of St. Victor, Abbot of Wigmore: A Twelfth-Century Hebraist," *Recherches de théologie ancienne et médiévale* 10 (1938): 358–73.

43. Frans van Liere, "Andrew of St. Victor, Jerome, and the Jews: Biblical Scholarship in the Twelfth-Century Renaissance," in *Scripture and Pluralism: Reading the Bible in the Religiously Plural Worlds of the Middle Ages and Renaissance*, ed. Thomas J. Heffernan and Thomas E. Burman, Studies in the History of Christian Traditions 123 (Leiden: Brill, 2005), pp. 59–75. See also Frans van Liere, "Andrew of Saint Victor and His Franciscan Critics," in *The Multiple Meanings of Scripture: The Role of Exegesis in Early-Christian and Medieval Culture*, ed. Ineke van 't Spijker, Commentaria: Sacred Texts and Their Commentaries, Jewish, Christian, and Islamic 2 (Leiden: Brill, 2008), pp. 291–309.

44. Rainer Berndt, "Pierre le Mangeur et André de Saint Victor. Contribution à l'étude de leurs sources," *Recherches de Théologie ancienne et médiévale* 61 (1994): 88–114.

45. David Weiss Halivni, *Peshat and Derash. Plain and Applied Meaning in Rabbinic Exegesis* (Oxford: Oxford University Press, 1991); Herman Hailperin, *Rashi and the Christian Scholars* (Pittsburgh: University of Pittsburgh Press, 1963).

46. Matthieu Cauwe, "La Bible d'Étienne Harding: Principes de critique textuelle mis en oeuvre aux livres de Samuel," *Revue bénédictine* 103 (1993): 414–44.

47. Vittorio Peri, "'Correctores immo corruptores,' un saggio di critica testuale nella Roma del XII secolo," *Italia medioevale e umanistica* 20 (1977): 19–125.

48. Franz Ehrle, "Die Handschriften der Bibel-Correctorien des 13. Jahrhunderts," in *Archiv für Literatur- und Kirchengeschichte des Mittelalters*, ed. Heinrich Denifle and Franz Ehrle (Freiburg im Breisgau: Herder, 1888), pp. 263–311; and Gilbert Dahan, "La critique textuelle dans les correctoires de la Bible du XIIIe siècle," in *Langages et philosophie: hommage à Jean Jolivet*, ed. Alain De Libera, A. Elamrani-Jamal, and A. Galonnier, Études de Philosophie Médiévale 74 (Paris: J. Vrin, 1997), pp. 365–92.

49. Martin Grabmann, *Die Geschichte der scholastischen Methode* (Freiburg im Breisgau: Herder, 1909–11), ii:476; Smalley, *Study of the Bible*, pp. 196–263.

50. Stephen A. Barney, "Peter the Chanter's Distinctiones Abel," in *Allegory, Myth, and Symbol*, ed. Morton W. Bloomfield (Cambridge: Harvard University Press, 1981), pp. 87–107.

51. Otto Schmid, *Über verschiedene Eintheilungen des Heiligen Schrift insbesondere über die Capitel-Eintheilung Stephan Langtons in XIII. Jahrhunderte* (Graz: Leuschner and Lubensky, 1892); and Paul Saenger, "The Anglo-Hebraic Origins of the Modern Chapter Division of the Latin Bible," in *La fractura historiografica: Edad Media y Renacimento desde el tercer milenio*, ed. Francesco Javier Burguillo and Laura Meier (Salamanca: Seminario de Estudios Medievales y Renacentistas, 2008), pp. 177–202.

52. Richard H. Rouse and Mary A. Rouse, "The Verbal Concordance to the Scriptures," *Archivum Fratrum Praedicatorum* 44 (1974): 5–30.

53. This was Beryl Smalley's collective title for Peter Comestor, Stephen Langton, and Peter the Chanter. Smalley, *Study of the Bible*, p. 196.

# Mendicant School Exegesis

*Bert Roest*

The two largest mendicant orders—the Friars Preachers (Dominicans) and the Friars Minor (Franciscans)—had very different beginnings. The Dominicans started out as a taskforce of well-trained preachers and priests eager to counter the influence of dualist heresies in southern France and Spain. They adopted a life of austerity modeled on the biblical message in order to be successful in their struggle against ascetic Cathar spokesmen.[1] Solid biblical learning was a cornerstone of the Dominican identity from the outset.

The Franciscans, on the other hand, began as a body of lay people identifying themselves with the message of the poor and suffering that Christ presented in the Gospel. Their initial submersion in the biblical message was akin to the meditative approach to the Bible found in earlier eremitical communities. Counter to the Dominicans, who adopted the rule of Augustine (which gave them the flexibility to be teachers, students, and itinerant preachers), the Franciscans built their first rule from biblical citations, thus emulating the Gospel message in their early regulations.[2]

Despite these differences, the Dominicans and the Franciscans soon became papally approved international orders of preachers, confessors, missionaries, and inquisitors. They adopted both a framework of communal religious life modeled on older monastic and canonical models and a regulated system of theological education that led to the creation of a hierarchical school network with local, custodial, provincial, and general *studia* (study houses). The mendicants' educational system also brought the friars to the principal centers of theological learning, namely, the theology faculties of the universities of Paris, Oxford, Cambridge, and elsewhere.[3]

As novices, professed friars, and priests, Dominicans and Franciscans encountered the biblical text every day in the liturgy and in their obligatory moments of private meditation. The conflict between the ambulant life of many friars and their liturgical and meditative obligations gave rise to the production in large numbers of concise "pocket" Bibles and breviaries, ideally one for each clerical friar in the order, leading to yet another change in the format of the biblical text. Beyond these liturgical and meditative settings, the Bible was central to the friars' preaching effort as well as to their confrontations with heretics and "infidels" (in Muslim territory). Many surviving mendicant sermon collections therefore have strong exegetical and catechetical characteristics, a phenomenon that presupposed a thorough emphasis on biblical study in the mendicant schools.[4] No wonder then, that in their schools the mendicants adopted and perfected programs of biblical teachings developed by the twelfth- and early thirteenth-century theology masters of the University of Paris and soon surpassed the secular masters (theology masters without ties to a religious order) in exegetical prowess.[5]

After the departure of the theology master Stephen Langton, who in 1206 became archbishop of Canterbury, academic exegesis at Paris lost some of its earlier appeal. Thanks to the labors of Hugh and Andrew of St. Victor, Peter the Chanter, Peter Comestor, Stephen Langton, early thirteenth-century secular masters had access to a decent number of recent biblical commentaries on top of the *Glossa ordinaria* and additional instruments to facilitate academic biblical teaching. (Such biblical teaching included basic cursory lectures provided by the *baccalaureus biblicus*— an adult "teaching assistant" of the ruling master—and in-depth biblical lectures by the master himself.) It was tempting to divert scholarly attention to discussions fueled by the influx of new philosophical ideas, following the translation of Aristotelian philosophical books and their Arab commentators. For these discussions, the format of the biblical commentary was not well suited. Hence, Parisian masters engaged in lengthy disputations, for which the privileged literary form was the academic *quaes-*

*tio* (literally "question"). Although cursory biblical lectures continued to take place (they still appear in Parisian faculty statutes of 1362), the secular masters in particular gradually abandoned the practice of lecturing ex cathedra on different biblical books and circulating their biblical lecture courses in extended published commentaries.[6]

Once the mendicants obtained a foothold in the university in the 1220s, however, they embraced the practice of biblical teaching espoused by Stephen Langton and his predecessors by lecturing extensively on most or all biblical books, creating so-called *postillae* and *lecturae* (more or less continuous commentaries on the biblical text geared to the needs of students and fellow theologians) on a larger scale than ever before. With the backing of the international study networks of the mendicant orders, these commentaries were disseminated all over Europe.[7]

Early milestones of mendicant academic exegesis were the postills created by the Dominican exegetical team led by Friar Hugh of St. Cher, who already held a doctorate in canon law and a bachelor's degree in theology before he joined the Dominicans at Paris in 1225. Hugh held the position of *sententiarius,* so called because it entailed giving lectures on the *Sentences* of Peter Lombard, which by then had become a prerequisite for attaining the degree of master of theology. After serving as *sententiarius* and a stint as order provincial, Hugh returned to Paris to teach the Bible as the Dominican master of theology between 1229 and 1233 (while also preparing his commentary on the *Sentences* for publication). He continued working on biblical materials with other Dominican friars during his position as prior of the Parisian Dominican friary between 1233 and 1236. In these years Hugh and his team "postillated" through the Bible from be-ginning to end, providing Dominican and non-Dominican students alike with an expanded version of the glossed Bible, known as the *Postilla super Totam Bibliam* (*Postill on the Whole Bible*), including comments and corrections that had not been part of the twelfth-century *Glossa Ordinaria* (which had privileged comments from the fathers).[8]

Hugh of St. Cher's *Postilla* avoided overtly "moralist" forms of biblical commentary that did not have a proper basis in the biblical text as well as the older practice of introducing numerous theological questions into biblical commentary, since such questions belonged to speculative theology, which by then was taught at Paris using the *Sentences* of Lombard. Hugh's *Postilla* project stayed close to the biblical text while providing a solid foundation for further exegetical and speculative theological work and homiletic applications.

The "up-to-date" biblical postills produced by Hugh and his team became a platform for subsequent biblical teaching and for larger biblical commentaries by mendicant theology masters until the 1330s, when the Franciscan master Nicholas of Lyra published his even more inclusive literal and moral postills on the Bible (including comments and theological elucidations from thirteenth-century masters), which in turn became the standard framework for biblical teaching in the theology schools until the sixteenth century.

The foundation provided by Hugh of St. Cher stimulated an outpouring of detailed biblical commentaries by Dominican and Franciscan theology masters, leading to the large and influential biblical works of Bonaventure and Thomas Aquinas in the 1250s and 1260s. Among the Dominican theologians who left their mark as academic exegetes in this period should be mentioned the Dominicans Guerric of Saint-Quentin (master of theology at Paris between 1233 and 1242), Geoffrey of Bléneau (d. 1250), the Oxford Dominican masters Robert Bacon (fl. c. 1230–48) and Simon of Hinton (fl. c. 1248–50), both of whom were inspired by the English scholar-bishop Robert Grosseteste (c. 1175–1253) and introduced the insights of natural philosophy into biblical exegesis, and Albertus Magnus (d. 1280), who likewise employed insights from the arts and sciences and the reading techniques used in the study of philosophy, avoiding allegorical and anagogical interpretations of the biblical text.[9] In the commentaries of these five Dominican friars (Guerric of Saint-Quentin, Geoffrey of Bléneau, Robert Bacon, Simon of Hinton, and Albertus Magnus), methods used in speculative theological and philosophical disputation replaced traditional, more meditative modes of monastic hermeneutic engagement with the biblical text.

The Franciscans also counted important exegetes in this period, although their commentaries from the 1230s and 1240s never reached the same status as the postills of Hugh of St. Cher. The first Franciscan master of theology at Paris, the Englishman Alexander of Hales, had been an innovative master of theology as a secular cleric between 1223 and 1227. He joined the Franciscans by 1236, and as their first regent master at the university of Paris returned both to systematic scholastic theology — leading to the great *Summa Theologiae*, finished after his death in 1245 by the Franciscans John of La Rochelle (died 1245), William of Meliton (died 1257), and others — and to biblical exegesis, finalizing his postills on the Gospels.[10]

John of La Rochelle and William of Meliton also produced biblical commentaries. John is best known for his Gospel commentaries and for his *Generalis Introitus ad Sacram Doctrinam* (*General Introduction to Sacred Learning*), a so-called *principium* (inaugural lecture) on scriptural teaching. Less keen than Alexander of Hales to separate theological argument from biblical commentary, he reintroduced the custom of inserting theological *quaestiones* into his Gospel lectures.[11] William of Meliton, on the other hand, did not concentrate so much on the Gospels but commented on the Apocalypse and on various books from the Old Testament with special significance for the Franciscan way of life, namely, Ecclesiastes, Job, the Song of Songs, and the twelve prophets.[12]

At Oxford, Franciscan biblical exegesis was promoted by Adam Marsh (d. 1259), whose biblical works have not survived, and by Thomas Docking (alias Thomas Good), who worked at Oxford in the 1250s and 1260s. Like his Dominican counterparts Simon of Hinton and Robert Bacon, Thomas Docking was inspired by Grosseteste to see theology first and foremost as biblical study, and he wrote voluminous commentaries on various books from the Old and New Testament. Following earlier traditions, Docking abandoned the "modern" postill format to include theological questions into his commentaries.[13]

Mendicant academic exegesis reached full maturity between the 1250s and the 1270s with the commentaries and parabiblical texts of the Franciscans Bonaventure, John Pecham, and John of Wales, and the Dominicans Thomas Aquinas and Peter of Tarantasia. Of these, Bonaventure and Thomas Aquinas concern us here, as they combined large exegetical endeavors with profound reflections on exegetical method.[14]

As a *sententiarius* in the early 1250s and during the years before he became master of theology, the future general minister Bonaventure of Bagnoregio (d. 1274) produced numerous theological *quaestiones* and a rather innovative *Sentences* commentary, in which he clearly distinguished between the study of Scripture and the study of doctrinal theology. Yet, in subsequent years, worried by philosophical developments that seemed to undermine Christian teachings and by polemics about the evangelical foundation of the mendicant way of life,[15] Bonaventure engaged in biblical studies, producing influential biblical commentaries on Ecclesiastes, Luke, and John that combined literal and spiritual exegesis with recourse to the Victorines, Bernard of Clairvaux, and Hugh of St.-Cher, as well as a handbook of biblical theology for Franciscan students (the so-called

*Breviloquium*) and exegetical collations or public evening lectures held before the assembly of students and teachers in the Franciscan friary at Paris (the *Collationes in Decem Preceptis*, or *Lectures on the Ten Commandments*, and the *Collationes in Hexaemeron*, or *Lectures on the Hexameron*).[16]

The Dominican Thomas Aquinas (d. 1274), now famous for his *quaestiones* and his *Summa Theologiae*, wrote most of his biblical works in the 1260s and the early 1270s, including a literal exposition of Job and commentaries on the Psalms, on the Lamentations of Jeremiah, and on the Epistles of Paul. Between 1263 and 1268 he produced a *Catena Aurea* (*Golden Chain*), a collection of extracts from the Latin and Greek fathers. It formed a continuous gloss on the Gospels in order to provide students with a study aid to interpret their literal and spiritual sense and to signal differences between Latin and Greek traditions of biblical interpretation. With the *Catena Aurea*, Thomas introduced students not familiar with Greek exegesis to texts by Athanasius, Basil the Great, John Chrysostom, and Gregory of Nyssa. Alongside the *Glossa ordinaria*, the *Sentences* of Lombard, and the postills of Hugh of St. Cher, Thomas's *Catena* became an important source for later medieval Gospel commentaries.[17]

The emphasis on the letter of the Gospels by mendicant commentators from this period does not mean that moral and allegorical exegesis of other biblical books was entirely rejected. Rather, for doctrinal purposes, the literal sense of the Gospel texts was privileged as the proper foundation for theological argumentation. Nevertheless, the same period saw a significant number of mendicant commentaries on Job, the Psalms, the Song of Songs, and on the sapiential books (Ecclesiasticus, Wisdom, Proverbs, and Ecclesiastes) focusing on lessons to be drawn for pedagogical, ethical, and political purposes.[18] Bonaventure's commentary on Ecclesiastes became a veritable classic.[19]

## Discussing Biblical Method

Both Thomas and Bonaventure wrote works dealing with exegetical method. In itself this was nothing new. Since the later twelfth century (at least since Peter Comestor), exegetical method was routinely addressed by academic theologians providing public biblical lectures at the university as biblical bachelor or as regent master. They started their lectures with an introductory sermon, or *principium*, in which they developed a methodological framework legitimizing the exegetical undertaking.

In these introductions it was common to use analytical terms borrowed from the teachings in the arts faculties to deal with issues of authorship, the utility of the text, the proper way to approach it, and the way one had to divide it in order to understand its meaning. Some *principia*, such as John of La Rochelle's *Generalis Introitus ad Sacram Doctrinam*, also include discussions of the biblical canon and the order and nature of the various biblical books.[20]

Around 1250, such *principia* incorporated the new Aristotelian scientific vocabulary describing, for instance, the exegetical enterprise with reference to the Aristotelian notion of the four causes, according to which the efficient cause dealt with the author of the text, the material cause with the subject matter, the formal cause with the so-called *modus agendi* or actual procedure, and the final cause with the ultimate intention or goal of the text and its correct *divisio*.[21]

Statements concerning exegetical method in *principia* texts could be standard academic exercises rather than extended reflections. This was not the case with Thomas Aquinas and Bonaventure, however, both of whom reflected on the nature of the exegetical enterprise as well as on the relationship between biblical exegesis and theological speculation. They had inherited a scholarly practice of distinguishing as clearly as possible between the literal and spiritual senses, setting theological questions apart for separate treatment and relating the outcome of well-established exegetical consensus by means of preaching. Hence they were heirs to a streamlined theological enterprise with a specific place and, increasingly, a specific format for exegetical work.[22]

Bonaventure and Thomas Aquinas realized that existing defenses of exegetical method needed refreshment. New Aristotelian works on logic, physics, and metaphysics (especially Aristotle's model of scientific knowledge put forward in his *Posterior Analytics*) threatened to disqualify biblical scholarship. After all, Aristotle had claimed that true scientific knowledge started with general first principles from which other truths could be derived logically. Since biblical exegesis (based as it was on events and stories from the Bible) seemed to deal with particulars rather than with universal truths from which other subalternated truths could be inferred logically, the scientific status of theology seemed to be in danger.

It was necessary to reformulate the status of the biblical text and its modes of exegetical understanding in response to the Aristotelian challenge. One had either to reposition the *res gesta* (events and occurrences) related in Scripture, as signifiers of universal acts and divine truths that in

and of themselves could form the basis of a truly scientific enterprise, or
to distinguish theology as a form of wisdom (*sapientia*), not necessarily
bound to the strictures of ordinary science (*scientia*). Both Thomas Aquinas and Bonaventure grappled with this, Thomas tending to reestablish
theology as a proper science and Bonaventure eventually leaning toward a
redefinition of theology as a form of wisdom beyond mere scientific
reasoning.

Thomas Aquinas took Hugh of St. Victor's definition of the literal
sense as a point of departure for his own doctrine on the extended *sensus
litteralis* ("literal sense") that could serve as a foundation for theological
argument. This concept, which he developed over a significant time
period in various writings (notably his seventh quodlibetal question *De
Sensibus Sacrae Scripturae* (*On the Senses of Holy Scripture*),[23] his commentary
on the Epistle to the Galatians, and his *Summa Theologiae* (Ia Pars, q. I, a.
10.),[24] started from the assumption that the Bible was ordered by God to
reveal to mankind what was necessary for salvation. This could be grasped
through a proper study of the meaning of the biblical words and the realities signified by these words. The first (the meaning of the words) yielded
the literal or historical sense, the second the spiritual sense. Thomas was
adamant that the spiritual senses should always start from and be supported by the letter, so as to attain a disciplined exegesis that overcame
confusion and revealed the univocal literal meaning of the biblical message on the basis of which scholarly argumentation was possible.

Whenever anything necessary for Christian faith and its proper understanding was contained in a scriptural passage under the spiritual sense, it
was also conveyed elsewhere in the Bible through the literal sense.
Thomas anchored this in a broad definition of the literal sense and in the
conviction that the ultimate author of the Bible was God, who understood everything at once in His intellect. Thomas agreed with Bonaventure that everything included under the authorial intention of the ultimate biblical author could be seen to pertain to the literal sense, signifying
divine truth either directly or through metaphor, parables, and symbols.
In this view, even messianic prophecies and typological prefigurations
from the Old Testament (or at least their proper meaning) pertained to
the literal sense as part of God's intended message concerning the coming
of Christ and His work of salvation.[25] The proper understanding of this
extended literal sense, founded on God's unerring and ultimately unambiguous authorial intention, provided theologians with knowledge con-

cerning the articles of faith that could function as axiomata for scientific reasoning in a truly Aristotelian fashion.[26]

In Bonaventure's "early" statements on biblical exegesis (his commentary on the *Sentences*, his *De Reductione Artium ad Theologiam* (*On Retracing the Arts to Theology*), and in the introductions to some of his biblical commentaries), he had developed lines of reasoning comparable to those of his Dominican colleague, and he used the Aristotelian notion of the four causes to speak at length about divine and human authorship of Scripture. Like Thomas, Bonaventure expounded the idea that the Bible's ultimate author was God, and that His authorial intention constituted the literal sense. As God intended to give man everything necessary for salvation in the Bible, either overtly or in veiled form, everything in the Bible pertaining to our salvation was part of the literal sense one way or another or could be seen as a direct or indirect product of the literal sense. On this basis, Bonaventure set forth rules for biblical exposition that allowed for a systematic foundation of the spiritual senses on the letter and for the recuperation of the dogmas of faith from their indirect manifestation in biblical allegorical and anagogical figures.[27]

In his *Breviloquium* (1254–57), a manual of theology for beginners and a program for biblical theology for students in the provincial schools of the Franciscan order, and increasingly in later writings as well (culminating in his *Collationes in Hexaëmeron*, 1273), Bonaventure was less interested in defending or presenting biblical exegesis in Aristotelian scientific terms and categories. He became convinced that biblical studies were not bound by "pagan" conceptions concerning the proper nature of scientific knowledge. Theology as *Sacra Scriptura* (Holy Scripture) should only use philosophical knowledge of the natural world and philosophical categories insofar as these could reveal divine truth. Otherwise, according to the mature Bonaventure, philosophy was irrelevant for the theologian. Hence theology students should go back to Scripture as the proper source for theological studies and, more existentially, as the foundation for a Franciscan life of evangelical perfection.

The *Breviloquium* therefore posited rather than argued that the Bible should be understood christologically, by accepting Christ's work of redemption with an act of faith, and that from this perspective the Bible described the complete universe (insofar as was necessary for man's salvation). The biblical text showed this through its amplitude (its variety of books), its longitude (its account of the trajectory of human history), its height (its display of the ecclesiastical, heavenly, and divine hierarchies), and its depth (its multiple senses or meanings). By understanding this depth, one could obtain all the knowledge necessary for salvation and an insight in God's wisdom.[28]

In his *Collationes in Hexaëmeron*, Bonaventure explored the amplitude and the depth of Scripture, discussing with a deliberately nonscientific vocabulary Scripture's *spirituales intelligentiae* ("spiritual significations," a significant amplification of the allegorical, tropological, and anagogical senses), its *sacramentales figurae* ("sacramental symbols," an expansion of the typological prefigurations and expressions of Christ in the Old and New Testament), and its *multiformes theoriae* ("multiple forms of contemplation," concerning the interpretation of time, the ages of man, and salvation history as a dynamic representation of the Divine). The latter amplified Bonaventure's ideas concerning the longitude of Scripture, first formulated in the *Breviloquium*.[29]

## Correcting the Biblical Text

The biblical text encountered by mendicant students in the schools was substantially different from the Bible digested in monastic reading. The mendicants were keen to professionalize biblical studies even further. Following Stephen Langton, they facilitated the study of the biblical text by dividing the books of the Bible into sections and chapters and by extending biblical wordlists, dictionaries, and concordances—thereby making the Bible a searchable text for those needing quotes or information on specific persons, events, or concepts. A major concern in this context was the "accountability" of the received biblical text.

Theologians knew that the Latin Bible used in the schools was a translation, and possibly not the best translation possible, especially taking into account the accumulation of mistakes and scribal errors in the course of centuries of copying. Since the times of Langton, more or less standardized one-volume versions of the Bible, the so-called Paris Bibles or Vulgate Bibles, circulated in the schools. (On the Bible in the thirteenth century, see Laura Light's chapter in this volume). Everybody acknowledged that these contained errors, a fact lamented most ferociously by the Franciscan Roger Bacon.[30] Although he did not produce lengthy Bible commentaries, he displayed a philological sensitivity to the deficiencies of the received biblical text. According to Bacon, these deficiencies resulted from a lack of proper linguistic training.

Inspired by Robert Grosseteste, who prior to his appointment to the Episcopal seat of Lincoln had taught the Franciscan friars at Oxford between 1229 and 1235, albeit without joining the order, and had emphasized the need for an adequate knowledge of Greek, Bacon argued that valid theological arguments needed to be based on a valid text checked against the original languages in which the Bible had been written. Therefore, in his *Opus Majus*, his *Opus Minus*, and his *Opus Tertium*, Bacon called for the study of languages and the development of philological tools. In addition, he worked on Greek and Hebrew grammars to facilitate the study of biblical languages.[31]

Such plans to put theological studies on a linguistic-philological footing never materialized. Medieval school programs did not leave room for the level of training in languages and philology required for a complete revision of the received recension of the Latin Bible. Plans for such an endeavor would bear fruit only with the establishment of the *Collegium Trilingue* ("trilingual college") in Louvain in 1517 for the study of Greek, Hebrew, and Latin under the aegis of humanist scholarship.[32] The various language *studia* founded by the mendicant orders in the later thirteenth and fourteenth centuries were more concerned with missionary efforts among the Arabs and Orthodox Christians than with raising levels of biblical scholarship.[33] These limitations notwithstanding, the mendicants tried to correct errors by compiling Greek and Hebrew wordlists and by checking and correcting biblical passages in the received translation using Greek and Hebrew versions.

Hugh of St-Cher and his Dominican team at St. Jacques had already taken the matter seriously as early as the 1230s. Hugh's own *Correctorium* displayed variant readings in existing copies of the Vulgate in order to evaluate discrepancies.[34] The work of Hugh and other Dominicans resulted in a revised biblical text, the so-called Bible of Saint-Jacques, with corrections and remarks for nearly all biblical books with the exception of the Psalms.[35] Roger Bacon did not approve of Hugh of St.-Cher's efforts, however, claiming that they lacked secure linguistic and philological foundations. Bacon was happier with the work of fellow Franciscan "correctors" from the 1250s and 1260s, several of whom were of English provenance and, like Bacon, steeped in a tradition of language scholarship in England that went back via Grosseteste to twelfth-century figures such as Andrew of St. Victor, Herbert of Bosham, Alfred of Sareshel, and Alexander Nequam.[36]

Two of the Franciscan "correctors" who earned Roger Bacon's approval were William of Mara/de la Mare, who knew Greek and Hebrew and wrote an influential *De hebraeis et graecis vocabulis glossarium Bibliae* (*Glossary of the Hebrew and Greek Words in the Bible*), and Gerard of Huy, a Belgian friar and author of both a *Liber Triglossos* (on the three biblical languages) and an interesting *Correctorium*.[37] Another important contribution was the lexicon of biblical terms issued in the 1260s by the Franciscan William Brito, which was revised in 1309 by Friar John of Erfurt.[38]

These "correctors" did not aim for a completely new edition of the Bible. They focused on outright translation or transmission mistakes and provided alternatives where the wording made the text difficult to understand. On the whole, the Dominican correctors were more radical in emending the text on the basis of available Greek, Latin, and Hebrew manuscripts, whereas the Franciscans tried to strike a balance between grammatical correctness and the weight of the tradition, driven by the idea that the Vulgate text was a translation with a transmission history and that slavish correction of individual words on the basis of a few available Greek and Hebrew "originals" was not philologically correct procedure (as Roger Bacon pointed out in his denunciation of Dominican correction practice).[39]

The apex of Franciscan Hebrew scholarship before the onset of humanism may be found in exegetical works of Nicholas of Lyra, who probably obtained his Hebrew knowledge before he joined the Friars Minor. Although he applied this expertise first and foremost to denounce Jewish "failures" to recognize the prefiguration of Christ in the Old Testament, he was one of the few later medieval biblical scholars to use the materials of the "correctors" more or less consistently and he routinely reached back to the *Hebraica Veritas* and Jewish commentary traditions to establish the literal sense of the Old Testament.[40]

## Exegesis and the Impact of Joachimism

The Dominicans and Franciscans took their form of religious life and their evangelical mission very seriously. They encountered staunch opposition from elements within the secular clergy who objected to the "innovative" lifestyle of the friars, finding fault with their mendicant status and the competition they represented in the field of pastoral care. The friars defended themselves with recourse to the biblical text, arguing that their way of life was vindicated by Christ's admonitions in the Gospels. Moreover, they became sensitive to forms of prophetic exegesis according to which the Bible seemed to announce their very existence at a critical moment in church history in order to battle the forces of the Antichrist and to prepare Christianity for Christ's return.

A major source of inspiration for such ideas was the lingering influence of the historical and typological exegesis of Joachim of Fiore, a twelfth-century abbot from Calabria (southern Italy). Joachim wrote commentaries and prophetic treatises, using the prophetic books in the Bible (notably Daniel, Jeremiah, and the Apocalypse) to seek insight into the course of history between the first and second coming of Christ (i.e., the period of church history since the time of the apostles). He argued that all major figures and events in the Old Testament could be read typologically to stand for important developments within that later period.

Joachim of Fiore combined his exegesis with a tripartite division of salvation history during which the Trinity manifested itself to mankind, and increasing insight into God's divine plan could be expected together with mounting tribulations that would culminate in the final onslaught of the Antichrist. Christ's first coming had ended the era of the Father and had ushered in the era of the Son. Yet Joachim foresaw an era of the Spirit: an epoch of spiritual renewal prepared by new "spiritual men" (*viri spirituales*) before a last confrontation with the forces of darkness, after which Christ's second coming would announce final judgment and the end of times.

It was tempting for the mendicants, with their "new" life of evangelical perfection and their quick missionary successes, to identify with Joachim's spiritual men and situate their pastoral ministry in the transition toward an age of spiritual renewal. Not surprisingly, some moderate forms of Joachimist typological exegesis, whether or not adapted through several pseudographs circulating under Joachim's name, found their way into early mendicant biblical commentaries often combined with other forms of exegesis that expanded the literal sense of prophetic visions in the book of Revelation to account for developments in church history since apostolic times.[41] An example of the latter is the Apocalypse commentary by Alexander Minorita of Bremen (fl. ca. 1250), whose "historical" reading of the Apocalypse seemed to explain all major events in Church history until his own time and which in an adapted form was used again in the "literal" exegesis of the Apocalypse by fourteenth-century exegetes Peter Aureol and Nicholas of Lyra.[42]

Joachimist and comparable forms of (para)biblical speculation became a liability when the Franciscan friar Gerard of Borgo San Donnino, sent to Paris by his order for a so-called lectorate course (a four-year nondegree theology course), published an *Introduction Into the Eternal Gospel* (*Introductorius in Evangelium Aeternum*) in 1254 without permission from his superiors. It proclaimed that the age of the Spirit was about to appear, that the mendicant orders (the Franciscans in particular) were to be its handmaidens because of their spiritual intelligence concerning God's plan with the world, that existing ecclesiastical hierarchies would give way, and that the Bible itself would be replaced by an eternal Gospel of spiritual truth (i.e., the works of Joachim of Fiore). Gerard's publication embarrassed the Franciscan order, not least because it gave ammunition for attacks on the friars' orthodoxy by their opponents among the secular clergy at the University of Paris and beyond.

The condemnation of Gerard's work by secular theologians from Paris and by a papal committee, Gerard's subsequent imprisonment, and the destruction of all copies of his work seemed to herald the end of Joachimist speculations among the mendicants.[43] However, it proved more difficult to exclude Joachimist ideas altogether. Bonaventure, who replaced the minister general John of Parma (under whose leadership Gerard had been able to announce his views), would himself adopt a sanitized version of Joachimism to portray the importance in world history of the order's founder, Francis of Assisi. In his later works, Bonaventure developed an alternative typological reading of Old Testament figures and biblical prophecies that would save both the historical significance of the mendicant orders and the primacy of the papacy (on the approval of which the mendicant orders were totally dependent).[44]

Bonaventure's solution appeased clerical elites but did not curb Joachimist and outright apocalyptical speculations by later mendicant authors. Still, in the 1270s, the Dominican friar John of Varzy speculated on the arrival of the Antichrist. Twenty years later, the Church found fault with the Franciscan Peter of John Olivi. The official condemnation of his Apocalypse commentary by the Franciscan order in 1319 and by Pope John XXII in 1326 signaled a watershed. From then onward, Joachimist apocalyptic schemes based on or passed off as biblical exegesis were associated with heretical groups that faced inquisitorial persecution. Yet this never thwarted the production of new prophecies and extravagant exegetical readings of selected biblical books, which continued well into the early modern period.[45]

## The Decline of Mendicant Exegesis?

The adoption of the *Sentences* of Lombard as a textbook of theology at Paris and Oxford after the 1230s and the disputation requirements for obtaining the doctorate of theology gradually changed the relative weight of biblical studies vis-à-vis *Sentences* lectures and advanced *quaestiones* literature within mendicant circles as well. This change was most notable in those *studia generalia* of the mendicant orders that were aligned with the universities (throughout the thirteenth century, especially Paris, Oxford, and Cambridge) where a selected number of friars could obtain their baccalaureate and doctorate degrees in theology.[46] Roger Bacon denounced this in the 1260s, complaining that *Sentences* commentaries and theological *quaestiones* had become preferred vehicles for distinction in the theology faculty and that lecturers in the *Sentences* were given the best lecturing hours, to the detriment of the lectures on the Bible.[47] Bacon interpreted this as a marginalization of the Bible in scholastic theology. Bonaventure would voice comparable concerns toward the end of his life, and in the 1290s the Franciscan friar Peter of John Olivi also deplored the phenomenon.

By the later thirteenth century, *Sentences* commentaries, *quaestiones disputatae* ("disputed questions"), and *quaestiones quodlibetae* ("quodlibetal questions") had become *the* vehicles for discussing new theological and philosophical ideas in the theology faculties and the associated mendicant degree schools. This practice agreed with the scientific method propagated by Aristotle's *Posterior Analytics* and used in other sciences at the medieval university. If the *Historia Sacra* provided the axiomata, the elaboration of consequences and inferences, especially concerning matters to be believed, could best be developed in more detail in theological genres independent of the biblical commentary. In fact, the *Sentences* of Lombard had originally been developed as a thematic gathering of important doctrinal statements derived from the patristic tradition, thereby furnishing theologians with a more streamlined basis for discussion than the biblical text. The latter confronted the reader with stories, events, sayings, and enigmas that did not lend themselves easily to proper scientific discourse in the Aristotelian sense.[48] For those interested in interpreting and defending the validity of Christian beliefs in light of the latest philosophical and scientific insights (concerning the creation of the world, human nature, Divine omnipotence, the nature of certain knowledge, etc.) that were being transformed under the influence of newly translated Aristotelian texts and their Arab commentators, sustained engagement with biblical commentary might have seemed counterproductive.

At the same time, friars interested in moral lessons to be derived from the biblical texts could by then rely on a wealth of thematically and/or alphabetically organized handbooks of moral theology in which the moral or tropological readings of the biblical texts had been condensed and geared to the demands of preachers and educators alike. Even for those desiring ready-made information on themes that could be linked to the assigned biblical readings throughout the liturgical year, it was now unnecessary to go back to the biblical text itself.[49]

Another limiting factor that concerned mendicant theology masters in particular was the short duration of their regency once they had obtained their degree. To boost the numbers of possible masters with only a limited number of faculty chairs assigned to them, the mendicants had settled by the 1250s for short regencies of one or two years, so that every year a new incepting master could take over. The outgoing master then would move on to teach elsewhere in the order's network of *studia* or make an administrative and ecclesiastical career in the order or the Church. Considering these developments, it is surprising how many friars going through the theology degree programs at Paris, Oxford, or Cambridge still bothered to produce lengthy biblical commentaries, particularly when we take into account the availability of commentaries produced by their immediate predecessors.

In the last quarter of the thirteenth and the first quarter of the fourteenth centuries, we still encounter a fair number of mature Dominican and Franciscan biblical exegetes.[50] The most influential of these was the Franciscan Nicholas of Lyra, who had joined the order after spending his formative years around Évreux (Normandy) where he became acquainted with Jewish biblical scholarship. Possibly because of his Hebrew knowledge, he was selected by the Franciscan minister general John of Murro to enter the theology degree program around 1301 as a *baccalaureus biblicus*.[51]

By 1308 he had become the Franciscan regent master at Paris, a position he held until 1310. Thereafter, he fulfilled various administrative posts within the order.

In between his administrative duties, Nicholas began in 1322 or 1323 with the compilation of his *Postilla Litteralis* (a commentary on the literal sense of the Bible), starting from the notes of his cursory lectures held at Paris between 1301 and 1302, expanding them into well-researched commentaries on all biblical books. The work was more or less completed in 1331. It was exceptional not only for its inclusiveness with regard to the medieval commentary tradition but also in its use of Hebrew exegetical scholarship (especially the works of Rabbi Schelomo Içaki, or Rashi, d. 1105). Once his *Postilla Litteralis* had been completed, Nicholas compiled commentaries on the spiritual senses, the so-called *Postilla Moralis seu Mystica* (*Moral or Mystic Postill*, more or less completed by 1339). Whereas the *Postilla Litteralis* was meant for use by theologians in the higher schools and universities, the *Postilla Moralis* was meant to be a concise handbook for order lectors and preachers in the provinces, providing short moral, typological, and allegorical notes on those Scripture passages that lend themselves to spiritual interpretation. Both the *Postilla Litteralis* and the *Postilla Moralis* have survived in many manuscripts and editions, as they became standard biblical textbooks in theological education throughout Europe until the early sixteenth century.[52]

Nicholas of Lyra's *Postilla Litteralis* was still frequently printed in the 1510s and 1520s, ordinarily in volumes that also contained the received Vulgate text and a version of the *Glossa ordinaria*, thus providing theologians of nearly every mold with a foundation for their own biblical studies. Even when early sixteenth-century humanists and the first Protestant scholars questioned the validity of the received biblical text and its apparatus of glosses and postills, Lyra's *Postilla Litteralis* proved to be difficult to ignore. There is some truth to the saying by Julius von Pflug (1499–1564) that "si Lyra non lyrasset, Lutherius non saltasset" ("Had Lyra not played, Luther would not have danced").[53]

At first glance, academic mendicant biblical exegesis went into sharp decline for several decades after the death of Nicholas in the 1340s. Plague epidemics, warfare, and socioeconomic troubles hampered mendicant recruitment for some time. More importantly, the availability of Nicholas's *Postilla Litteralis* in nearly every mendicant library, whether or not it was complemented by Hugh of St. Cher's postills and commentaries by other well-regarded mendicant exegetes from the thirteenth and the early fourteenth century, made it less urgent to write additional commentaries at a time when the orders faced numerous challenges.

Upon closer examination, however, this apparent gap in mendicant exegesis needs to be qualified. First of all, there was an ongoing production of exegetical instruments of an encyclopedic nature, continuing a tradition brought to fruition already in the thirteenth century in the Dominican and the Franciscan orders, alongside the massive production of concordances, distinctions collections, and additional biblical handbooks.[54]

Exegesis also continued to be practiced within homiletic contexts. Mendicant preaching had always been a direct continuation of mendicant exegesis. Hugh of St. Cher and his team, following Peter Comestor's adage that the ultimate goal of exegesis was preaching, had created their postills to give fellow preachers the materials to expound the word of God in the world. (On sermons, see Eyal Poleg's chapter in this volume.) Other exegetes had expressed the same motivation (as in Nicholas of Lyra's *Postilla Moralis* from the 1330s). This tied in with mendicant convictions concerning the importance of teaching the biblical message and especially the Gospel message to the people, which also stimulated their promotion of popular devotions to the Virgin Mary and the passion of Christ. Mendicant preachers stayed close to the biblical text, and their most elaborate sermons can be seen as exegetical treatises in their own right. This is also true for early fourteenth-century master preachers such as the Franciscan Francis of Meyronnes (d. 1328) and the Dominican Dominic Cavalca (d. 1342).

The availability of homiletic instruments in mendicant libraries providing piecemeal biblical themes and examples rendered strictly exegetical encounters with the biblical text superfluous. Yet the turn toward a more practically and biblically oriented theology from the late fourteenth century onward also signaled recourse to genuine biblical scholarship in homiletics, especially in Dominican and Franciscan Observant circles. The Observant movements within these religious orders aimed to recapture the orders' pristine religious fervor. This led to a disavowal of the technicalities of higher learning and rekindled interest in the biblical foundation of the mendicant religious life.

Various Franciscan and Dominican Observant preachers never earned an advanced degree in theology (for which reason they remain invisible to scholars basing their surveys of late medieval intellectual life on the matriculation lists of medieval universities). These Observants received their education in provincial study houses that stressed biblical and moral theology more than the renowned *studia generalia*, reserving their exegetical energies for their sermons. A famous case in point is Bernardino of Siena (d. 1444), who relied on the exegetical works of Hugh of St. Cher, Bonaventure, and Olivi to build his own sermon collections.[55]

At Europe's main universities, inspired by the aforementioned turn toward a more practically and biblically oriented theology, secular academic theologians once again began to comment on the Bible in the 1370s. Some scholars maintain that their commentaries from this later period surpass in quantity and quality the commentaries of the religious orders.[56] Yet the apparent lack of mendicant biblical commentaries in the decades after the death of Nicholas of Lyra and the observed dominance of secular theologians in academic exegesis in the period after 1370 are misleading. After around 1347, the monopoly of established universities (i.e., Paris, Oxford, and Cambridge) was seriously undermined due to the emergence of many new ones. The mendicant study houses integrated into theology departments of these newer universities were at times less speculatively oriented. More to the point, mendicant biblical output was not limited to the mendicant *studia generalia* integrated into the major universities. Beneath these schools where mendicant friars could pursue theology degrees, there existed internationally organized networks of *studia*. Although a number of these *studia* were eventually incorporated into university theology faculties of new universities for their degree programs, many such study houses and additional provincial and custodial schools with programs of biblical study based on the exegetical legacy of the thirteenth-century postillators primarily catered to nondegree students. An inventory of the exegetical initiatives of teachers active in these heterogeneous study networks between the later fourteenth and the early sixteenth centuries yields a much larger harvest of Dominican and Franciscan commentaries and exegetical instruments than has, up to now, been apparent to scholars focusing solely on the masters who can be traced through academic theology degree programs of Paris, Oxford, or Cambridge.[57]

Finally, at least from the later fifteenth century onward, mendicant exegetes were active at Louvain, Alcalá (Spain), and other new centers of theological learning, where these friars took a stance in the discussions regarding humanist biblical philology and the emerging Protestant biblical orientations. Cases in point are Cardinal Cisneros (d. 1517), who commissioned the influential Complutensian Polyglot Bible, the Louvain

professor Frans Titelmans,[58] Adam Sasbout,[59] Zweder Zeegers, Francis
Zorzi of Venice (1460–1540),[60] Andreas de Vega (1498–1549),[61] and Diego
Estella (1524–78).[62] These Franciscan exegetes defended the Catholic tradition against Erasmian and early Protestant biblical scholarship.[63] For
that reason, modern scholars automatically assume that the exegetical
work of these Franciscan theologians was traditional and second-rate.
Nearly all scholarly attention to this period is given to the protagonists of
humanist and Protestant innovation, and the works of their mendicant
opponents is not studied in depth. Considering the fact that their exegetical positions helped establish the Catholic Counter-Reformation, this is
a lamentable oversight.

Only a few decades after their foundation, the Dominicans and Franciscans dominated the field of biblical theology both within and beyond
the university setting. They came to the schools when major innovations
in biblical school exegesis had already been implemented. Their raison
d'être as religious orders with a commitment to a life of evangelical perfection and with specific responsibilities for universal mission and pastoral care made them perfect beneficiaries of this scholarly legacy. Between
the postills of Hugh of St. Cher in the 1230s and the compilation of the
*Postilla Litteralis* by Nicholas of Lyra a century later, mendicants dominated the production of biblical commentaries and an array of exegetical instruments. Within limits, they also developed ways of correcting
the biblical text, thereby taking the first steps toward a process of biblical
textual criticism that would come to fruition with the humanist scholarship of the sixteenth century.

After Nicholas of Lyra the dominance of mendicant biblical scholarship seemed on the wane, yet on closer examination that impression
might be misleading. Whereas the most renowned fourteenth-century
mendicant theologians at Paris, Oxford, and Cambridge were indeed
more interested in speculative theology than in biblical exegesis, there
was an ongoing mendicant involvement with the production of exegetical
instruments and commentaries in other, less well-researched centers of
learning. Moreover, the massive mendicant output of sermon collections
in the fourteenth century and later, an output not yet sufficiently
explored, had strong exegetical roots. From the closing decades of the
fifteenth century onward, mendicant theologians became involved in
the controversies surrounding humanist and early Reformation biblical

scholarship. Their contribution to these later discussions has not received the scholarly attention it deserves.

## Notes

I would like to express my gratitude to Dr. Frans A. van Liere and Dr. Susan Boynton for their insightful comments and editorial remarks on earlier drafts of this chapter.

1. Catharism was a dualist religious movement with a strong presence in southern France around 1200. It distinguished between a pure realm of the spirit (the work of God) and a tainted material realm (the work of an evil power). The world and the human body were prisons from which the soul had to be liberated by adopting a rigorously ascetical lifestyle. Most Cathars negated the incarnation of Christ and the Catholic doctrine of bodily Resurrection.

2. Maria Conti, "La Sacra Scrittura nell'esperienza e negli scritti di san Francesco. Criteri ermeneutici," in *Lettura biblico-teologica delle fonti francescane*, ed. Gerardo Gardaropoli and Maria Conti (Rome: Ed. Antonianum, 1979), pp. 36–48.

3. See M. Michèle Mulchahey, *"First the Bow is Bent in Study": Dominican Education Before 1350*, PIMS Studies and Texts 132 (Toronto: Pontifical Institute of Mediaeval Studies, 1998); Bert Roest, *A History of Franciscan Education (c. 1210–1517)*, Education and Society in the Middle Ages and the Renaissance 11 (Leiden and Boston: Brill, 2000).

4. See the first chapter of Bert Roest, *Franciscan Literature of Religious Instruction before the Council of Trent*, Studies in the History of Christian Traditions 117 (Leiden: Brill, 2004); as well as David L. D'Avray, *The Preaching of the Friars: Sermons Diffused from Paris Before 1300* (Oxford: Clarendon, 1985).

5. Beryl Smalley, *The Gospels in the Schools c. 1100–c. 1280* (London: Hambledon, 1985), p. 190.

6. Smalley, *The Gospels*, p. 121. See also Jacques Verger, "L'exégèse de l'Université," in *Le Moyen Âge et la Bible*, ed. Pierre Riché and Guy Lobrichon, Bible de tous les temps 4 (Paris: Beauchesne, 1984), pp. 199–232; John Van Engen, "Studying Scripture in the Early University," in *Neue Richtungen in der hoch- und spätmittelalterlichen Bibelexegese*, ed. Robert E. Lerner and Elisabeth Müller-Luckner, Schriften des Historischen Kollegs, Kolloquien 32 (Munich: Oldenbourg, 1996), pp. 17–38.

7. This form of textual glossing, called a *postilla*, may be derived from the Latin *post illa verba*, or "after this word," to signify the practice of inserting comments in the body of the biblical text, expounding the meaning of individual words and (parts of) sentences. It can be seen as an intensification of the interlinear gloss. In the course of the thirteenth century, the word *postilla* came to be used for nearly all continuous commentaries, whereas the word *glossa* remained in use to designate more modest forms of marginal and interlinear annotation or to

signify the more or less standardized *Glossa ordinaria*. Alessandro Ghisalberti, "L'esegesi della scuola domenicana del secolo XIII" in *La Bibbia nel Medio Evo*, ed. Giuseppe Cremascoli and Claudio Leonardi, La Bibbia nella storia 16 (Bologna: Dehoniane, 1996), pp. 291–304, at 293.

8.  Smalley, *The Gospels*, pp. 118–20; Lesley Smith, "What Was the Bible in the Twelfth and Thirteenth Centuries?" in *Neue Richtungen in der hoch- und spätmittelalterlichen Bibelexegese*, ed. Robert Lerner, Elisabeth Müller-Luckner, Schriften des Historischen Kollegs, Kolloquien 32 (Munich: Oldenbourg, 1996), pp. 1–15, at 8–9.

9.  On the Dominicans, see Gilbert Dahan, *L'exégèse chrétienne de la Bible en Occident médiéval, XIIe–XIVe siècle*, Patrimoines, christianisme (Paris: Cerf, 1999), passim; Ghisalberti, "L'esegesi della scuola domenicana," pp. 294–96, 301–3; Smalley, *The Gospels*, pp. 241–43; Albert Fries, "Zur Entstehungszeit der Bibelkommentare Alberts des Grossen," in *Albertus Magnus, Doctor Universalis, 1280–1980*, ed. Gerbert Meyer and Albert Zimmermann (Mainz: Matthias-Grünewald-Verlag, 1980), pp. 119–39.

10. On Alexander's postills, see: *Repertorium Biblicum Medii Aevi,* ed. Friedrich Stegmüller with the assistance of Nicolaus Reinhardt, 11 vols. and *Supplement* (Madrid: Consejo Superior de Investigaciones Científicas, 1950–1980), 1:1151–54 and suppl. 1151–54, I; Smalley, *The Gospels*, pp. 144–66; Gian Luca Potestà, *I francescani e la Bibbia nel' 200* (Milano: Biblioteca francescana, 1994), passim.

11. Smalley, *The Gospels*, pp. 175–77, 191.

12. See the information on William in my Franciscan Authors Catalogue (http://users.bart.nl/-roestb/franciscan/) as well as *Repertorium Biblicum 2*, nos. 418–28 and no. 2960, and 9, no. 2927 and no. 2966.

13. Johannes Madey, "Thomas Good von Docking," *Biographisch-Bibliographisches Kirchenlexikon* XVII, 1370–71; Monika Rappenecker, "Thomas Gude (Good) v. Docking," *Lexikon für Theologie und Kirche*, 3d. ed., 9:1527–28.

14. On Pecham, John of Wales, and other Franciscan exegetes, see Jenny Swanson, *John of Wales: A Study of the Works and Ideas of a Thirteenth-Century Friar*, Cambridge Studies in Medieval Life and Thought, Fourth Series 10 (Cambridge: Cambridge University Press, 1988); Friedrich Stegmüller, "Der Johanneskommentar des Johannes Pecham O. M.," *Franziskanische Studien* 31 (1949): 396–414; Friedrich Stegmüller, "Eine weitere Handschrift mit dem Johanneskommentar des Johannes Peckam O. M.," *Franziskanische Studien* 35 (1953): 440–42; Potestà, *I francescani e la Bibbia*, passim.

15. In particular, he was troubled by philosophical discussions concerning the eternity of the world and the survival of the soul after death, and the polemics of secular masters regarding mendicant privileges in the church.

16. The collation was originally a monastic tradition recapitulating the main theme of the day's biblical reading during the evening. The mendicants adopted the collation as part of their religious life and at times developed it into lengthy conferences in which leading theologians elaborated upon important exegeti-

cal and spiritual themes. Ignatius Brady, "Sacred Scripture in the Early Franciscan School," in *La Sacra Scrittura e i Francescani* (Rome-Jerusalem: Antonianum, 1973), pp. 74–76; Smalley, *The Gospels*, pp. 202–5; C. Bérubé, "De la théologie à l'Écriture chez Saint Bonaventure," *Collectanea Franciscana* 40 (1970): 5–70; Robert J. Karris, "St. Bonaventure as Biblical Interpreter: His Methods, Wit and Wisdom," *Franciscan Studies* 60 (2002): 159–208.

17. Henri de Lubac, *Exégèse médiévale. Les quatre sens de l'Écriture*, 4 vols. (Paris: Aubier, 1959–64), 4:273–302; Smalley, *The Gospels*, pp. 257–59; Ghisalberti, "L'esegesi della scuola domenicana," pp. 296–301.

18. Ghisalberti, "L'esegesi della scuola domenicana," p. 303.

19. Beryl Smalley, *Medieval Exegesis of Wisdom Literature: Essays by Beryl Smalley*, ed. Roland E. Murphy (Atlanta: Scholars, 1986), pp. 40, 43, 45.

20. Smalley, *The Gospels*, pp. 62–64.

21. Dahan, *L'exégèse chrétienne*, pp. 113, 266–67; Ferdinand Maria Delorme, "Deux leçons d'ouverture de cours biblique données par Jean de la Rochelle," *La France Franciscaine* 16 (1933): 345–60; Albert Fries, "Principium Biblicum Alberti Magni," in *Studia Albertina: Festschrift für Bernard Geyer*, ed. Heinrich Ostlender (Münster: Aschendorff, 1952), pp. 128–47; Peter of John Olivi, *Peter of John Olivi on the Bible: Principia Quinque in Sacram Scripturam, Postilla in Isaiam et in I ad Corinthios*, ed. D. Flood and G. Gal (St. Bonaventure: Franciscan Institute, 1997), pp. 17–151; Athanasius Sulavik, "*Principia* and *Introitus* in Thirteenth-Century Christian Biblical Exegesis with Related Texts," in *La Bibbia del XIII secolo: Storia del testo, storia dell'esegesi*, ed. Giuseppe Cremascoli and Francesco Santi (Florence: Edizioni del Galluzzo, 2004), pp. 269–321.

22. Dahan, *L'exégèse chrétienne*, pp. 91–108, 156–59.

23. Quodlibetal questions were specific academic exercises in which the theologian did not discuss a preassigned topic (as was the case with other disputed questions or *quaestiones disputatae*), but rather could address any topic (*de quolibet*).

24. See Paul Synave, "La doctrine de Saint Thomas sur le sens littéral des Ecritures," *Revue biblique* 35 (1926): 40–65; Dahan, *L'exégèse chrétienne*, pp. 271–90.

25. Thomas spoke of the meaning of messianic "figures" or their *virtus operativa*. See Synave, "La doctrine de Saint Thomas," pp. 44–45, 48, 58; see also Edward Synan, "The Four 'Senses' and Four Exegetes," in *With Reverence for the Word: Medieval Scriptural Exegesis in Judaism, Christianity, and Islam*, ed. Jane Dammen McAuliffe, Barry D. Walfish, and Joseph W. Goering (Oxford: Oxford University Press, 2003), pp. 225–32.

26. Ghisalberti, "L'esegesi della scuola domenicana," p. 301.

27. Smalley, *The Gospels*, pp. 203–4; Hans-Josef Klauck, "Theorie der Exegese bei Bonaventura," in *S. Bonaventura, 1274–1974*, 4 vols. (Grottaferrata: Collegio S. Bonaventura, 1974), 4:71–128, at 91, 94.

28. Bonaventura de Bagnoreggio, *Breviloquium*, in *Opera Omnia edita studio et cura PP. Collegii a S. Bonaventura*, 11 vols. (Ad Claras Aquas: Ed. Quaracchi, 1882–1902) 1:2 and 5. See also Klauck, "Theorie der Exegese," pp. 84–94.

29. Klauck, "Theorie der Exegese," pp. 102–5; Bérubé, "De la théologie," pp. 5–70.

30. Bacon, *Opus Minus*, in *Fr. Rogeri Bacon Opus Tertium, Opus Minus, Compendium Philosophiae*, ed. John S. Brewer (London: Longman, Green, and Roberts, 1859), pp. 330–33; *The Opus Majus of Roger Bacon*, ed. John H. Bridges, 3 vols. (Oxford: Oxford University Press, 1897), 1:77–78.

31. *The Greek Grammar of Roger Bacon and a Fragment of His Hebrew Grammar*, ed. Edmond Dolan and Stephen A. Hirsch (Cambridge: Cambridge University Press, 1902); Deeana Copeland Klepper, "Nicholas of Lyra and Franciscan Interest in Hebrew Scholarship," in *Nicholas of Lyra: The Senses of Scripture*, ed. Philip D. W. Krey and Lesley Smith, Studies in the History of Christian Thought 90 (Leiden: Brill, 2000), pp. 289–311, at 291–93.

32. Franco Alessio, "Ruggero Bacone fra filologie e grammatiche," in *Aspetti della letteratura latina nel secolo XIII*, ed. Claudio Leonardi and Giovanni Orlandi (Perugia: Regione dell'Umbria/Firenze: "La Nuova Italia," 1986), pp. 281–317.

33. André Berthier, "Les écoles de langues orientales fondées au XIIIe siècle par les Dominicains en Espagne et en Afrique," *Revue Africaine* 73 (1932): 84–102; Berthold Altaner, "Die Fremdsprachliche Ausbildung der Dominikanermissionare während des 13. und 14. Jahrhunderts," *Zeitschrift für Missionswissenschaft* 23 (1933): 233–41.

34. Verger, "L'exégèse de l'Université," p. 203. Another person to be mentioned here is Thibaud of Sézanne, a converted Jew with a profound knowledge of Hebrew.

35. Dahan, *L'exégèse chrétienne*, pp. 181–83.

36. Copeland Klepper, "Nicholas of Lyra," p. 302.

37. Dahan, *L'exégèse chrétienne*, pp. 184–87; Arduin Kleinhans, "De studio sacrae Scripturae in ordine fratrum minorum saeculo XIII," *Antonianum* 7 (1932): 413–40, at 436–37; Copeland Klepper, "Nicholas of Lyra," p. 298. See these authors also on later biblical correctors, such as Gerard of Buxo and John of Cologne.

38. *Summa Britonis sive Guillelmi Britonis Expositiones vocabulorum Bibliae*, ed. Lloyd W. Daly and Bernardine A. Daly, 2 vols. (Padua-Rome: Editrice Antenore, 1975).

39. Gilbert Dahan, "La critique textuelle dans les correctoires de la Bible du XIIIe siècle," in *Langages et philosophie: Hommage à Jean Jolivet*, ed. Alain de Libera, A. Elamrani-Jamal, and A. Galonnier, Études de Philosophie Médiévale 74 (Paris: J. Vrin, 1997), pp. 365–92; Gilbert Dahan, "La connaissance du grec dans les correctoires de la Bible du XIIIe siècle," in *Du copiste au collectionneur: Mélanges d'histoire des textes et des bibliothèques en l'honneur d'André Vernet*, ed. Donatella Nebbiai-Dalla Guarda and Jean-François Genest, Bibliologia 18 (Turnhout: Brepols, 1998), pp. 89–10; Dahan, *L'exégèse chrétienne*, pp. 114–15, 181–90, 223–335.

40. Copeland Klepper, "Nicholas of Lyra ," pp. 297–99.

41. For vestiges of apocalypticism in Hugh of St. Cher, see Robert E. Lerner, "Poverty, Preaching, and Eschatology in the Revelation Commentaries of 'Hugh of St. Cher,'" in *The Bible in the Medieval World: Essays in Memory of Beryl Smalley*, ed. Katherine Walsh and Diana Wood (Oxford: Basil Blackwell, 1985), pp. 157–89. Traces of Joachimist interpretations can also be found in the works of John of La Rochelle, Roger Bacon, and Adam Marsh. Smalley, *The Gospels*, pp. 183–85.

42. Alexander developed a specific "historical," nonrecapitulative reading of the major apocalyptical visions. See Sabine Schmolinski, *Der Apokalypsenkommentar des Alexander Minorita: Zur frühen Rezeption Joachims von Fiore in Deutschland* (Hanover: Deutsches Institut für Erforschung des Mittelalters, 1991).

43. Heinrich Denifle, "Das *Evangelium aeternum* und die Commission zu Anagni," *Archiv für Literatur-und Kirchengeschichte des Mittelalters* 1 (1885): 49–142; Ernst Benz, "Die Excerptsätze der Pariser Professoren aus dem *Evangelium aeternum*," *Zeitschrift für Kirchengeschichte* 51 (1932): 415–55; Bernhard Töpfer, "Eine Handschrift des *Evangelium aeternum* des Gerardino von Borgo San Donnino," *Zeitschrift für Geschichtswissenschaft* 8 (1960): 156–63.

44. Joseph Ratzinger, *Die Geschichtstheologie des heiligen Bonaventura* (Munich-Zürich: Schnell and Steiner, 1959); Paolo Vian, "Bonaventura di Bagnoregio di fronte a Gioacchino da Fiore e al gioachimismo: Qualche riflessione su recenti valutazioni," *Antonianum* 65 (1990): 133–60.

45. For the mendicant production of such texts (such as the works of the Dominican Robert of Uzès and the Franciscan friars John of Rupescissa and Telesphorus of Coscenza), see Francesco Santi, "La Bibbia e la letteratura profetico-apocalittica," in *La Bibbia nel Medio Evo*, ed. Giuseppe Cremascoli and Claudio Leonardi, La Bibbia nella Storia 16 (Bologna: Edizioni Dehoniane, 1996), pp. 389–408; Harold Lee, Marjorie Reeves, and Giulio Silano, *Western Mediterranean Prophecy: The School of Joachim of Fiore and the Fourteenth-Century Breviloquium*, Studies and Texts 88 (Toronto: Pontifical Institute of Mediaeval Studies, 1989).

46. Dahan, *L'exégèse chrétienne*, pp. 108–20; James McEvoy, *Robert Grosseteste* (Oxford and New York, 2000), pp. 164–67; Deeana Copeland Klepper, "Nicholas of Lyra," pp. 304–7.

47. Roger Bacon, *Opus Minus*, ed. John Brewer (London: Longman, Green, and Roberts, 1859), p. 328.

48. Bonaventure, *Breviloquium* V, nos. 14, 16; Smith, "What Was the Bible," p. 9.

49. Louis-Jean Bataillon, "Early Scholastic and Mendicant Preaching as Exegesis of Scripture," in *Ad litteram: Authoritative Texts and Their Medieval Readers*, ed. Mark Jordan and Kent Emery, Notre Dame Conferences in Medieval Studies 3 (Notre Dame, IN: University of Notre Dame Press, 1992), pp. 165–98.

50. For exegetical works by Dominicans such as Bernard of Trilia (d. 1292), Nicholas of Gorran (d. 1295), Jacques of Lausanne (d. 1322), Nicholas Trivet (d. 1330), Pierre de la Palu (d. 1342), Dominique Grima from Toulouse (d. 1347), Thomas Waleys (1349), and others, see Thomas Kaepelli, *Scriptores Ordinis Praedicatorum Medii Aevi*, 3 vols. (Rome: ad S. Sabinae, 1970–80). For Franciscan exegetes such as Peter of John Olivi (d. 1298), Matthew of Aquasparta (d. 1302), Alexander of Alexandria (d. 1314), Peter Auriol (d. 1322), Henry of Cossey/Costesy (d. 1336), and Poncio Carbonell (d. 1350), see the references in the Franciscan author catalogue mentioned in note 11. Olivi and Peter Auriol combined exegetical works with innovative forms of speculative theology.

51. On John of Murro's exegetical interests regarding biblical history and the literal

sense of old-testamental prophecies, see Copeland Klepper, "Nicholas of Lyra," pp. 289–91, 299–300, 310.

52. See for instance *Postilla Litteralis*, 5 vols. (Rome: Sweynheym and Pannartz, 1471– 72); *Biblia cum Glosa ordinaria et Nicolai de Lyra Postilla*, 6 vols. (Basel, 1506–8).

53. See *Nicholas of Lyra: The Senses of Scripture*.

54. Late-medieval examples worth mentioning are the *Speculum morale totius sacrae Scripturae* by Vital du Four (d. 1327), the *Distinctiones in Sacram Scripturam* by Arnald Royard (d. 1334), the *Biblia Pauperum* by Peter of Udine (d. 1360), the anonymous *Allegoriae et tropologiae in utrumque Testamentum*, Petrus Berchorius's *Repertorium morale seu reductorium morale super totam Bibliam*, Angelus of Lemposa's *Opus de concordantia Veteris et Novi Testamenti*, Anthony Belengarius's handbook on biblical figures, the *Bibliorum anacephalaeosis* by Anthony of Assisi (fl. 1466), the *Lexicon Biblicum* written by Andreas Plach (d. 1548), and the *Concordantiae materiarum ex Sacris Bibliorum Libris* (Paris, 1544) by Anthony Broick of Koenigstein (d. 1541). Plach's works were reprinted by the Calvinists in the late 1550s to serve as a foundation for their own biblical scholarship.

55. See his *Sermones de Tempore*, edited in *S. Bernardini Senensis Opera Omnia (...)*, ed. Coll. S. Bonaventurae, 9 vols. (Ad Claras Aquas: Quaracchi, 1950–65), vol. 7, and his *Postillae in Epistolas et Evangelia*, and selected sermons in his *Quadragesimale de Evangelio Aeterno (Opera Omnia)*, vols. 9 and 3–5 respectively.

56. William Courtenay, "The Bible in the Fourteenth Century: Some Observations," *Church History* 54 (1985): 176–87.

57. This impression is based on a scrutiny of the Franciscan author Web site (see note 11). Among the Franciscans we can trace are the biblical commentaries of Landulfus Caraccioli (d. 1355), John of Sommerfeld (d. 1361), John of Lathbury (d. 1362), Marquard of Lindau (d. 1392), John Quaia of Parma (d. 1398), John Vasco (fl. late 14th cent.), Christian of Hiddestorf (fl. ca. 1400), and John Hilten (fl. later 15th cent.). The exegesis of John Hilten was a source of inspiration for Luther, Melanchthon, and Calvin.

58. Titelmans disputed the statements of Erasmus and Lefèvre d'Étaples regarding the Vulgate text and the biblical canon, for instance, in his *Prologus apologeticus pro veteri et ecclesiastica Novi Testamenti Latina interpretatione* (Antwerp: W. Vorsterman, 1530). See Irena Backus, "The Church Fathers and the Canonicity of the Apocalypse in the Sixteenth Century: Erasmus, Frans Titelmans, and Theodore Beza," *Sixteenth Century Journal* 29 (1998): 651–55.

59. His *In Isaiam* (Louvain, 1558) in fact departed from "traditional" allegorical exegesis.

60. *In Scripturam Sacram Problemata* (Venice, 1536).

61. *Commentarius in Psalmos* (Alcalà, 1599).

62. *In Sacrosanctum Iesu Christi Domini Nostri Evangelium Secundum Lucam Enarrationes*, 2 vols. (Salamanca, 1574–75/Lyons, 1592 [1580]).

63. Some Franciscans came to defend exegetical positions that brought them into the camp of Luther (such as Johan Pelt, Conrad Pellican, and Francis Lambert of Avignon).

# "A Ladder Set Up on Earth"

THE BIBLE IN MEDIEVAL SERMONS

*Eyal Poleg*

D irect access to the Bible was the exception rather than the rule in medieval Europe. Limitations imposed by cost, sacrality, and degrees of literacy determined one's ability to own or consult the Christian Scriptures. Sermons stood out among the multitude of events and objects that offered mediated access to the Bible. At a time when the Bible was written in Latin and biblical translations were frowned upon, sermons presented the laity with biblical texts in languages they were able to understand. Preachers, while relying on biblical exegesis, simplified complex biblical texts, paraphrased their narratives, and interpreted the archaic words of the Vulgate. Sermons were among the few occasions on which the clergy was instructed to accommodate the biblical text to its audience, and priests constantly aimed to make the biblical text relevant for their listeners, interspersing their sermons with contemporary examples and adjusting specific texts to distinct groups. The place of the Bible in sermons was unequivocal. It served as an inexhaustible source of narratives, exempla, role models, and texts that were woven into the very fabric of the sermon, to such an extent that dozens of biblical quotations and references frequently appear in a single sermon.

Medieval preachers and modern scholars alike acknowledged the centrality of the Bible to medieval preaching.[1] The ways in which sermons mediated the Bible for its medieval audiences are less evident. Preachers did not simply elucidate the biblical text. Rather, the Bible was employed for different aims, such as moral injunction and commentary on the liturgy. For these diverse purposes preachers explored the depth of the biblical text, employed various means of exegesis and analysis, and in turn influenced the evolution of biblical scholarship. The place of the Bible in medieval sermons can thus be seen in the image of Jacob's Ladder (employed by medieval preachers), which linked heaven and earth and enabled preachers to connect tenets of Christian faith to their audience. However, both Jacob's Ladder and the Bible were not the ultimate goal but rather the means of achieving it.

This chapter will explore the role of the Bible in medieval sermons, tracing the dynamics of preaching the Bible alongside changes in medieval preaching. These changes, set against the background of the transformation of church and society in the high Middle Ages, led preachers to reassess the role of the Bible in sermons and to prefer, eventually, the textual rather than narrative qualities of the biblical text. But first the context of the sermon itself will be presented in connection to another important mediator of biblical knowledge in the Middle Ages: the liturgy. A discussion of preachers' awareness of their audiences will lead to the question of the gap between extant sources and the medieval reality. Detailed analysis of the way the Bible was presented in sermons establishes the centrality of the Bible in sermons and the various manners in which preachers expanded on the biblical text and will also enable us to reassess the claims advanced during the Reformation that the role of the Bible had deteriorated in late-medieval sermons.

## The Liturgical Setting for Medieval Preaching

Christian preaching is rooted in the Bible itself. Medieval preachers emulated the prophets in their moral admonitions and followed Christ's commandment to the apostles: "Go ye into all the whole world, and preach the gospel to every creature" (Mark 16:15). One episode in particular, Luke's description of Christ's own preaching (4:16–30), has influenced Christian preaching ever since. On the Sabbath, Christ entered a synagogue in Nazareth and read from the book of Isaiah. He connected Isaiah's "the Spirit of the Lord is upon me, because the Lord hath anointed me: he hath sent me to preach to the meek" (Isa. 61:1–2) to his own preaching at the synagogue. Alluding to the stories of Elijah and Elisha (1 Kings 17, 2 Kings 5), Christ claimed that prophets had never been accepted by their own communities. As it happened, he incurred the wrath of his audience, who drove him out of the synagogue and sought to take his life. Luke's brief description presents a view of preaching familiar to medieval audiences. Christian preachers, like Christ, combined biblical quotations and narratives in elucidating a biblical text; they too connected the biblical text to their own situations , although theirs were more mundane. The liturgical setting of Christ's sermon provided a context that has defined medieval sermons.

Sermons were typically preached during Mass, between the Gospel reading, which was expounded in the sermon, and the Canon of the Mass. (For a description of the Mass, see Boynton's chapter in this volume.) The sermon was thus surrounded by liturgical actions. The priest, responsible for administering the sacraments, was also responsible for preaching. The connection between preaching and heterodoxy, evident in the example from the Gospel of Luke, led to an emphasis on the identity of preachers and on the regulation of preachers by the church; the office of preacher was assigned to bishops in the early Middle Ages and delegated by them to licensed clergymen in the high and late Middle Ages.[2] Traditional preaching took place within the confines of the church from pulpits, or from sacred locations on its outskirts, such as the churchyard cross. Thus, through text and time, actors and locations, sermons were intertwined with church rituals. The Eucharistic context of preaching was challenged in the late Middle Ages as popular preachers delivered sermons in marketplaces and license was given to orthodox secular preachers. The connection between biblical readings and sermons influenced the use of the Bible in preaching. The Gospels and Epistles—the biblical books most commonly employed as readings for the Mass—were also the ones that appeared most frequently in medieval sermons.[3] Pericopes (the technical term for the biblical reading at Mass) followed the liturgical cycles of the *temporale* and *sanctorale* to furnish liturgical occurrences with appropriate biblical passages. In some instances the narrative recounted in a pericope was substantially reenacted through the texts and actions of the liturgy. However, in the many extrabiblical events of the Christian liturgy, the juxtaposition of pericope and feast followed an intricate allegorical interpretation.[4] For example, the story of Christ's entry into Jerusalem was read on Palm Sunday—the liturgical commemoration of the biblical event—and on the first Sunday in Advent, when Christ's entry was seen in the light of the first and second coming. Pericopes thus supplied preachers with a biblical excerpt, creating tension between text and liturgical occurrence. Preachers commented on the biblical text as well as its occasion within church rituals. Thus preaching was a continuation of the exegetical impulse that linked pericopes and liturgical worship. The centrality of the liturgy to preaching influenced the compilation of medieval sermon collections, which frequently follow the sequence of the liturgical year rather than a biblical sequence.[5]

The liturgy permeated the text of sermons in other ways as well.[6] Some sermons made direct reference to liturgical occasions, whether biblical or extrabiblical. One example is the elaborate comparison of the processions of Purification, Palm Sunday, and Ascension, made in a sermon for the first Sunday of Advent by Odo of Cheriton (d. 1246).[7] There the biblical narrative, actors, and complex imagery were invoked alongside a description of the feast day's ceremonies, including their timing, ritual actions, and paraphernalia. This enabled the audience to recognize biblical events through their well-known liturgical reenactments. Sermons also had embedded liturgical echoes and prayers: early medieval sermons ended with benedictions, while late medieval sermons integrated an additional prefatory prayer, known as the prologue or *antetheme*. The blurring of the boundaries was known to preachers in late antiquity and the Middle Ages, who punned on the Latin word *orator*, which can mean both an orator and one who prays: "[the preacher] must become an orator/man of prayer before becoming a man of words" (*sit orator antequam dictor*).[8]

An important change in medieval preaching altered the very place of the Bible within sermons. In late antiquity and the early Middle Ages preachers commented upon the entire pericope. Known today as homilies, their sermons provided a line-by-line reading of the pericope interspersed with commentaries, exempla, and citations. The pericope structured the entire sermon and was gradually elucidated in its course. Homilies of church fathers, from Augustine of Hippo (d. 430) and Gregory the Great (d. 604) to the Venerable Bede (d. 735), were known, copied, and read privately and publicly throughout the Middle Ages, especially in monastic communities. By the thirteenth century a new form of preaching had evolved, sometimes called a university sermon. Rather than following the entire pericope, preachers employed only a segment of the pericope—a line or even a single word—as the sermon's core. This biblical nucleus, known as a *thema*, was then developed in major and minor divisions, each verified by a biblical or extrabiblical quotation or allusion—the proof. In theory, this "modern sermon" adhered to a highly rigid structure: it began with the *protheme*, which commented upon preaching in general; then came the thema, sometimes accompanied by the headings of the major divisions; an appeal for divine assistance followed, known as *antetheme* or prologue; then a repetition of the thema and a short introduction preceded the major divisions of the thema, accompanied by their own subdivisions, each verified by a proof. The sermon concluded with a repetition of the thema, a short admonition, and a prayer.

The function of major and minor divisions is demonstrated by figure 10.1, which is based on Jacobus de Voragine's (d. 1298) sermon for the feast of St. Bartholomew. The sermon, taking as its thema a verse from Job—"Skin for skin: and all that a man has he will give for his life" (Job 2:4)—expanded upon the saint's skin and his flaying.[9] Voragine employed four definitions of skin for his major divisions, which were related both to the martyrdom of Bartholomew and the verse from the book of Job. Two of the major divisions (nature and blame) were subdivided into minor divisions to elucidate the reasons for shedding one's skin and the variety of sinners. The structure of the sermon utilized only a fraction of the biblical text, and its divisions were far removed from the biblical narrative of the book of Job. This is indicative of the move from pericope to thema: whereas the pericope was comprised of several verses commonly consti-

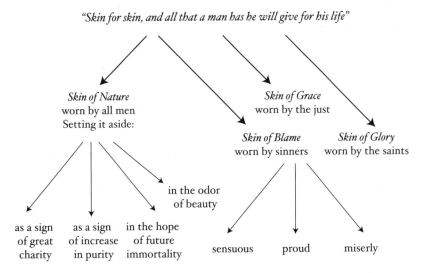

10.1. Structure of Jacobus de Voragine's Fourth Sermon for the Feast of St. Bartholomew.

tuting an identifiable narrative unit, the thema retained only a fragment of the pericope.

## Preaching to the Populace

The evolution of medieval preaching was contemporaneous with a transformation in medieval church and society. The beginning of the thirteenth century saw the establishment of the first universities in Italy, France, and England. There sermons and lectures were a common means of disseminating knowledge, and students were expected to deliver a public sermon upon their graduation. The strong emphasis on biblical exegesis in university curricula befitted the education of preachers. Lecture notes were taken by students, reorganized according to a liturgical sequence, and made into sermons.[10] At the same time that universities offered new opportunities for the education of preachers, a dedicated cadre of preachers came into the limelight. The mendicant orders, and especially the Franciscans and Dominicans, followed the examples of Francis and Dominic in making preaching one of their key objectives. University trained, itinerant, and skilled in disputation and rhetorical arts, the friars brought preaching to new heights and new audiences.[11] (On biblical exegesis and university training among the mendicants, see Roest's chapter in this volume.) Their convents spread across Europe and combined with changes in scribal practices and the rise of preacher's aids to disseminate ideas and sermons quickly and efficiently, creating a form of "mass communication in a culture without print."[12]

The new form of preaching was promulgated in rhetorical treatises, many of which were written by friars. Although not part of the official university curriculum, *ars praedicandi* ("art of preaching") treatises supplied preachers with concrete advice and theoretical background for the use of the Bible in sermons.[13] These treatises were based on the works of church fathers, including Augustine of Hippo's *De doctrina Christiana* (*On Christian Doctrine*), which was read and copied extensively throughout the Middle Ages. In the fourth book, Augustine explored the link between rhetoric, the Bible, and Christian preaching.[14] The book was divided in two: interpretation and communication (*modus inveniendi* and *modus proferendi*), a division that reflected the connection between preaching and the Bible: preachers were to be aware of the biblical text as well as its audience, and they were to address both questions of exegesis and of dissemination. While biblical exegesis was widely employed by Augustine's contemporaries, he laid a special emphasis on eloquence. Augustine warned Christian orators of the danger of boring their audiences and advocated the value of the pagan *artes* (liberal arts), predominantly rhetoric, in making the Christian message palatable. Anticipating objections, Augustine assured his readers that both form and content were to be found in the Bible, especially in the words of the Prophets. Less than two centuries later the value of Christian eloquence was reaffirmed by Gregory the Great. In his *Cura pastoralis* (*Pastoral Care*), he advanced the means of communication available to Christian orators.[15] Breaking away from classical rhetoric, Gregory highlighted the importance of accommodating one's message to specific audiences and provided examples of themes appropriate for discrete publics.

Medieval ars praedicandi treatises built upon these early works, and supplied biblical texts appropriate for diverse audiences alongside general discussions regarding the place of the Bible in sermons. Some treatises delineated a corpus of biblical texts based on authenticity or applicability. Thus a widespread ars praedicandi composed possibly in Oxford in 1322 questioned the use of several biblical texts (such as the Third and Fourth Esdras or Paul's Epistle to the Laodiceans) in sermons, because of their dubious authorship.[16] Other means of delineating a suitable group of biblical texts for preaching were based on dissemination rather than exegesis. Alan of Lille, in his *Summa de arte praedicatoria* (*Summa on the Art of Preaching,* c. 1199), considered only the Gospels, Psalms, Paul's Epistles, and the books of Solomon to be fit to serve as *themata* (plural of thema); their moral injunctions enabled preachers to instruct effectively in faith and behavior.[17] Following in Augustine's footsteps, ars praedicandi treatises found a role model for preachers in the Bible, suggesting that even the new form of preaching originated in the biblical text itself.

The introduction to Alan of Lille's *Summa de arte praedicatoria* addresses the place of the Bible in sermons and in the education of preachers. The biblical image of Jacob's Ladder (Gen. 28:12 "And he [Jacob] saw in his sleep a ladder standing upon the earth, and the top thereof touching heaven: the Angels also of God ascending and descending by it") was recalled twice in this context. At first its rungs were likened to man's ascent in faith: confession to prayer, thanksgiving, the study of Scriptures, of the church fathers, of biblical exegesis, and, lastly, preaching the Bible.[18] Preaching was thus seen as the culmination of Christian life and education, with biblical study, both of text and of exegesis, as a prerequisite. The same biblical image was then invoked in a description of the act of preaching. Preachers were likened to the angels of God ascending the ladder in preaching heavenly things, but descending in preaching morality: "This is what is meant by the angels ascending and descending. Preachers are the angels who ascend when they preach about heavenly matters, and descend when they bend themselves to earthly things in speaking on behavior."[19]

Preachers were presented as mediators par excellence, as they actively bridged the gap between heaven and earth. Like angels (with the implied moral and sacral parallels), they constantly moved between the two realities. The place of the Bible in this image, however, is not evident. Was it the "heavenly matters" to which the ascending angels were drawn, or was it the ladder, which enabled the connection between the two realities? Alan of Lille's own definition of preaching supplies the answer. Earlier in the treatise he presented a definition of sermons that was common among his contemporaries and used by modern scholars of medieval preaching: "an open and public instruction in faith and behavior, whose purpose is the forming of men; it derives from the path of reason and from the fountainhead of the 'authorities.'"[20] In this definition, the Bible stands in the shadow. It was faith and behavior, doctrinal matter rather than biblical, to which preachers aspired. The Bible supplied the means to do so, alongside other authorities, such as the church fathers or even pagan writers. The Bible was thus similar to Jacob's Ladder, on which medieval preachers trod in their moral admonitions.

Biblical interpretation and moral admonition were not seen as contradictory by medieval preachers. Following the tenets of allegorical interpretation, it was the very nature of the biblical text that promoted Christian life and faith. This is evident in the protheme of an Advent Sunday sermon by the Austin canon John Waldeby (d. after 1372). The protheme, located at the very beginning of the sermon, provided Waldeby with the opportunity to reflect upon his own actions and the value of preaching the Bible.[21] Each of Waldeby's assertions is validated by a proof—a biblical citation:

The Gospel should be preached and elucidated to the laity for three reasons: first as this fulfills God's commandment; second, the audience becomes worthy of God's blessings; third, the Gospel itself holds good tidings. First we find in the last chapter of Mark: "preach the Gospel to every creature" (Mark 16:15); second Luke 12: "blessed are they who hear the word of God and keep it" (Luke 11:28); third we find that the Gospel is interpreted as good tidings:

Luke 2: "I bring you good tidings of great joy &c" (Luke 2:10). Therefore this Gospel, which described the Advent of Christ in the flesh is for us good tidings, that is so that it shall lead us to salvation.[22]

Waldeby, like Augustine and authors of ars praedicandi treatises, demonstrated the value of preaching as embedded in the biblical text itself. There was no distinction between the biblical text and the admonition of his audience. Rather, it was the very essence of the Bible that was preached. Waldeby expanded upon the motivation of preachers and hearers alike: the audience, by hearing the sermon and adhering to its articles of faith, was ensured of its future salvation; preachers, on the other hand, followed Christ's injunction to the apostles. This differentiation reflected the unique status of priests, whose proximity to the sacred word was inherently different from that of the laity.

## Preaching to the Different Estates

While the difference between clergy and laity was evident in Waldeby's protheme, another type of distinction was prevalent in medieval sermons and treatises. Following in the footsteps of Gregory the Great, medieval preachers differentiated between discrete audiences in their sermons. Sermons known as *ad status* addressed specific audiences—groups with a particular social position (*status*)—such as merchant, monks, soldiers, or virgins. Each audience was allocated an appropriate theme or biblical narrative: the poor were shown the merits of poverty, while the rich were confronted with the value of almsgiving; pilgrims were reminded of the story of the Magi, and Crusaders were taught about God's chosen people.[23]

Ad status sermons are indicative of a much broader phenomenon that is crucial to understanding the place of the Bible in medieval sermons. By connecting specific audiences to particular topoi, preachers aimed at modifying their message according to their audience. Sermons were a dynamic form of biblical mediation that could be adjusted in order to enhance its reception. Biblical narratives were linked to world events in a connection, still prevalent today, that Lawrence T. Martin described as "[a good preacher] has a Bible in one hand and a newspaper in the other."[24] Thus in late medieval England ruling monarchs were likened to Rehoboam, who tormented the Israelites following the advice of his young councillors (1 Kings 12). In the sermon of Thomas Wimbledon, preached on Quinquagesima Sunday 1388, it was Richard II who was likened to the ill-advised king; Henry de Harkeley, chancellor of the University of Oxford, equated Edward II with Rehoboam, himself with Jeremiah, and Thomas Becket, on whose day the sermon was preached (December 29, 1314), with both Josiah and John the Baptist.[25]

References to world events and ad status sermons are not particularly frequent among extant medieval sermons. Most sermons built upon liturgical occasions and made little reference to external events. These sermons employed other means of connecting the Bible to the reality of the audience. The sermon of Odo of Cheriton, mentioned earlier, refers to a village (*castellum*) to which Christ sent his disciples (Matt. 21:2). This village was seen as a fortified castle, dominated by the devil. It had four turrets, each guarded by a variety of sinners; the apostles assailed each by a siege engine—an act of charity.[26] The allusion to medieval warfare, which assisted Odo in establishing a minor division, was lacking in the Gospel narrative. It enabled him to connect a verse from the pericope to the reality of his listeners. Another vivid image of medieval life appealed to a very different audience. Bernardino of Siena (d. 1444), in a sermon to the women of Florence, utilized the image of a trousseau—a bridal box containing jewelry, pearls, and a ring—to expand upon the various qualities of the mystical union with Christ:

> David says, *Desponsavit animam meam Deus*: —God has married my soul. Surely I want to show that all may understand it. This consciousness was made just as a trousseau that you women have with you when you go to your husband: that small one, I am not speaking of those large ones; you known that you hold inside them your ring, pearls, jewels and other similar things; and also sometimes you put inside the letter, which your lover sends you, and he puts inside musk and carnations, so that when you open it a strong perfume permeates the whole house, and you close it with a key, wanting to keep it for yourself. And thus God has made to his own trousseau. That he places inside a ring that signifies the faith; but see that when we are baptized, we are asked: *Quid quaeris?*—What are you seeking?—and we have to answer—Faith. And then he puts the ring in this ark.[27]

The link between audience and Bible is evident in the language of sermons. At a time when the liturgy was in Latin and biblical translations scarce, sermons presented the Bible in a language the laity was able to understand. While sermons for the clergy were delivered in Latin, the laity was exposed to sermons in the vernacular. Latin and vernacular even cohabited in the space of a single sermon. A linguistic hybrid, known as macaronic or code switching, is defined by a change of language in between passages or even mid-sentence. This is evident in an example from a fourteenth-century sermon, which moved between Middle English and Latin. I have emphasized the Latin to assist in differentiating the two:

> *Pater enim mittit appropriate loquendo* wit a selli miht, *Filius* wit a semli riht, *Spiritus sanctus* wyt a seli lyht. *Et correspondenter his venit Filius primo* onto mans kynd, *secundo* onto mans mind, *tercio* onto the demyng.[28]

The Father sends, by his own speech, with wonderful might, the Son with pure right, the Holy Ghost with blessed light. Correspondingly by this went the Son, at first into mankind, secondly into man's mind, thirdly into Judgment.

The transition between Latin and Middle English is immediate. It preserves the rhyming of the English (*riht, riht, lyht*) alongside the religious terminology and logical conjunctions of the Latin (*Pater, Filius, Spiritus sanctus; correspondenter*). In the past, scholars saw in these sermons evidence for a decline in priestly education, but recently a more complex understanding of bilingualism has emerged in which clerics are seen as competent in both languages.[29]

A gap exists between the delivery of the sermon, a speech act with performative traits, and its preservation in manuscript form. Without supporting evidence, it is difficult to infer whether a sermon recorded in macaronic form or in Latin was actually delivered in the vernacular. The gap between language, performance, and preservation extends even to the rare instances in which we hold a record for the delivery instead of a compilation of sermons: the few extant *reportationes* (lecture notes) in which French sermons were recorded in Latin reflect scribal conventions and education rather than mere transcription of a sermon.[30] Most sermon manuscripts were compiled to assist preachers in future sermons and at times provide a skeletal structure upon which the preacher expanded extemporaneously. The gap between oral event and textual testimony influenced the place of the Bible in sermons: biblical verses are often truncated in the manuscripts, accompanied by book and chapter number. It is possible that in delivery these verses were expanded and read aloud; although the new form of preaching utilized only a fragment of the pericope, there is evidence to suggest that the entire pericope was read and translated without leaving a reference in our sources.

## Themata and Proofs

Extant sermons contain two discrete types of biblical references, based on their function rather than biblical origin: a single thema stood at the core and supplied the rationale for the entire sermon, while a multitude of proofs permeated the sermon, providing in some cases dozens of biblical references and quotations. Ars praedicandi treatises and extant sermons agree that themata were to be taken solely from the Bible and not from church fathers, saints' lives, or the classics. This injunction was safeguarded at times by listeners, as illustrated by an incident in which a new preacher was reproached by his parishioners for a sermon whose thema was taken from classical literature.[31] Themata were restricted by authors of ars praedicandi treatises to specific books of the Bible, based on their moral applicability. They were to follow the biblical text closely without any alterations, even minor or grammatical ones.[32]

Biblical quotations employed as proofs were not subjected to the rigorous rules for themata. A comparison between the Bible and biblical proofs from Waldeby's Advent Sunday sermon demonstrates the relative freedom of the preacher in employing biblical proofs:[33]

| Waldeby's Advent Sunday Sermon | Bible |
| --- | --- |
| The Lord did not think [it] worthy to sit on a naked horse or ass, because on such he was forced to sit, led in contempt, to his own hanging. | |
| Last (chapter) of the Apocalypse "Blessed is he that watcheth his garments, lest he walk naked." | Behold, I come as a thief. Blessed is he that watcheth, and keepeth his garments, lest he walk naked, and they see his shame (Apoc. 16:15) |
| As though he was to say similarly "blessed is he that hears the word of God and keeps it." | But he said: Yea, rather, blessed are they who hear the word of God, and keep it (Luke 11:28) |
| About these vestments spoke the Apostle (Col. 5) "put on as the elect of God mercies and kindness etc." | Put ye on, therefore, as the elect of God, holy, and beloved, the bowels of mercy, benignity, humility, modesty, patience (Col. 3:12) |

Themata were not to be altered, no matter how small or trivial the change might be, whereas proofs were modified constantly in sermons, as plural was changed to singular, singular to plural, cases were modified, adverbs and conjunctions were omitted, and verses truncated. While sermons were constructed to suit a thema, proofs were modified to assist preachers in integrating biblical quotations to the structure of the sermon. Removing biblical quotations from their context led to juxtaposing well-known biblical episodes alongside abstruse texts and episodes. Proofs drew not only on the Bible but also on church fathers, saints' lives, exegetical works, the classics, fables, and natural phenomena. This wealth of sources enabled preachers to connect their sermons to vogues in preaching and scholastic knowledge and to appeal to the taste of their audiences. However, as studies of quotations and allusions in late medieval sermons demonstrate, the Bible retained its centrality as the most prevalent source of proofs.[34]

While the thema structured the entire sermon, proofs validated each and every argument made by the preacher. In accordance with Aristotelian logic, which gradually attained prominence in the high Middle Ages, the Bible can be seen as apodictic or "necessary" proof.[35] Dozens of quotations were linked by logical conjunctions and constituted the "fabric" of the sermon. The analogy between weaving and preaching was employed by medieval preachers, who saw their sermons as woven (*texitur*) from biblical materials.[36] This concept enabled preachers and hearers to approach sermons not as a new creation but rather as a manifestation of a divine, biblical truth.

Beyond techniques of quotation, the excerpt taken from Waldeby's sermon provides insight into the construction of a medieval sermon. The clothes addressed by Waldeby's array of proofs originated in the day's pericope. The garments (*vestimenta*) laid on the ass by the apostles (Matt. 21:7) were seen by Waldeby as a sign of the love of Christ; the ass was likened to the soul, which should be adorned with pious deeds. The ways of expanding upon the thema, structuring proofs, and weaving them into a sermon, were known as means of amplification. Several such means are evident in the excerpt: the connection between the apostles' garments and Revelation rested upon a repetition of word (*vestimenta*); the admonition against nakedness was linked to pious deeds by a verbal echo (assisted by a slight modification of the proof)—"Blessed is he" (*Beatus qui*). The appeal to contemporary imagery is another means of amplification, which assisted the preacher in the division of the thema.

Means of amplification were explored in medieval treatises. An anonymous thirteenth-century Franciscan treatise enumerated ten means of
amplification, which expanded upon the thema through division, argument, and logical connections or applied the use of concordances, verbal
echoes, and definitions.[37] These means of amplification necessitated a
close reading of the biblical text, examining the definition of its words, its
grammar, morphology and etymology, the sound of its words or the links
between the words of the thema, and other biblical texts.

Allegorical interpretation of the biblical text was a prerequisite for the
elaboration of themata. A tenacious and perennial link exists between
preaching and biblical exegesis. Leading Christian exegetes, from Origen
(d. c. 254) and Augustine to Bernard of Clairvaux (d. 1153), were also
preachers and presented parts of their work in the form of sermons; early
biblical commentaries were written for preachers, and the form of the
homily, with its line-by-line expansion of the pericope, replicated the layout of exegetical works.[38] Allegorical interpretation guided preachers in
their understanding of the biblical text and supplied a rationale for the
connection between Christian belief and Old Testament texts, between
the Bible and its audience.

The new form of preaching provided preachers with numerous ways of
incorporating biblical exegesis into their sermons, from direct references
to exegetical works to the deployment of allegorical analysis of biblical
narratives. Let us turn again to Jacobus de Voragine's sermon for the feast
day of St. Bartholomew, with an excerpt that exemplifies these trends:

> "Skin for skin, and all that a man has he will give for his life." (Job 2:4).
> According to the Gloss, skin is given for skin, because often when a blow is
> directed toward an eye, we put our hand to it, so as to be hurt in the hand
> rather than the eye, as if it were said: Job resisted exteriorly many blows,
> because he preferred not to be struck interiorly.
>
>     . . .
>
>    Firstly, he set it aside as a sign of fervent charity. People who suffer from
> excessive heat have the habit of removing their clothes. When the blessed
> Bartholomew set aside his skin, that fire of love that filled him was made
> clear. This is what is meant when it is said: "Jonathan loved David like his
> soul." In fact he removed his tunic and he gave it to David. By Jonathan who
> signifies the gift of the dove, the blessed Bartholomew is signified, for he
> was filled by the Holy Spirit. Thus he who loved David (that is, Christ) like

his soul, removed his tunic and he gave it to David when due to the love of Christ he allowed himself to be skinned alive.[39]

Jacobus linked the martyrdom of Bartholomew, in which he was flayed, with the verse from Job through allegorical interpretation. His first proof was taken from the *Glossa ordinaria*, the university textbook for biblical exegesis, and enabled him to make the transition from external skin to inward piety.[40] Allegorical interpretation also furnished the connection between Jonathan's gift of his tunic to David (1 Sam. 18:4) and the martyrdom of Bartholomew. David was seen as a prefiguration of Christ, Jonathan a prefiguration of Bartholomew. The giving of the tunic to David symbolized Bartholomew's relinquishing his own skin out of love for Christ in the course of his martyrdom.[41]

The identification of Jonathan and Bartholomew relied upon a widespread biblical glossary—the *Interpretation of Hebrew Names* (*Interpretationes nominum Hebraeorum*)—in which Jonathan was defined as the "gift of the Dove" (*donum columbe*).[42] This glossary became a standard addendum to biblical manuscripts in the late Middle Ages and had a special appeal to medieval preachers.[43] It provided preachers with several short and allegorical definitions for a single Hebrew or Aramaic name and enabled them to efficiently employ a common means of amplification—definition. Preachers' aids, much like their education, eluded the dichotomy of preaching and exegesis. Dictionaries, concordances, and patristic works befitted both uses; whereas exegetes employed them in an in-depth analysis of the biblical text, preachers relied on them as a mean of amplification.

The new form of preaching was characterized by an elaborate structure that expanded an excerpt from the pericope in an array of biblical and extrabiblical proofs. This style, and especially its use of the Bible, elicited criticism from reformers both inside and outside the Catholic Church. John Wyclif (d. 1384) and his followers lamented the state of preaching and accused preachers of preferring rhetoric to the biblical truth.[44] During the Reformation the "university sermons" were attacked repeatedly, and even modern scholars have lamented the decline of the place of the Bible in medieval sermons.[45] Such criticism, combined with attacks on the mendicant orders and the rediscovery of classical rhetoric in the Renaissance, led to the rejection of this form of preaching and the reintroduction of the homily.

The dichotomous view of the Bible in medieval sermons adopted by church reformers can be misleading. Throughout the Middle Ages, sermons relied on the Bible. They employed intricate rules that evolved over the course of the Middle Ages. The change, however, was not from strict adherence to the biblical text to mere rhetoric; rather it presented a growing emphasis on the textual qualities of the biblical text, through definition of words, morphology, and repetition at the expense of the Bible's narrative qualities, which diminished with the move away from the pericope. The connection between preaching and other forms of biblical mediation, most notably the liturgy, persisted throughout the Middle Ages and shaped the place of the Bible in sermons. With the mendicant orders, orthodox preaching was more widely disseminated than ever before, and lay audiences throughout Europe were presented with common topoi and similar means of expanding upon the biblical text. The modern form of preaching removed biblical proofs from their original contexts and highlighted textual elements at the expense of the biblical narrative. In so doing, however, it raised awareness of the complexity of the biblical text and its Semitic origins. These developments influenced the proliferation of biblical manuscripts and provided an important audience for them. (For the development of university Bibles, see Light's chapter in this volume.) Their portability, layout, and especially their frequent inclusion of glossaries suited the needs of preachers and provided them with the means of amplification. Thus medieval preaching predated the works of humanists and reformers in celebrating difficult and contradictory biblical readings and bringing increased attention to the Semitic roots of the Vulgate. Preaching served to promulgate a notion of the Bible similar to that of early modern reformers, who lamented the decline of the use of the Bible by medieval preachers.

## Notes

1.  There is no definitive study of the Bible in medieval sermons. Among the most useful introductory works are *De Ore Domini: Preacher and the Word in the Middle Ages*, ed. Thomas L. Amos, Eugene A. Green, and Beverly Mayne Kienzle (Kalamazoo: Western Michigan University, 1989), in which the introduction (John W. O'Malley, S.J., "Introduction: Medieval Preaching," pp. 1–11) is a useful survey of medieval preaching. See also Marie Anne Mayeski, "Reading the Word in a Eucharistic Context: The Shape and Methods of Early Medieval Exegesis," in *Medieval Liturgy: A Book of Essays*, ed. Lizette Larson-Miller (New York: Garland, 1997), pp. 61–84. Recent studies on sermons include Nicole Bériou,

*L'avènement des maîtres de la Parole: La prédication à Paris au XIIIe siècle*, 2 vols. (Paris: Institut d'études augustiniennes, 1998), which identifies a key moment in the evolution of medieval sermons in connection with the place of the Bible; Hughes Oliphant Old, *The Reading and Preaching of the Scriptures in the Worship of the Christian Church*, vol. 3: *The Medieval Church* (Grand Rapids, MI: Eerdmans, 1999), a descriptive history of medieval preaching; and *The Sermon*, ed. Beverly Mayne Kienzle (Turnhout: Brepols, 2000), which, although less biblically oriented, provides a comprehensive introduction to medieval preaching, comprised of in-depth analyses and texts of extant sermons.

2. The licensing of preachers is most evident in canons 3 (*On Heretics*) and 10 (On Appointing Preachers) of the Fourth Lateran Council (1215): *Decrees of the Ecumenical Councils*, vol. 1: *Nicea I to Lateran V*, ed. Norman P. Tanner (Washington, DC: Georgetown University Press, 1990), pp. 234–35 and 239–40. On heterodox and orthodox preaching, see John H. Arnold, *Belief and Unbelief in Medieval Europe* (London: Hodder Arnold, 2005), pp. 41–50.

3. For a detailed survey of late medieval sermons according to their biblical theme, see Johannes Baptist Schneyer, ed., *Repertorium der lateinischen Sermones des Mittelalters für die Zeit von 1150–1350*, 11 vols. (Münster, Westfalen: Aschendorff, 1969–90). An analysis based on mendicant preaching and liturgy can be found in Louis-Jacques Bataillon, "Early Scholastic and Mendicant Preaching as Exegesis of Scripture," in *Ad Litteram: Authoritative Texts and their Medieval Readers*, ed. Mark D. Jordan and Kent Emery, Notre Dame Conferences in Medieval Studies 3 (Notre Dame, IN: University of Notre Dame Press, 1992), pp. 165–98.

4. The development of the pericope is presented in Boynton's chapter in this volume.

5. For a survey and analysis of late-medieval sermon collections, see Siegfried Wenzel, *Latin Sermon Collections from Later Medieval England: Orthodox Preaching in the Age of Wyclif* (Cambridge: Cambridge University Press, 2005).

6. An analysis of the connection between liturgy and preaching in a specific milieu can be found in Chrysogonus Waddell, "The Liturgical Dimension of Twelfth-Century Cistercian Preaching," in *Medieval Monastic Preaching*, ed. Carolyn Muessig (Leiden: Brill, 1998), pp. 335–49.

7. Odo's Latin sermon was revised and translated to Middle English by the turn of the fifteenth century. See H. Leith Spencer, "Middle English Sermons," in *The Sermon*, pp. 597–660, at 657–60.

8. Augustine, *De Doctrina Christiana*, ed. and trans. R. P. H. Green (Oxford: Oxford University Press, 1995), pp. 234–35.

9. Iacobus de Voragine, "Sermon IV for the Feast of Saint Bartholomew," trans. George Ferzoco (http://www.semones.net/spip.php?article24&lang=fr), accessed October 4, 2008. A detailed study of the sermon appears in Nicole Bériou, "Pellem pro pelle (Job 2,4): Les sermons pour la fête de saint Barthélemy au XIIIe siècle," *Micrologus: Natura, scienze e società medievali; Nature, Sciences and Medieval Societies* 13 (2005): 267–84.

10. Beryl Smalley, *English Friars and Antiquity in the Early Fourteenth Century* (Oxford: Blackwell, 1960), pp. 28–44; and *The Study of the Bible in the Middle Ages*, 3d. ed. (Oxford: Blackwell, 1983), pp. 196–213.

11. On biblical exegesis and university training among the Mendicants, see Bert Roest, "Mendicant School Exegesis," in this volume.

12. David L. d'Avray, "Printing, Mass Communication and Religious Reformation: The Middle Ages and After," in *The Uses of Script and Print, 1300–1700*, ed. Julia Crick and Alexandra Walsham (Cambridge: Cambridge University Press, 2004), pp. 50–70, which builds upon d'Avray, *Medieval Marriage Sermons: Mass Communication in a Culture without Print* (Oxford: Oxford University Press, 2001); and d'Avray, *The Preaching of the Friars: Sermons Diffused from Paris Before 1300* (Oxford: Oxford University Press, 1985).

13. On rhetoric, see Martin Camargo, "The Long and the Short of Geoffrey of Vinsauf's Documentum de modo et arte dictandi et versificandi," *Speculum* 74 (1999): 935–55; and John O. Ward, "Rhetoric in the Faculty of Arts at the Universities of Paris and Oxford in the Middle Ages: A Summary of the Evidence," *Bulletin du Cange: Archivum Latinitatis Medii Aevi* 54 (1996): 159–231. I thank Rita Copeland for her assistance in the matter. An up-to-date introduction to ars praedicandi treatises is Marianne G. Briscoe, *Artes praedicandi* (Turnhout: Brepols, 1992). The treatises were described in Th. M. Charland, *Artes praedicandi: Contribution à l'histoire de la rhétorique au moyen âge* (Paris: Vrin; Ottawa: Institut d'études médiévales, 1936); and James J. Murphy, *Rhetoric in the Middle Ages: A History of Rhetorical Theory from Saint Augustine to the Renaissance* (Berkeley: University of California Press, 1974), pp. 269–355. Caution in utilizing ars praedicandi treatises in the study of sermons was advocated by d'Avray, *Preaching of the Friars*, pp. 178–79, 206.

14. Augustine, *De doctrina Christiana*.

15. Gregory the Great, *The Book of Pastoral Rule and Selected Epistles of Gregory the Great Bishop of Rome*, ed. and trans. James Barmby (Oxford, 1895), pp. 24–71.

16. Robert of Basevorn, "The Form of Preaching," trans. Leopold Krul, in *Three Medieval Rhetorical Arts*, ed. James J. Murphy (Berkeley: University of California Press, 1971), pp. 109–215, at 150–51; Latin text in Charland, *Artes praedicandi*, pp. 264–66.

17. Alan of Lille, *The Art of Preaching*, trans. Gillian R. Evans (Kalamazoo: Cistercian, 1981), p. 20; Latin text in Alanus de Insulis, *Summa de arte prædicatoria*, PL 210:111.

18. Alan of Lille, *The Art of Preaching*, pp. 15–16; PL 210:111.

19. "Quod significatur per angelos ascendentes et descendentes: angeli enim hi sunt prædicatores, qui tunc ascendunt cum cœlestia prædicant; descendunt, quando per moralia se inferioribus conformant," *The Art of Preaching*, pp. 17–18; PL 210:111. This image was employed in a recent study of preachers. See Claire M. Waters, *Angels and Earthly Creatures: Preaching, Performance, and Gender in the Later Middle Ages* (Philadelphia: University of Pennsylvania Press, 2004).

20. Alan of Lille, *The Art of Preaching*, pp. 16–17; PL 210:111. Similar definitions guided Alan of Lille's contemporary, Alexander of Ashby in his *Alexandri Essebiensis Opera theologica*, CCCM 188:1, ed. Franco Morenzoni and Thomas H. Bestul (Turnhout: Brepols, 2004), pp. 29–30, as well as the recent introduction to sermons by Beverly Kienzle: "The sermon is essentially an oral discourse spoken in the voice of the preacher who addresses an audience to instruct and exhort them on a topic concerned with faith and morals and usually based on a sacred text" ("Introduction," in *The Sermon*, pp. 150–59). For an analysis of Alan's definition and its place and time, see Mark A. Zier, "Sermons of the Twelfth Century Schoolmasters and Canons," in *The Sermon*, pp. 325–62, at 325–27.

21. On *prothemes*, see Johannes Baptist Schneyer, *Die Unterweisung der Gemeinde über die Predigt bei scholastischen Predigern: Eine Homiletik aus scholastischen Prothemen* (Munich: Schöningh, 1968).

22. "Evangelium est laycis exponendis & predicandis triplici de causa: primo que talis implet dei preceptum, secundo audiens meretur dei benedictiones, tertio ipsum Evangelium continet bonum nuntium. Primum patet marci ultimo 'predicate Evangelium omni creatore'. Secundum lucas .12. 'Beati qui audiunt verbum dei et custodiunt illud'. Tertium patet que Evangelium interpretatur bonum nuntium lucas 2 'evangelizo vobis gaudium magnum &c'. Igitur evangelium illud quod describit adventum Christi in carnem est nobis bonum nuntium, ideo ut nobis presit ad salvationem": Oxford, Bodleian Library Laud. misc. MS 77 (hereafter Laud. Misc. 77), fol. 26r; Oxford Bodleian Library Bodley MS 687 (hereafter Bodl. 687), fol. 79ra. On the author and the collection, see Yuichi Akae, "A Study of the Sermon Collection of John Waldeby, Austin Friar of York in the Fourteenth Century," (Ph.D. diss., University of Leeds, 2004); Akae, "A Library for Preachers: The *Novum opus dominicale* of John Waldeby OESA and the Library of the Austin Friars at York," *Medieval Sermon Studies* 49 (2005): 5–26; and Wenzel, *Latin Sermon Collections*, pp. 40–44, 625–30.

23. Examples of *topoi* appropriate for specific audiences can be found in Gregory the Great, *The Book of Pastoral Rule*; Alan of Lille, *Art of Preaching*; Servus of Sint Anthonis, "Preaching in the Thirteenth Century: A note on MS Gonville and Caius 439," *Collectanea Franciscana* 32 (1962): 310–24 (I thank Bill Campbell for this reference); and Bériou, *L'avènement des maîtres*, I:501–2.

24. Lawrence T. Martin, "The Two Worlds in Bede's Homilies: The Biblical Event and the Listeners' Experience," *De Ore Domini*, pp. 27–40, at 27–28. A similar statement, again with reference to modern preachers, was made by Amaury d'Esneval, "Le perfectionnement d'un instrument de travail au début du XIIIe siècle: Les trois glossaires bibliques d'Etienne Langton," in *Culture et travail intellectuel dans l'Occident médiéval*, ed. Geneviève Hasenohr and Jean Longère (Paris: Editions du Centre national de la recherche scientifique, 1981), p. 164.

25. Eric W. Kemp, "History and Action in the Sermons of a Medieval Archbishop: The Bishop of Chichester," in *The Writing of History in the Middle Ages: Essays Presented to Richard William Southern*, ed. Ralph H. C. Davis and John M.

Wallace-Hadrill (Oxford: Oxford University Press, 1981), pp. 349–65, at 351–52; and Patrick J. Horner, "Preachers at Paul's Cross: Religion, Society, and Politics in Late-Medieval England," in *Medieval Sermons and Society: Cloister, City, University, Proceedings of International Symposia at Kalamazoo and NY*, ed. Jaqueline Hamesse et al. (Louvain-la-Neuve: Fédération Internationale des Instituts d'études médiévales, 1998), pp. 261–82, at 275–76.

26. Spencer, "Middle English Sermons," pp. 645–46.

27. Dice David: *Desponsavit animam meam Deus*:—Iddio ha sponsata l'anima mia.— per certo, io vel voglio mostrare che tutta lo 'ntenda. Questa conscienzia è fatta proprio come quello goffanuccio [cofanetto] che voi, donne, avete quando andate a marito: quel piccolino, non dico quelli grandi; sapete, che voi vi tenete dentro le vostre anella e pierle e gioiette, et altre simili cose; et anco talvolta vi mettete la lettera che vi manda el vostro innamorato, e mìttevi dentro del moscado e de' garofani, che quando l'aprite gitta grande odore per tutta la casa, e sèrrolo colla chiave, e vuo'la tenere per te. E così ha fatto Iddio a questo suo goffanuccio. Che ci metta l'*anella*, che significa la fede; e però, vedi, che quando noi ci battezziamo, noi siamo domandati: *Quid quaeris?*—Che vai tu cercando?— E noi doviamo respóndare:—Fede.—Et allora mette l'anella in questa arca . . .

　　Bernardino da Siena, *Le Prediche volgari inedite, Firenze 1424, 1425, Siena 1425*, ed. P. Dionisio Pacetti, I Classici Cristiani 56 (Siena: E. Catagalli, 1935), p. 413. I thank Suzy Knight for this reference. On this metaphor see Adrian W. B. Randolph, "Performing the Bridal Body in Fifteenth-Century Florence," *Art History* 21 (1998): 182–200. Many other visual images in Bernardino's sermons are analyzed by Lina Bolzoni, *The Web of Images: Vernacular Preaching from Its Origins to St Bernardino da Siena*, trans. Carole Preston and Lisa Chien [from *La rete delle immagini: Predicazione in volgare dalle origini a Bernardino da Siena* (Torino: Einaudi 2001)] (Aldershot: Ashgate 2004), pp. 120–95.

28. Alan J. Fletcher, "'Benedictus qui venit in nomine Domini': A Thirteenth-Century Sermon for Advent and the Macaronic Style in England," *Mediaeval Studies* 56 (1994): 217–45, supplies the text of the sermon and a discussion.

29. Linda E. Voigts, "What's the Word? Bilingualism in Late-Medieval England," *Speculum* 71 (1996): 813–26; and Siegfried Wenzel, *Macaronic Sermons: Bilingualism and Preaching in Late-Medieval England* (Ann Arbor: University of Michigan Press, 1994). For further examples of sermons from fourteenth-century England, see Siegfried Wenzel, ed. and trans., *Preaching in the Age of Chaucer: Selected Sermons in Translation* (Washington D.C.: Catholic University of America Press, 2008).

30. Nicole Bériou, "Latin and the Vernacular. Some Remarks About Sermons Delivered on Good Friday During the Thirteenth Century," in *Die deutsche Predigt im Mittelalter. Internationales Symposium am Fachbereich Germanistik der Freien Universität Berlin vom 3.–6. Oktober 1989*, ed. Volker Mertens and Hans-Jochen Schiewer (Tübingen: Niemeyer, 1992), pp. 268–84. On reportationes and preservation, see the various articles in *Medioevo e Rinascimento* 3 (1989); and especially (for technical aspects) Malcolm B. Parkes, "Tachygraphy in the Middle Ages: Writ-

ing Techniques Employed for 'Reportationes' of Lectures and Sermons," *Medioevo e Rincascimento* 3 (1989): 159–69; reprinted in Parkes, *Scribes, Scripts and Readers: Studies in the Communication, Presentation and Dissemination of Medieval Texts* (London: Hambledon, 1991), pp. 19–34.

31. H. Leith Spencer, *English Preaching in the Late Middle Ages* (Oxford: Oxford University Press, 1993), pp. vi–vii.

32. For prohibitions on altering the Biblical text in *themata*, see Basevorn, "The Form of Preaching," §7, §15, §31 (Krul, *Three Medieval Rhetorical Arts*, pp. 127–28, 133–34, 154–58, Charland, *Artes praedicandi*, pp. 244–45, 249–50, 268–72).

33. Laud misc. 77, fols. 27v–28r; Bodl. 687, fol. 79va–b. The Latin is provided below to present the verbal echoes.

| *Waldeby (D 27v–28r; B 79va–b)* | *Bible* |
|---|---|
| Non enim dominus dignatur nudo sedere equo vel asino que in contemtum ductus ad suspendium taliter cogitur sedere | |
| Apocalypse ultimo: "Beatus qui custodit vestimenta sua ne nudus ambulet." | *Ecce venio sicut fur. Beatus qui vigilat, et custodit vestimenta sua, ne nudus ambulet, et videant turpitudinem ejus* (Apoc. 16:15) |
| Quasi diceret equivalenter "beatus qui audit verbum dei & custodit' illud." | *at ille dixit Quinimmo beati qui audiunt verbum Dei et custodiunt* (Luke 11:28) |
| De hiis vestibus locutio apostolus ad col. 5 dicens "induite vos sicut electi dei misericordias & benignitatem &c" | *Induite vos ergo, sicut electi Dei, sancti, et dilecti, viscera misericordiæ, benignitatem, humilitatem, modestiam, patientiam* (Col. 3:12) |

34. Larissa Taylor, *Soldiers of Christ: Preaching in Late Medieval and Reformation France*, (New York: Oxford University Press, 1992), pp. 73–76. Taylor examined 1,337 late-medieval sermons, and found that 76 percent of the quotations were taken from the Bible. Similar conclusions were reached by Hervé Martin, *Le métier de prédicateur en France septentrionale à la fin du moyen âge (1350–1520)* (Paris: Cerf, 1988), p. 246.

35. James J. Murphy, "Rhetoric in Fourteenth-Century Oxford," *Medium Aevum* 34 (1965): 1–20, at 9 n.41. Reprinted in Murphy, *Latin Rhetoric and Education in the Middle Ages and Renaissance* (Aldershot: Ashgate, 2005) §ix.

36. Simon Tugwell traced this analogy to Bernard of Clairvaux (d. 1153) and Humbert of Romans (d. 1277), the fifth master general of the Dominican Order. See "*De huiusmodi sermonibus texitur omnis recta predicatio*: Changing Attitude Towards the Word of God," *De l'homélie au sermon: Histoire de la prédication médiévale*, ed.

Jacqueline Hamesse and Xavier Harmand (Louvain-la-Neuve: Publications de l'Institut d'études médiévales, 1993), pp. 159–68.

37. Servus, "Preaching in the Thirteenth Century." Similar means were suggested by Basevorn, "The Form of Preaching," §39 (Krul, *Three Medieval Rhetorical Arts*, pp. 180–84; Charland, *Artes praedicandi*, pp. 291–95).

38. On the connection between preaching and exegesis, see Louis-Jacques Bataillon, "Similitudines et exempla dans les sermons du XIIIème siècle," in *The Bible in the Medieval World: Essays in Honour of Beryl Smalley*, ed. Katherine Walsh and Diana Wood (Oxford: Blackwell, 1985), pp. 191–205; reprinted in Bataillon, *La Prédication au XIIIe siècle en France et Italie* (Aldershot: Ashgate, 1993), §x; Bataillon, "De la lectio à la predicatio: Commentaires bibliques et sermons au XIIIe siècle," *Revue des sciences philosophiques et théologiques* 70 (1986): 559–75; reprinted in Bataillon, *La Prédication*, §v; and Bataillon, "Early Scholastic and Mendicant Preaching." Other works that engage with the connection between preaching and exegesis are Marie Anne Mayeski, "Reading the Word"; and Harry Caplan, "The Four Senses of Scriptural Interpretation and the Mediaeval Theory of Preaching," *Speculum* 4 (1929): 282–90. For the question of the delivery of Bernard's sermons on the Song of Songs, see Christopher Holdsworth, "Were the Sermons of St. Bernard on the Song of Songs Ever Preached?" in *Medieval Monastic Preaching*, pp. 295–318.

39. *Primo eam deposuit in signum feruide charitatis. Solent enim homines calore nimio estuantes exponere uestimenta. In hoc ergo quod B. Bartholomeus pellem suam deposuit, ostenditur quanto igne amoris plenus fuit. Hoc significatum est, ubi dicitur: Diligebat Ionathas Dauid quasi animam suam. Nam expoliauit se tunica sua, et dedit eam Dauid. Per Ionatham qui donum columbe interpretatur, beatus Bartholomeus intelligitur, qui dono Spiritus sancti fuit repletus. Iste ergo qui diligebat Dauid, id est Christum sicut animam suam, tunica se expoliauit, et dedit Dauid, quando propter Christi amorem se excoriari permisit.* Iacobus de Voragine, "Sermon IV for the feast of Saint Bartholomew."

40. *Biblia cum glossa ordinaria: Facsimile Reprint of the editio princeps Adolph Rusch of Strassburg 1480/81*, ed. Karlfried Froehlich and Margaret T. Gibson, 4 vols. (Turnhout: Brepols, 1992), ii:380.

41. For this process, see Bériou, "Pellem pro pelle."

42. Following the common *Aaz* version of the *Interpretations* (London, BL Stowe MS 1 fol. 449rb): *Columba veniens vel columbe donum sive columba dans aut columbe donatio.* On the Interpretationes, see d'Esneval, "Perfectionnement d'un instrument de travail," pp. 163–75.

43. These manuscripts are described in Laura Light's chapter in this volume.

44. Anne Hudson, *The Premature Reformation: Wycliffite Texts and Lollard History* (Oxford: Clarendon, 1988), pp. 269–70. This is evident in Wyclif's Latin sermons §30 and §31: *Iohannis Wyclif Sermones: Now First Edited from the Manuscripts*, ed. Iohann Loserth, 4 vols. (London, 1887–90), 4:256–62, 262–75. Interestingly, while admonishing preachers for overly rhetorical sermons, the structure of

Wyclif's sermons follows the new form of preaching and some of his proofs are taken from extrabiblical sources or modified the biblical text itself. See Marsden's chapter in this volume.

45.  This is evident in the similarity between the words of John Hooper (d. 1555), a sixteenth-century reforming bishop, and G. R. Owst, a twentieth-century biblical scholar. Hooper wrote, "a copy of vain glory and crafty connexion of words, to satisfy the most part of the audience and to flatter the richest; wrestling and writing the simple verity of God's words into as many forms and divers sentences, as be vain and carnal affections wrought within his ungodly heart." See "A Declaration of the Ten Holy Commandments of Almighty God," in *Early Writings of John Hooper, D. D., Lord Bishop of Gloucester and Worcester, Martyr, 1555*, ed. Samuel Carr Parker Society Publications 11 (Cambridge: Cambridge University Press, 1843), pp. 249–430, and also 325–26, 335–39. Centuries later, Owst wrote, "The sacred page had clearly fallen, in the general decadence of preaching, to the mere level of any hand-book of collected narrations or moralized Properties of Things. Its living historic continuity of thought and action was being ruthlessly ignored. Its various characters and objects were being wrenched from their context, distorted or mutilated into mere passive conveniences for moral dilation, a mere lifeless framework to be set up and arranged, as the preacher pleases, to suit the formal superstructure of his discourse." G. R. Owst, *Literature and Pulpit in Medieval England: A Neglected Chapter in the History of English Letters and of the English People*, 2d. ed. (Oxford: Blackwell, 1961), p. 66. See Spencer, *English Preaching*, pp. 321–34; and John W. Blench, *Preaching in England in the Late Fifteenth and Sixteenth Centuries: A Study of English Sermons, 1450–c.1600* (Oxford: Blackwell, 1964), pp. 87–94.

# The Bible and the Individual

## THE THIRTEENTH-CENTURY PARIS BIBLE

*Laura Light*

The transformation of the Bible in the thirteenth century was a European-wide phenomenon that in many respects represents the beginning of the Bible as we know it today. For the first time in the Middle Ages, thirteenth-century Bibles were, like modern Bibles, usually pandects, that is, books that contained the complete Old and New Testaments in one volume. Thirteenth-century Bibles, like modern Bibles, varied in size, but many were very small indeed. Finally, for the first time in the Middle Ages, in the thirteenth century Bibles were copied in significant numbers, making them much more widely available to individuals than they had been earlier. These developments are true of Bibles produced everywhere in Western Europe. The history of the Bible known as the Paris Bible, in contrast, is the story of one particular type of Bible, defined in terms of its text, that was very important in Paris and for the development of the modern Bible.

The number of thirteenth-century Bibles surviving from Paris that belong to the same general textual type—that are, in other words, examples of Paris Bibles—is remarkable. We will examine what this means, beginning with a description of the Paris Bible, and explore the questions

of its origin and use in the thirteenth century.[1] It is, however, also important to remember that the tendency to see the history of the thirteenth-
century Bible exclusively through the lens of the Paris Bible distorts the
history of the Latin Vulgate during these years; the histories of the Bible
in England, Spain, Italy, and indeed in the rest of France, although they
have received less attention, are important in their own right and are
areas that deserve further research.[2]

The importance of Paris both as a large and vibrant urban center and,
more particularly, as a center for commercial book production forms
the background of our discussion.[3] Together these factors made the
Paris Bible possible. The Capetian kings made Paris their capital, and
as royal power grew, so did the city. During the reigns of Louis VII (1137–
80), Philip Augustus (1180–1223), and Saint Louis (1226–70), building projects included the Cathedral of Notre Dame, the royal chapel (Sainte-
Chapelle), and new walls encircling the city, all testifying to the city's
unique importance and wealth. Paris was known throughout Europe as a
center of learning. In 1210 William the Breton proclaimed: "In that time
the study of letters flourished in Paris. Never before at any time or in any
part of the world, neither in Athens nor Egypt, had there been so many
scholars. The reason for this is not only the special beauty of the city and
its affluence but also the freedom and special privileges that King Philip
and his father before him conferred upon the scholars."[4] The University
of Paris attracted students and masters from everywhere in Europe; its
faculty of theology was certainly preeminent.

All these factors—the presence of the monarchy and the members of
the royal court, the wealth and security of the city, and the flourishing
university—made Paris the home of the most important commercial
book trade in Europe in the thirteenth century. This fact is crucial to the
understanding of the history of the Paris Bible. The Paris Bible was a
product of the commercial book trade, a book purchased by students and
masters from the university (including many from the new mendicant
orders), as well as by other members of the church, the monarchy, and the
court, and by many others who did business in Paris.

The designation *Paris Bible* is directly based on the observation that
numerous Bibles copied in Paris in the thirteenth century share certain
common features. It is, in other words, a description of a common type of
Bible. Some knowledge of the methodology used by historians of the
medieval Vulgate is a necessary preliminary to our discussion of the thirteenth-century Bible. Scholars begin by asking which books of the canon

are included and in what order they are arranged. In contrast to today's Bible, medieval Bibles were arranged according to many different orders. Samuel Berger, the great nineteenth-century historian of the medieval Bible, recorded 212 orders in an appendix to his *Histoire de la Vulgate pendant les premiers siècles du moyen âge.*[5]

Next, historians of the Bible examine the prologues. In medieval Bibles the majority of the biblical books were preceded by nonbiblical prologues. Some of these prologues were by the translator of the Vulgate, St. Jerome, or circulated in the Middle Ages attributed to him. Other prologues were even older; some were more recent. Their content also varied, ranging from Jerome's discussions of his translations to introductions to the actual content of the biblical book.[6] The reference tool used to identify prologues is Stegmüller's *Repertorium biblicum medii aevi,*[7] which provides the opening and closing words of approximately 560 prologues, each identified by a number. Stegmüller's *Repertorium* was designed to bring together information from many sources. It was not intended to be the final word on the topic or to contribute new research. There are prologues that were not included in the *Repertorium,* and the notes on the authors and editions of prologues, are not, and were not intended to be, authoritative. The study of biblical prologues requires careful attention to details. Many begin with identical or very similar phrases, and since it is sometimes impossible to identify prologues only from their opening words, it is good scholarly practice to record both the beginnings and endings of prologues.

It is also important to examine how the text of the Bible is divided into chapters. Many different systems of chapters were used in manuscripts of the Bible during the Middle Ages.[8] Most manuscripts dating before c. 1230 also included lists at the beginning of each biblical book, known as *capitula* lists, that summarized the contents of the book, chapter by chapter, and provided the reader with a summary of the text. These lists originally corresponded to the actual chapter divisions found in the accompanying biblical book. Later in the Middle Ages, however, because of the complexities of transmission, even this basic agreement cannot be taken for granted, and manuscripts can include capitula lists that are unrelated to the actual divisions found in the biblical text.[9]

The order of the books, the prologues, the chapter lists, and the chapter divisions throughout the Bible are the essential extrabiblical elements studied by historians of the medieval Bible. They provide a window into what the users and makers of any given Bible considered to be important and can also point to the origin of the Bible. Textual families—that is Bibles descending from a common exemplar or exemplars—tend to share the same order, choice of prologues, and chapters. This evidence, however, has to be weighed carefully. Scribes sometimes introduced changes into the manuscripts they were copying. Exact, uniform copies are relatively rare in the world of the manuscript Bible, and small differences do not mean two Bibles are not related. Conversely, manuscripts with similar (or even identical) orders, prologues, and chapters do not always have a real textual affinity. All these external textual features could—and did—circulate independently of the actual biblical text. Moreover, before the thirteenth century, pandects were relatively rare. Most Bibles were multivolume, and the circulation of single books such as the Psalms, or groups of related books, such as the Gospels, the Pauline Epistles, or the Prophets, was numerically more important during most of the Middle Ages than the circulation of the complete Bible (whether in one or many volumes).[10] Consequently, many Bibles have different parent manuscripts for different biblical books and for different parts of the accompanying extrabiblical apparatus.

Studying the actual text of the Bible presents challenges. We are, however, fortunate to have good critical editions to guide our work. In a manuscript culture, any written text is likely to change slightly in successive copies. These textual alterations can be caused by many factors: scribes made simple copying mistakes and misread their exemplars or inadvertently skipped words or lines of the text. The influence of the scribe's memory also played a part. When copying a text that you know well, it is easy to copy what you think is correct rather than copying your exemplar word for word. Much of the Bible was known to medieval scribes through the liturgy, which sometimes included versions of the Bible predating Jerome's Vulgate translation. All these errors inadvertently introduced changes into the text. Scholars throughout the Middle Ages also corrected the text with varying outcomes. Critical editions record the differences in the surviving manuscripts. By comparing these differences, it is possible to reconstruct the original text. Critical editions of the Latin Vulgate include the Oxford edition of the New Testament, which was begun in 1898, and the critical edition of the Old Testament prepared by the Benedictine monks of the monastery of St. Jerome in Rome; the first volume appeared in 1926 and the last in 1994.[11] The formidable research into the text of the versions predating Jerome by the Vetus Latina Institute at Beuron has resulted in a number of superb editions; their research (still in progress) often touches on the history of the Vulgate.[12] The Bible is a long text. Collating—that is, comparing the readings of the text, word by word with the critical edition of the Bible, and/or other manuscripts—is time-consuming indeed and impossible from a practical point of view. A common solution is to focus either on short passages in a small number of biblical books or on selected "test" readings, known to be textually interesting, from a wider range of different books. These solutions allow us a certain degree of insight into the biblical text but are not perfect.

Since the late nineteenth century, historians of the Bible have recognized that many of the Bibles copied in Paris during the thirteenth century share certain common characteristics.[13] These characteristics allow us to identify Bibles that we can call examples of the Paris Bible. The order of the books in Paris Bibles is almost identical with that of the modern Bible, with the exception that the Pauline Epistles follow immediately after the Gospels and before Acts: Octateuch (Genesis, Exodus, Leviticus, Numbers, Deuteronomy, Joshua, Judges, and Ruth), 1–4 Kings, 1–2 Chronicles (followed by the Prayer of Manasses, Stegmüller 93.2), Ezra, Nehemiah, 2 Ezra (= 3 Ezra), Tobit, Judith, Esther, Job, Psalms, the Sapiential books (Proverbs, Ecclesiastes, the Song of Songs, Wisdom, and Ecclesiasticus), the Prophets (Isaiah, Jeremiah, Lamentations, Baruch, Ezekiel, Daniel, and the twelve minor prophets), 1–2 Maccabees, the Gospels, the Pauline Epistles, Acts, the Catholic Epistles, and the Apocalypse.

This order, which was new to the history of the Latin Vulgate (Bibles copied before the thirteenth century were not arranged in this way), groups all of the historical books at the beginning of the Old Testament, thus emphasizing the literal sense of the text and the importance of biblical history. The only exception are the two books of Maccabees, which recount events closest in time to the New Testament and are placed at the end of the Old Testament. It was an order that was well suited to the way the Bible was studied in the schools starting in the second half of the twelfth century.[14] The popularity of the *Historia Scholastica* by Petrus Comestor (died c. 1178), for example, a convenient retelling of biblical history, similarly testifies to the importance placed on studying the literal and historical sense of the biblical text (on the interpretation of the Bible, see the chapters by Harris and van Liere in this volume).[15]

Paris Bibles also include a set of sixty-four prologues.[16] These prologues are important because they circulated together as a set found in numerous Bibles with little variation. It is the number of Bibles with these same prologues (more than the actual prologues included, most of which are found in earlier manuscripts) that sets them apart, both from earlier medieval Bibles and from Bibles copied elsewhere in Europe during the thirteenth century. This set does include, however, six prologues of special interest that are not found in manuscripts of the unglossed Vulgate before the thirteenth century: the prologue to Ecclesiastes, "Memini Me" (Stegmüller 462) from Jerome's commentary on Ecclesiastes; the prologue to Amos by an unknown author, "Hic Amos" (Stegmüller 513); two prologues to Maccabees by Rabanus Maurus, "Cum sim promptus," and "Memini me" (Stegmüller 547 and 553); the prologue to Matthew, "Matheus cum primo" (Stegmüller 589), which is a revision of the longer prologue by Jerome to his commentary on the Gospels; and the prologue to the Apocalypse, "Omnes qui pie" (Stegmüller 839).[17] The origin of these prologues has never been investigated thoroughly, but there is a link between them and the prologues in the *Glossa ordinaria*. The Glossed Bible was created by twelfth-century schoolmen who gathered together the most important commentaries on the various books of the Bible and arranged them alongside the text of the Bible.[18] Glossed Bibles typically include many more prologues before each biblical book than does the Paris Bible, but the new prologues to Ecclesiastes, Amos, and Matthew circulated first in twelfth-century Glossed Bibles.[19]

The Paris Bible is also associated with the use of chapters that differ only slightly from the chapters still used today.[20] Traditionally, Stephen Langton, who taught in the Paris schools from c. 1180 until 1206 when he left to become archbishop of Canterbury, has been considered the author of the new chapters;[21] new research calls this attribution into question, however.[22] Chapter divisions themselves were not new, and many different systems of chapters circulated in earlier manuscripts. Earlier chapters, however, were used primarily to aid in reading and analyzing the biblical text. The practice of identifying biblical citations by book and chapter, which continues to be the primary use of biblical chapters today, dates only from the middle of the twelfth century. These first references were to one of the older systems of chapters. Early in the thirteenth century, references to modern chapters and to older chapters are found in the writings of Paris theologians. From around 1225, references to modern chapters are common.[23] As the practice of using chapters as the means of identifying citations (and conversely, of finding citations) became more widespread, it was inevitable that one system replaced the many in circulation. The modern chapters are found as early as the opening decades of the thirteenth century in some Parisian Bibles that also include older chapter divisions. In Bibles copied after c. 1230, modern chapters are typically the only chapters used.

The final extrabiblical element associated with the Paris Bible is the text known as the *Interpretation of Hebrew Names,* usually found at the end of the Bible after the Apocalypse. The widespread circulation of this text, not only in examples of the Paris Bible but also in Bibles produced throughout Europe after c. 1230, may seem odd from a modern perspective. It consists of interpretations of thousands of transliterated names found in the Bible—that is, the literal meaning of the name in Hebrew or its allegorical significance—and provided users of the Bible with a handy key to unfamiliar names to be used in biblical commentaries and sermons. The version beginning, "Aaz aprehendens vel apprehensio" ("Aaz [who is mentioned in Nehemiah] means taking hold, or seizing upon") is traditionally attributed to Stephen Langton and is based on a work by St. Jerome, though considerably expanded and reorganized in complete alphabetical order.[24] With only a few exceptions, the *Interpretation of Hebrew Names* is found in Bibles only after c. 1230; earlier versions are found in nonbiblical manuscripts.[25]

It is more difficult to study the actual text of the Bible, and most research on the text of the Paris Bible has been based on a comparison of a small number of selected passages in many manuscripts or, alternatively, by studying longer passages in only a few Bibles.[26] Real progress in our understanding of this aspect of the Paris Bible, and indeed, of the text of the late medieval Vulgate as a whole, depends on future scholars who are willing to study carefully the text of many Bibles through actual collations of representative sections of the biblical text. Nonetheless, one can cautiously observe that Bibles with the extrabiblical characteristics associated with the Paris Bible often, although by no means always, circulated with an identifiable text that was descended in part from three important earlier biblical recensions: the ninth-century Alcuinian and Theodulfian Bibles, and the Italian recension, which circulated in Italy in the tenth and eleventh centuries. (On the early text recensions, see van Liere's chapter in this volume.)[27] Twentieth-century scholars, including Niels Haastrup and Rainer Berndt, have demonstrated that the text found in examples of the Paris Bible was not a new text created in the thirteenth century but simply the textual type current in the schools, which had also circulated in many twelfth-century Glossed Bibles and commentaries.[28]

In the critical edition of the Old Testament Vulgate, three manuscripts were chosen as examples to represent this text, which the prominent member of the commission, and the editor in chief of the Pentateuch, Henri Quentin, called the "University Bible": Paris, Bibliothèque Mazarine MS 5, Paris, Bibliothèque nationale de France MSS Lat. 16719–22, and BNF MS Lat. 15467.[29] These Bibles were chosen by the Benedictine editors for reasons that can almost be considered random: the Mazarine manuscript was likely chosen because it includes a note that allows us to date it before 1231; Lat. 16719–22 is an important corrected Bible from the Dominican Convent of St. Jacques in Paris, and the third Bible, Lat. 15467, is also dated, 1270. They are examples of a textual type and should not be regarded as the source of the Paris text or as more important than many of the other hundreds of manuscripts that could have been chosen. Nonetheless, they teach us valuable lessons about the circulation of the Paris text and illustrate the fact that it was not confined only to Paris; the earliest of the three manuscripts, Mazarine 5, is English. Moreover, they also show that the Paris text circulated in Bibles without the extrabiblical elements of the Paris Bible (Mazarine 5 is arranged in a different order and includes other prologues; the Dominican Bible, Lat. 16719–22, also does not include the exact set of Paris prologues). Lastly, although all three of these Bibles can be grouped together in the same general textual family, their texts do differ.[30] Too little attention has been paid to the introductions to the later volumes of the Benedictine Vulgate, which include a careful reassessment of the text of these three Bibles. The editors concluded that the text of Lat. 15467 most accurately reflected the common Paris text; the text of Mazarine 5 was possibly closer to the text of twelfth-century Glossed Bibles, and the text and the marginal notes in Lat. 16719–22 were both the product of Dominican efforts to correct the Bible.[31]

The evolution of the Paris Bible was a two-stage process. The first Bibles with most of its characteristics were produced in Paris c. 1200.[32] These new one-volume Bibles, the proto-Paris Bibles, were among the most important products of the commercial booksellers, scribes, and illuminators who were establishing themselves in the city.[33] They are arranged according to the new order of the biblical books and include a related set of prologues (not identical to the Paris set of sixty-four, but notably including the six new prologues).[34] An examination of selected test passages indicates their text is the text that circulated in copies of the mature Paris Bible. They do not include the *Interpretation of Hebrew Names*.

The chapters used in this group distinguish them from the mature Paris Bible. In common with earlier manuscripts of the Vulgate, their text is divided according to older chapters, and they include *capitula* lists at the beginning of the biblical book. Indeed (and this is rare in the history of the Vulgate), they include the same set of capitula lists from Genesis to the Apocalypse, with little variation. This set was new, created for the proto-Paris Bible from new capitula lists, revisions of older lists, and unrevised older lists.[35] I know of no Bibles from this period that are divided only according to modern chapters, but some include both older chapter divisions and modern chapters. This is a feature found not only in some proto-Paris Bibles but also in Bibles that are textually unrelated to the mature Paris Bible.[36]

Proto-Paris Bibles were the product of a significant revision of the Vulgate, including the creation of a new order of the biblical books, a new set of prologues, and a new series of capitula lists. Their biblical text, like the text in the mature Paris Bible, was not new, but one current in the schools and found in manuscripts of the Glossed Bible. We do not know the exact circumstances surrounding the creation of this Bible, but it was a success. The overall number of Bibles copied in Paris in the opening decades of the thirteenth century is significant, although certainly smaller than the remarkable number of Bibles copied after c. 1230. I have studied twenty-seven Bibles from this period; fourteen are examples of the proto-Paris Bible, and another five are closely related; the remaining eight are unrelated. These eight Bibles, although outside our present focus, are evidence of the innovation and experimentation that characterize this period.

The transition to Bibles that are examples of the mature Paris Bible can be found as early as the end of the 1220s and the early 1230s. They were the result of only minor changes to the proto-Paris Bibles: slight changes in the set of prologues, the addition of the *Interpretation of Hebrew Names* at the end of the Bible, and, most importantly, the exclusive use of modern chapter divisions. Three Bibles from these years, a Bible sold at Sotheby's,[37] Paris, Bibliothèque de l'Arsenal MS 70,[38] and Baltimore, Walters Art Gallery MS 60,[39] are among the earliest examples of Parisian Bibles divided only according to modern chapters; the capitula lists and older chapter divisions of proto-Paris Bibles are absent. The earliest dated example (although not the earliest surviving example) of a Bible with all the features of the mature Paris Bible is Dôle, Bibliothèque municipale MS 15; we know this Bible was copied in 1234 because it was signed and dated by its scribe, Thomas.[40]

There is a remarkable increase in the number of Bibles copied in Paris after ca. 1230. We lack a definitive survey of all these Bibles, but the number included in Robert Branner's study of thirteenth-century illumination in Paris gives an idea of the volume of production. Branner identified seventeen complete one-volume Bibles that he dated c. 1200–30; he found over one hundred that he dated approximately between 1230 and the middle of the century, and around sixty that he dated from the 1230s and later.[41] These represent only a fraction of the Bibles copied in Paris in the thirteenth century. There are illuminated Bibles that were unknown to Branner, and, more importantly, Branner was interested only in Bibles with painted initials.[42]

Since the nineteenth century, scholars have noted the relative uniformity observable in Bibles copied in Paris after c. 1230.[43] The number of Bibles that include the features we have associated with the Paris Bible is an important development that is unprecedented in the earlier history of the medieval Vulgate. Equally important, however, is the fact that the texts of many Bibles copied in Paris show significant variations. This is demonstrated in the sample of sixty-nine Parisian Bibles studied here. All the Bibles studied include the new order of the biblical books—with only one exception (and one Bible that includes Ezra 4–6)—and all include the modern chapters. The *Interpretation of Hebrew Names* is found in all but ten of the Bibles. Interestingly, this text circulated independently of the Paris prologues and the characteristic text; there are "typical" Paris Bibles without the *Interpretations*, and unrelated Bibles that include them. Thirty-three Bibles are typical examples of Paris Bibles and include the new order, the set of prologues, modern chapters, and the characteristic readings. An additional eighteen Bibles are closely related and differ only in the prologues included (although they all include the six "new" prologues). Seven Bibles were copied from exemplars differing from the Paris Bible in important respects; all but one includes the new order, but they do not include the Paris prologues, nor the textual variants characteristic of the Paris text. The remaining eleven Bibles are difficult to characterize simply, but in general are mixed, with some features of the Paris Bible and others that are unrelated. Five of these Bibles include the Paris prologues but lack some of the characteristic readings, serving as important reminders that extrabiblical characteristics are not always a reliable guide to the biblical text.[44]

The pattern of circulation seen in the texts of these Bibles is key to understanding the Paris Bible. Roger Bacon, the thirteenth-century Franciscan scientist and social critic, refers to the Paris Bible as the "Bible in common use, that is, of Paris" ("exemplar vulgatum, hoc est parisiensis").[45]

Moreover, he links the origin of this Bible with the commercial booksell-ers (booksellers he describes scathingly as *illiterati et uxorati*, "illiterate and married") and complains that they were completely unconcerned with the quality of the text.[46] The Paris Bible was not a Bible established to bring uniformity to the Bibles used in the Paris classroom, and it was certainly not an "official" Bible in any sense of the term.[47] It was simply the most common Bible copied in Paris and a significant commercial suc-cess. The pattern of textual uniformity, together with an important degree of textual diversity, can be explained most easily if we remember the sheer quantity of Bibles copied in Paris after c. 1230. Every Bible had to be copied from a preexisting copy; in the context of such rapid produc-tion, a relative degree of uniformity was inevitable, but it was never a requirement. Although this scenario is only hypothetical, we can perhaps imagine that someone—a master from the theology faculty, a student, or a former student, possibly a Franciscan or Dominican—commissioned a Bible from a Paris bookseller and specified that it include the features we associate with the Paris Bible. This Bible, whose text and other features answered the needs of scholars, preachers, and collectors, proved to be much in demand, and in the context of a flourishing commercial book-trade it was inevitable that numerous similar Bibles would be produced.[48]

The Paris Bible was thus a product of the commercial booktrade. It is also true that thirteenth-century theologians were interested in the text of the Bible, and aware that the text in various manuscripts differed. The Franciscans and Dominicans were especially active in this respect and produced a number of biblical *correctoria*, manuals listing variant readings from Latin Bibles as well as comparing these readings with the biblical text as it is transmitted in patristic writings as well as in Hebrew and Greek Bibles. The correctoria are important, but they were most likely used primarily as exegetical tools by commentators and preachers. They were collections of useful variants rather than guides for producing new, corrected Bibles.[49]

The Paris Bible is a descriptive term denoting a certain textual type; copies vary widely in terms of size and other details of their physical pre-sentation. The Bible copied in 1234 mentioned earlier (Dôle 15), for exam-ple, is an example of the remarkable thirteenth-century invention, the "pocket Bible." It is a small, compact volume, copied on extremely thin, almost translucent parchment, and measures only 158 x 105 (written space, 110 x 70) mm.[50] Many other Bibles copied in Paris in the thirteenth century were larger, and the sample of Bibles studied here suggests no one format was dominant. These Bibles also differ in the amount of decoration they contain, varying from very expensive volumes with exquisite historiated initials to much humbler manuscripts with simple pen initials marking the beginning of the biblical books.

The Paris Bible, as well as other textually related Bibles copied in Paris (and indeed, throughout Europe in the thirteenth century), was embraced and used by many segments of society. Paris Bibles were owned by the very wealthy members of the court and church hierarchy and were treasured for their beauty and the holiness of their text.[51] Paris Bibles were also used by the masters and students of the Paris schools and by the mendicant friars, the Franciscans and Dominicans, who needed Bibles they could bring with them on their travels.[52]

The use of the Paris Bible by students and masters in the theology faculty needs to be treated carefully. The Bible used *in* the classroom throughout the thirteenth century was almost certainly the Glossed Bible. Classroom lectures and commentaries on the Scriptures started with the Bible and its accompanying commentary and added another layer of interpretation on top of that base.[53] Nonetheless, we need to remember that the same students and masters who studied the Bible and its accompanying gloss were also using the Bible in preaching and disputations (it also seems probable that students who could not afford to own a multivolume set of the complete Bible with the gloss did own one-volume unglossed Bibles). The one-volume Bible was searchable; it was, in other words, not only a book to read and to meditate upon but also (and perhaps more importantly) a book to use to find the passage needed for a sermon or commentary. The thirteenth century is known for new tools such as the biblical concordance, other indexes to the Bible, and alphabetical distinction collections (guides to the figurative meanings of biblical words) that reflect the new pastoral mission of the Church and the promotion of preaching as a means of meeting the challenge of heresy.[54] The one-volume Bible was the most important of all these tools and, as such, was used not only by the mendicant friars, but also by the church as a whole, including the secular masters and students of theology (on preaching from the Bible see Poleg's chapter in this volume).

The Paris Bible never became the only biblical text copied in Paris, and it was certainly not the only Bible copied elsewhere in Europe; indeed, although the modern chapters and the *Interpretation of Hebrew Names* and, to some extent, the new order of the biblical books, are found in Bibles copied throughout Europe, the influence of the new set of prologues and the characteristic text was much less.[55] The Paris Bible was a text, however, that was destined to have an enduring place in the history of the Vulgate. The text printed by Johann Gutenberg (c. 1400–68) in the Gutenberg Bible (printed in Mainz around 1453–55), which was not only the first printed Bible but the first book printed with movable type, is a direct descendant of the Paris Bibles of the thirteenth century.[56] Moreover, the text of the Clementine Bible of 1592, which remained the official text of the Roman Catholic Church until 1979, is also essentially an example of a Paris Bible.[57]

## Notes

1. This study is based on twenty-seven Bibles from c. 1200–30, and sixty-nine Bibles dating ca. 1230–1300, which are assigned to Paris based on the evidence of their script and decoration. This is a fraction of the total number of Bibles that may have been copied in thirteenth-century Paris, but the story they tell is, I believe, generally true. Not all of these Bibles are illuminated, but I am especially indebted to the studies of Parisian illumination in the thirteenth century by Patricia Stirnemann, François Avril, and Robert Branner. See Patricia Stirnemann, "Nouvelles pratiques en matière d'enluminure au temps de Philippe Auguste," in *La France de Philippe Auguste. Le Temps des Mutations*, ed. Robert-Henri Bautier, Colloque internationaux du Centre National de la Recherche Scientifique 602 (Paris: CNRS, 1982), pp. 955–80; François Avril, "À quand remontent les premiers ateliers d'enlumineurs laïcs à Paris?" *Les Dossiers de l'Archéologie. Enluminure gothique* 16 (1976): 36–44; and "Un Manuscrit d'auteurs classiques et ses illustrations," in *The Year 1200. A Symposium* (New York: Metropolitan Museum of Art, 1975), pp. 267–68, n. 3; and Robert Branner, *Manuscript Painting in Paris During the Reign of Saint Louis: A Study of Styles,* California Studies in the History of Art 18 (Berkeley: University of California Press, 1977).

2. In general, see Laura Light, "The Thirteenth-Century Bible: The Paris Bible and Beyond," in *The New Cambridge History of the Bible*, ed. E. Ann Matter and Richard Marsden (Cambridge: Cambridge University Press, 2011). On the text of English Bibles, see Adelaide Bennett, "The Place of Garrett 28 in Thirteenth-Century Illumination," (Ph.D diss., Columbia University, 1973), pp. 36–113; and "Additions to the William of Devon Group," *Art Bulletin* 54 (1972): 31–40, at 31. On Italian Bibles, see Sabina Magrini, "Production and Use of Latin Bible Manuscripts in Italy During the Thirteenth and Fourteenth Centuries," *Manuscripta* 51 (2007): 209–57, especially 236–47; and Sabina Magrini, "La Bibbia all'università (secoli XII–XIV): La 'Bible de Paris' e la sua influenza sulla produzione scritturale coeva," in *Forme e modelli della tradizione manoscritta della bibbia,* ed. Paolo Cherubini (Vatican City: Scuola Vaticana di Paleografia, Diplomatica e Archivistica, 2005), pp. 407–21, at 419–21.

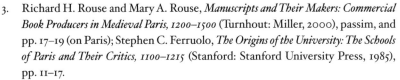

3. Richard H. Rouse and Mary A. Rouse, *Manuscripts and Their Makers: Commercial Book Producers in Medieval Paris, 1200–1500* (Turnhout: Miller, 2000), passim, and pp. 17–19 (on Paris); Stephen C. Ferruolo, *The Origins of the University: The Schools of Paris and Their Critics, 1100–1215* (Stanford: Stanford University Press, 1985), pp. 11–17.

4. Quoted in Ferruolo, *Origins of the University*, p. 12, from *Historia de vita et gestis Philippi Augusti*, ed. Henri-François Delaborde, in *Oeuvres de Rigord et de Guillaume le Breton, historiens de Philippe-Auguste*, 2 vols. (Paris: Librairie Renouard, H. Loones, successeur, 1882–85), 1:230.

5. Samuel Berger, *Histoire de la Vulgate pendant les premiers siècles du moyen âge* (Paris: Librarie Hachette, 1893), pp. 301–6, and 331–39; updated in *Vetus Latina: Die Reste der altlateinischen Bibel nach Petrus Sabatier neu gesammelt und herausgegeben von der Erzabtei Beuron* (Freiburg im Breisgau: Herder, 1949–), XI/1:222–300, although Berger is still useful; see also Pierre-Maurice Bogaert, "La Bible latine des origins au Moyen Âge: Aperçu historique, état des questions," *Revue théologique de Louvain* 19 (1988): 137–59 and 276–314, at 301–3; and Richard Marsden, *The Text of the Old Testament in Anglo-Saxon England*, Cambridge Studies in Anglo-Saxon England 15 (Cambridge: Cambridge University Press, 1995), pp. 37–39.

6. For editions of prologues, see Donatien de Bruyne, *Préfaces de la Bible latine* (Namur: A. Godenne, 1920; not widely available); some are edited in *Biblia sacra iuxta latinam vulgatam versionem ad codicum fidem . . . cura et studio monachorum abbatiae pontificiae Sancti Hieronymi in urbe O. S. B. edita*, ed. Henri Quentin et al., 18 vols. (Rome: Typis polyglottis vaticanis, 1926–94); and in *Novum testamentum domini nostri Iesu Christi latine secundum editionem sancti Hieronymi*, ed. John Wordsworth and Henry J. White (Oxford: Clarendon, 1889–1954). See also Samuel Berger, *Les Préfaces jointes aux livres de la bible dans les manuscrits de la Vulgate* (Paris: Impr. Nationale, 1902); and Maurice Schild, *Abendländische Bibelvorreden bis zur Lutherbibel*, Quellen und Forschungen zum Reformationsgeschichte 39 (Gütersloh: G. Mohn, 1970).

7. *Repertorium biblicum Medii Aevi*, ed. Friedrich Stegmüller (Madrid: Consejo superior de Investigaciones científicas, 1950–61), and *Supplement*, with the assistance of Nicolaus Reinhardt (Madrid: Consejo Superior de Investigaciones Cientificas, 1976–80), 1:253–306 and 8:220–29.

8. Edited in Donatien de Bruyne, *Sommaires, divisions et rubriques de la Bible latine* (Namur: A. Godenne, 1914; not widely available); some are edited in *Biblia sacra* and *Novum testamentum*. See also Berger, *Histoire*, pp. 307–15.

9. Early in the Middle Ages, capitula lists and the chapter divisions were usually carefully numbered; by the twelfth and early thirteenth centuries there are many examples of Bibles with unnumbered capitula lists and chapter divisions (capitula lists are rare after c. 1230); the topic deserves further study.

10. Marsden, *Text of the Old Testament*, pp. 30–31, and 39–49; Rosamund McKitterick, "Carolingian Bible Production: the Tours Anomaly," in *The Early Medieval Bible: Its Production, Decoration and Use*, ed. Richard Gameson (Cambridge: Cam-

bridge University Press, 1994), pp. 63–77, at 76; and Patrick McGurk, "The Oldest Manuscripts of the Latin Bible," in *Early Medieval Bible*, pp. 1–23, at 2–4.

11. *Novum testamentum*, and *Biblia sacra*; *Biblia sacra iuxta vulgatam versionem*, ed. Robert Weber et al., 4th. ed. (Stuttgart: Deutsche Bibelgesellschaft, 1994), is a compact edition convenient for personal use; its text is based on the two earlier critical editions, with some revisions, and it includes an abbreviated critical apparatus.

12. *Vetus latina*; founded in 1945, the goal of the Vetus Latina Institute is to completely collate and provide critical editions of all surviving fragments of the Old Latin translations.

13. Jean Pierre Paulin Martin, "Le texte parisien de la Vulgate latine," *Le Muséon* 8 (1889): 444–66, at 446–47 and 456; Berger, *Les Préfaces*, p. 28; more recently, see Laura Light, "Versions et révisions du texte biblique," in *Le Moyen Âge et la Bible*, ed. Pierre Riché and Guy Lobrichon, Bible de tous les temps 4 (Paris: Beauchesne, 1984), pp. 55–93, at 79–80; Light, "Roger Bacon and the Origin of the Paris Bible," *Revue bénédictine* 111 (2001): 483–507, at 498–99; Guy Lobrichon, "Les éditions de la Bible latine dans les universités du XIIIe siècle," in *La Bibbia del XIII secolo: Storia del testo, storia dell'esegesi. Convegno della Società Internazionale per lo studio del Medioevo Latino (SISMEL) Firenze, 1–2 giugno 2001*, ed. Giuseppe Cremascoli and Francesco Santi (Florence: SISMEL, Edizioni del Galluzzo, 2004), pp. 15–34, at 19–22; and Sabina Magrini, "La 'Bible parisienne' e i Vangeli," in *I Vangeli dei popoli. La parola e l'immagine del Cristo nelle culture e nella storia*, ed. Franceso D'Aiuto, Giovanni Morello, and Ambrogio M. Piazzoni (Vatican City, Rome: Biblioteca Apostolica Vaticana, Rinnovamento nella Spirito Santo, 2000), pp. 99–105, at 99–100.

14. Laura Light, "French Bibles c. 1200–30: A New Look at the Origins of the Paris Bible," in *The Early Medieval Bible*, pp. 155–76, at 159–63. The thirteenth-century order is almost exactly that of the fourth-century Greek Bible, the Codex Vaticanus (Vatican City, Biblioteca Apostolica Vaticana MS Graec. 1209), but there is no reason to think this manuscript had any influence on the thirteenth-century order (see Berger, *Histoire*, p. 304; and Marsden, *Text of the Old Testament*, p. 203).

15. David Luscombe, "Peter Comestor," in *The Bible in the Medieval World: Essays in Memory of Beryl Smalley*, ed. Katherine Walsh and Diana Wood, Studies in Church History Subsidia 4 (Oxford: Blackwell, 1985), pp. 109–29, at 110–12, 118–21; Beryl Smalley, *The Study of the Bible in the Middle Ages* (Notre Dame, IN: University of Notre Dame Press, 1964), pp. 83–106 and 196–263.

16. Listed in Neil R. Ker, *Medieval Manuscripts in British Libraries*, 5 vols. (Oxford: Clarendon, 1969–2002), 1:96–98, and in Branner, *Manuscript Painting*, pp. 154–55.

17. Light, "French Bibles," pp. 163–68; Lobrichon, "Les éditions," pp. 20–21 and 29; see also Guy Lobrichon, "Une nouveauté: les gloses de la Bible," in *Le Moyen Âge et la Bible*, pp. 95–114, at 113.

18. Smalley, *Study of the Bible*, pp. 46–66; Lobrichon, "Une nouveauté," pp. 95–114; Christopher de Hamel, *The Book: A History of the Bible* (New York: Phaidon,

2001), 107–11; de Hamel, *Glossed Books of the Bible and the Origins of the Paris Booktrade* (Woodbridge: Brewer, 1984); Margaret T. Gibson, "The Place of the *Glossa Ordinaria* in Medieval Exegesis," in *Ad Litteram, Authoritative Texts and their Medieval Readers*, ed. Mark D. Jordan and Kent Emery (Notre Dame, IN: University of Notre Dame Press, 1992), pp. 5–27; and *Biblia latina cum glossa ordinaria. Facsimile Reprint of the editio princeps Adolph Rusch of Strassburg 1480/81*, ed. Margaret T. Gibson and Karlfried Froehlich (Turnhout: Brepols, 1992).

19. Light, "French Bibles," pp. 164–65; and Lobrichon, "Les éditions," pp. 20–21; the remaining "new" prologues are also found in the gloss, but appear later, ca. 1200–30.

20. The use of numbered verses dates from the sixteenth century; Paul Saenger, "The Impact of the Early Printed Page on the Reading of the Bible," in *The Bible as Book: The First Printed Editions*, ed. Paul Saenger and Kimberly van Kampen (London: British Library, 1999), pp. 31–51, at 43.

21. Otto Schmid, *Über verschiedene Eintheilungen der Heiligen Schrift insbesondere über die Capitel Eintheilungen Stephan Langtons im XIII. Jahrhunderts* (Graz: Leuschner and Lubensky, 1892), pp. 56–103; Martin, "Le texte parisien," pp. 458–65; Amaury d'Esneval, "La division de la vulgate latine en chapitres dans l'édition parisienne du XIIIe siècle," *Revue des sciences philosophiques et théologique* 62 (1978): 559–68, at 561.

22. Paul Saenger, "The Birth of Modern Chapters," in "The Latin Bible as Codex," A. S. W. Rosenbach Lectures, April 2008; and Paul Saenger, "The Anglo-Hebraic Origins of the Modern Chapter Division of the Latin Bible," in *La fractura historiográfica: Las investigaciones de Edad Media y Renacimento desde el tercer milenio*, ed. Javier San José Lera, F. Javier Burguillo, and Laura Mier (Salamanca: Seminario de Estudios medievales y renacentistas, 2008), pp. 177–202.

23. Artur Landgraf, "Die Schriftzitate in der Scholastik um die Wende des 12. zum 13. Jahrhundert," *Biblica* 18 (1937): 77–94, especially 77–90; and Smalley, *Study of the Bible*, pp. 221–24.

24. *Repertorium*, 5:234, no. 7709; Martin, "Le texte parisien," pp. 66–70; Amaury d'Esneval, "Le perfectionnement d'un instrument de travail au début du XIIIe siècle: Les trois glossaires bibliques d'Etienne Langton," in *Culture et travail intellectuel dans l'occident médiéval*, ed. Geneviève Hasenohr-Esnos and Jean Longère (Paris: CNRS, 1981), pp. 163–75; Gilbert Dahan, "Lexiques hébreu/latin? Les receuils d'interprétations des noms hébraïques," in *Les manuscrits des lexiques et glossaires de l'antiquité tardive à la fin du moyen âge*, ed. Jacqueline Harnesse, Textes et études du moyen âge 4 (Louvain-la-Neuve: Fédération internationale des instituts d'études médiévale, 1996), pp. 480–526, at 486–89; and de Hamel, *The Book*, 112–13.

25. For example, Paris, Bibliothèque de l'Arsenal MS 65, a Bible dating before c. 1230, includes an early version of the *Interpretation of Hebrew Names*.

26. My research is based on an analysis of selected passages identified as characteristic of the Paris text by Henri Quentin, *Mémoire sur l'établissement du texte de la Vulgate*, Collectanea biblica latina 6 (Rome: Desclée; Paris: J. Gabalda, 1922), pp.

385–88; and Hans H. Glunz, *History of the Vulgate in England from Alcuin to Roger Bacon* (Cambridge: Cambridge University Press, 1933), pp. 259–84. The results are therefore by necessity only preliminary, but not without value.

27. For an overview of the Carolingian Bibles, see Marsden, *Text of the Old Testament*, pp. 18–24. For the Italian Bibles, see Quentin, *Mémoire*, pp. 361–84; Larry Ayres, "The Italian Giant Bibles: Aspects of Their Touronian Ancestry and Early History," in *The Early Medieval Bible*, pp. 125–54; and Emma Condello, "La Bibbia al tempo della riforma gregoriana: Le Bibbie atlantiche," in *Forme e modelli*, pp. 347–72.

28. First suggested by Glunz, *History of the Vulgate*, pp. 259–84 (esp. 262–63, and 277); Light, "Versions," pp. 81–82, summarizing and critiquing Glunz; Niels Haastrup, "Zur frühen Pariser Bibel—auf Grund Skandinavischer Handschriften," *Classica et mediaevalia: Revue danoise de philologie et d'histoire* 24 (1963): 242–69; Niels Haastrup, "Zur frühen Pariser Bibel—auf Grund Skandinavischer Handschriften," *Classica et mediaevalia: Revue danoise de philologie et d'histoire* 26 (1965): 394–401; and Rainer Berndt, *André de Saint-Victor (d. 1175): Exégète et théologien*, Biblioteca Victorina 2 (Turnhout: Brepols, 1991), pp. 119–48. See also Heinrich Schneider, *Der Text der Gutenbergbibel, zu ihrem 500 jährigen Jubiläum untersucht*, Bonner biblische Beiträge 7 (Bonn: P. Hanstein, 1954), pp. 19–78; his collations support the fact that the Paris text is found in earlier Glossed Bibles, though he did not advance this claim; see p. 21.

29. Quentin, *Mémoire*, pp. 385–88.

30. Schneider, *Text der Gutenbergbibel*, pp. 20–21 and 74–75; Haastrup, "Zur frühen Pariser Bibel" (1963), pp. 243 and 263.

31. *Biblia sacra*, 13:xlii–xliii.

32. This group is studied in greater depth in Light, "French Bibles," pp. 155–76.

33. For discussions of commercial book production in Paris in the late twelfth and early thirteenth centuries, see Rouse and Rouse, *Manuscripts and Their Makers*, pp. 17–49; Branner, *Manuscript Painting*, pp. 22–31 and appendix VA; Avril, "À quand remontent les premiers ateliers," pp. 36–44; and Avril, "Un Manuscrit d'auteurs classiques," pp. 267–68, note 3.

34. Light, "French Bibles," pp. 166–68; and Lobrichon, "Les éditions," p. 21. Proto-Paris Bibles lack the prologue to 2 Chronicles (Stegmüller 327) and the prologue to Wisdom (Stegmüller 468). They also show considerable variation in the prologues used before the Pauline Epistles.

35. Light, "French Bibles," pp. 168–71.

36. Ibid., pp. 171–72; and "Versions," pp. 85–86.

37. London, June 22, 2004, lot 52; Margot McIlwain Nishimura, *Important Illuminated Manuscripts* (Akron, OH and Paris: Bruce Ferrini and Les Enluminures, 2000), pp. 18–22, present location unknown (I have studied photographs only).

38. See Branner, *Manuscript Painting*, appendix VA, p. 204. This manuscript is certainly early and shows some variation in the books included, the prologues, and the text.

39. Branner, *Manuscript Painting*, p. 210, appendix VC, p. 210 and fig. 125; Lilian M. C. Randall, *Medieval and Renaissance Manuscripts in the Walters Art Gallery*, vol. 1: *France, 875–1420* (Baltimore: John Hopkins University Press, 1989), pp. 37–40; this Bible does include some additional prologues that I have not examined personally.

40. Charles Samaran and Robert Marichal, *Catalogue des manuscrits en écriture latine portant des indications de date, de lieu ou de copiste* (Paris: CNRS, 1959– ), 5:41, pl. 23.

41. Branner, *Manuscript Painting*, passim.

42. I have not examined all of the Bibles in Branner, *Manuscript Painting*; of the sixty-nine Bibles studied here dating after c. 1230, forty were also studied by Branner.

43. See note 13.

44. The text of five of the Bibles in this sample was not studied.

45. "Quintum peccatum est majus omnibus praedictis. Nam textus est pro marjori parte corruptus horribiliter in exemplari Vulgato, hoc est Parisiensis." Roger Bacon, *Opus minus*, in *Opera quaedam hactenus inedita*, ed. John S. Brewer, Rerum britannicarum medii aevi scriptores (London: Longman, Green and Roberts, 1859; reprint, London: Kraus Reprints, 1965), p. 330. See also *The Opus Majus of Roger Bacon*, ed. John H. Bridges (Oxford: Clarendon, 1879–1900; repr. Frankfurt: Minerva, 1964), pp. 77–78. For an English translation, see *The Opus Majus of Roger Bacon*, trans. Robert Burke (Philadelphia: Univerisity of Pennsylvania Press, 1928), pp. 87–88.

46. Bacon, *Opus minus*, ed. Brewer, p. 333; the full passage has often been cited. For example, see Light, "Roger Bacon," pp. 484–85.

47. These are statements that are still current, though unsupported; see for example, Branner, *Manuscript Painting*, p. 16. Bacon's writings are also not evidence that the Paris Bible was created and disseminated early in the thirteenth-century by the university stationers who rented exemplars of texts used in the university. University control over the book trade did not exist c. 1230, and the production of manuscripts by exemplars divided into small sections, or *peciae*, can be dated only to c. 1260 or later in Paris; see Rouse and Rouse, *Manuscripts and Their Makers*, pp. 87–88; for a general discussion of this type of book production, see pp. 75–81, 85–89, and 24–25. The question of whether Bibles were ever copied from *pecia* exemplars later in the century is enigmatic; see Giovanna Murano, *Opere diffuse per Exemplar e pecia*, Textes et Études du Moyen Âges 29 (Turnhout: Brepols, 2005), pp. 318–19. The Bible was included on the lists of exemplars rented in Paris in 1275 and 1304; see Murano, *Opere diffuse*, 87 (no. 87) and 123 (no. 68). Very few Bibles with *pecia* marks survive, however. See Light, "The Thirteenth-Century Bible"; and "Roger Bacon," pp. 486–87 and 503–4, discussing Paris, BNF MSS Lat. 28, Lat. 14238, and Lat. 9381 and Paris, Bibliothèque Mazarine MS 37; cf. de Hamel, *The Book*, pp. 136–37. There is also an Italian Bible with *pecia* marks; see Magrini, "Production and Use," pp. 214–15.

48. Light, "The Thirteenth-Century Bible"; and "Roger Bacon," p. 501; Lobrichon, "Les éditions," pp. 33–34; cf. de Hamel, *The Book*, pp. 131–38.

49. Roger Bacon, for example, whose remarks on the Paris Bible have been mentioned earlier, was chiefly concerned with discussing the *correctoria*; Gilbert Dahan is currently investigating the *correctoria* and has published numerous articles related to them, most recently *L'exégèse chrétienne de la Bible en occident médiéval XIIe–XIVe siècle* (Paris: Cerf, 1999), pp. 175–228; and Gilbert Dahan, "Sorbon II," in *La Bibbia del XIII secolo*, pp. 114–53. See also Heinrich Denifle, "Die Handschriften der Bibel-Correctorien des 13. Jahrhunderts," *Archiv für Literatur- und Kirchengeschichte* 4 (1888): 263–311 and 474–601. On the question of the use of correctoria, see Light, "Versions," p. 90; Lobrichon, "Les éditions," p. 25; and Dahan, *L'exégèse*, pp. 223–28.

50. Light, "The Thirteenth-Century Bible," pp. 276–77. They appeared in France and England virtually simultaneously (c. 1230) and spread to Italy and Spain very early. See also Rosanna Miriello, "La Bibbia portabile di origine italiana del XIII secolo: Brevi considerazione e alcuni esempi," in *La Bibbia del XIII secolo*, pp. 47–77.

51. A famous example is Paris, BNF MS Lat. 10426, said to have belonged to St. Louis. Pierre Petitmengin, "La Bible de Saint Louis," in *Mise en page et mise en texte du livre manuscrit*, ed. Henri-Jean Martin and Jean Vezin (Paris: Cercle de la Librairie-Promodis, 1990), pp. 84–89; Lobrichon, "Les éditions," pp. 35–36.

52. de Hamel, *The Book,* pp. 131–36; Kenneth W. Humphreys, *The Book Provisions of the Medieval Friars, 1215–1400* (Amsterdam: Erasmus, 1964).

53. Lobrichon, "Les editions," pp. 26–29; de Hamel, *The Book*, p. 136, but see also p. 138; Mark Zier, "The Development of the Glossa Ordinaria to the Bible in the Thirteenth Century: The Evidence from the Bibliothèque Nationale, Paris," in *La Bibbia del XIII secolo*, pp. 155–84, at 157–60 and 171.

54. Mary A. Rouse and Richard H. Rouse, "The Development of Research Tools in the Thirteenth Century," in *Authentic Witnesses: Approaches to Medieval Texts and Manuscripts*, ed. Mary A. Rouse and Richard H. Rouse (Notre Dame, IN: University of Notre Dame Press, 1991), pp. 221–55; and Light, "The New Thirteenth-Century Bible and the Challenge of Heresy," *Viator* 18 (1987): 275–88, analyzing a group of Bibles (not examples of the Paris Bible) used for preaching.

55. See note 1; and Light, "Thirteenth-Century Bible."

56. A good introduction to the subject is found in de Hamel, *The Book*, pp. 190–215 and 201. The Gutenberg Bible does not reproduce typical Paris Bibles exactly. For example, it includes 4 Esdras, it does not include the exact set of Paris prologues, and lacks the *Interpretation of Hebrew Names*; its text was the ancestor for most of the fifteenth-century printed Bibles. See Paul Needham, "The Text of the Gutenberg Bible," in *Trasmissione dei testi a stampa nel periodo moderno: II, Il seminario internazionale Roma-Viterbo 27–29 Giugno 1985*, ed. Giovanni Crapulli (Rome: Ateneo, 1987), pp. 43–84; and Quentin, *Memoire*, p. 89–94.

57. *Biblia sacra vulgatae editionis Sixti Quinti iussu recognita (et auctoritate Clementis Octavi edita)* (Rome, 1592 and 1593, 1598).

# The Illustrated Psalter

LUXURY AND PRACTICAL USE

*Stella Panayotova*

Of all the biblical books, the Psalter was the one whose very beginning offered medieval readers practical advice on the way they should live their lives. Psalm 1 encouraged them to follow "the way of the just" and to steer clear from "the way of sinners" (Ps 1:1, 6). There was hardly a text more widely used and better known to medieval audiences, be they religious or lay, learned or barely literate.[1] This chapter will examine the texts and images in medieval Psalters as witnesses to the experiences, beliefs, anxieties, and aspirations of those who made and used them.

Crucial in Judaic worship and celebrated as the summit of Hebrew poetry, the psalms were commonly ascribed to King David throughout the Middle Ages, although some commentators, following St. Jerome (c. 342–420), recognized them as the work of different authors. An Old Testament type of Christ, David was the biblical king on whom the ideal image of the wise and pious ruler was modeled. Before the Book of Hours came of age in the late thirteenth century, and even afterward, the Psalter was the standard primer and the most popular devotional reading because of the overwhelming presence of the psalms in the core and optional texts of the hours. Heavily drawn upon in theology, exegesis, and liturgical practices, the Psalter doubled as a religious encyclopedia and was used as a vehicle for politics, ideology, and popular belief.[2]

## The Psalms in the Circle of Life

Children's first encounter with the Bible was through the Psalms.[3] King Louis IX (1215–70) learned to read from a Psalter.[4] It is also in a Psalter (one belonging to Jeanne II of Navarre and made around 1335–40) that we see St. Louis hard at work over a book under his mother's supervision.[5] While neither manuscript was originally intended as a royal ABC, proper Psalter-primers were custom made for medieval children. The Copenhagen Psalter, probably presented to the seven-year-old Canute VI on the occasion of his coronation in 1170, includes the alphabet.[6] It also contains the Lord's Prayer (which appears in numerous Books of Hours made for children, hence the English name *Primer*, after the office of Prime, which was prayed in the morning) along with the alphabet and the Apostles' Creed, all core elements of primers proper, as in the early sixteenth-century picture ABC of Claude de France.[7] In 1401–2 Michelle of France, who was also seven, owned a book of the alphabet followed by psalms.[8] A thirteenth-century Psalter made by nuns in the Rhineland includes practice alphabets, mnemonic verses, the Apostles' Creed, and the Lord's Prayer.[9] A contemporary English Psalter contains a carefully penned alphabet, an Anglo-Norman commentary and translation of the Apostles' Creed and *Our Father*, short devotions with minimal abbreviations, and bright images—all emphatically large on the tiny pages.[10] Intended for a female owner, the book may have been designed to meet her changing needs over a long period of time, from her first acquaintance with the ABC until she was ready to learn a moral lesson from the vividly depicted story of Joseph and Potiphar's wife. Or perhaps a mother used the manuscript for her own devotions while teaching her children the alphabet and basic prayers. The worn-out margins and rubbed images show how heavily the book had already been thumbed by the fifteenth century, when the damaged sections were patched up.

Having prepared their young owners for adulthood, Psalters celebrated crucial events in their lives. As wedding gifts, they sanctified the bond between bride and groom with shared devotions and sealed dynastic alliances through ostentatious armorial displays. The borders of the Bohun

Psalter, one of the finest late fourteenth-century English manuscripts, are studded with the arms of Henry de Bohun, Earl of Hereford and Sussex (d. 1373), and of Henry Bolingbroke, the future Henry IV of England (1399–1413).[11] The Psalter was most probably commissioned for the marriage of Henry Bolingbroke and Mary, daughter of Henry de Bohun, in 1380. Psalters also alluded to the more intimate aspects of marriage by populating their margins with courting scenes and erotically charged imagery.[12] While such marginalia reflected moral values and social obligations, they also created a *frisson* and offered entertainment.[13] Psalters were presented as tokens of affection outside conventional marital bonds, too. Abbot Geoffrey of St. Albans prepared the St. Albans Psalter as a magnificent gift for the edification and delight of his close friend the anchoress Christina of Markyate.[14] Abelard sent what was probably a modestly illuminated but truly scholarly book (now lost) to his former lover, Heloise, whose inquiring mind joined Jerome's in questioning David's authorship of the Psalms.[15]

The Psalms were thought to defend life and health. Legend has it that St. Columba (c. 521–97) carried an early seventh-century Psalter into battle as a talisman; it is known as the famous *Cathach* (Old Irish: "battler") of St. Columba.[16] Some scholars recognize a talismanic function in later Psalters, too, interpreting their marginal grotesques as apotropaic images.[17] A Byzantine official used his Psalter as a fortune-teller amidst the shifting climate of court politics in eleventh-century Constantinople.[18] Monastic manuscripts from eleventh-century Winchester and twelfth-century Canterbury coupled the Psalms with texts on onomancy (a form of divination employing the letters of a name) and chiromancy (palm reading).[19]

The Psalms completed the circle of life; with them, children grew up into this world and adults left it behind. Victor Leroquais offered numerous examples of psalms being chanted as death approached.[20] Often recording the deaths of family members in their calendars, Psalters preserved the memory of the departed and reminded the living of their own mortality. Some Psalters and especially Psalter-Hours, a hybrid particularly popular in the thirteenth century, included the Office of the Dead, which comprised mainly psalm verses and had originated as a text for private mourning.[21] The first of its three liturgical hours, or offices— Vespers—was effectively a vigil for the dead said over the body during the night before the burial, while the other two, Matins and Lauds, were recited in church the following morning. In addition to this public use, the Office of the Dead was also read as part of a private devotional routine, a reflection on the *memento mori*, which offered solace at the deathbed of relatives and nurtured the hope for salvation.

## The Psalms in the Church

If the Psalter marked important moments in the life of the laity, it fully dominated the life of the religious. In its synthesis of monastic practices and the traditions of the secular Church, the Rule of St. Benedict (c. 540) structured the offices so as to accommodate the reading of the entire Psalter within a week (for more on the psalms in Mass and Office, see Boynton's chapter in this volume).[22] While compromising the standards of the desert fathers who recited all 150 psalms daily, St. Benedict's Rule offered healthy spiritual servings, wisely rationed throughout the day, the week, and the year. This "monastic" division resulted in groups of psalms that were often marked in manuscripts by singling out with a decorated or historiated initial the first psalm assigned to each Nocturn sung during Matins from Sunday through Saturday (Pss. 20, 26, 32, 38, 45, 52, 59, 68, 73, 79, 85, 95, 101, and 105) and at Sunday Vespers (Ps. 109).[23] The illustrations to these psalms reflect the focal points of monastic devotion, learning, and daily routine. But they also resonate with echoes from the world outside.[24]

The clergy in secular cathedrals and parish churches also recited all 150 psalms each week, but grouped them differently. Theirs was the so-called liturgical or eightfold division. Of the various systems of Psalter division, this was the most common and received the most systematic figural decoration of initials embellished with figures or stories, especially drawn from the Bible.[25] Artists singled out the first psalm of the groups chanted daily at Matins (Pss. 1, 26, 38, 52, 68, 80 and 97) and at Vespers on Sundays (Ps. 109).[26] In Germany, the Southern Netherlands, and especially England, it was often combined with the traditional "threefold division" (Pss. 1, 51, and 101), which had long been signaled by its own set of historiated initials or full-page illustrations.[27] Since Psalm 1 participated in both systems, the combination resulted in the so-called tenfold division.

The conspicuous presence of the psalms in the daily offices and in the celebration of major feasts had a considerable impact on their illustration. Psalters were commissioned and made by people who were equally familiar with the use of the Psalms in commentaries, sermons, the Mass, and the daily offices. Liturgy and exegesis were reconciled in medieval commentaries on the offices, and in liturgical drama, and these also could inspire Psalter decoration.[28] Prefatory cycles of full-page miniatures featuring scenes from the Old and New Testaments had first been joined to English Psalters, usually before the first psalm, in the eleventh century.[29] Prefatory cycles of miniatures depicting Christ's life placed the Psalter in a general messianic and liturgical context.[30] But it fell to images linked with specific verses to remind readers when to use individual psalms and how to reactivate their prophetic meaning in church ceremonial and private prayer. The initial to Psalm 8 in an early thirteenth-century Canterbury Psalter (to which we shall return shortly) shows the Massacre of the Innocents.[31] Verse 3 of the psalm, "Out of the mouth of infants and of sucklings thou hast perfected praise," is linked to its use on the feast of the Holy Innocents (December 28). In the Bury Psalter of c. 1050 the same subject appears as a marginal drawing beside Psalm 78, whose third verse ("They have poured out their blood as water") was also part of the office on December 28.[32] Liturgical associations could be conveyed through depictions of rituals performed by the celebrant. The initial to Psalm 25 in the St. Albans Psalter shows a priest washing his hands at the Offertory, the section of the Mass during which the psalm verse "I will wash my hands among the innocent" was recited.[33] Depictions of the Annunciation to the shepherds at Psalm 97 reflect a long tradition of interpreting the psalm as a prophecy about the Incarnation and of using "The Lord hath made known his salvation" from verse 2 as an antiphon, *Notum fecit dominus,* at the feast of the Nativity.[34] Similarly, depictions of the Coronation of the Virgin at Psalm 109 married biblical text with theology, exegesis, and liturgical practice. A Marian subject was suggested by the "rod of virtue" of verse 2, *Virgam virtutis tuae emittet Dominus ex Sion,* and by the imagery of birth mentioned in verse 3, "From the womb before the day I begot thee," linked by commentators with the Virgin since the early Christian period. Psalm 109 opened Vespers at the feast of the Assumption. In the course of the twelfth century, the Coronation of the Virgin was established as the visual formula for the Assumption throughout the Latin West.[35] Dogma, liturgy, and exegesis converge in the humorous pragmatism of a fifteenth-century scribe: a three-headed grotesque embellishes his catchword for the quire that begins with the Trinitarian Psalm 109, "The Lord said to my Lord" (fig. 12.1).[36]

12.1. Cambridge, University Library, Ff.4.5, fol. 73v (detail), Catchword for Psalm 109. *By permission of the Cambridge University Library.*

## Word Illustration and Thirteenth-Century Psalters

Medieval artists and viewers would have conceived of Psalter illustrations in a variety of ways, often simultaneously. They would have found them useful as markers of major text divisions and mnemonic aids; enjoyable as embellishments of their treasured books and reminders of their piety, status, and wealth; helpful as focal points for meditation and incentives to examine the biblical text in minute detail; instructive in their moral messages and visual interpretations of Scripture; or amusing in their secular, frivolous, obscene, even blasphemous connotations.

Intimate knowledge of the psalms and their immense authority inspired a long tradition of word illustration in which individual words or verses from the Psalms were depicted more or less literally. Some of the most celebrated examples are the manuscripts of the Utrecht Psalter family. The first example, the Utrecht Psalter (Utrecht, Universiteitsbibliothek MS Nr. 32), was embellished in the ninth century with elaborate strips of pen-drawn word illustrations before each Psalm.[37] It was copied at least three times in England over the course of the next three centuries.

Much more common, however, is the system of word illustration developed to illustrate Psalters in Parisian Bibles from c. 1200 onward.

No two identical Psalters survive from the medieval period, but nowhere else could we come closer to standardization and feel less uneasy with the term *iconographic program* than in thirteenth-century Paris. The eight initials marking the psalms of the "liturgical" division developed for priests and secular canons in these Bibles were historiated with subjects suggested by the psalm heading or opening verses.[38] Physically bound by the letter, David points to his eyes while exclaiming "The Lord is my light" (Ps. 26) or, submerged in water, prays: "Save me, O God: for the waters are come in even unto my soul" (Ps. 68).

While the stimulus for these iconographic choices came from the biblical text, the uniform application of the *ad verbum* (or literal) technique was the product of a new intellectual and commercial environment. The burgeoning book trade of the early thirteenth century transformed Paris into Europe's leading center of manuscript production, and the increasing demand for multiple copies of Scripture and the small size of the Paris Bibles called for the adoption of a straightforward program.[39] The artists' knowledge of established schemes and acceptable variations ensured its fast and accurate reproduction. The Parisian program was assembled for the Bible in its entirety, not for its individual books. A set of images that responded to a wide spectrum of stimuli and encouraged infinite variations was conceivable within the limits of a biblical book, but it was less practical as part of a large-scale program covering the whole Bible and intended for mass production.

The establishment of the program coincided with the rise of Paris as the leading university center of the time and with a major revision of the biblical text. The first three decades of the thirteenth century, the formative period of the Parisian cycle of initials, were crucial for the emergence of the one-volume Paris Bible.[40] (On the Bible in the thirteenth century, see Light's chapter in this volume.) Surviving commentaries and students' *reportationes* (lecture notes) reveal that lectures on the Bible at the beginning of the thirteenth century combined exposition of the text with an introductory *summa*, bringing together different exegetical techniques and various theological strands—dogmatic, sacramental, and moral.[41] (On biblical studies in this period, see van Liere's chapter in this volume.)

If a parallel development could be detected between the emerging Paris Bible and literal Psalter illustration, it is in the close attention to the biblical text and the manifest attempt at standardization. By the 1250s, however, more overlap can be found between university teaching practices and the illustrations in the Bibles undoubtedly used by many of the students. The Bible was read first *cursorie*, with narrative summaries and explanations of the literal meaning, and only then *ordinarie*, with the spiritual sense built onto the literal and followed by lectures on Peter Lombard's *Sentences*. The same order was followed when students began to teach: starting with cursorie lectures, they had to qualify as regent masters before lecturing on the Bible ordinarie.[42] (On the study of the Bible in university curricula during the thirteenth century, see Roest's chapter in this volume.) The illustration of the Parisian Bibles seems to correspond to the first part of the theology course. Repetitive and predictable as a memory aid, the straightforward ad verbum technique corresponds with the method of biblical exposition offered to beginners.

By mid-century, the French sequence of initials was adopted in other university centers that created a similar market for the book trades, notably Oxford and Bologna,[43] and continued to spread rapidly throughout Latin Christendom. The English cycle of historiated initials was the most eclectic to flourish in thirteenth-century Northern Europe and also the most resilient, since its salient features survived well into the fourteenth century. Close attention to the biblical text was combined with a tendency to extend its meaning toward exegesis, dogmatic theology, and liturgical and devotional practices. Drawing on the biblical *tituli* (titles) to Psalms 26, "The Psalm of David before he was annointed," and 51, "David condemneth the wickedness of Doeg, and foretelleth his destruction," the initials showed, respectively, the anointing of David and Doeg slaying the priests of Nob. The fool who declared, at the beginning of Psalm 52, "There is no God" became the devil in representations of Christ's Temptation. The story of Jonah for Psalm 68 was suggested by the nearly identical wording of the second verse, "Save me, O God, for the waters are come in even unto my soul," and Jonah's prayer (Jon. 2:6). It was also a well-known prefiguration of Christ's Passion and Resurrection alluded to in verse 22 and sanctioned in the Gospels by Jesus himself. The illustration for Psalm 109 drew on the psalm text, exegesis, and doctrine. Central to the Trinitarian dogma, this psalm was commonly illustrated with an image inspired by its opening verse, "The Lord said to my Lord: you shall sit at my right hand": the Holy Spirit descending in the form of a dove between the seated figures of the Father and the Son. The alternative subject for Psalm 109, the Coronation of the Virgin, and the Annunciation to the shepherds for Psalm 97 have already been mentioned as visual intersections of biblical text, commentary, and liturgy.

This eclectic approach invited the infiltration of current fashions and foreign elements. By the 1230s, the Parisian program for Bible illustration was welcomed in Oxford. As the international prestige of the university grew, its links with Paris were strengthened and its provision of books was established on an increasingly commercial basis. The dissemination of the university Bible coincided with the attempt to provide historiation in English Bibles for each of the ten psalms that initiated a major division of the Psalter. Some of the subjects in the English cycle had appeared in twelfth-century Psalters, but the earliest manuscripts to display a complete set of the ten historiated initials date from the first two decades of the thirteenth century and combine liturgical, stylistic, and iconographic features suggesting that they were produced in Winchester or Oxford.[44]

A home for centuries of important political, ecclesiastical, and artistic traditions, and an important royal residence, Winchester attracted wealthy patrons and leading artists at the beginning of the century. It had close connections with Oxford, which was emerging as the major intellectual center of the kingdom.[45] The University of Oxford's growing demand for books lured manuscript makers with prospects for long-term employment.[46] Yet the first two decades of the century, the formative period of the English cycle, were a time of crisis for the university. An interdict imposed on England between 1208 and 1214 coincided with the exodus of Oxford scholars after a violent clash between town and gown, with consequences that were not remedied until 1218. The amorphous beginning and uncertain future of the university could hardly have provided the intellectual and artistic climate necessary for the creation and dissemination of the program of ten historiated initials found in English Bibles of this period. However, the program manifests high standards of learning and a concerted effort to balance a close attention to the biblical text with imagery referring to the exegetical, devotional, and liturgical uses of the Psalms. While the existence of a centralized university was not a sine qua non for the establishment of the English cycle of historiated initials, it could not have originated in an intellectual vacuum.

As we have seen, scholars are right to reject the simplistic use of the term *literal illustration*. They can easily reveal the "shock effect" and "visual charades" produced by playful indulgence of the ad verbum technique.[47] Exegetical, political, social, and ideological layers of meaning can be found in seemingly straightforward images. Biblical and even pagan history could assume a political inflection, particularly in free-standing Psalters made for upper-class patrons, as Madeleine Caviness demonstrated in her work on the Little Canterbury Psalter.[48] She interpreted its iconographic program as a political allegory—a pictorial invective against King John's rule. The context, she proposed, was his confrontation with Rome over the election of Stephen Langton as archbishop of Canterbury, which brought the papal Interdict on England in 1208. It is intriguing that a contemporary manuscript—the Ashmole Psalter, almost identical in content and structure with the Little Canterbury Psalter and illustrated by the same group of artists—should offer a strikingly different perspective on kingship.[49] It is one of the few surviving Psalters with extrabiblical tituli, collects, and historiated initials to every psalm, all of which were features characteristic of deluxe manuscripts.[50] The image of a man presenting a book to a king in the initial to Psalm 14 (fig. 12.2) amounts to a pictorial dedication. The titulus echoes the opening words of the psalm and doubles as a caption for the image: "This psalm reveals those who will live in the kingdom of God." In contrast to the pictorial program of the Little Canterbury Psalter, the numerous royal images in the Ashmole Psalter adopt the tone of reconciliation that marked the correspondence between

12.2. Oxford, Bodleian Library, Ashmole 1525, fol. 13r (detail), king presented with a book. *By permission of the Bodleian Library, University of Oxford.*

King John and Pope Innocent III after May 1213. The initials illustrate the psalm text or tituli so faithfully that we could brand them "literal" if unaware of their historical and political overtones. This Psalter is a reminder of how deceptively straightforward text-bound images could appear.

## Personalization and Self-promotion

Likewise in France, the Parisian program was, at its height, often modified to suit personal preferences in Psalters more than in Bibles. The Parisian subjects were supplemented with both a creation cycle within the initials and also courtly scenes in the margins of a Psalter from about 1280–90 from Amiens.[51] Their seemingly uniform presence in the Psalter of St. Louis[52] and the Psalter-Hours of Isabelle of France[53] was subtly altered in line with the private circumstances and public roles of the manuscripts' owners, Louis IX of France and his sister Isabelle, respectively.[54] The image of David tempted by the bathing Bathsheba and repenting before God at the opening of the psalm text in both manuscripts is consonant with the renunciation of carnal pleasure and the austere devotional routines cherished by St. Louis and his sister.[55] Isabelle's vow of chastity caused her to break off her engagement with a count and turn down the marriage offer of the son of the German emperor, Frederick II. With St. Louis's support, she founded a Franciscan convent outside Paris (the later Longchamp) in 1255. The Franciscans, who compiled the rule for her convent, feature in the calendar, litany, suffrages, and initials of her prayer book. To them, and to their fellow protagonists, the artists entrusted the acting out of the psalm text in both manuscripts. The king (no doubt St. Louis empathizing with David) was free to pray to the Lord above: his figure, invariably shown in God's presence, dominates the initials and reinforces the message about divinely ordained kingship exemplified by the prefatory miniatures.[56]

As we have already seen in England, though the Parisian program of Psalter illustrations made a strong impact across Europe through the books and ideas that international students brought home from Paris, the initials for the psalms of the liturgical division display significant variations among different regional schools. Local traditions flourished in Flemish, Mosan, German, Italian, and English Psalters.[57] The Parisian subjects were combined with Byzantine iconography in thirteenth-century Bolognese Psalters.[58] In the 1280s a woman from Liège had her Psalter expanded, textually and visually, into the ultimate book that would secure the salvation of her soul and the well-being of her body.[59] She could recite the Psalms, Offices of the Virgin, and Office of the Dead in the privacy of her home or during communal celebrations of the major Marian feasts. She had prayers, penned in both Latin and French, to say during confession and communion. While the Easter table allowed her to find the date of the Resurrection every year, the table of health rules advised her on bloodletting, diet, and purgation month after month (fig. 12.3). She was able to follow the liturgical, astronomical, and agricultural year from

12.3. Cambridge, Fitzwilliam Museum, 288, fol. 6v, women visiting apothecary beneath the table of instructions for bloodletting. *By permission of the Fitzwilliam Museum, Cambridge.*

the church feasts, zodiac images, and labors of the month in the calendar. The images of saints in the psalm initials and the Passion and Marian cycles in the Offices of the Virgin would help her focus during meditation, and she had her own portrait included in the initials to the French devotions to the Virgin and in the confession and Mass prayers. She also saw herself visiting the apothecary to obtain the herbs prescribed by the health table—a physical counterpart to the healing properties of spiritual reading. One of the most complex Mosan Psalters in existence, this manuscript preserves features from Flanders, Brabant, and Hainaut as well as Paris, all of which contributed to its stylistic, iconographic, and textual eclecticism.

Equally international in its conception and execution is a manuscript illuminated for a lady at the ducal court of Breslau between 1255 and 1269.[60] The Infancy, Passion, and Marian cycles represent the liturgical and devotional use of the Psalms; their full-page miniatures are rich in Byzantine iconographic schemes and distributed at the major text divisions as was customary in contemporary German Psalters and Flemish Psalters.[61] The large historiated initials of the tenfold division combine Christological scenes with Parisian-inspired literal subjects. The most extraordinary is the *Beatus* initial for Psalm 1 (fig. 12.4). Its two compartments represent the Old and New Testaments reconciled by David's psalmody on the left. On the right, Solomon refers to God's wisdom while Isaiah predicts the Incarnation of the Word below. Interceding for humankind (and for the manuscript's owner), the Virgin and John the Baptist introduce the theme of the Last Judgment through the Byzantine image of the Deësis. The dove of the Holy Spirit in the intersection, symbolic of the double procession, unites the two tiers into a vertical Trinity. This is transformed into Christ's baptism by the alignment of John's figure with the Father's scroll: "This is my beloved Son" (Matt. 3:17). As a visual frontispiece that interconnects central tenets of dogmatic theology, the initial parallels the importance of Psalm 1 celebrated by exegetes as an introduction to the entire Psalter, a prophecy about Christ, and a guide to eternal life. The program blends aristocratic splendor with religious fervor and combines Byzantine, Parisian, and Saxon iconography with Italian style.

An important circumstance of the early Winchester-Oxford-related Psalters containing the basic cycle of ten historiated initials is that many of them were made for women. This is the case, notably, in one of the earliest manuscripts firmly associated with Oxford, the Arundel Psalter.[62] It

12.4. Cambridge, Fitzwilliam Museum, 36-1950, fol. 23v, *Beatus* initial for Psalm
1. *By permission of the Fitzwilliam Museum, Cambridge.*

is an early example of the hybrid Psalter-Hours, and two of the prayers
reveal that it was made for a woman, perhaps a wealthy patron of the priory. The same is true of two contemporary books associated with the
Benedictine convent at Amesbury.[63] The Amesbury-Fontevrault litany
and the obit of Margaret de Quincey, *priorissa nostra* ("our prioress"),
added later in the century, confirm that the more imposing one, the Imola
Psalter, belonged to the convent. The other Psalter is a tiny book for private devotion, dependent on the style and iconography of the Imola Psalter, but with several alterations. The most intriguing of these is the decision to evoke the theme of the Incarnation for Psalm 97 through an image
of the Virgin and Child (fig. 12.5). The iconographic type is that of the
*Hodegetria*, the palladium of Constantinople and the most highly vener-

12.5. Oxford, Bodleian Library, Liturg. 407, fol. 137r (detail), Virgin and Child at Psalm 97. *By permission of the Bodleian Library, University of Oxford.*

ated Marian icon in the Byzantine world. Deriving from its home, the Hodegon Monastery in Constantinople, its name was associated with the hand of the Virgin pointing at Christ and showing the right way.[64] This is relevant to the beginning of the psalm, *salvavit sibi dextera eius*, "His right hand hath wrought for him salvation," and to a marginal gloss on Psalm 97, *de ostensione salvatricis dexterae* ("concerning the showing of the salvific right hand") found in numerous copies of the *Glossa ordinaria*. The *Hodegetria* initial shows close attention to biblical text and authoritative exegesis, as well as an understanding of the Byzantine image. Though rare in Western manuscripts, the *Hodegetria* appears in several contemporary English Psalters.[65] The artist would have had exemplars at hand, and he was also familiar with another image of the Virgin and Child popular in the Byzantine East, the Madonna of Kykkos. Its salient feature, the Child's bare kicking legs symbolic of His eager preparation for the

Passion, is skillfully incorporated in the *Hodegetria* initial to a psalm interpreted as a prefiguration of both the first and second coming of Christ.

The *Hodegetria* icon in Constantinople was the talk of the day. Immediately after the fall of Constantinople on April 13, 1204, it was the focus of a major conflict between the Venetian doge, Patriarch Morosini, and the local population, a conflict that provoked the hurling of anathemas, the use of military power, and the anger of Pope Innocent III.[66] The icon was one of the few Constantinopolitan treasures the Venetians failed to acquire. The *Hodegetria* initial in the Bodleian Psalter may well reflect the owner's interest in the events just as two unusual features in the calendar, both penned by the original scribe, probably reveal her family's involvement in the Crusades. *Expugnatio Ierusalem a francis*, "Storming of Jerusalem by the Franks," on July 15, commemorates the fall of Jerusalem to the First Crusade in 1099. January 26 marks the feast of John Chrysostom, the fourth-century archbishop of Constantinople whose relics were taken to San Marco together with the Venetian booty in 1204. The artist's familiarity with an unusual iconographic formula linked the psalm text to its commentary, offered a hieratic visual expression of the dogma of the Incarnation and Redemption, and met the patron's need for a powerful devotional stimulus, while hinting at her interest in contemporary events and perhaps at her family background.

Numerous medieval Psalters were personalized through the inclusion of specially requested texts and images celebrating the wealth, wisdom, and piety of their patrons or the skill of their makers. But few manuscripts preserve traces of their "designers," these notoriously evasive "artistic directors." A four-volume set written and illuminated in Sens between 1173 and 1177 is exceptional in allowing us to observe its "project manager" in action.[67] This monumental copy of Peter Lombard's *Magna glossatura* (*Great Gloss*) on the Psalms and the Pauline Epistles was commissioned by Thomas Becket probably as a gift for Christ Church, Canterbury.[68] It was masterminded by Herbert of Bosham, Becket's secretary and theological adviser (c. 1120–c. 1194). After Becket's death, Herbert remained in exile in France, striving to establish himself as an academic in Paris. Desperate for the patronage of powerful ecclesiastics, he pressed his erudition and close relationship with Becket into service. He designed the *Magna glossatura* set as a critical edition, a monument to his biblical scholarship. Herbert supplemented the Gallican text of the Psalms with Jerome's translation from the Hebrew and had the margins filled with cross-references between the Psalms, the Pauline Epistles, and other bib-

lical books. More importantly, he identified passages wrongly attributed
to commentators, relegating his corrections to the margins out of defer-
ence for his former Parisian master, Peter Lombard, but drawing attention to them with clever visual devices. The figures of Augustine, Cassiodorus, or Jerome stand watch in the borders, holding scrolls inscribed "I
did not say that" and stabbing the wrong attributions with sharp lances
(fig. 12.6). Finally, Herbert added another unique feature: the themes of
individual psalms are signaled by striking marginal images, such as a man
engulfed in the fire of Purgatory or a personification of Aristotle's *Ethica*
(fig. 12.7), which drew on recently rediscovered texts and on ideas hotly
debated at the time. As with the authority figures, Herbert used pictures
to stimulate a critical study of the text in order to showcase his own scholarship and ultimately further his career.

Medieval manuscripts preserve tangible evidence about the people
who conceived, wrote, illustrated, and read the Psalms throughout their
lives. Almost every discussion of Psalter illustration contains a statement
about the challenge the highly poetic, non-narrative text of the Psalms
presented to medieval artists, patrons, readers, and viewers. Yet, it was
one of the most frequently and most richly illuminated books of the Middle Ages. The examples in this chapter are a reminder that the challenge
artists and users faced was not the lack of clues as to Psalter illustration
and interpretation, but rather the multiple choices. These were choices of
text and image, as well as unlimited opportunities to allude to historical

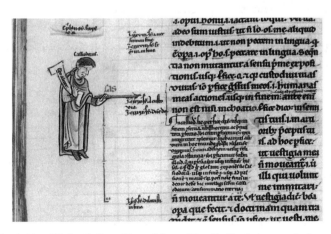

12.6. Cambridge, Trinity College, B.5.4, fol. 43v (detail), Cassiodorus pointing at a wrong
attribution. *By permission of Trinity College Cambridge.*

12.7. Cambridge, Trinity College, B.5.4, fol. 15r (detail), *Ethica*.
*By permission of Trinity College Cambridge.*

events, political figures, social changes, ideological controversies, intellectual developments, personal circumstances, and career moves: in short, opportunities to allude to the practical concerns and realities that make up the rich kaleidoscope of life.

## Notes

I am grateful to Greti Dinkova-Bruun and Jennifer Harris for editing an early draft of this chapter.

1. Victor Leroquais's introduction to vol. 1 of his monumental *Les psautiers manuscrits latins des bibliothèques publiques de France* (Macon: Protat Frères, 1940), pp. v–cxxxvi, remains a key text on the central place of the Psalter in medieval life. The most comprehensive recent treatment of Psalter illustration in the medieval West is *The Illuminated Psalter: Studies in the Content, Purpose and Placement of Its Images*, ed. Frank O. Büttner (Turnhout: Brepols, 2004).

2. The multifaceted role of the psalms in intellectual life is reflected in *The Place of the Psalms in the Intellectual Culture of the Middle Ages*, ed. Nancy van Deusen (Albany: State University of New York Press, 1999).

3. Psalm verses were inscribed on the oldest specimen of writing to survive from Ireland, the Springmount Bog wax tablets from which children learned to read and write in the early seventh century. Martin McNamara, "The Psalms in the Irish Church," in *The Bible as Book: The Manuscript Tradition*, ed. John L. Sharpe III and Kimberly van Kampen (London and New Castle, DE: British Library and Oak Knoll, 1998), pp. 89–103.

4. Leiden, Bibliotheek der Rijksuniversiteit MS Lat. 76A; Nigel Morgan, *Early Gothic Manuscripts 1190–1250*, 2 vols. (London and Oxford: Harvey Miller and Oxford University Press, 1982–88), no. 14.

5. Paris, Bibliothèque Nationale de France (hereafter BNF), MS Lat. 3145, fol. 85v.

6. Copenhagen, Royal Library MS Thott 143 20; Patricia Stirnemann, "The Copenhagen Psalter Reconsidered as a Coronation Present for Canute VI (Kongel. Bibl., MS Thott 143 20)," in *The Illuminated Psalter*, pp. 323–28.

7. Cambridge, Fitzwilliam Museum MS 159; Roger S. Wieck, "Special Children's Books of Hours in the Walters Art Museum," in *"Als ich can": Liber amicorum in Memory of Professor Dr. Maurits Smeyers*, ed. Bert Cardon et al., 2 vols. (Leuven: Peeters, 2002), 2:1629 39; and Roger S. Wieck, "The Primer of Claude de France and the Education of the Renaissance Child," in *The Cambridge Illuminations: The Conference Papers*, ed. Stella Panayotova (London: Harvey Miller, 2007), pp. 267–77.

8. Leroquais, *Les psautiers manuscrits*, p. vii.

9. London, British Library Add. MS 60629; and Judith H. Oliver, "A Primer of Thirteenth-Century German Convent Life: The Psalter as Office and Mass Book (London, BL, MS Add. 60629)," in *The Illuminated Psalter*, pp. 259–70.

10. Paris, BNF MS Lat. 1315; and François Avril and Patricia D. Stirnemann, *Manuscrits enluminés d'origine Insulaire, vii$^e$–xx$^e$ siècle* (Paris: Bibliothèque Nationale, 1987), no. 78.

11. Cambridge, Fitzwilliam Museum MS 38–1950; Francis Wormald and Phyllis M. Giles, *A Descriptive Catalogue of the Additional Illuminated Manuscripts in the Fitzwilliam Museum* (Cambridge: Cambridge University Press, 1982), pp. 431–36; and Lucy F. Sandler, *Gothic Manuscripts 1285–1385*, 2 vols. (London and Oxford: Harvey Miller and Oxford University Press, 1986), no. 139.

12. Lucy F. Sandler, "A Bawdy Betrothal in the Ormesby Psalter," in *Tribute to Lotte Brand Philip: Art Historian and Detective*, ed. William W. Clark et al. (New York: Abaris, 1985), pp. 155–59; and Sandler, *Gothic Manuscripts*, no. 43.

13. The literature is extensive, but two works can be quoted as representative of extreme perspectives: Michael Camille's *Image on the Edge* (London: Reaktion, 1992) celebrates the creative outbursts of artistic self-expression, humorous as well as licentious, often to the point where imaginative reading becomes a subjective interpretation. Madeline H. Caviness, "Anchoress, Abbess, and Queen:

Donors and Patrons or Intercessors and Matrons," in *The Cultural Patronage of Medieval Women*, ed. June H. McCash (Athens: University of Georgia Press, 1996), pp. 105–54, reads the same sexually charged marginalia as the oppressive instruments of male power, not only denying female owners any role in the creation of their manuscripts but also depriving them (and us) of the delights offered by brilliantly provocative works of art. For a balanced view of such interpretations, see Lucy F. Sandler, "The Study of Marginal Imagery: Past, Present, and Future," *Studies in Iconography* 18 (1997): 1–49.

14. Hildesheim, Dombibliothek MS God. 1; Jane Geddes, *The St. Albans Psalter: A Book for Christina of Markyate* (London: British Library, 2005), http://www.abdn.ac.uk/stalbanspsalter/.

15. I thank Sister Benedicta Ward for bringing this to my attention.

16. Dublin, Royal Irish Academy, s.n.; and Christopher F. R. de Hamel, *A History of Illuminated Manuscripts* (London: Phaidon, 1994), p. 22, plate 12.

17. Ruth Mellinkoff, *Averting Demons: The Protecting Power of Medieval Visual Motifs and Themes*, 2 vols. (Los Angeles: privately published, 2004).

18. Washington, DC, Dumbarton Oaks MS 3; and Henry Maguire, "Images of the Court," in *The Glory of Byzantium: Art and Culture of the Middle Byzantine Era, A.D. 843–1216*, ed. Helen C. Evans and William D. Wixom (New York: Metropolitan Museum of Art, 1997), pp. 183–91.

19. Charles Burnett, "The Prognostications of the Eadwine Psalter," in *The Eadwine Psalter: Text, Image and Monastic Culture in Twelfth-Century Canterbury*, ed. Margaret Gibson, Tony A. Heslop, and Richard W. Pfaff (London: Modern Humanities Research Association, 1992), pp. 165–67.

20. Leroquais, *Les psautiers manuscrits*, pp. x–xi.

21. Knud Ottosen, *The Responsories and Versicles of the Latin Office of the Dead* (Aarhus: Aarhus University Press, 1993).

22. *La règle de S. Benoît*, ed. Jean Neufville and Adalbert de Vogüé, 7 vols., SC 181–182 (Paris: Cerf, 1971–77), 2:528–535 (chapter 18, on the distribution of psalms over the week).

23. Andrew Hughes, *Medieval Manuscripts for Mass and Office: A Guide to Their Organization and Terminology* (Toronto: University of Toronto Press, 1982), pp. 226–31; and Robert Taft, *The Liturgy of the Hours in East and West: The Origin of the Divine Office and Its Meaning for Today* (Collegeville, MN: Liturgical, 1993 [1986]), pp. 134–40.

24. Jonathan J. G. Alexander, "Iconography and Ideology: Uncovering Social Meanings in Western Medieval Christian Art," *Studies in Iconography* 15 (1993): 1–44.

25. Rainer Kahsnitz, *Der Werdener Psalter in Berlin, MS theol. Lat. Fol. 358: Eine Untersuchung zu Problemen mittelalterlicher Psalterillustration* (Düsseldorf: Schwann, 1979).

26. Kahsnitz, *Der Werdener Psalter*, pp. 134–35; and Hughes, *Medieval Manuscripts*, pp. 226–31.

27. Kahsnitz, *Der Werdener Psalter,* pp. 115–33, and Kathleen M. Openshaw, "The Symbolic Illustration of the Psalter: An Insular Tradition," *Arte Medievale* n.s. 6 (1992): 41–60.

28. On the relationship between commentaries on the Office and Psalter illustration, see Alfred Büchler, "Zu den Psalmillustrationen der Haseloff-Schule: Die Vita Christi-Gruppe," *Zeitschrift für Kunstgeschichte* 52 (1989): 215–38. On the convergence of liturgical and exegetical traditions in medieval religious plays, see Susan Boynton, "Performative Exegesis in the Fleury *Interfectio puerorum,*" *Viator* 29 (1998): 39–64.

29. Kathleen M. Openshaw, "The Battle Between Christ and Satan in the Tiberius Psalter," *Journal of the Warburg and Courtauld Institutes* 52 (1989): 14–33.

30. Kristine E. Haney, *The Winchester Psalter* (Leicester: Leicester University Press, 1986), pp. 47–69; and Büchler, "Zu den Psalmillustrationen."

31. Oxford, Bodleian Library MS Ashmole 1525, fol. 10r; and Madeline H. Caviness, "Conflicts Between *Regnum* and *Sacerdotium* as Reflected in a Canterbury Psalter of ca. 1215," *The Art Bulletin* 61 (1979): 38–58.

32. Vatican City, Biblioteca Apostolica Vaticana MS Reg. Lat. 12, fol. 87v; and Robert M. Harris, "The Marginal Drawings of the Bury St. Edmunds Psalter (Rome, Vatican Library MS Reg. Lat. 12)," (Ph.D. diss., Princeton University, 1960), pp. 234–35.

33. See Hildesheim, Dombibliothek MS God. 1, reproduced in Geddes, *The St. Albans Psalter.*

34. A Nativity scene replaced the Annunciation to the Shepherds in Oxford, Bodleian Library MS Arundel 157, fol. 82r; the altarlike manger emphasizes the Eucharistic dimension of the image. On the equation of Christ in the crib with the Eucharist on the altar, see Ursula Nilgen, "The Epiphany and the Eucharist: On the Interpretation of Eucharistic Motifs in the Medieval Epiphany Scenes," *Art Bulletin* 49 (1967): 311–16; and Robert Deshman, *The Benedictional of St. Ethelwold* (Princeton: Princeton University Press, 1995), pp. 19–24.

35. Philippe Verdier, *Le couronnement de la Vierge: Les origines et les premiers développements d'un thème iconographique* (Paris: Institut d'études médiévales, 1980); and Marie-Louise Thérel, *Le triomphe de la Vierge-Église: Sources historiques, littéraires et iconographiques* (Paris: Centre nationale de la recherché scientifique, 1984).

36. Cambridge, University Library MS Ff.4.5, fol. 73v.

37. *The Utrecht Psalter in Medieval Art: Picturing the Psalms of David,* ed. Koert van der Horst, William Noel, and Wilhelmina C. M. Wüstefeld (Westrenen: HES, 1996); *The Eadwine Psalter;* William Noel, *The Harley Psalter* (Cambridge: Cambridge University Press, 1995); and *Anglo-Catalan Psalter,* ed. Nigel Morgan, Rosa Alcoy, and Klaus Reinhardt (Barcelona: Manuel Moleiro, 2006).

38. Günther Haseloff, *Die Psalterillustration im 13. Jahrhundert* (Kiel, 1938), pp. 104–17; and Frank O. Büttner, "Der illuminierte Psalter im Westen," in *The Illuminated Psalter,* pp. 1–106.

39. Robert Branner, *Manuscript Illumination in Paris during the Reign of Saint Louis*, California Studies in the History of Art 18 (Berkeley: University of California Press, 1977), pp. 15–21; and Mary A. Rouse and Richard H. Rouse, *Manuscripts and Their Makers: Commercial Book Producers in Medieval Paris, 1200–1500* (London: Harvey Miller, 2000), pp. 17–49.

40. Laura Light, "French Bibles c. 1200–1230: A New Look at the Origins of the Paris Bible," in *The Early Medieval Bible: Its Production, Decoration, and Use*, ed. Richard Gameson (Cambridge: Cambridge University Press, 1994), pp. 155–76.

41. This lack of differentiation, inherited from the schools of the late twelfth century, is noted as the "uncharted territory" of c. 1200–30 in Beryl Smalley, *The Study of the Bible in the Middle Ages* (Oxford: Blackwell, 1983), pp. 264–68, and admirably discussed with original sources in Joseph W. Goering, *William de Montibus (ca. 1140–1213): The Schools and the Literature of Pastoral Care*, Studies and Texts 108 (Toronto: Pontifical Institute of Medieval Studies, 1992), pp. 36–38 and 497–99.

42. Palémon Glorieux, "L'enseignement au moyen âge: Techniques et méthodes en usage à la Faculté de Théologie de Paris, au XIIIe siècle," *Archives d'histoire doctrinale et littéraire du moyen âge* 43 (1968): 65–186; and John Van Engen, "Studying Scripture in the Early University," in *Neue Richtungen in der hoch- und spätmittelalterlichen Bibelexegese*, ed. Robert E. Lerner and Elisabeth Müller-Luckner, Schriften des Historischen Kollegs. Kolloquien, 32 (Munich: Oldenbourg, 1996), pp. 17–38.

43. Karl-Georg Pfändtner, *Die Psalterillustration des 13. und beginnenden 14. Jahrhunderts in Bologna* (Neuried: Ars Una, 1996); and Stella Panayotova, "Typological Interpretation and Illustration in English Psalters, ca. 1150–1250" (Ph.D. Diss., Oxford University, 1998).

44. Morgan, *Early Gothic Manuscripts*, 1:72–76.

45. Richard W. Southern, "From Schools to University," in *The History of the University of Oxford*, vol. 1: *The Early Oxford Schools*, ed. Jeremy I. Catto (Oxford: Clarendon, 1984), pp. 1–36.

46. Southern, "From Schools to University"; and Michael A. Michael, "The Artists of the Walter of Milemete Treatise," (Ph.D. Diss., University of London, 1987), app. 2.

47. William Noel, "Medieval Charades and the Visual Syntax of the Utrecht Psalter," and Lucy F. Sandler, "The Images of Words in English Gothic Psalters," in *Studies in the Illustration of the Psalter*, ed. Brendan Cassidy and Rosemary Muir Wright (Stamford: Shaun Tyas, 2000), pp. 34–41 and 67–86, respectively. Jonathan Alexander emphasized the need to inquire into the social models encoded in religious imagery. See Alexander, "Iconography and Ideology." Michael Camille's analysis of the Luttrell Psalter demonstrated how fruitful this approach could be in his *Mirror in Parchment: The Luttrell Psalter and the Making of Medieval England* (London: Reaktion, 1998). In a series of exemplary studies of manuscripts commissioned by the Bohun family between the 1350s and the 1390s,

Lucy Sandler unveiled the political realities behind "literal" and Davidic imagery. The most recent and comprehensive study, with earlier bibliography, is her *The Lichtenthal Psalter and the Manuscript Patronage of the Bohun Family* (London: Harvey Miller, 2004).

48. Paris, BNF MS Lat. 770; Caviness, "Conflicts between Regnum and Sacerdotium"; and Avril and Stirnemann, *Manuscrits enluminés*, no. 79.

49. Oxford, Bodleian Library MS Ashmole 1525; Caviness "Conflicts Between Regnum and Sacerdotium," pp. 52–56; Morgan, *Early Gothic Manuscripts*, no. 33; and Stella Panayotova, "Art and Politics in a Royal Prayerbook," *Bodleian Library Record* 18 (2005): 440–59.

50. Just over fifty medieval manuscripts with illustrations to each psalm survive. Thirty-nine of them are Western and, with the exception of a French group of Psalters that shared a list of captions, their images differ significantly in format and relationship to biblical and exegetical texts. Elizabeth A. Peterson, "Iconography of the Historiated Psalm Initials in the Thirteenth-Century French Fully Illustrated Psalter Group" (Ph.D. Diss., University of Pittsburgh, 1991); and "The Textual Basis for Visual Errors in French Gothic Psalter Illustration," in *The Early Medieval Bible*, pp. 177–204.

51. Paris, BNF MS Lat. 10435; see *L'art au temps des rois maudits Philippe le Bel et ses fils 1285–1328*, ed. Danielle Gaborit-Chopin et al. (Paris: Réunion des musées nationaux, 1998), pp. 298–99.

52. Paris, BNF MS Lat. 10525.

53. Cambridge, Fitzwilliam Museum MS 300.

54. Sydney C. Cockerell, *A Psalter and Hours Executed Before 1270 for a Lady ... Probably Isabelle of France* (London: Chiswick, 1905); Marcel Thomas, *Psautier de Saint-Louis*, Codices selecti 37 (Graz: Akademische Druck-u. Verlagsanstalt, 1972); Branner, *Manuscript Painting*, pp. 132–37, 176–77, 238–39; Francis Wormald and P.M. Giles, *A Descriptive Catalogue*, pp. 280–84; and Harvey Stahl, "Bathsheba and the Kings: The Beatus initial in the Psalter of Saint Louis (Paris, BNF, ms lat. 10525)," in *The Illuminated Psalter*, pp. 427–34.

55. Cockerell, *A Psalter and Hours*; Jacques Le Goff, *Saint Louis* (Paris: Gallimard, 1996).

56. William C. Jordan, "The Psalter of Saint-Louis (BN Ms. lat. 10525): The Program of the Seventy-Eight Full-Page Illustrations," in *The High Middle Ages*, ed. Penelope C. Mayo (Binghamton: Center for Medieval and Early Renaissance Studies, 1983), pp. 65–91; Philippe Büttner, "Bilderzyklen in englischen und französischen Psalterhandschriften des 12. und 13. Jahrhunderts: Visuelle Realisationen persönlich gefärbter Heilsgeschichte?" in *Für irdischen Ruhm und himmlischen Lohn*, ed. Hans-Rudolf Meier, Carola Jäggi, and Philippe Büttner (Berlin: Dietrich Reimer, 1995), pp. 131–54; and Gerald B. Guest, "The People Demand a King: Visualizing Monarchy in the Psalter of Louis IX," *Studies in Iconography* 23 (2002): 1–27.

57. Hanns Swarzenski, *Die lateinische illuminierten Handschriften des XIII. Jahrhun-*

*derts in den Ländern an Rhein, Main, und Donau,* 2 vols. (Berlin: Deutscher Verein für Kunstwissenschaft, 1936); Haseloff, *Die Psalterillustration;* Kersten B. E. Carlvant, "Thirteenth-Century Illumination in Bruges and Ghent," (Ph.D. Diss., Columbia University, 1978); Judith H. Oliver, *Gothic Manuscript Illumination in the Diocese of Liège (ca. 1250-ca. 1350),* 2 vols. (Leuven: Peeters, 1988); Büchler, "Zu den Psalmillustrationen der Haseloff-Schule: Die Vita Christi-Gruppe"; Alfred Büchler, "Zu den Psalmillustrationen der Haseloff-Schule II. Psalter mit eklektischen Programmen," *Zeitschrift für Kunstgeschichte* 54 (1991): 145–80; Pfändtner, *Die Psalterillustration*; Panayotova, "Typological Interpretation"; and Büttner, "Die illuminierte Psalter."

58. Karl-Georg Pfändtner, "Zwischen Frankreich und Byzanz: Zwei Bologneser Psalter des 13. Jahrhunderts und ihr Illustrationssystem (Bologna, Bibl. Univ., ms 346 und Paris, BNF, ms Smith-Lesouëf 21)," in *The Illuminated Psalter*, pp. 181–92.

59. Cambridge, Fitzwilliam Museum MS 288; Wormald and Giles, *A Descriptive Catalogue*, pp. 252–58; Oliver, *Gothic Manuscript Illumination*, no. 9; and Judith H. Oliver, "*Te Matrem Laudamus*: The Many Roles of Mary in a Liège Psalter-Hours," in *The Cambridge Illuminations*, pp. 159–72.

60. Cambridge, Fitzwilliam Museum MS 36–1950; Wormald and Giles, *A Descriptive Catalogue*, pp. 414–29; and *The Cambridge Illuminations*, no. 71.

61. Alison Stones, "The Full-Page Miniatures of the Psalter-Hours New York, PML, ms M. 729," in *The Illuminated Psalter*, pp. 281–307 and appendix.

62. London, BL MS Arundel 157, c. 1200–c. 1210; and Morgan, *Early Gothic Manuscripts,* no. 24.

63. Imola, Biblioteca comunale MS 100; Oxford, Bodleian Library MS Liturg. 407; and Morgan, *Early Gothic Manuscripts*, nos. 26 and 27.

64. Victor N. Lazarev, *Istoriia Vizantiiskoi Zhivopisi*, 2 vols. (Moscow: Iskusstvo, 1986), 1:84, 97, and 299; Hans Belting, *Likeness and Presence* (Chicago: University of Chicago Press, 1994), pp. 73–77 and 389–90; and C. Angelidi and T. Papamastorakes, "The Veneration of the Virgin *Hodegetria* and the Hodegon Monastery," in *Mother of God: Representations of the Virgin in Byzantine Art*, ed. Maria Vassilaki (Milan: Skira, 2000), pp. 373–87.

65. Despite its monumental scale, the full-page miniature in the c. 1200 Westminster Psalter (London, BL MS Royal 2.A.XXII) is the closest parallel as an iconic image. The prefatory cycle of the contemporary Great Canterbury Psalter (Paris, BNF MS Lat. 8846), the third manuscript in the Utrecht family, shows the *Hodegetria* within the Flight into Egypt miniature. She appears in the same context in two related Oxford Psalters: London, BL MSS Arundel 157 and Royal I.D.X.

66. Robert L. Wolf, "Footnote to an Incident of the Latin Occupation of Constantinople: The Church and the Icon of the Hodegetria," *Traditio* 6 (1948): 319–28.

67. Beryl Smalley, *The Becket Conflict and the Schools* (Oxford: Oxford University Press, 1973), pp. 59–86; Christopher F. R. de Hamel, *Glossed Books of the Bible and*

the *Origins of the Paris Booktrade* (Woodbridge: Brewer, 1984), pp. 42–43, 60; and "A Contemporary Miniature of Thomas Becket," in *Intellectual Life in the Middle Ages: Essays Presented to Margaret Gibson*, ed. Lesley Smith and Benedicta Ward (London: Hambledon, 1992), pp. 179–84; Monique Peyrafort-Huin and Patricia Stirnemann, *La Bibliothèque médiévale de l'Abbaye de Pontigny (XIIe–XIXe siècles): Histoire, inventaires anciens, manuscripts* (Paris: Institut de recherche et d'histoire des textes, 2001), pp. 17–22, 55–78, 110–112; Stella Panayotova, "Tutorial in Images for Thomas Becket," in *The Cambridge Illuminations*, pp. 77–86; and Patricia Stirnemann, "En quête de Sens," in *Quand la peinture était dans les livres: Mélanges en l'honneur de François Avril*, ed. Mara Hofmann and Caroline Zöhl (Turnhout: Brepols, 2007), pp. 303–11.

68.   On the Psalms: Cambridge, Trinity College MS B.5.4; Oxford, Bodleian Library MS Auct. E.inf.6; on the Pauline Epistles: Cambridge, Trinity College MSS B.5.6 and B.5.7.

# 13

# The Bible in English in the Middle Ages

*Richard Marsden*

No complete Bible in the English language was produced until the end of the fourteenth century (in the version known as the Wycliffite Bible), but for more than a thousand years, since at least the ninth century, speakers of English have been able to read or hear in their own language many of the pivotal biblical narratives—the story of creation in Genesis, the crossing of the Red Sea in Exodus, the life of Christ in the four Gospels. Indeed, English has one of the longest continuous traditions of biblical translation of any of the modern Western languages.[1] Linguistically, however, this continuity has inevitably been compromised by the evolution of English, with the greatest change occurring in the twelfth to fourteenth centuries. There is consequently a considerable gulf between texts written in the Old English period (i.e., that of the Anglo-Saxons, c. 450–c. 1150) and those written in the Middle English period (c. 1150–c. 1500).[2] There is another significant difference between the earlier and later medieval periods, too, relating to the audience for vernacular Scripture: in general, we may say that the earlier translations were made for the "professional" religious (monks and clerics) and certain aristocratic laypeople (who probably commissioned the translations), whereas the Wycliffite and later English Bibles were aimed at "everyman," ordinary men and women desiring direct access to Scripture.

When we talk of "vernacular" Scripture, we mean, of course, Scripture in the language or dialect spoken by ordinary people in a particular region or country, but in the context of medieval Christianity the term also means more specifically "not Latin." The effects of the cultural imperialism of Latin on Western Christendom cannot be overstated: it was *the* language of Christianity—and thus, ipso facto, of learning—from the fourth century until the Reformation. It came to be revered as a sacred language on a par with the original scriptural languages, Hebrew (the language in which most of the Old Testament was written) and Greek (the language of the New Testament). The very words of Scripture, the Word of God, were considered inviolable, and translation was potentially a heretical undertaking. Furthermore, as knowledge of Latin declined, a gap was created between the professional religious, who still learned the sacred language, and the great majority of the Christian flock, who did not.[3] But this would come to be considered by many in the Church as not so much a barrier to understanding as an essential safety buffer, for it allowed priests and preachers to control access to the biblical narratives and to interpret them according to current orthodoxies. Such mediation would eventually become a contentious issue. Reformers from the later fourteenth century onward saw it as a pernicious means to hide the naked truth of Scripture from the people. They would point out that Latin itself was once simply a vernacular into which the Hebrew and Greek Scriptures had of necessity been translated to allow direct access. However, any challenge to the hegemony of Latin as a scriptural and devotional language was also a challenge to the church itself as an institution. Thus the use of the vernacular in the Middle Ages had huge cultural and theological implications for Christians, which we must bear in mind in our survey.[4]

## The Anglo-Saxon Period (c. 500–c. 1100)

When the Anglo-Saxons were converted to Christianity, first through the mission of Augustine of Canterbury in the south (beginning in 597) and then by Aidan in the north (from 635), they acquired literacy as well as a new faith. Their own language, which today we know as Old English (really a group of mutually intelligible dialects), had been recorded until then in a very limited way in the runic alphabet, carved on stone, wood, or bone; now it could be written in the Latin alphabet, adapted by Christian monks to accommodate sounds in Old English that were absent from Latin itself. We have no clear evidence of any systematic attempts to provide Scripture in the vernacular during the earliest years of Anglo-Saxon Christianity, but the conversion process must have relied on preaching in English and the regular citation in translation of key biblical episodes and the themes of Christian history. The missionaries were literate in Latin and presumably will have spoken it among themselves, and they brought with them volumes of Scripture in Latin. Once they had established monastic schools, they had to start training native Anglo-Saxon boys to become competent users of Latin also, in order for them to be able to understand and take part in the liturgy of the monastic offices (the daily round of church services) that punctuated their lives. The Venerable Bede (c. 673–735), a native Northumbrian with English as his mother tongue, fills out the picture a little in a letter he wrote to Bishop Egbert of York, recommending the use of the vernacular to teach the Creed and the Lord's Prayer both to laypeople and to monks and clerics.[5] One of his followers even records that Bede was working on a translation of part of the Gospel of John (as far as 6:9, it seems) as he lay dying in the spring of 735 at the twin monastery of Wearmouth-Jarrow, where he had spent all his life from the age of seven.[6] This has sometimes been taken as an indication that Bede translated all four of the Gospels, and even the whole Bible, into English, but such an idea is far-fetched. It is possible that he was simply "glossing" a section of John—that is, dictating a word-by-word Old English version to be inserted between the lines of a Latin text. This might have been a way of facilitating the reading of the latter by learners of Latin as part of a program of teaching the language.

Such glossing did become a regular feature of monastic practice in later centuries, above all in Psalters. These small, portable volumes of the biblical psalms for devotional and liturgical use survive in greater numbers (forty) than any other type of manuscript book from the Anglo-Saxon period.[7] Psalms had a central role in the life of monks. A selection was used in all the daily offices, and the whole corpus of 150 was sung over the course of every week (on the Psalms in the Mass and Office, see Boynton's chapter in this volume). Eleven of the extant Anglo-Saxon Psalters are more or less continuously glossed in Old English, and four others partly so. The Old English version of each Latin word is written immediately above it in the interlinear space, thus producing a word-for-word crib of the Latin. This is not, of course, the same as a true translation, for the syntax and word order of Latin are often very different from those of Old English, and the latter version, read continuously, may be almost incomprehensible in places. The gloss was there to help readers to understand the Latin, not replace it. The oldest extant example is one added in the ninth century to a Latin Psalter whose original text had been copied in the eighth century, possibly at Canterbury (the "Vespasian Psalter," London, BL Cotton Vespasian A. i).

As for other biblical manuscripts, vernacular glossing is conspicuously absent from the two complete Latin Bibles and the handful of Old Testament "part-Bibles" that have survived from the Anglo-Saxon period (for more on "part-Bibles," see Gyug's chapter in this volume).[8] Nor are there glosses in the approximately thirty extant gospel books from this period, with just two exceptions. One of these is among the most famous Anglo-Saxon manuscripts: the magnificent Lindisfarne Gospels (London, BL Cotton Nero D. iv), produced probably at the island monastery of Lindisfarne, off the Northumbrian coast, to mark the exhumation in 698 of the remains of Cuthbert, Northumbria's most important saint.[9] It was not until the mid tenth century that the original Latin text was supplied with a continuous word-for-word Old English gloss, by Aldred, provost of a community established in honour of Saint Cuthbert at Chester-le-Street in County Durham. The other glossed gospel book from Anglo-Saxon England is the Rushworth or Macregol Gospels (Oxford, Bodleian Library Auct. D. 2. 19), produced in the late eighth or early ninth century, possibly in Ireland; this, too, received its gloss only in the tenth century. The two scribes involved are named in the manuscript as Owun and Farmon, but we do not know where they worked. Consistent similarities indicate that they used a version of the Lindisfarne gloss as the model for much of their work, but in the sections done by Farmon (Matthew and John 18:1–3) there is a tendency for the word-for-word technique to be abandoned in favor of an Old English version more in accord with native syntax and thus readable in itself without recourse to the Latin.[10]

From what we have seen, extensive biblical glossing did not become the norm in England until the ninth century (and then mainly in Psalters). It may be that in the earlier centuries the teaching of Latin had been more rigorous and more successful, but, when these circumstances changed, it was recognized that more help was needed. There is indeed ample evidence for a severe decline in both the quantity and the quality of Latin learning by the middle of the ninth century, as we shall have occasion to note in discussing King Alfred. But another way of "translating" the Bible was already by this time well established, namely, the poetic paraphrase. The fashion for making dramatic poems, often very long, from the key narratives of Scripture more or less died out among English poets after the seventeenth century (Milton being the last notable exponent), but it was highly popular throughout the Middle Ages. We have "historical" evidence of its beginning as early as the late seventh century, and again it is from the invaluable Bede, in his *Historia ecclesiastica gentis Anglorum* ("Ecclesiastical History of the English People"). He tells how a cowherd named Cædmon at the monastery of Whitby, in Northumbria, received divine inspiration to make vernacular songs out of the books of Latin Scripture. After first showing his mettle with a lyric about creation (known as "Cædmon's Hymn"), Cædmon was received into the monastery as a monk and went on to compose a poetical portfolio of major biblical themes. As Bede tells it:

> He sang about the creation of the world, the origin of the human race, and the whole history of Genesis, of the departure of Israel from Egypt and the entry into the promised land and of many other of the stories taken from the sacred Scriptures: of the incarnation, passion, and resurrection of the Lord, of his ascension into heaven, of the coming of the Holy Spirit and the teaching of the apostles. He also made songs about the terrors of future judgement, the horrors of the pains of hell, and the joys of the heavenly kingdom. In addition he composed many other songs about the divine mercies and judgements.[11]

This is a remarkably comprehensive overview of biblical history. A number of poems in Old English treating these very themes are extant, but they cannot be attributed to Cædmon himself (about whom we know only what Bede tells us), and in fact appear to be by several different poets. On Old Testament themes, we have (using their modern titles) *Genesis A*, *Genesis B*, *Exodus*, *Daniel*, and *Judith*; and on New Testament themes, *Christ and Satan*, *Christ* (I, II, and III), *Andreas* (about the apostle Andrew), *The Fates of the Apostles*, *The Dream of the Rood* (about Christ's crucifixion), *Elene* (about Helen, finder of the "true cross" of the crucifixion), *The Descent into Hell* (about Christ's "harrowing of hell"), and *Judgement Day*.[12] The narratives on which some of these are based are categorized today as apocryphal or noncanonical, because they were not later accepted as part of the official canon of Scripture by either the Roman Catholic or the Protestant Churches; the Book of Judith is in fact accepted by the former but not the latter.

Some of the poetic paraphrases (especially those based on the Old Testament) follow the Bible quite closely; others treat their themes more loosely or tangentially. All have an explicit purpose beyond a simple retelling of the biblical stories: the narratives are rearranged, shaped, and often elaborated in such a way that a clear doctrinal message is conveyed. This is thus a sort of exegesis, and it is the orthodoxies of the great church fathers such as Augustine, Jerome, and Gregory that are usually (but not invariably) followed. For instance, the 349-line *Judith* retains from the Old Testament story only the episode in which Judith has her fateful meeting with the Assyrian general Holofernes, the enemy of the Hebrew people. She is a "type" of faith, whose righteousness God rewards by endowing her with the strength to cut off the general's head. To enhance the effect, Judith is transformed by the poet from the feisty widow of the Bible to a pious virgin, and Holofernes is thoroughly demonized as a lecherous ogre (which may explain the poem's inclusion in the manuscript containing *Beowulf* and other "monster" texts). In *Genesis A*, a poem of almost 3,000 lines, the focus is on the working out of the promises made by God to Abraham. Lines 235–851 were originally a separate poem, which we label *Genesis B*; its theme is obedience, and the highly emotive narrative, full of psychological insights, links the fall of the rebellious Satan and his followers with the fall of Eve and Adam. In the case of *Exodus* (590 lines), the raw material for the poet is the pivotal crossing of the Red Sea by the fleeing Israelites. This is told economically in the Bible (Exod. 13:20–14) but here is extended into an exciting drama of deliverance in which God fulfills his covenant with Moses by saving his chosen people and destroying Pharaoh with his army. The message of *Daniel* (764 lines) is about salvation; highlighted are the miraculous survival of the three boys in the fiery furnace, Daniel's part in the conversion of Nabuchodnezzar, and the prophetic happenings at Balshazzar's feast (featuring "the writing on the wall"). *Genesis*, *Exodus*, and *Daniel* are collected in the so-called Junius codex (Oxford, Bodleian Library Junius 11), along with *Christ and Satan*, a poem that complements the others by carrying us forward to New Testament themes: the Harrowing of Hell, Resurrection, Ascension, and the Day of Judgment.[13]

For the Anglo-Saxon audience of these poems, the characters, as well as the language, are made "familiar." The male characters often seem to be taken straight from the traditional heroic world recreated so memorably in *Beowulf*. Thus in *Genesis A* Abraham leads his people as a doughty battle-hardened chieftain, famous for his deeds; in *Exodus* Moses is a vaunting helmeted warrior, and the tribes of Israel march in their mail-coats, brandishing shield and spear; and in *Genesis B* even Satan is a lord whose followers owe him loyalty in return for his gifts of treasure.

*Genesis B* is of particular interest because it is actually not an original Old English work at all but the close translation of a poem written in Old Saxon, the language of the inhabitants of Saxony, which was the home-land of many of the original Anglo-Saxon settlers (in part of what is now Germany). We know this because a twenty-five-line fragment of the Old Saxon version is preserved in a manuscript in the Vatican Library; the lan-guage is remarkably similar to Old English.[14] We are thus reminded of the close contacts between England and the Continent during much of the Anglo-Saxon period. From the end of the seventh century, Anglo-Saxon missionaries evangelized among the Germanic peoples of the Continent, including the Frisians and the Saxons. But there was traffic in the other direction too. We know, for instance, that a monk called John the Saxon was one of King Alfred's helpers when he was seeking to restore learning in England during the closing decades of the ninth century. When the Old Saxon poem reached England is unknown, but certainly it was not the only biblical poem known to the Saxons. Another survivor is the *Heliand* (Old Saxon for "savior"), a versified life of Christ apparently based on an early "gospel harmony" (a narrative made from a conflation of the accounts of Christ in the four gospels).[15]

Neither of the "translation" methods so far discussed, interlinear gloss-ing and versified paraphrasing, is translation as normally understood. In the former case, the Latin remains in place, and its primacy is not chal-lenged; the Old English version serves mainly as a crib to help in reading it. In the latter case, selected passages of Latin Scripture are simply the starting point for the dramatic amplification and exploration of the bare narrative. The earliest substantial continuous "plain" translation of Scrip-ture that we know about is associated with the reign of King Alfred of Wessex (877–99). This is not surprising, given the king's central role in promoting the English language as a viable and flexible medium both of learning and communication in Anglo-Saxon England. He saw how dra-matically Latin learning in the monasteries had declined during the decades preceding his accession to the throne, and he took the opportu-nity, once he had achieved some political stability by halting the encroachment of settling Danes, to instigate a program of education for the young men of his kingdom.[16] This was not to be in the time-honored language of learning, Latin, but in English.

The first evidence of vernacular Scripture is a prefatory section that the king prepared, or had prepared, to introduce his Old English law code. It consists of translated extracts from Exodus 20–23 (chapters of Mosaic law that include the ten commandments) and Acts 15:23–29 (a reference to the apostles' preaching of the law to the fledging churches). The explicit object of these extracts is to give scriptural authority to Alfred's own laws. A far more substantial work is the translation that Alfred made of the first fifty psalms. Our only copy of the text is one made long after the king's death, in the mid eleventh century, as part of a manuscript known as the "Paris Psalter" (Paris, Bibliothèque nationale de France MS. lat. 8824), a book which is three times as tall as wide (526 x 186 mm), with two narrow columns of text per page.[17] Originally it had a frontispiece of King David playing the harp and a number of colored decorative pages, but these have all disappeared. The fifty prose psalms, which stylistic and circumstantial evidence allows us to be fairly confident were translated by Alfred himself, are followed by the other one hundred psalms in metrical versions, but these are unlikely to be Alfred's. The volume also has a Latin text for all the psalms, supplied in the left-hand column of each page, in parallel with the Old English text, but this is not the one that had been used by the translators of the Old English texts.[18] In other words, the Old English and Latin versions were united arbitrarily at a later date, and there is no reason to think that Alfred had originally included a parallel Latin text. An explanation for this unusual and costly book might be that it was compiled for a wealthy and pious nobleman or noblewoman who wanted to emulate religious in having his or her own Latin Psalter but was unable to read that language and so needed a continuous Old English version.

Alfred's translation is consistently accurate and mostly follows the Latin closely in sense, but sometimes he amplifies the text or adds short explanations. This may be illustrated with his version of the start of what was Psalm 22 in Alfred's Vulgate numbering but is more widely known today as Psalm 23.[19] We shall use our own interlinear glossing system to put a literal modern rendering over the Old English words. Such have been the changes in English since Alfred's day that, for the modern reader unfamiliar with the older language, this modern version works rather as the interlinear Old English glosses in Latin psalters would have done in the Anglo-Saxon period for those not knowing Latin.[20]

Lord　　me guides not is to-me of-none good lacking And  he  me  put
Drihten mē rǣt,  ne byð mē nānes gōdes wan.　　Ond hē mē geset

in  very  good cattle-land and fed　　me by waters' banks　　and
on swȳðe good feohland ond fēdde mē be wætera staðum ond

my  heart  turned  from unhappiness to  joy  He me  led
mīn mōd gehwyrfde of unrōtnesse　on gefēan. Hē mē gelǣdde

over the ways of-righteousness for his name　 Though I now walk　in
ofer þā wegas rihtwīsnesse for his naman. Þēah  ic nū  gange on

midst　the shadow of-death not dread  I me none evil  because　 thou
midde þā sceade dēaðes ne ondrǣde ic mē nān yfel, for þām  þū

be  with me  Lord　　 Thy yard and thy staff me　 comforted
byst mid mē Drihten. Þīn gyrd ond þīn stæf mē āfrēfredon,

that is thy correction and also thy consolation
þæt is þīn þrēaung ond eft þīn frēfrung.

A more idiomatic version of the interlinear modern English is: "The Lord guides me; to me nothing in the way of good is lacking. And he placed me in very good pasture land and fed me beside the banks of streams, and turned my heart from sadness to joy. He led me along the paths of righteousness, in his name. Though I now walk in the middle of the shadow of death, I (will) fear no evil, because you are (or will be) with me, Lord. Your rod and your staff comforted me; that is, your correction and also your consolation."

Notable in Alfred's version is the redefining of what in the Latin is simply "place of pasture" as "very good cattle land." Another addition is the explanation of the symbolic meaning of "rod and staff," which offers an interpretation common among the established church commentators on Scripture, such as Augustine of Hippo. Before each of the psalms except the first (and the lack here is certainly due to loss in transmission), Alfred also placed a short introduction to explain the psalm's historical and theological significance. The one that prefaces Psalm 22 (23) begins: "David sang this twenty-second psalm when he prophesied about the freedom of the Israelites and how they were to be led out from Babylonian captivity, and how they should thank God for the mercies which they would receive on the way home; and also [he sang] about his own return from his journey of exile." For Alfred it is important that the devotional impulse of psalm-reading be complemented with sound teaching.

We should not leave Alfred without mentioning an important document written by him in which he discusses some of the problems of scriptural translation. It is a letter that he sent to bishops around the kingdom to accompany copies of one of the translations of Christian works that he had authorized, Gregory the Great's *Cura pastoralis* ("pastoral care").[21] In it, while asserting the need for turning sacred works into English, he shows that he is nevertheless concerned about possible criticism. He forestalls this by citing precedent: that is, the Hebrew Scriptures had been put into Greek and then into Latin to meet the needs of the people whose vernaculars these were; English is merely the latest such case. Alfred alludes also to a question that has exercised biblical translators since Jerome and continues to do so in modern times: how close should the target language stay to the source language? Can one risk tampering with the "literal" word of God? Alfred's solution is characteristically pragmatic: he tells us that sometimes he translated "word for word," sometimes "sense for sense," as seemed necessary.[22]

Our next named Anglo-Saxon translator of parts of the Bible, Abbot Ælfric of Eynsham, similarly worried about what he was doing. Ælfric translated the first half of Genesis, a part of Numbers, and Joshua, but expressed his misgivings in a preface to the Genesis translation.[23] Genesis is composed exactly as God gave it to Moses, he declares, and therefore "I dare not write any more in the English than the Latin has, or change the order of things, except only when the Latin and the English do not have the same way of doing things." In other words, while he does try to keep to a strictly "word for word" translation, he knows full well that he must substitute English syntax if the translation is to make "sense," which is the prime object. Ælfric's translations are in fact remarkably close to the Latin, and yet literalism is never allowed to obscure meaning, and he, like Alfred, occasionally makes small amplifications in order to clarify the scriptural narrative.

In the early years of the eleventh century, Ælfric's renderings of Genesis, part of Numbers, and Joshua were gathered together with Old English versions of Exodus, Leviticus, the rest of Numbers, and Deuteronomy to make a "Hexateuch," a compilation of the first six books of the Old Testament. The non-Ælfrician pieces may have been made especially for the compilation, but who did this is unknown. One full copy of the Hexateuch survives in a beautiful manuscript packed with nearly four hundred miniature paintings, illustrating the scriptural narrative step by step (London, BL Cotton Claudius B. iv).[24] The only other surviving complete copy is in a smaller and more workaday manuscript to which the seventh book of the Old Testament, Judges, has been added, making an *Old English Heptateuch.* Judges is again by Ælfric and is more of a homily than a strict translation, though it does contain extended passages of plain text. Parts of the Hexateuch compilation survive in five or six other manuscripts or manuscript fragments, suggesting that this vernacular part-Bible was popular.[25]

More or less contemporary with the Old Testament translations— though unconnected, as far as we can tell—is a complete version of the four Gospels. There are six eleventh-century manuscripts of *Old English Gospels* extant, four of them complete, and two more not copied until the twelfth century, perhaps at Canterbury. In the case of the latter two, the language has been revised to bring it in line with twelfth-century usage. We have no idea who made the translations, but several people were probably involved, to judge from stylistic variation. Overall, the translation is very accurate and close to the Latin.[26]

Who was the audience for these substantial translations of Scripture in Old English? We know from Ælfric's writings that his own versions of Genesis 1–24:26 and Joshua were made for his patron, Æthelweard, ealdorman of the southwestern part of England (who had already, according again to Ælfric's account, commissioned a translation of the later part of Genesis from someone else). It is worth noting also that the luxurious illustrated Hexateuch volume must have been made for someone wealthy, though not for Æthelweard himself, to judge from the probable date of the manuscript's production in the second quarter of the eleventh century. In part, then, an audience of aristocratic people for vernacular Scripture may be surmised, but there is good evidence in several of the manuscripts themselves, in the form of additions and annotations, that they were used also in the monasteries. In one gospel manuscript, Latin headings have been added to some passages to indicate the liturgical occasions on which they were to be read, but this does not necessarily mean that the translations were actually used in services. It is unlikely that the Old English translations circulated beyond the monasteries and the houses of the pious nobility. Although there were no other substantial translations of Scripture into Old English, as far as we know, we should not forget that a major source of snippets of translation was the homily or sermon (on sermons, see Poleg's chapter in this volume). Many of the items in Ælfric's two volumes of *Catholic Homilies*, for example, begin with a biblical passage, given first in Latin and then in translation; there then follows a detailed explanation of the significance of the passage in the church year and in the lives of Christian people.[27] This sort of translation is of course tightly controlled: it is not read independently of interpretation and commentary, and often, as noted earlier, the original Latin is the starting point.

## The Later Medieval Period (c. 1150–1500)

The Norman Conquest of 1066 brought cataclysmic political and ecclesiastical change to England. A Norman French aristocracy took over the running of the country, and Norman French bishops and abbots soon occupied most positions of leadership in church and monastery. The primacy of Latin as the language of Christianity was reinforced. It had in fact never lost its prestige, but the vernacular had enjoyed an easy parallel relationship with it. English remained, of course, the language of the native people after the Conquest and although the natural processes of language change would now accelerate, both the *Old English Heptateuch* and the *Old English Gospels* were among the texts that continued to be copied and/or annotated until the early thirteenth century. However, by about 1250 the older language would have become rather difficult for most readers. One problem, apart from obvious changes such an increasing loss of inflections, new spelling conventions, and a gradual, but accelerating, introduction of new words (mostly from French), was that written English had lost the control of a "standard" form—a form used with small variation by most educated people writing it, wherever they might live in the country. The standard during the Anglo-Saxon period had been based on West Saxon (the variety of Old English spoken in Wessex), but now regional varieties asserted themselves just as strongly and the language of the old biblical translations became merely one dialect among many.[28]

No efforts appear to have been made during the thirteenth and earlier fourteenth centuries to update or recreate the substantial OE prose translations we have noted (of the Heptateuch or the Gospels) or to add further biblical books to them. In contrast, during this time French vernacular versions—including complete Bibles—became well established (see Sneddon's chapter in this volume). This, however, is not surprising.

For some two hundred years after the conquest, the stratum of society in which a desire for translations was combined with the wealth to commission or buy them was the French-speaking ruling elite. Furthermore, for the reasons noted, it would take some time for anything like a new standard English to develop, one that would be intelligible to most English people, no matter where they lived. Essential, too, for the emergence of a complete English biblical translation would be the political (as well as devotional) will to provide it; this would eventually come from the Wycliffites in the 1390s.

Yet this is not to say that the Middle English–speaking people of England were deprived of access to Scripture in their own language; far from it. The later twelfth, thirteenth, and fourteenth centuries saw the production of an astonishing quantity and variety of Christian devotional, instructional, and regulatory literature in the vernacular, in both prose and verse. Most of it of necessity quoted or paraphrased the Bible freely.[29] As in the Anglo-Saxon centuries, it was a case of Scripture transmitted piecemeal (and usually in paraphrase)—to meet specific devotional or didactic demands and in whatever form seemed fit for purpose. Many of the texts were translations of existing works in French that were in use among the French-speaking upper classes. As in Anglo-Saxon times, sermon and homily provided some of the most pervasive methods of exposure to the Bible in English. Major collections of such works continued the Old English tradition exemplified above all by Ælfric.

Some of the metrical works were massive, attempting to present the whole conspectus of biblical (and thus human) history, from Creation and Fall, through exile, covenant, and prophecy, to fulfillment in the life and passion of Christ, the evolution of the church, and onward, ultimately, to the Last Judgment. One of the earliest was the *Ormulum*, dating from 1170–80 and named after its author, Orm, an Augustinian canon who probably lived in the "Danelaw" area of the north and east of England, to judge from his language. The work is 20,000 lines long as we have it but was apparently intended to be far longer. It has 31 substantial New Testament readings in verse paraphrase, followed by long passages of amplification and interpretation, but no fewer than 242 readings are listed in the introductory part of the poem. Another vast metrical work is the *Cursor mundi* (Runner of the world), of which there are ten surviving manuscripts preserving various versions, the longest of which has 30,000 lines. The work may have originated in the north of England around 1300. Its narrative of biblical history is based on the seven "ages" of the world and is filled out with extra material taken from legend. Elucidation is provided by extracts from the *Historia scholastica*, a hugely influential work by the French theologian Peter Comestor, written in the twelfth century for students in the great university schools. Middle English poems restricted to parts of the Old Testament include the 4,000-line *Genesis and Exodus* (which incorporates material from Numbers and Deuteronomy also), extant in an early fourteenth-century manuscript but probably originally composed c. 1250. It is again based on the *Historia scholastica*.

There are many shorter works also, which isolate and epitomize single themes or events, such as the Beatitudes, the Ten Commandments, the *Pater noster* ("Our Father"), or stages in the life of Christ (very frequently the Passion). The *Ballad of the Twelfth Day*, for instance, extant in one mid-thirteenth-century copy, tells the story of the three magi and Herod from Matthew 2:1–12 in eighty lines. An Old Testament example is *Iacob and Iosep*, a five-hundred-line poem again in the ballad tradition, the earliest of the two extant manuscripts dating from the later thirteenth century. Starting with a reference to Noah's flood, which is presented as a punishment for gluttony, it then alludes mainly to the events of Genesis 37–47, including Joseph's dream, Pharaoh's dream, and the famine in Egypt. Its aim is to contrast the present time of sinful over-indulgence with events in the biblical age.

The works so far mentioned are paraphrases of, and usually commentaries on, selected parts of the biblical narratives. In the earlier Middle English period, only the Psalms circulated in complete and continuous translations (as well as individually and in numerous small selections), but these, too, were rarely without additional explicatory material of some sort.[30] Several vernacular versions became available, but by far the most popular was the prose Psalter produced by the Yorkshire scholar and hermit Richard Rolle of Hampole (d. 1349). Nearly forty copies of it survive in various forms. Rolle was a mystic whose emotionally charged writings (most of them in Latin) expressed his burning passion for God and Christ. A verse prologue in one copy of the Psalter tells us that Rolle composed it (probably c. 1340) for his friend Margaret Kirkeby, whom he had cured of a disease. His Psalter included a Latin text, along with an extensive commentary (in English) based on that of Peter Lombard, the great Italian theologian who studied and then taught at Paris during the twelfth century (on biblical commentary in this period, see van Liere's chapter in this volume). In an introduction, Rolle says that in his Psalter he uses simple English and where possible words that are near to the Latin, as a help for devout people who do not know that language. This may explain why the English is often, to modern minds at least, stilted, and it has been suggested that this version (like others, in all probability) began life as an interlinear gloss. Nevertheless, Rolle states clearly (echoing the words of Ælfric 350 years earlier) that he will abandon strict literalism where necessary and follow only the sense of the Latin.

This is the opening of Psalm 22 (23) in Rolle's version:[31]

| | |
|---|---|
| Lord gouerns me and nathynge sall me want; | *sall* shall |
| in sted of pasture thare he me sett. On the | *sted* place |
| watere of rehetynge forth he me broght; my | *rehetynge* refreshment |
| saule he turnyd. He led me on the stretis of | *stretis* "streets," paths |
| rightwisnes, for his name. For whi, if I had | *For whi* Wherefore |
| gane in myddis of the shadow of ded, I sall | *gane* gone, walked; *ded* death |
| noght dred illes, for thou ert with me. | *noght* not; *illes* ill, harm |
| Thi wand and thi staf, thai haf confortyd me. | |

The English here is indeed remarkably close to the Latin (too much so for our comfort), yet it is not a completely literal version—which would, for instance, have produced "for thou with me ert" in the seventh line.

We move finally to the Wycliffite Bible, which gave England for the first time the complete Old and New Testaments in the vernacular, a translation designed unequivocally to take the place of Latin Scripture for lay Christians. It was made by scholars associated with the theologian and reformer John Wyclif, working mostly at Oxford in the closing decades of the fourteenth century. An astonishing total of about 250 manuscripts survive, though some are fragmentary; two-thirds of them are part-Bibles, including gospel books, and it is clear that these always outnumbered complete Bibles.[32]

The production of the Wycliffite Bible can only be understood in the context of contemporary theological debate and ecclesiastical politics. The beginning of the Protestant Reformation is usually pinpointed to the decisive challenge to the papacy launched by Luther in Germany in 1517, when he nailed his ninety-five "theses" against indulgences to the door of the Schlosskirche in Wittenberg; but one of the fundamental issues that provoked his challenge—dissatisfaction with spiritual failings and administrative abuses in the church—had long been identified. Criticisms of members of the church hierarchy, from local priests right up to the pope himself, were rife (as readers of Langland's *Piers Plowman* and Chaucer's

*Canterbury Tales* will know well enough). For Wyclif, human salvation depended on individual faith, and the Bible was the guide to that faith, the one and only source of Christian truth. The elaborate hierarchical structures used by the ecclesiastical authorities to sustain their power were without basis in Scripture. Wyclif was angered by the stranglehold that priests, and, especially, the preaching friars, had on the practice of religion among the laity. False preachers had corrupted the law of God for their own ends. As one Lollard tract put it, they are known as Christians and "þei prechen sumwhat of þe gospel" but they "gloson it as hem likeþ"—they preach something of the Gospel but gloss (i.e., interpret) it as they please.[33]

It was the desire to make available to every man and woman the direct word of God, without tampering by priest or speculative theologian, that lay behind the enterprise to translate the Bible in its entirety. The Wycliffites did not reject interpretation of the Bible; indeed, most of the long prologue that was attached to some late copies of their version was taken up with the principles of proper interpretation, based on the church fathers, and sometimes the translation itself offered explanatory readings. Rather, they saw the contemporary overworldly church, with its self-serving priests and friars, as inadequate to interpret Scripture in a traditional Christ-centered way.

Not surprisingly, the church authorities condemned Wyclif for his unorthodox views. In 1382 he was obliged to retire to his parish at Lutterworth, in Warwickshire, but he was still writing angry pamphlets until his death in 1384. Thereafter, his followers continued to preach and practice his ideas. They would become known as Lollards—a contemptuous term (used also of earlier sects) derived from a Dutch verb meaning to mumble or mutter.

The extent to which Wyclif himself participated in the production of what we now call the Wycliffite Bible has been a matter of dispute.[34] Direct evidence of his day-to-day involvement is lacking, yet it is hard to imagine that he was not involved; it is indeed likely that he initiated and encouraged the project, and he may have actively supervised it. Other collaborators among the Oxford Lollards certainly included Nicholas of Hereford (according to the evidence of several manuscripts) and probably John of Trevisa and John Purvey. Preparatory work may have begun in the early 1370s and the whole project was extended in several stages over a number of years (the latest datable copy appears to have been produced in 1408). Viewed as a whole, the extant manuscripts of the Wycliffite Bible, many of which underwent revision and alteration, seem to constitute a work in progress, but the full details are all but impossible to unravel fully now. Broadly speaking each manuscript falls into one of two groups.[35] The smaller first group has an "earlier version" of the English text very close to the Latin, to the extent that literalism may render sense obscure; the far larger second group has a "later version," which seems to have been revised to produce a more idiomatic English text. The general difference between earlier and later versions may be illustrated with a short passage from the opening of Genesis 8, which recounts the later stages in the story of Noah's flood. The usual Latin Vulgate version is given first (with significant words italicized), along with a modern translation:[36]

*Recordatus* autem Deus Noe cunctarumque *animantium* et omnium *iumentorum* quae erant cum eo in arca, *adduxit spiritum* super terram et inminutae sunt aquae:

[God moreover remembered Noah and all the living things and all the animals which were with him in the ark, (and) he brought a wind on the earth and the waters were diminished.]

*Earlier version:*

Þe lord forsoþ recordyde of noe
& of all hauyng souleȝ & of all
iumenteȝ þat wern with hym in þe
ark / & he brouȝte to a spyrit vpon
þe erþ. and þe watris ben lassed.

*Later version:*

Forsoþe þe lord hadde mynde on noe
& of alle lyuinge beestis. & of alle
werk bestis þat weren with him in þe
schip: and brouȝte a wynd on
þe erþe / and watris weren decreesid

In the earlier version, "recordyde of" renders literally the Latin *recordatus* (and in fact the verb is regularly used in the sense of "remember" in Middle English). The translation of Latin *cunctarum animantium* as "of all having souls" in the earlier version is precise, but awkward. In "iumenteȝ," we see the straight borrowing of another Latin word, probably its first occurrence in English.[37] As for "brouȝte to," this precisely renders the prefixed Latin verb, *ad-duxit*, but is not idiomatic here, and the literal "spirit" is not what is meant in this context by *spiritum* ("a breathing" or "breeze," and thus by extension the "breath of life"). Overall, although it is true that the later version may still seem to us rather defective, some of the extreme literalisms of the earlier version have been removed in the revision, and there is greater clarity.

The simple "earlier" or "later" division between versions of the Wycliffite Bible in fact often breaks down, for there are manuscripts that show elements of both versions, but the model of an evolving work remains valid. An invaluable "general prologue" attached to a handful of the later manuscripts includes a section that details the painstaking labor that went into the project. It tells how the scholars first had to establish a reliable Latin text (for the quality of Latin Bibles was notoriously variable in the medieval period); then they used all the resources they could find, including ancient commentaries, to understand fully what the Latin meant before actually translating, and then they passed the work among themselves for careful revision. This was a team effort.

The prologue also refers to the specific difficulties of the Latin language and raises the old problem of whether to translate word for word or sense for sense:

> First it is to knowe þat þe beste translating is, out of Latyn into English, to translate aftir þe sentence [sense] and not oneli aftir þe wordis, so þat þe sentence be opin eiþer openere [clear or clearer] in English as in Latyn, and go not fer fro [far from] þe lettre; and if þe lettre mai not be suid [followed] in þe translating, let þe sentence euere [ever] be hool [whole] and open, for þe wordis owen [ought] to serue [serve] to þe entent [intention] and sentence, and ellis [else] þe wordis ben superflu [are superflous] eiþer false.[38]

This is the practical approach we are familiar with from the testimony of Alfred and Ælfric, but there is an added (and provocative) dimension—namely, the implicit claim that the English translation may communicate the truth of Scripture more clearly than the Latin itself.

We have already noted that, while the avowed aim of the Wycliffites was to make available "naked" Scripture, they were not against interpretation. The principle of *sola scriptura* ("by scripture alone") has often been wrongly ascribed to them.[39] Many copies of the Wycliffite Bible, especially those of the later version, carry extensive glossing of various kinds, including alternative translations of specific words and explanatory amplifications (often of the sort that we have seen that both Alfred and Ælfric used). Sometimes they are in the margins, sometimes incorporated in the text, usually underlined, and the most frequent source for the content of the additions is Nicholas of Lyra, the Paris-based Fransciscan scholar (d. 1340). There appear to be several series of glosses, shared by various groups of manuscripts, and it is likely that some, at least, were made by the translators themselves and thus may be considered to have special authority. In addition, there survive separate Wycliffite commentaries in English on the four Gospels and on the book of Psalms.[40]

Although we have seen that translators such as Alfred and Ælfric had already in the Anglo-Saxon period been sufficiently uneasy about translating God's word from Latin that they felt it necessary to justify themselves, the church never seems to have issued an official ban against translation at any time. Papal decrees sometimes hinted at it, but in general it is clear that it was not the availability of vernacular Scripture in itself that caused anxiety but the possibility of "wrong" interpretations by laypeople and also a real concern that the role of priests might be usurped.[41] As far as England is concerned, the wide circulation of translations such as Rolle's Psalter seems to prove that, until late in the fourteenth century, there was no official opposition to the vernacularization of Scripture per se. But the Wycliffite Bible project, closely identified with a known heretic, was a highly visible symbol of a real threat to the established church and so it created its own opposition.

In 1409, a ban was included in the so-called *Constitutions* (i.e., regulations) issued by Archbishop Arundel. There were thirteen of them, and they dealt (in Latin) with a whole range of ecclesiastical matters, but the crucial one was the seventh. This forbade the translation of any text of Scripture into English and the ownership of any translation made in the time of Wyclif or later, without the express permission of a bishop, which would be granted only after inspection of the translation. The wording of the regulation does not make it clear whether or not the prohibition extended to books merely containing quotation in English.[42] Very little is known about how, and to what extent, the regulation was implemented. What is beyond doubt is that Wycliffite Bibles did continue to circulate, and often among respectably orthodox people, including, for instance, several religious communities. Royal owners, too, were common throughout the fifteenth century, including Henry IV (d. 1413), Henry VI (d. 1471), and Henry VII (d. 1509). It seems that the orthodoxy of the owner was enough to sanction the owned translation itself as orthodox. Even among lay people, owning an English Bible was probably not by itself likely to condemn the owner as a heretic—but it might certainly identify the owner as a Lollard and thus a heretic.[43]

Despite the clear evidence that large numbers of manuscript Wycliffite Bibles produced during the close of the fourteenth and the early years of the fifteenth centuries continued to be used, the official restrictions on the use of the Bible in English would stay in force for another 120 years. By the early sixteenth century, however, the Protestant Reformation was spreading through Europe, catalyzed by Luther's defiance of the pope. The issue of the vernacularization of Scripture again became prominent, especially in England, where it was championed most famously by William Tyndale, a scholar and ordained priest, who had vowed that he would provide access to the Bible even for the simple ploughboy.[44] He duly set about making a new translation and, for the first time among English translators, he used the original Hebrew and Greek Scriptures as his primary source texts, not the Latin Vulgate. Accused of heresy by the church authorities, he was soon forced to flee to the Continent for his safety, and there his New Testament was printed in 1526, with copies being smuggled back across the channel into England. Tyndale then began work on the Old Testament but had published only the Pentateuch (1530) and Jonah (1531) when, in 1535, he was betrayed and arrested.

In fact, the tide of opposition to biblical translation had already turned, to the extent that, in 1536, a complete English Bible produced on the Continent by another reformer, Miles Coverdale, began to circulate in England with little opposition; it was even dedicated to King Henry VIII.[45] Yet that did not prevent Tyndale himself from being executed in Brussels in October 1536, a martyr for English Scripture. The cruelest irony is that the translations of the New Testament and the Pentateuch used in Coverdale's Bible were taken directly from Tyndale's.

## Notes

1. The Goths had a vernacular Bible as early as the fourth century, but their language (in the eastern Germanic language family) had died out by the ninth century. A version of Psalms in Old Frisian (part of the western Germanic family of languages to which English and modern German belong) is reported to have

been made as early as the end of the eighth century, but the earliest extant fragment is a much later copy.

2. Politically, the Anglo-Saxon era ends with the Norman Conquest of 1066, but the division between the language of the Anglo-Saxons, Old English, and the next stage of the language, Middle English, is usually put by linguists about a century later.

3. From the third century onward, spoken Latin began to evolve into the various mutually unintelligible languages of the Romance family—French, Spanish, Italian, etc.; the written language remained, with some modifications, as a sort of lingua franca for the educated.

4. For background on the pervasive use of the Bible in both the early and late medieval periods, David C. Fowler's wide-ranging *The Bible in Early English Literature* (Seattle: University of Washington Press, 1976) is recommended.

5. Translated in *English Historical Documents c. 500–1042*, ed. Dorothy Whitelock, 2d ed., English Historical Documents 1 (London and Oxford: Eyre Methuen and Oxford University Press, 1979), pp. 799–810, at 801.

6. Letter from Cuthbert, a later abbot of Bede's monastery of Wearmouth-Jarrow, to a colleague. "Epistola de obitu Bedae," in *Bede's Ecclesiastical History of the English People*, ed. Bertram Colgrave and Roger A. B. Mynors, Oxford Medieval Texts (Oxford: Oxford University Press, 1969), pp. 580–86, at 582 (Latin text with English translation).

7. See Phillip Pulsiano, "Psalters," in *The Liturgical Books of Anglo-Saxon England*, ed. Richard W. Pfaff, Old English Newsletter, Subsidia 23 (Kalamazoo: Medieval Institute, 1995), pp. 60–85.

8. *Part-Bibles* is a useful term for designating small volumes of Scripture—the Pentateuch, the Prophets, the four Gospels, the Pauline Epistles, etc. Such volumes, practical to use and cheaper to produce, were far more common than cumbersome and expensive complete Bibles in the earlier medieval period.

9. For a facsimile, see *Evangeliorum Quattuor Codex Lindisfarnensis. Musei Britannici Codex Cottonianus Nero D. iv*, ed. Thomas D. Kendrick et al., 2 vols. (Olten: Urs Graf, 1956–60).

10. Both glosses can be found in *The Lindisfarne and Rushworth Gospels now first printed from the Original MSS. in the British Museum and the Bodleian Library*, ed. Joseph Stevenson and George Waring, 4 vols., Surtees Society 28, 39, 43, 48 (Durham: Published for the Society by G. Andrews, 1854–65). Interestingly for historians of the English language, Farmon wrote in a Northumbrian dialect, Owun in Mercian.

11. *Bede's Ecclesiastical History*, ed. Colgrave and Mynors, IV: 24, 419.

12. All are put into modern English in S. A. J. Bradley, *Anglo-Saxon Poetry*, 2d ed. (London: Everyman, 1995).

13. For a fuller overview of these biblical poems, with references, see Robert D. Fulk and Christopher M. Cain, *A History of Old English Literature* (Oxford: Blackwell, 2003), pp. 110–19.

14. For the text of the Old Saxon poem alongside the Old English, see *The Saxon Genesis: An Edition of the West Saxon Genesis B and the Old Saxon Vatican Genesis*, ed. Alger N. Doane (Madison: University of Wisconsin Press, 1991).

15. See *Heliand; Text and Commentary*, ed. James E. Cathey, Medieval European Studies 2 (Morgantown: West Virginia University Press, 2002); and for a translation and commentary, see G. Ronald Murphy, *The Saxon Savior: The Germanic Transformation of the Gospel in the Ninth-Century Heliand* (New York: Oxford University Press, 1989).

16. This meant basically Wessex, but Alfred's rule by now encompassed Mercia also as a unified England began to take shape. Good introductions to Alfred are *Alfred the Great: Asser's* Life of King Alfred *and Other Contemporary Sources*, ed. and trans. Simon Keynes and Michael Lapidge (Harmondsworth: Penguin, 1983); and Allen J. Frantzen, *King Alfred* (Boston: Twayne, 1986).

17. For a facsimile, see *The Paris Psalter (MS Bibliothèque Nationale fonds latin 8824)*, ed. Bertram Colgrave et al., Early English Manuscripts in Facsimile 8 (Copenhagen: Rosenkilde and Bagger, 1958); and, for an edition of Alfred's psalms, *King Alfred's Old English Prose Translation of the First Fifty Psalms*, ed. Patrick P. O'Neill (Cambridge: Medieval Academy of America, 2001). Four psalms are edited in *The Cambridge Old English Reader*, ed. Richard Marsden (Cambridge: Cambridge University Press, 2004), 116–21.

18. Three different Latin versions of the Psalms circulated in the earlier medieval period.

19. The numbering in the Latin Vulgate Bible varies from that in the Protestant Bible because, in several instances, what is presented as a single psalm in one version is divided into two in the other. However, both systems end with exactly 150 psalms, and the variation in numbering affects only a small range of them.

20. Text in *Old English Reader*, p. 120. The macrons (bars) on some vowels are editorial and indicate "long" pronunciation.

21. The letter (commonly known as Alfred's "preface" to the *Cura pastoralis*) is translated in *Alfred the Great*, pp. 124–26; for the Old English text, with notes, see *Old English Reader*, pp. 30–36.

22. On approaches to biblical translation, including crucially those of Jerome, see Richard Marsden, "Ælfric as Translator: The Old English Prose Genesis," *Anglia* 109 (1991): 319–58, especially 322–8. A useful discussion of patristic theories will be found in Robert Stanton, *The Culture of Translation in Anglo-Saxon England* (Cambridge: Brewer, 2002), ch. 4. For a more challenging account of medieval translation theory in general, see Rita Copeland, *Rhetoric, Hermeneutics, and Translation in the Middle Ages: Academic Traditions and Vernacular Texts* (Cambridge: Cambridge University Press, 1991).

23. On Ælfric's approach to translation, see "Ælfric as Translator." For the Old English text with notes, see *Old English Reader*, pp. 122–29.

24. For a facsimile of the *Hexateuch*, see *The Old English Illustrated Hexateuch: British Museum Cotton Claudius B. IV*, ed. C. R. Dodwell and Peter Clemoes, Early En-

glish Manuscripts in Facsimile 18 (Copenhagen: Rosenkilde and Bagger, 1974). There is a CD-ROM of the same manuscript in Benjamin C. Withers, *The Illustrated Old English Heptateuch, Cotton Claudius B.iv: The Frontier of Seeing and Reading in Anglo-Saxon England* (Toronto: University of Toronto Press, 2007).

25.  The *Heptateuch* is edited, with introduction, in *The Old English Version of the Heptateuch and Ælfric's Libellus de ueteri testamento et nuovo*, ed. Richard Marsden, Early English Text Society 330 (Oxford: Oxford University Press, 2008). For an annotated extract, see *Old English Reader*, pp. 106–9.

26.  The work is edited in *The Old English Version of the Gospels*, ed. Roy M. Liuzza, 2 vols., Early English Text Society 304 and 314 (Oxford: Oxford University Press, 1994–2000), vol. 1. For an annotated extract, see *Old English Reader*, pp. 110–15. See also Roy M. Liuzza, "Who Read the Gospels in Old English?" in *Words and Works: Essays for Fred C. Robinson*, ed. Peter S. Baker and Nicholas Howe (Toronto: University of Toronto Press, 1998), pp. 3–24.

27.  A translation of the homilies is given in parallel with the Old English text in *The Homilies of the Anglo-Saxon Church*, ed. Benjamin Thorpe, 2 vols. (London: Ælfric Society, 1844–46).

28.  Good surveys of English language history include Thomas Pyles and John Algeo, *The Origins and Development of the English Language,* 5th ed. (Florence, KY: Heinle, 2004); and Dennis Freeborn, *From Old English to Standard English*, 3d ed. (Basingstoke: Palgrave Macmillan, 2006).

29.  For an indispensable systematic survey of Middle English biblical works (with editions) including those noted in the following paragraphs, see James H. Morey, *Book and Verse: A Guide to Middle English Biblical Literature* (Urbana: University of Illinois Press, 2000). On the use of English for Scripture, see especially Morey's introduction, pp. 24–55.

30.  From the mid fourteenth century, there is another rare example of continuous translation preceding the Wycliffite Bible in the form of two separate versions of Revelation, both based on an Anglo-Norman text; they are extant in seventeen manuscripts in all.

31.  Text in *The Psalter of the Psalms of David and Certain Canticles, with a Translation and Exposition in English by Richard Rolle of Hampole*, ed. H. R. Bramley, rev. W. W. Skeat (Oxford: Clarendon, 1884), pp. 83–84 (punctuation normalized).

32.  On all aspects of the Wycliffite Bible, including doctrinal issues, the starting point is Mary Dove, *The First English Bible: The Text and Context of the Wycliffite Versions* (Cambridge: Cambridge University Press, 2007).

33.  *Selections from English Wycliffite Writings*, ed. Anne Hudson (Cambridge: Cambridge University Press, 1978), p. 107.

34.  For a judicious review of the question of Wyclif's involvement and the identity of other translators, see Dove, *First English Bible*, pp. 68–82, whose views I accept here. See also Anne Hudson, *The Premature Reformation: Wycliffite Texts and Lollard History* (Oxford: Clarendon, 1988), pp. 240–41.

35. This was established in the pioneering edition *The Holy Bible Containing the Old and New Testaments with the Apocryphal Books, in the Earliest English Versions Made from the Latin Vulgate by John Wycliffe and His Followers*, ed. J. Forshall and F. Madden, 4 vols. (Oxford: University Press, 1850; repr. New York: AMS, 1982). In recent years, Conrad Lindberg (see next note) has separately edited representative manuscripts of the whole Bible in both the earlier and the later versions.

36. The earlier version is in Oxford, Bodleian Library MS. Bodley 959, the later in Bodley 277; the latter manuscript once belonged to Henry VI, who later gave it to an unidentified Carthusian monastery somewhere outside London. The texts are from *MS Bodley 959. Genesis–Baruch 3.20 in the Earlier Version of the Wycliffite Bible*. Vol. 1: *Genesis and Exodus*, ed. Conrad Lindberg, Stockholm Studies in English 6 (Stockholm: Almquist and Wiksell, 1959), p. 44; and *King Henry's Bible MS Bodley 277: The Revised Version of the Wyclif Bible*. Vol. 1: *Genesis–Ruth*, ed. Conrad Lindberg, Stockholm Studies in English 89 (Stockholm: Almquist and Wiksell, 1999), p. 55.

37. Later spelled *jument*, it would continue to occur occasionally until the beginning of the nineteenth century with the sense "beast (of burden)."

38. Hudson, *Selections from English Wycliffite Writings*, p. 68.

39. See on this topic especially Dove, *First English Bible*, pp. 193–98.

40. For an overview of Wycliffite glossing, see Dove, *First English Bible*, pp. 152–72; also Hudson, *Premature Reformation*, pp. 247–64.

41. On this issue, see Dove, "The Bible Debate," in *First English Bible*, pp. 6–36, especially 6–14.

42. Nicholas Watson, "Censorship and Cultural Change in Late-Medieval England: Vernacular Theology, the Oxford Translation Debate, and Arundel's Constitutions of 1409," *Speculum* 70 (1995): 822–64, at 826. Constitution 7 is translated in Margaret Deanesly, *The Lollard Bible and Other Medieval Biblical Versions* (Cambridge: Cambridge University Press, 1920; repr. 1966), p. 296. See also Anne Hudson, "Lollardy: The English Heresy?" in her *Lollards and Their Books* (London: Hambledon, 1985), pp. 141–63, at 146–48.

43. Dove, *First English Bible*, pp. 37–58; see also Hudson, *Premature Reformation*, p. 166.

44. A good account of Tyndale's biblical endeavors is in David Daniell, *William Tyndale: A Biography* (New Haven: Yale University Press, 2001).

45. Coverdale's own text of the Psalter, which includes the best-known form of Psalm 22 (23), became the favored version in the Church of England until modern times.

# 14

# The Old French Bible

THE FIRST COMPLETE VERNACULAR BIBLE IN WESTERN EUROPE

*Clive R. Sneddon*

T he purpose of this chapter is to introduce the earliest complete translation of the Bible into French and to contextual-
ize it by a brief presentation of other French biblical works.
This translation, which we will call the *Old French Bible*, was made in the
thirteenth century and appears to have been quite successful in its day,
but was not chosen for publication by the earliest printers when they published biblical texts in French in the late fifteenth century.[1] The French
scholar and theologian Samuel Berger identified the translation again at
the end of the nineteenth century,[2] but there is no complete modern edition, and as a result, even today, the existence of this translation is still not
widely recognized by scholars.

The *Old French Bible* is not the only neglected medieval Bible translation in French. The existence of genuine Bible translations before the
Reformation has been obscured by the popularity from 1314 on of the
"Bible historiale complétée" and, in the fifteenth and early sixteenth centuries, of the "Bible abrégée."[3] Neither of these was a Bible in the strict
sense. However, the entire Bible was translated into French three times in
all during the Middle Ages. For the bibliographers of the seventeenth and

eighteenth centuries, the earliest translation of the Bible into French was the translation of Raoul de Presles, done for King Charles V, apparently in the 1370s, but that no longer survives complete. This was one of a whole series of texts translated for the king for his library in the Louvre.[4] Both library and translations remained well known to scholarship, so that there is an identifiable historiographical tradition for Raoul de Presles and his fellow translators, which is simply lacking for the *Old French Bible*. This fourteenth-century translation by Raoul de Presles survives in six principal manuscripts, to which should be added some copies of his version of the Psalms.[5] The fullest manuscript of the Raoul de Presles translation ends in Matthew 19.27. A third translation, this time into Anglo-Norman, survives in three manuscripts only, none of which is earlier than the fourteenth century, and the most complete of which ends in Hebrews 13.17.[6] Another text that contains many passages from the Bible is the missal, and this exists in a complete fourteenth-century translation into French, which survives in five manuscripts.[7] The only Bible to survive complete is the *Old French Bible*.

The relative neglect of this thirteenth-century translation can reasonably be ascribed to two factors. The first of these is the physical complexity of its transmission in the Middle Ages, when books from the complete Bible were from the early fourteenth century on combined with material from a totally different work, the "Bible historiale" by Guiart des Moulins.[8] This creates difficulties for the would-be modern editor, especially when the sheer bulk of the complete Bible text is already awe-inspiring. The second factor is that the apparent circumstances of the Bible's translation do not fit with the generally accepted history of Bible translation in the West, where the Roman Catholic Church is perceived to have resisted Bible translation until its hand was forced in the sixteenth century. The contentious nature of the Wycliffite translation into English in the late fourteenth century (for more information on English Bible translations, see the chapter by Marsden in this volume), as well as the controversies about Bible translation that appeared at the time of the Reformation, make it seem reasonable to assume that it was St. Jerome's translation of the Bible into Latin that was the last translation of the Bible to be made and accepted before modern times. The particular translation into French that is the subject of this chapter was made more than a century before Wyclif's translation of the Bible into English. What is more, it was doctrinally orthodox, not inspired by heretics and not suppressed by the church authorities.[9]

## Early Scholarship on the Bible in Old French

Scholars have long been aware of the existence of two translations of the Bible into French: the complete Bible commissioned in the fourteenth century by King Charles V from Raoul de Presles, already mentioned,[10] and the "Bible historiale" by Guiart des Moulins, which would from the early fourteenth century be combined with the *Old French Bible* in manuscripts. Guiart said in his translator's preface that he had done the work of translation between 1291 and 1295; he also mentioned in the preface his election in 1297 as dean of the collegiate church of St. Peter in Aire, which is in Artois in northern France.[11]

Strictly speaking, the "Bible historiale" is not a Bible, because it translates a twelfth-century university textbook, the *Historia scholastica* by Peter Comestor (for more information on the *Historia scholastica*, see the chapter by Harris in this volume). However, Comestor's work was intended to act as a companion to the study of the literal meaning of the Bible. It is organized broadly by biblical book, from Genesis to Acts, and amplifies the Bible narrative with other material Comestor regarded as casting light on the historical information in the Bible. Guiart edited the *Historia scholastica* to make it more accessible to his intended lay readers. In particular, he included substantial extracts from the Bible itself and presented the result in his preface as a Bible organized on the model of the *Historia scholastica*. Beginning with Genesis, he worked his way through the historical books of the Old Testament, to a Gospel Harmony and Acts, ending with a short series of apocryphal texts, such as a Life of Pilate. His translation is thus a hybrid with two principal sources, and it is not surprising that his work was regarded as a commented French Bible text, even though it does not contain the complete Bible.

The manuscripts of Guiart's "Bible historiale" fall into two principal groups. The first group, which comprises only a small number of manuscripts, consists of manuscripts containing the "Bible historiale" more or less as Guiart had composed it.[12] The second and much more substantial group contains most, but not all, of the "Bible historiale" as found in the first group.[13] It also contains at least half the Bible itself, in a translation which cannot be by Guiart.[14] This is because not all these biblical books belong in Guiart's declared program for the "Bible historiale," and some must therefore have been added. All parts of the Bible, including those added to Guiart's translation, can be found in thirteenth-century manuscripts; this implies that their texts existed before Guiart's late-thirteenth-century "Bible historiale."[15] This is why Berger concluded that there must have been a complete translation of the Bible made in the second quarter of the thirteenth century and that this translation was copied into two volumes containing Genesis to Psalms and Proverbs to Revelation respectively.[16]

Therefore, the second group of "Bible historiale" manuscripts was a new composite work termed by Samuel Berger the "Bible historiale complétée."[17] This consists of Guiart's "Bible historiale" up to and including Esther, which is then completed up to the end of the Bible by books from the *Old French Bible*, but with a preface apparently identifying the entire work as being by Guiart des Moulins. This new composite work belongs to the early fourteenth century and complicates the transmission of both the *Old French Bible* and the "Bible historiale." By the age of printing, the new combination had replaced both of its predecessors, and this version continued to be printed until the Paris edition of 1544–46, by which time two modern translations existed to replace it, those of Lefèvre d'Étaples and Olivetan.[18]

The complete thirteenth-century Bible was probably the work of more than one translator, yet since no translator's preface of the type provided by Guiart for his "Bible historiale" exists for this translation, the exact identity of the translators is unknown, as is the milieu in which they worked and the audience for which they were writing. It was not uncommon for translators to remain anonymous in the thirteenth century. As a rapid consultation of Bossuat's bibliography of Old French literature will show,[19] a number of substantial texts were translated in the thirteenth century, including the *Code* of Justinian, and a range of historical, scientific and medical works.[20] The earlier translations are mostly anonymous, with named translators such as Guiart des Moulins or Jean de Meung only becoming the norm at the end of the thirteenth century. Given that the *Old French Bible* belongs, as will be seen in a moment, to the period of the earlier translations, it follows that its anonymity is simply a function of contemporary translating practice. This anonymity seems to mask a team effort, undertaken according to Berger within the University of Paris, which had the human and material resources for such a project.[21]

The question of whether the Old French Bible translation was the result of a single project has remained vexed. The decision to produce a complete Bible translation for the first time would require a series of choices to be made in order to implement that decision. These choices should be regarded as akin to those made by a modern publisher who plans the production of a new Bible translation. To achieve a manuscript ready to be published, the publisher has three broad options, which may or may not involve directly in the work of translation the person or group instigating the new vernacular Bible.

The first option would be to have the entire Bible translated by one individual. This seems unlikely in the case of the *Old French Bible* because more than one translator worked on the text. The second option would be to commission a team of translators to translate the whole text. If, in the case of the *Old French Bible,* the individual translators were responsible for blocks of books, such as the Prophets or the Gospels, it seems preferable to consider such blocks as evidence for a single project and to regard the *Old French Bible* as a single project carried out by a team of translators. This does not preclude the production of a new translation of an individual book by revising older translations, nor does it preclude the early production of manuscripts containing individual parts of the *Old French Bible*, such as the New Testament.[22]

The third option would be to collect together those existing partial translations that are available and then commission translations of the rest. It would require singular good fortune as well as good library resources to discover that every single part of the Bible had already been translated independently and that all that remains is the purely editorial task of combining the existing texts into a single copy. Nonetheless, Alan Robson has argued that the *Old French Bible* was not a unified text produced as a single project but rather that the work of a series of independent anonymous translators was brought together, presumably by a publisher, some time between 1280 and 1300,[23] in much the same way as the composite "Bible historiale complétée" was produced in the 1310s.[24]

Robson's position equates the compilation of the "Bible historiale complétée" with the more positive step of producing a complete Bible translation for the first time. The oldest extant format of the "Bible historiale complétée" shows that it was in essence produced by a simple juxtaposition.[25] The first volume (Genesis to Esther) was taken from Guiart des Moulins's "Bible historiale," and the second volume (Proverbs to Revelation) from the *Old French Bible*.

What is the relative importance of the two original texts, the *Old French Bible* and the "Bible historiale," as evidenced by their manuscript transmission? Why was the *Old French Bible* translation produced, and why was it then combined with Guiart's "Bible historiale" to produce a composite text?

There remain only eleven "Bible historiale" manuscripts, none of which is complete with Guiart des Moulins's original order and contents. However, the *Old French Bible* is preserved in part in another nineteen manuscripts including three complete Bibles, New York, Pierpont Morgan Library MS M 494; Chantilly, Musée Condé MSS 4–5, and London, British Library Harley MS 616 and Yates Thompson MS 9[26] (excluding two copies of the first volume which were not copied with an *Old French Bible* volume 2).[27] In addition to these manuscripts, there is also one manuscript each of the Old and New Testaments, and individual copies of Tobit, Job, the Gospels, and Revelation in non-Bible miscellanies.[28] The *Old French Bible* is thus quantitatively twice as well attested as Guiart's "Bible historiale" and qualitatively much better attested if one considers the lack of any complete "Bible historiale" manuscript in Guiart's original format, with his preface and apocryphal texts, and the recourse to *Old French Bible* or "Bible historiale complétée" texts in many of the extant "Bible historiale" manuscripts.[29]

The *Old French Bible* uses the Stephen Langton chaptering, and thus, as the Langton chapters become more usual and then from c. 1230 on standard, the *Old French Bible* cannot be older than c. 1200–1230.[30] The *Old French Bible* must also have been completed before around 1260, when Paris, BNF Fr. 899, the oldest surviving manuscript of the text, though now incomplete, was written.[31] Overall this gives us a date of composition of, say, c. 1220–1260.

In the case of both the *Old French Bible* and the "Bible historiale," extracts from glosses and commentaries that were included in the surviving translations of the Bible into French can give us evidence for the motivation behind the original translation.[32] The translators of the *Old French Bible* used material from the *Glossa ordinaria*, including the short paragraph preceding Genesis that is a slightly edited translation of a section of the Prothemata to the *Glossa ordinaria*.[33] This paragraph was read by some *Old French Bible* scribes as being a preface to or even part of Genesis, but its intention is clearly to demonstrate the essential unity of the entire Bible, the New Testament fulfilling what is in the Old; in particular the book of Matthew is explained as the counterpart of Genesis through its account of the origins of the second man who leads Christians to spiritual life, as compared to the account in Genesis of the first man who was created from the earth after the creation of the world.[34] This prologue is sufficiently important for our understanding of the *Old French Bible* for it to be transcribed in full, in Latin and Old French, followed by a full translation of the Old French text.[35]

| *From the Prothemata to the Glossa ordinaria* | *Prologue* |
| --- | --- |
| Liber iste more hebreorum a principio genesis appellatur: quia in eo de celi et terre generatione agitur: licet alia multa sequantur sicut euangelium Matthei: Liber generationis Jesu christi. Jnducit enim Moyses primum hominem formam futuri de terra virgine conditum: qui generaret terrenos in vitam transitoriam: sic et euangelium secundum hominem scilicet christum de matre virgine genitum: qui generaret celestes in vitam eternam. Hic ergo figura: in euangelio veritas. | Cist liures est apelez genesis. por ce que il est de la generacion du ciel. et de la terre ou comancement. Ja soit ce que il parole apres de pluseurs autres choses. Aussi come lesuangile saint Matheu est apelee li liures de la generation ihesucrist. Et aussi come Moyses dist en ce liure. Commant li premiers homs fu criez de la terre qui estoit uirge qui pot engendrer les terriens homes en ceste uie trespassable. Autressi lesuangile saint Matheu moustre ou coumancement. commant li seconz homs fu nez de la beneoiste uirge marie. Ce est ihesucrist. qui les homes celestieux peust bien engendrer en uie pardurable. |

This book is called Genesis, because it concerns the generation of heaven and earth in the beginning, even though it talks afterward of many other things; similarly the Gospel of St. Matthew is called the book of the generation of Jesus Christ. And just as Moses says in this book how the first man was created from the virgin earth who could beget earthly men in this transient life, so the Gospel of St. Matthew shows in the beginning how the second man was born of the blessed Virgin Mary, i.e., Jesus Christ, who would be very well able to beget celestial men in eternal life.

This initial presentation of the spiritual purpose of the Bible allowed the *Old French Bible* translators to use some further spiritual material in the glosses they added to Genesis, Judges, Joshua, and Ruth. Once this spiritual purpose was established in these early books, the glosses added to Psalms or the Gospels were more literal or occasionally moral in character, and many books have virtually no glosses at all. Work done by Elaine Higgleton on the sources of the Gospel glosses shows that the translator of the Gospels did not use a single source, but rather compiled material from the gloss tradition to, in effect, create a new commentary.[36] Some of the Gospel glosses are found in the *Postills* of Hugh of St. Cher, which, if they were only found there, could perhaps be taken as a source for the *Old French Bible* and thus bring the *terminus a quo* down to c. 1235. However, a range of sources was clearly used, and it may well be that the translator of the Gospels was simply drawing on a similar range of commentaries to the ones used by Hugh of St. Cher and his team.[37] The tradition of Bible commentary to which the glosses in the Four Gospels belong is one that flourished in the twelfth and early thirteenth centuries. In particular, its interest in morality and good works, and also in establishing the literal meaning of the Bible text, may be traced back to the Victorines.[38]

The most likely reason that the *Old French Bible* and Guiart's "Bible historiale" were combined was to maximize the historical commentary available on the Bible while losing as little as possible of the Bible text itself. The most significant effect of the creation of the composite "Bible historiale complétée" was to replace the Octateuch from the *Old French Bible*, which has extensive spiritual glosses to Genesis, Joshua, Judges, and Ruth,[39] with the more historically focused and, in the case of Leviticus, shortened Octateuch by Guiart. Both the *Old French Bible* and the "Bible historiale" contain 1–4 Kings, Tobit, Judith and Esther, but none of them are glossed in the *Old French Bible*, so that Guiart's text had the advantage, made up in part as it was of a translation of Peter Comestor's *Historia scholastica*, of offering additional historical information. Guiart's work, however, lacked substantial portions of the Bible, and, paradoxically for works which are not and did not set out to be complete Bibles, the major process that can be observed in both the "Bible historiale" and in the "Bible historiale complétée" is the effort to produce a text that is as close as possible to the Bible in its contents. Some manuscripts of Guiart's "Bible historiale" itself already took Acts and other extracts from the *Old French Bible*.[40] This process was taken further in the "Bible historiale complétée" after its initial creation. In the course of the fourteenth century, those biblical books that had been abridged or omitted by Guiart were simply borrowed from the *Old French Bible* and added to the "Bible historiale complétée." The result was that, although the inclusion of Guiart's translator's preface ensured that he continued to be regarded as the author of the "Bible historiale complétée," about two thirds of the new composite work came in its fullest versions from the *Old French Bible*.[41] By the end of the fourteenth century, the desire for completeness went beyond simply combining the two thirteenth-century texts. Translations of many of the standard set of prologues from the thirteenth-century Paris Vulgate were added[42] in order to enhance the resemblance of the "Bible historiale complétée" to an ordinary Bible.[43]

The conclusion to be drawn from this is that the fourteenth century wanted a more completely commented text than the *Old French Bible* alone could provide. Overall, the history of the "Bible historiale complétée" shows that historical information was part of the motive for reading Bible texts, but that there was also a strong desire for a complete version of the Bible that had sufficient but not excessive commentary.

In light of these conclusions about the existence, unity, and importance of the *Old French Bible*, what aspects of the translation seem most significant? It is the oldest complete Bible translation into the vernacular to survive in Western Europe and, since the Second World War, has been the subject of increasing scholarly interest. Initially, this interest focused on the possibility of exploiting the *Old French Bible* as a resource for improved understanding of philological issues relating to Old French, which can also be seen as preparing the ground for editing the text.[44] The vocabulary of the *Old French Bible* translation of the New Testament was studied,[45] while Genesis has now been published in a modern edition,[46] and the Four Gospels have been edited based on six early manuscripts representing two recensions of the text.[47]

The translation has also been studied with a view to identifying its readership.[48] The question of who the translation was made for is certainly affected by the nature of the glossing, which focuses on the literal understanding of the text, showing the basic spiritual importance of the Old Testament for the New, and indicating on more than one occasion the moral imperative of performing good works. A natural interpretation of this would be that the translation was intended for a lay, relatively wealthy, audience. For the composite "Bible historiale completée," ownership evidence from the fourteenth and fifteenth centuries shows that the work was owned by members of the aristocracy, by royalty, and, in the later period, by commoners; one late fourteenth-century manuscript of the composite work, Copenhagen, Royal Library MS Thott 6, has at the end (fols. 473–4) a list of liturgical readings beginning with the first Sunday of Advent, so that the manuscript could have been used to follow Gospel readings or to read them as an act of private devotion.[49]

It would be a reasonable assumption that a similar pattern of use goes back to the *Old French Bible* in the thirteenth century, but our unambiguous evidence for this is limited to Paris, BNF MS Fr. 899; the workshop for the illumination of this manuscript has been localized to the Île de la Cité, where luxury manuscripts for the wealthy were produced.[50] An early owner of Fr. 899, apparently still within the thirteenth century, added letters beside Gospel passages that seem to identify reading passages and thus private devotional use.

To summarize so far, it would appear that the *Old French Bible* is a product of the period c. 1220–1260, that its most likely but not certain place of composition is Paris, and that it was written for wealthy lay people for their edification and possible devotional use. The scale of the work involved in not only translating the Bible but going through commentaries and deciding on the extent and choice of glossing in any individual book makes this a very substantial enterprise, which seems inevitably to have involved more than one translator.

## Precedents for the *Old French Bible*

Before the *Old French Bible*, the only large-scale Bible project involving the vernacular is the work known now as the *Bible moralisée*, which, as John Lowden shows, was conceived to be read through its medallions, text, and commentary.[51] Four major manuscripts have survived from the thirteenth century, the two one-volume manuscripts Vienna 2554 and 1179, and two three-volume manuscripts now respectively in Toledo and divided between Oxford, Paris, and London.[52] The two Vienna manuscripts are respectively in French and Latin; it is possible that they were conceived as a sort of diptych, with one in each language, though the loss of the final portion of the French manuscript Vienna 2554 makes that difficult to establish beyond a reasonable doubt. The two three-volume manuscripts may originally have been intended to contain both Latin and French texts, as Lowden argues, but only the Toledo manuscript contains any French, and fully bilingual *Bibles moralisées* were not produced until the fourteenth and fifteenth centuries, with Paris, BNF MSS Fr. 167 and Fr. 166.[53]

The exact dating of the four thirteenth-century *Bibles moralisées* has been debated among scholars. Branner proposed c. 1212–25 for Vienna 1179 and 2554, in that order, c. 1225–35 for Toledo, and c. 1235–45 for Oxford-Paris-London.[54] Lowden proposed c. 1220–30 for Vienna 2554, though he regards it as older than Vienna 1179, which he places in the mid

1220s, and proposed late 1220s, mid 1230s for Toledo and the mid 1230s for Oxford-Paris-London.[55] In either case, these *Bibles moralisées* were roughly contemporary with the *Old French Bible*. All four manuscripts are characterised by a profusion of illuminated images, setting out typological links between Bible and commentary. The cost of physically producing such manuscripts, and the work involved in creating the images and text, suggest a wealthy patron, of such wealth as to make it difficult to imagine a nonroyal patron. Duly, we find at the end of two of the manuscripts, Vienna 1179 and the New York quire from the Toledo manuscript, a patron portrait.[56] Vienna 1179 shows a king, who could perhaps, if the portrait is idealized, represent Philippe Auguste (1180–1223), but whom Haussherr and Lowden agree to be Louis VIII (1223–26), an identification that is supported partly by the apparent age of the king but also by a now largely erased quotation on f. 246r beside the king taken from Rigord's dedication of his *De Gestis Philippi Augusti* to the future Louis VIII.[57] The better-known image from the Toledo *Bible moralisée* shows a throned and youthful king and a perhaps older queen. From the gestures of the queen, she appears to be addressing the king, perhaps admonishing or exhorting him. This would be consistent with Blanche de Castille as queen regent rather than queen, with the king being her son Louis IX (1226–70) and not her husband Louis VIII.[58] The *Old French Bible*, like the *Bibles moralisées*, expressed a recognition of the fulfillment of the Old Testament by the New and the need for good works. Once this interpretative framework is fully established in the *Old French Bible*'s Octateuch, the rest of the Bible is presented on the basis that the literal sense is largely self-explanatory, requiring only minimal glossing, except for the most frequently read texts, Psalms and the Gospels, for which a certain number of mostly literal glosses are supplied.

It is the present author's view that the in some ways smaller project of the *Old French Bible* could have originated during the period c. 1220–1260, as a result of the royal interest preserved in the *Bibles moralisées*.[59] Once complete, the work was seized upon by others, female or male, became available on the lay book market in Paris by 1260, and was revised, though not by the original translators, there being four states of this text by c. 1300.[60] Regardless of whether the patrons of the original translation were royal or of lesser standing, it was, to judge from the number of surviving copies, quite widely available to the laity for devotional reading and was thus an important vehicle for the transmission of religious knowledge among those with education or access to books. This is confirmed by the selective commentary included in some books of this Bible translation. The translation is not heretical, but acceptable to the church authorities.[61]

## Notes

This chapter is a composite, adapted for the present volume, of a substantial 2002 revision of the author's "A Neglected Mediaeval Bible Translation," *Romance Languages Annual* 5 (1993): 111–16, made for a book that never appeared, and his "On the Creation of the *Old French Bible*," *Nottingham Medieval Studies* 46 (2002): 25–44.

1. Bettye Thomas Chambers, *Bibliography of French Bibles: Fifteenth- and Sixteenth-Century French-Language Editions of the Scriptures*, Travaux d'Humanisme et Renaissance 192 (Geneva: Droz, 1983). Chambers (her nos. 1, 13, 4, 26, and 33) identifies in her catalogue the following pre-Reformation Biblical texts, printed at various dates from the 1470s on: 1. "La Bible abrégée," an abridged version of a thirteenth-century Bible history identified in note 3 of this chapter; 2. part or all of the "Bible historiale complétée" which will be introduced later in this chapter; 3. "L'exposicion de la Bible," which is derived from the "Bible moralisée," discussed most recently by John Lowden, *The Making of the "Bibles Moralisées"*, 2 vols. (University Park: Pennsylvania State University Press, 2000); 4. the "Biblia Pauperum" with a commentary in French. Chambers also includes 5. an apparent edition of the "Vengeance Nostre Seigneur," a text whose various prose versions, with their manuscripts and twenty-three early editions, are identified in *La Vengeance de Nostre-Seigneur. The Old and Middle French Prose Versions: The Version of Japheth*, ed. Alvin E. Ford, Studies and Texts 63 (Toronto: Pontifical Institute of Mediaeval Studies, 1984), pp. 1–3, 18–24.

2. Samuel Berger, *La Bible française au moyen âge: Étude sur les plus anciennes versions de la Bible écrites en prose de langue d'oïl* (Paris: Imprimerie nationale, 1884; repr. Geneva: Slatkine, 1967), pp. 109–56. The existence of a complete translation of the Bible into Old French in the second quarter of the thirteenth century was first asserted by Samuel Berger in his prizewinning entry for the 1879 *concours* of the *Académie des Inscriptions et Belles-Lettres*. For the details of this competition, see Berger, *La Bible française*, p. vii; and Clive R. Sneddon, "A Critical Edition of the Four Gospels in the Thirteenth-Century Old French Translation of the Bible," 2 vols. (Ph.D. dissertation, University of Oxford, 1978), 1:48, n. 1, and Sneddon, "The 'Bible du XIIIe siècle': Its Medieval Public in the Light of its Manuscript Tradition," in *The Bible and Medieval Culture*, ed. W. Lourdaux and D. Verhelst, Mediaevalia Lovaniensia Series 1, Studia 7 (Leuven: Leuven University Press, 1979), pp. 127–40, at 127. Berger asserted the existence of this text after studying a large number of manuscripts, which he described and classified. This translation was called by Berger the "Bible du XIIIe siècle," though some more recent French-speaking scholars have preferred the more explicit "Bible française du

XIIIe siècle." See for example Wilfried Decoo, "La Bible française du XIIIe siècle et l'Evangile selon Marc: Remarques critiques," *Romanica Gandensia* 12 (1969): 53–65; and Michel Quereuil, *La Bible française du XIIIe siècle: Edition critique de la Genèse*, Publications romanes et françaises 183 (Geneva: Droz, 1988).

3.   The "Bible abrégée" is a thirteenth-century Bible history preserved in Paris, BNF MS Fr. 24728 and in Vatican City, Biblioteca Apostolica Vaticana MS Pal. lat. 1957, a reduced version of which appears in nine fifteenth-century manuscripts and the editions listed by Chambers.

4.   Léopold Delisle, *Recherches sur la Librairie de Charles V, Roi de France, 1337–1380*, 2 vols. (Paris: A. Champion, 1907), 1:82–119.

5.   Berger, *La Bible française*, pp. 206–9 and 244–57.

6.   Berger, *La Bible française*, pp. 230–37.

7.   See L. M. J. Delaissé, "A Liturgical Problem at the End of the Middle Ages: The 'Missale Gallicum,'" in *Miniatures, Scripts, Collections, Essays Presented to G. I. Lieftinck*, ed. J. P. Gumbert and M. J. M. de Haan, 4 vols. (Amsterdam: van Gendt, 1972–76), 4:16–27.

8.   Berger, *La Bible française*, pp. 157–86.

9.   For internal evidence of the orthodox attitude shown by the translator, see the gloss on the role of Lot and Abraham in Genesis 13.8 (Berger, *La Bible française*, pp. 149–50).

10.  Berger, *La Bible française*, pp. 244–57.

11.  For the full text of Guiart's preface, see Eduard Reuss, "Fragments littéraires et critiques relatifs à l'histoire de la Bible française. Seconde série. Les Bibles du quatorzième et du quinzième siècle et les premières éditions imprimées," *Revue de théologie et de philosophie chrétienne* 14 (1857): 12–14, though the dates given there should be corrected by Berger, *La Bible française*, pp. 158–61.

12.  Berger, *La Bible française*, pp. 161–77. This first group can be further subdivided into two subgroups, identifiable in the first instance by the presence or absence of the translator's preface. Berger suggests that the subgroup without this preface was the older of the two (*La Bible française*, p. 166), but he may have been influenced in this by the fact that the majority of the manuscripts without the preface preserve a Picard form (*La Bible française*, pp. 161–64), whereas the manuscripts with the translator's preface are more likely to be in Central French (Berger, *La Bible française*, pp. 162 and 177). No single manuscript now survives with the complete contents of Guiart's original text.

13.  It is the subgroup with the translator's preface that has supplied the "Bible historiale" material in all manuscripts of this second group (Berger, *La Bible française*, p. 177).

14.  Reuss, "Fragments littéraires," pp. 78–80.

15.  Berger, *La Bible française*, pp. 113–19 and 156.

16.  Berger does not comment on the possibility that Psalms appeared instead at the beginning of the second volume, though this could be deduced from the contents of two of the manuscripts he describes (*La Bible française*, pp. 407–8 and 425–26): Cambridge, University Library MS Ee. 3. 52, and Copenhagen, Royal

Library, MS Thott 7. These *Old French Bible* manuscripts are described more fully in Sneddon, "A Critical Edition," 1:152–53 and 165–66.

17. Berger, *La Bible française,* pp. 187–99 and 210–20.

18. Lefèvre's translation began to appear in 1523 (Chambers, *Bibliography of French Bibles,* no. 31), and first appeared complete in 1530 (Chambers, no. 51). Olivetan's translation first appeared in 1535 (Chambers, no. 66).

19. Information on translations may be found in Robert Bossuat, *Manuel bibliographique de la littérature française du moyen âge* (Melun: Librairie d'Argences, 1951), pp. 247–357, 578–86, especially for Old French, pp. 266–88, 325–27, 356–57, updated by supplements for 1949–53, 1954–60, 1960–80, published respectively in 1955, 1961, and 1986–91; more recent bibliography may be found in Otto Klapp, *Bibliographie der französischen Literaturwissenschaft* (Frankfurt: Klostermann, 1960– ).

20. By way of example, see Bossuat, *Manuel bibliographique* (1951), nos. 2959 and 2960bis for the *Code* and *Institutes* of Justinian, 2986–91 for medical works and 2905 for a survey of encyclopedias; the massive three-volume work of Vincent de Beauvais, also translated into Old French, had not been worked on in the references known to Bossuat, though a Middle French use of Vincent is mentioned in no. 6479 of the third supplement. For a survey of Old French translations of texts from the classical world, see Jacques Monfrin, "Humanisme et traductions au moyen âge," in *L'Humanisme médiéval dans les littératures romanes du XIIe au XIVe siècle: Colloque organisé par le Centre de Philologie et de Littératures romanes de l'Université de Strasbourg du 29 Janvier au 2 Février 1962,* ed. Anthime Fourrier, Actes et Colloques 3 (Paris: Klincksieck, 1964), pp. 217–46, at 217–24.

21. Berger, *La Bible française,* pp. 108 and 145–48.

22. Berger, *La Bible française,* p. 147. Robson, "Vernacular Scriptures in France," pp. 445–48, treats the now incomplete Paris, BNF MS Fr. 899 as showing that a partial compilation existed before the completion of the *Old French Bible.* A codicological examination of this manuscript (Sneddon, "A Critical Edition," 1:148–51) shows that it could originally have contained the complete text. Sneddon, "The Origins of the *Old French Bible*: The Significance of Paris, BN, MS Fr. 899," *Studi Francesi* 43 (1999): 1–13, considers Robson's arguments in more detail and concludes that Robson's evidence is not substantive, among other reasons because some parts at least of the text of Fr. 899 represent a revision of the translator's original work, as Quereuil, *La Bible française,* in editing Genesis also concluded (Sneddon, "Origins," 7 n. 35 and 10 n. 38).

23. Possible dates are discussed in Sneddon, "A Critical Edition," 1:35–40, concluding that the *Old French Bible* can be dated c. 1235–60. Elaine Patricia Higgleton, "Latin Gospel Exegesis and the Gospel Glosses in the Thirteenth-Century Old French Translation of the Bible," 2 vols. (Ph.D. dissertation, University of St. Andrews, 1992), 1:9–17, has shown that the criterion used by Sneddon for a *terminus a quo* of c. 1235 is not valid and that the latest date for a *terminus a quo* is c. 1220.

24. Robson, "Vernacular Scriptures in France," pp. 446–48.

25. See the detailed discussion in Sneddon, "A Critical Edition," 1:6–8, and also the description at 1:241–42 of Edinburgh, University Library MS 19, which is dated 1314 and confirms the original format. Guiart's Genesis to Esther is complete except for the omission of his abridged text of Proverbs after 4 Kings; this is due to the presence of the complete text of Proverbs from the *Old French Bible*.

26. See C. A. Robson, "Vernacular Scriptures in France," in *The Cambridge History of the Bible*, vol. 2: *The West from the Fathers to the Reformation*, ed. G. W. H. Lampe (Cambridge: Cambridge University Press, 1969), 2:436–52 and 528–32, at 448 and 530–31. The manuscripts in question are New York, Pierpont Morgan Library MS M 494 (not 484 as stated in Pierre-Maurice Bogaert, *Les Bibles en français: Histoire illustrée du moyen âge à nos jours* [Turnhout: Brepols, 1991], p. 30), Chantilly, Musée Condé MSS 4–5, and London, British Library Harley MS 616 and Yates Thompson MS 9 (formerly Additional 41751). Berger, *La Bible française*, pp. 112–13, suggests that Paris, BNF MSS Fr. 6–7 is a complete manuscript of the *Old French Bible*, but recognizes that Fr. 7 is copied from a volume 2 of the "Bible historiale complétée." Sneddon, "A Critical Edition," 1:79–81, 155–57 and 332, confirms this.

27. Philadelphia, Pa., Free Library, MS Widener 2 copied with a "Bible historiale complétée" Gospels and an otherwise unknown translation of Revelation, and Paris, BNF MS Fr. 6, copied with MS Fr. 7, a "Bible historiale complétée" volume 2.

28. Sneddon, "A Critical Edition," 1:2–19, contains a revision of Berger's analysis of the contents of the *Old French Bible*, "Bible historiale," and "Bible historiale complétée"; 1:128–469 presents a detailed description of all the manuscripts known to the author in 1978.

29. Bogaert asserts that Guiart's "Bible historiale" is a more significant text than the *Old French Bible* because more manuscripts survive. To show this, he has to discount all copies of Proverbs to Revelation from both the *Old French Bible* and the "Bible historiale complétée." Pierre-Maurice Bogaert, "Adaptations et versions de la Bible en prose (langue d'oïl)," in *Les genres littéraires dans les sources théologiques et philologiques médiévales: Définition, critique et exploitation, Actes du Colloque international de Louvain-la-Neuve, 25–27 mai 1981*, ed. Robert Bultot, Publications de l'Institut d'études médiévales, 2d series: Textes, Études, Congrès 5 (Louvain-la-Neuve: Université catholique de Louvain, 1982), pp. 259–77, at 274–75. He justifies this rather drastic procedure on the grounds that a manuscript containing only Proverbs to Revelation cannot reliably be assigned to either of these two texts. Yet a more nuanced textual classification reveals that the "Bible historiale complétée" can be distinguished from the *Old French Bible* (Sneddon, "A Critical Edition," 1:64–82) and thus the approximately one hundred surviving "Bible historiale complétée" manuscripts can be eliminated from a numerical comparison between surviving *Old French Bible* and "Bible historiale" manuscripts. Absolute precision is difficult because the contents of individual "Bible historiale complétée" manuscripts often combine material from more than one

source, but Sneddon, "A Critical Edition," 1:238–469, lists eighty-four known manuscripts, of which sixty-two are complete, and the remaining thirteen volume 1s and nine volume 2s can safely be assumed to have been complete. This total ignores sixteen fragments, of which four are in miscellany manuscripts but the other twelve will no doubt have come from complete manuscripts, and also ignores four Old Testaments, ten Psalms, five New Testaments, and four Gospels.

30. See Laura Light, "French Bibles c. 1200–30: A New Look at the Origins of the Paris Bible," in *The Early Medieval Bible: Its Production, Decoration and Use*, ed. Richard Gameson, Cambridge Studies in Palaeography and Codicology 2 (Cambridge: Cambridge University Press, 1994), pp. 155–76, at 171–73.

31. See Robson, "Vernacular Scriptures in France," pp. 445–48; Sneddon, "The Origins of the *Old French Bible*; Berger, *La Bible française*, p. 112; and Robert Branner, *Manuscript Painting in Paris During the Reign of Saint Louis: A Study of Styles*, California Studies in the History of Art 18 (Berkeley: University of California Press, 1977), p. 106.

32. Robson's view of the origins of the *Old French Bible* was taken up by Pierre-Maurice Bogaert in 1981, as part of an argument that tends to diminish the importance of this complete Bible. Bogaert argues from a range of surviving texts that the main purpose of Bible translation in the Middle Ages was historical and that this is confirmed by what he sees as the absorption of the *Old French Bible* into Guiart's "Bible historiale." Bogaert, "Adaptations," p. 261. In saying this, he seems to be confusing the undoubted success of the composite "Bible historiale complétée" in replacing its two predecessors with the relative importance of these two original texts. Bogaert, "Adaptations," pp. 265–75, and "Bibles," pp. 29–30, describe Paris, BNF MS Fr. 899 and some *Old French Bible* manuscripts, restating his view of the limited diffusion of the *Old French Bible* on the grounds of the rarity of volume 1 manuscripts and the difficulty of distinguishing an *Old French Bible* volume 2 from a volume 2 of the "Bible historiale complétée." Bogaert, "Bibles," p. 33, provides a chronological table of "Bible historiale" and "Bible historiale complétée" manuscripts, from which he has excluded the eight manuscripts he regards as probably being volume 2s of the *Old French Bible*, but in which he conflates "Bible historiale" and "Bible historiale complétée" manuscripts.

33. See *Repertorium Biblicum Medii Aevi*, ed. Friedrich Stegmüller with the assistance of Nicolaus Reinhardt, 11 vols. and *Supplement* (Madrid: Consejo Superior de Investigaciones Científicas, 1950–80), 9:465, no. 117814. The Old French text modifies 117814 slightly, by omitting two phrases and its final sentence.

34. Clive R. Sneddon, "Translation Technique and the *Old French Bible*," in *Forum for Modern Language Studies* 35 (1999): 339–49, at 348.

35. Author's translation. The extract from the Prothemata to the *Glossa ordinaria* is taken from *Textus biblie. Cum Glosa ordinaria, Nicolai de lyra postilla, [ . . . ]* (Basel: Iohannes Petrus et Iohannes Frobenius, 1506), i, f. 21v1, and the Old French

Prologue from Paris, Bibl. de l'Arsenal, MS 5056, f. 111–2. Both extracts are presented in a diplomatic transcription, except for abbreviations, which have been silently expanded.

36. See Higgleton, "Latin Gospel Exegesis."

37. Beryl Smalley, *The Study of the Bible in the Middle Ages* (Oxford: Blackwell, 1983), pp. 269–73.

38. See Higgleton, "Latin Gospel Exegesis," 2:367–70 and 549–54.

39. Berger, *La Bible française*, pp. 121–27, who also identifies literal glosses in Genesis and Joshua.

40. The subgroup without the translator's preface changes the end of the "Bible historiale" after the Gospel Harmony by replacing Guiart's Acts and apocryphal texts with Acts, Lam., Matt. ch. 1, John 1.1–14, Dan. 3.51–90 and chs. 8–12, all from the *Old French Bible* (see Sneddon, "A Critical Edition," 1:5).

41. Sneddon, "A Critical Edition," 1:8–23 details and dates the successive enlargements of the "Bible historiale complétée," beginning with the addition of Psalms to create Berger's so-called Petites Bibles, the addition of Job to create his "Bibles moyennes," and finally the addition on two separate occasions of 1–2 Chronicles and 1–3 Esdras to create his "Grandes Bibles" and "Bibles à prologues" respectively (Berger, *La Bible française*, pp. 212–19).

42. See Neil R. Ker, *Medieval Manuscripts in British Libraries*, 5 vols. (Oxford: Clarendon Press, 1969–2002), 1:96–97, for the standard set of sixty-four prologues; and Sneddon, "A Critical Edition," 1:407–10, for the standard set in the "Bibles à prologues" group, more than fifty of which are in Ker's list.

43. See Sneddon, "A Critical Edition," 1:352–55 and 374–78, for two individual efforts at further completeness within Berger's "Grandes Bibles" group, respectively Brussels, Bibl. Royale MSS 9001–02, which intercalates as a commentary the "Bible moralisée," and Paris, BNF MSS Fr. 15370–71, which adds its own selection of prologues and also extracts from the post-Maccabees parts of the "Bible historiale."

44. For example, the language of Acts, chapters 20–24, was studied by Guy De Poerck, in his lecture course *Notions de grammaire historique du française exercices philologiques*, 2 vols. (Ghent: Story, 1955). This was reproduced at least until 1973, by which time it was entitled *Grammaire historique du français*. In 1961 it was intended to be the basis of vol. 3 of G. De Poerck and L. Mourin, *Introduction à la morphologie comparée des langues romanes basée sur des traductions anciennes des Actes des Apôtres ch. XX à XXIV*, (Bruges: De Tempel, 1961–64), but only vols. 1, 4, and 6 seem ever to have appeared.

45. Martin von Orelli, *Der altfranzösische Bibelwortschatz des Neuen Testamentes im Berner Cod. 28 (13 Jh.)* (Zürich: Juris Druck, 1975).

46. Quereuil, *La Bible française*. Unfortunately, the editor uses only four of the five manuscripts of Genesis known to Berger, when eleven substantially complete manuscripts and two fragments survive as well as brief extracts from two manuscripts destroyed respectively in 1870 and 1944. These manuscripts have been

previously referred to, and, of the eleven substantially complete manuscripts, all but the Old Testament manuscript London, BL Add. MSS 40619–20 are also listed in Quereuil 37, which does not explain why he chose to restrict his edition to four manuscripts. For a study of the vocabulary of Genesis, see Quereuil, "La Traduction du vocabulaire dans *La Bible française du 13eme siècle*," *Romanica Wratislaviensia* 30 (1989): 177–84.

47. See Sneddon, "A Critical Edition," 1:64–71, for these four recensions, identified by the manuscript sigla used there as the recensions found respectively in MSS A-D, EFLM, JK and N-R. A fuller account of the projected edition is given in Sneddon, "Pour l'édition critique de la Bible française du XIIIe siècle," in *La Bibbia in italiano tra Medioevo e Rinascimento: La Bible italienne au Moyen Âge et à la Renaissance, Atti del Convegno internazionale, Firenze, Certosa del Galluzzo, 8–9 novembre 1996*, ed. Lino Leonardi, Millenio Medievale 10: Agiografia e Bibbia in lingua italiana 1 (Florence: SISMEL, Edizioni del Galluzzo, 1998), pp. 229–46, though contrary to what is said there at 242 n. 3, a sample manuscript from each of the three "Bible historiale complétée" states of text will now be included. These states of text are briefly identified in Sneddon, "Rewriting the *Old French Bible*: The New Testament and Evolving Reader Expectations in the Thirteenth and Early Fourteenth Centuries," in *Interpreting the History of French: A Festschrift for Peter Rickard on the Occasion of His Eightieth Birthday*, ed. Rodney Sampson and Wendy Ayres-Bennett, Faux titre 226 (New York: Rodopi, 2002), pp. 37–38, esp. n. 15.

48. See Sneddon, "The 'Bible du XIIIe siècle.'"

49. See also ibid., p. 136.

50. Mary A. Rouse and Richard H. Rouse, "The Book Trade at the University of Paris, ca. 1250–ca. 1350," in *La production du livre universitaire au moyen age: Exemplar et pecia, Actes du symposium tenu au Collegio San Bonaventura de Grottaferrata en mai 1983*, ed. L. J. Bataillon, B. G. Guyot, and R. H. Rouse (Paris: CNRS, 1988), pp. 41–114, at note 56; repr. in *Authentic Witnesses. Approaches to Medieval Texts and Manuscripts*, ed. Mary A. Rouse and Richard H. Rouse (Notre Dame, IN: University of Notre Dame Press, 1991), 259–338.

51. See Lowden, *The Making of the "Bibles Moralisées"*, esp. 1:27–30.

52. Lowden discusses these manuscripts in considerable detail: Vienna, Österreichische Nationalbibliothek, MS 2554 in *The Making of the "Bibles Moralisées,"* 1:11–54; Vienna, Österreichische Nationalbibliothek, MS 1179 in 1:55–94; Toledo, Tesoro del Catedral, *Biblia de San Luis* and its final quire, now New York, Pierpont Morgan Library, MS M 240, in 1:95–137; Oxford, Bodleian Library, Bodley MS 270b, Paris, BNF MS Lat. 11560 and London, BL Harley MSS 1526–27 in 1:139–87. The Oxford-Paris-London manuscript was copied in England in the late thirteenth century, and the copy is now London, BL Add. MS 18719, discussed by Lowden, *The Making of the "Bibles Moralisées,"* 1:189–219, though it will have been in France when it was in turn copied at the instance of King John II for Paris, BNF MS Fr. 167, which in its turn was copied for the fifteenth-

century never-completed Paris, BNF MS Fr. 166. See Branner, *Manuscript Painting in Paris,* pp. 32–57, 157–75; and *Bible moralisée: Faksimile Ausgabe im Originalformat des Codex Vindobonensis 2554 der Österreichischen Nationalbibliothek,* ed. Reiner Haussherr, 2 vols., Codices Selecti XL–XL* (Graz: Akademische Druck-u. Verlagsanst , 1973). Lowden, *The Making of the "Bibles Moralisées,"* 1:2–3, explains why he does not consider in his study some of the manuscripts listed by Haussherr, essentially because they are not fully illustrated.

53. See Lowden, *The Making of the "Bibles Moralisées,"* 1:122–27, for a discussion of the quires containing French in the Toledo manuscript and the apparent abandonment of the projected bilingual text. The use of pressure-traced underdrawings in both the three-volume *Bibles moralisées,* first identified by Lowden, means that the two manuscripts were produced in rapid succession, so there is no question of the Oxford-Paris-London manuscript including any French.

54. See Branner, *Manuscript Painting in Paris,* pp. 48, 64–65.

55. See Lowden, *The Making of the "Bibles Moralisées,"* 1:50–52, 90–94, 127–32, 183–85.

56. See ibid., vol. 1, color plates 3 and 9–10. The end of Vienna 2554 has not survived, and neither has the outer bifolium of the last quire of MS Harley 1527, which would have contained any patron portrait, and which Lowden, ibid., 1:187, suggests may have been the model for a patron image in Oxford, Christ Church Library, MS 92.

57. See ibid., 1:90–94.

58. See ibid., 1:127–32. Lowden, ibid. 1:52 and 94, makes the very tempting suggestion that Blanche de Castille was the sponsor of Vienna 2554, and intended Vienna 1179 as a complementary gift for her husband Louis VIII; Lowden, ibid., 1:132, further suggests that Blanche intended Toledo for her son Louis IX, and commissioned Oxford-Paris-London at short notice for her daughter-in-law Marguerite de Provence for her marriage to Louis.

59. Sneddon, "On the Creation of the *Old French Bible.*"

60. For the manuscripts attesting these four states, see Sneddon, "Pour l'édition," p. 241, notes 1–3, and 242, note 1.

61. For confirmation of the generally tolerant attitude of the Church authorities to translations where there was no challenge to the Church's role of interpreting and preaching the word of God, see Leonard E. Boyle, "Innocent III and Vernacular Versions of Scripture," in *The Bible in the Medieval World: Essays in Memory of Beryl Smalley,* ed. Katherine Walsh and Diana Wood, Studies in Church History: Subsidia 4 (Oxford: Ecclesiastical History Society by Basil Blackwell, 1985), pp. 97–107.

# Castilian Vernacular Bibles in Iberia, c. 1250–1500

*Emily C. Francomano*

Historical linguistics, religion, and literary history intersect in the complex phenomenon of vernacular biblical production in medieval Iberia. From the eighth to the fifteenth centuries, three canonical languages coexisted in medieval Iberia: Arabic, Hebrew, and Latin were the languages of "The Book" for Muslims, Jews, and Christians. Each language along with its biblical tradition played a role in the shifting relationships of tolerance, indifference, and persecution between the three main groups living in al-Andalus, *Espanna*, and their overlapping geographical and conceptual territories.[1]

In the context of the expansion of territories under the control of Christian monarchs, population shifts, and religious conversions of the thirteenth century, however, Alfonso X the Wise, king of Castile and Leon (1252–84), built upon his forbears' earlier use of the vernacular in legal and literary texts and promoted the use of Castilian as the canonical language in his realms. Indeed, throughout the thirteenth century, many historical, scientific, literary, and scriptural texts were translated into Castilian as part of the Alfonsine cultural enterprise.[2] Alfonso X famously called his new canonical language *el castellano drecho,* meaning that it was correct, clear, Castilian.[3] The same period is marked by the appearance of Castilian translations of the Bible from Hebrew and Latin, some of which are associated with the scriptoria of Alfonso X. Given that the Bible is, as Francis E. Peters notes, the equivalent of "the charter document of the three faiths,"[4] the emergence of a vernacular biblical tradition in Iberia reflects the particular cultural politics at work in the changing demographics of the region. Indeed, history for all three religious worldviews begins with the covenant of Abraham. The Bible, in addition to narrating the common past of the three religions, is, to quote Peters again, "something that must be made to yield sense no less than satisfaction."[5] The Christian New Testament is in many ways a rewriting and a revision of the Hebrew Bible, and the Qur'an is in part a response to and a recasting of the Hebrew and Christian canons, which, according to Muslim belief, had both been doctored over the centuries in order to excise all references to Muhammad.

In light of the long history of Christians', Jews', and Muslims' mutual accusations of misreading and falsification of Scripture as well as misguided abrogation of the Bible,[6] the materialization of a Castilian canon raises interesting questions about the transmission of vernacular biblical material during the later Middle Ages—a period that saw the intensification of the Christian *reconquista*, the eventual overthrow of the last surviving Muslim-ruled kingdom in the Iberian peninsula, and the Expulsion of the Jews.[7] Nevertheless, and notwithstanding Muslim interest in the Hebrew and Christian Bibles, the Romance translations of the Bible in the later Middle Ages in Iberia reveal more about Jewish-Christian relations and polemics than about Muslim relations with either of the two groups. Romance vernacular Bibles were the products of collaboration between Christian and Jewish scholars and translators. For Christians, such collaboration was seen as an important factor in the transmission of *Hebraica veritas,* or "Hebrew truth." However, throughout the later Middle Ages and in the thirteenth century in particular, Christian tolerance for Jews as the guardians of the Hebraica veritas waned. In part, this change in attitude stemmed from contact between Christian and Jewish scholars.[8]

This chapter will explore the cultural politics at work in the production and reception of Castilian vernacular Bibles, or *Biblias romanceadas*, produced in the thirteenth through the fifteenth centuries, insofar as such information may be gleaned from the extant manuscripts. (For Romance translations of the Bible outside the Iberian peninsula, see Sneddon's chapter in this volume.)[9] While the number of extant Biblias romanceadas is small (especially in comparison with other traditions), the extant manuscripts reveal the continuing activity of translators working from both Latin and Hebrew texts in the later Middle Ages in Iberia. It is important to note that prior to Romance translations the Bible was translated into another vernacular language of the peninsula, Arabic, perhaps as early as the ninth century.[10]

## The Origins of Romance Translation in the Kingdom of Leon and Castile

Romance translations of the Bible begin with the significant figure of Herman the German, active in Toledo between 1240 and 1256, who, in addition to translating Arabic commentaries on Aristotle, translated the Psalter from Hebrew to Romance. The first complete Biblias romanceadas of the early thirteenth century also emerged within the context of the so-called School of Toledo, which was not a formal institution, but rather refers to the diverse translation activities in the twelfth and thirteenth centuries that took place in Toledo and in other sites throughout the peninsula.[11]

For several centuries before its conquest by the Christian monarch Alfonso VI in 1085, Toledo had been a cultural and intellectual center of al-Andalus, housing the famed library of Al-Hakam II, estimated to have held some four hundred thousand volumes. The conquest of Toledo not only allowed the monarch to consolidate his realms but it also gave Christian intellectuals access to Andalusian libraries and scholars. Following the fall of Toledo to Alfonso VI, the city that had once mainly been home to Muslims and Jews became a city of Christians, Muslims, and Jews. Toledo became the capital and center of intellectual power in the expanding kingdom of Leon-Castile. The translation activities centered around Toledo are marked by two distinct phases. The first, beginning in the twelfth century, is characterized by church patronage and the translation of scientific works from Arabic into Latin. The second wave of translations, in which Castilian rather than Latin was the prime target language, began in the mid thirteenth century and is intimately linked with the Alfonsine cultural enterprise. The rise of Romance translations did not mean the decline of Latin in ecclesiastical work, however; Toledo also remained a center for Latin translations well into the fifteenth century.[12]

Although some of the earlier patrons and commissioners are known, such as the Archbishop Raymond of Toledo (1126–52) and Peter the Venerable (c. 1092–1156), many translators from the period were unknown clerics who worked at the behest of the church in relative isolation from other translators and without the direct editorial intervention of a team or superior.[13] It was during the first period of the "school" that the Qur'an was translated into Latin at the request of Peter the Venerable by a team composed of the Christian clerics Herman of Carintia and Robert of Chester and the Jewish scholar Pedro de Toledo. The composition of this translating team typifies the modus operandi of the Toledo translators, who worked in teams including Arabic- and romance-speaking Jews and Latinists from other countries. It is thought that the teams typically translated from Arabic to romance orally and then from romance to Latin, recording this final version in writing. Consequently, an ephemeral tradition of romance translations of scientific and religious texts existed even before the production of romance texts.

Under the patronage and editorial direction of Alfonso X, translators gathered together to adapt and appropriate scientific, sacred, and literary texts from Arabic, Hebrew, and Latin. While prologues to the translations tell us that Alfonso grouped experts—in large part Jewish—together to work collaboratively on most of the translations he commissioned (suggesting a sort of "school" or workshop), there is no evidence that Alfonso's translators worked in Toledo as opposed to Seville (the monarch's preferred city of residence) or Murcia (where he had another scriptorium).[14] The result of the collaborative translations was the production of new works composed in what the Alfonsine collaborators called el castellano drecho. As Clara Foz points out, authority rested in the source language during the twelfth and early thirteenth centuries, but by the later thirteenth century authority lay not only within the truth of the text but also emanated from the use of Castilian as the external target language. Castilian was the language of the authority of the crown.[15]

Three kinds of biblical translations are generally included in discussions of the Biblias romanceadas: the translations that seek to present complete Bibles, those that weave literal and extensive translations of biblical passages into other narratives, and, last, moralized Bibles. Thanks to the endeavors of twentieth-century scholars working under the aegis of the Hispanic Seminary of Medieval Studies, critical editions of many of the Biblias romanceadas are accessible to students and researchers today.[16] These scholars' painstaking textual criticism reveals that the production of the Biblias romanceadas led not to any miracle stories about divine revelation (i.e., the story of the miraculous translation of the Septuagint) but rather produced a varied set of biblical texts in the vernacular that would provoke ecclesiastical censure. As Margherita Morreale has noted, the variety of texts translated from Latin and Hebrew created a complicated panorama of romance biblical production spanning three centuries in which no two extant Bibles are alike.[17] Indeed the relative paucity of extant manuscripts is balanced by the diversity of those that survived.

The first romance translations of biblical texts originated in the decades after the Fourth Lateran Council and would seem to follow the catechistic spirit of its proposed reforms. The second wave of translations began in the later fourteenth century or early decades of the fifteenth century and would culminate in the late-medieval biblical masterpiece the Alba Bible. By the end of the fifteenth century, however, the Spanish Inquisition prohibited the ownership of vernacular Bibles and burned many copies. Following mass conversions and the 1492 Expulsion of the Jews ordered by Ferdinand and Isabella I, known as the Catholic monarchs, vernacular Bibles became increasingly suspect in the eyes of the Inquisition because they were thought to be the tools of crypto-Jews and heretics. While many of the Bibles circulating in the vernacular have been lost, the versions that have come down to us demonstrate the complexity of the phenomenon of biblical translation into the vernacular in medieval Iberia.

## The Extant Biblias Romanceadas

The earliest surviving extensive translation of Biblical passages into Castilian appears to have been incorporated into the *Fazienda de Ultramar* (Deeds from Across the Seas, c. 1230), a historical and geographic description of the Holy Land and the wonders to be found there. According to its prologue, the Bishop Remont of Toledo (d. 1151), a leader of the so-called School of Toledo, commissioned the *Fazienda* from Almerich, archdeacon of Antioch. The original text produced by Almerich was probably in Latin and the *Fazienda,* found in a single manuscript witness, is a translation made after Remont's death.[18]

Significantly, Almerich's translation of biblical passages derives almost entirely from Hebrew texts. The biblical material incorporated into the *Fazienda* includes the historical and prophetic books of the Hebrew Bible (at times literally translated, at other times abbreviated and summarized), excerpts translated from the Deutero-canonical books, and the Gospels and Epistles. Almerich also privileged prophetic verses of key importance for the Christian typological interpretation of the Hebrew Bible, such as those found in Isaiah, Micah, Zechariah, Amos, and Daniel. The romance *Fazienda* is clearly a text produced within the context of the Crusades, wherein vernacular audiences are provided access to information about the contended Holy Land as well as the Scriptural background justifying its conquest. Nevertheless, as Fernando Gómez Redondo observes, the *Fazienda* was never meant to be a practical guide for crusaders or pilgrims. Rather, it presents a spiritual topography and a textual concretization of biblical history and legend.[19]

Further thirteenth-century biblical translation is represented by three manuscripts now housed in the Escorial Monastery Library. These translations, dating from the thirteenth century, were made from the Vulgate, most likely from the Paris Bible version (on the Paris Bible, see Light's chapter in this volume). However, in addition to the Paris Bible, these manuscripts also contain what Gómez Redondo has identified as "echoes" of earlier Visigothic Bibles and the Hebrew Bible.[20] The three manuscripts, known as E8 (San Lorenzo de El Escorial, Monasterio I.I.8), E6 (Monasterio I.I.6), and E2 (Monasterio I.I.2), each contain a different configuration of books of the Bible and appear to derive from a common source translation. According to Margherita Morreale, whose essay "Vernacular Scriptures in Spain" remains essential reading for scholars entering into the complicated world of Iberian romance translations of the Bible, the texts contained in these three manuscripts inaugurate the creation of a new biblical vocabulary and show what the language of the Spanish Bible might have become if a true vernacular tradition had established itself prior to the Council of Trent.[21]

E8 is a thirteenth- or fourteenth-century manuscript from the region of Navarre containing the books of Leviticus through Job according to the order and chapter divisions of the Paris Bible. It may have once contained the earlier books as well.[22] After Job, E8 contains a translation of Psalms in a different hand and demonstrating a different *mise en page* than the rest of manuscript. Though the manuscript states that the

Psalter is translated from Hebrew and attributes it to Herman the German, Mark G. Littlefield asserts that, despite the occasional term from the Hebrew Bible, it is in fact based on Jerome's translation from Hebrew and a Latin adaptation of the Septuagint.[23] E6, which contains Proverbs through 2 Maccabees, was copied in the second half of the thirteenth century and appears to have been copied in one of the scriptoria of Alfonso X.

Indeed, the production of the three thirteenth-century Castilian Bibles is closely related to the ambitious historiographic project of Alfonso X, the *General estoria* (World History), composed over the decade 1270–80 and ultimately left unfinished. E8, as Littlefield has observed, is closely related to an early fifteenth-century copy of the *General estoria*.[24] E2, while considered a *Biblia romanceada,* is in fact a thirteenth-century manuscript containing parts V and VI of Alfonso's *General estoria.* These sections narrate the "fifth age" of mankind—the transmigration of Babylon and the Jews' loss of self-governance—and incorporate vernacular translations of the final books of the Hebrew Bible as well the Gospels and Epistles.

Like the *Fazienda de Ultramar,* the *General estoria* uses the Bible as a structural and literary backbone. Alfonso's historiographic collaborators worked with all the authorities they had access to in order to produce a complete history of the world. Their use of the Bible is, of course, not surprising, for, in addition to its importance for the liturgy, the Bible was one of the most, if not the most, accessible source for historical information in the Middle Ages. However, the *General estoria* transforms the Bible by romancing, prosifying, and glossing the text. The *General estoria* interweaves biblical narratives with translations and adaptations from other sources, including Ovid, the fourth-century *Chronici canones (Chronological Canons)* by Eusebius of Cesarea, Josephus's *Antiquities of the Jews,* and Peter Comestor's *Historia scholastica.* (For these and other historical works see Harris's chapter in this volume.) The *matiere* of literary romances is also incorporated. Roberto González-Casanovas, one of the preeminent scholars on Alfonsine historiography, characterizes the *General estoria* as "a vernacular and secularized reconstruction of the Old Testament that is placed within synchronous annals of classical antiquity and within the pluralistic contexts of medieval Iberia."[25] According to the authorial voice of Alfonso X in his prologue to book 10 of the first part of the *General estoria*:

Nos en tod este libro la estoria de la Biblia avemos por arvol a que acordamos de nos tornar toda uia como a linna, cada que acabamos las razones delos gentiles, que contamos en medio; et por ende, quanto es en la estoria de la Biblia en quanto pudieremos, queremos dezir como Moysen dixo; et dezimos uos esto por que non seamos tenudos que de nuestro somos dobladores dela razon.

(General estoria 1:288)

Throughout this entire book, we have used the history of the Bible as a tree, to which we ever return, as to an outline, each time that we conclude the words of the gentiles, which we tell in between; thus, all that is in the history of the Bible, as far as we will be able, we will say as Moses said. We tell you this so that we will not be taken for manipulators of our truth.

The *General estoria,* as a history of the world composed from the perspective of a thirteenth-century Christian monarch, begins with a version of Genesis. Part 1 of the *General estoria* contains the Pentateuch, paraphrased and interwoven with other historical sources about the ancient world. Parts 2 through 6, which remained unfinished, contain most of the books of the Bible, some paraphrased and others translated as complete units. The complete *General estoria,* as envisioned by Alfonso and his collaborators, was supposed to conclude with what was for them the present day; it was intended to cover all the events of the Christian New Testament and link the new covenant to the rule of Alfonso's line in Castile and beyond. The history, vast as it is, only reaches the birth of the Virgin Mary, however.[26]

The biblical translators of the Alfonsine scriptoria remain anonymous, but their familiarity with rabbinical and Arabic sources is evident. Translators of other works commissioned by Alfonso, such as Bernardo el Arábigo, a convert from Islam, and Rabbis Isaq B. Sid and Juda B. Mosé, are named in their texts. It is possible that these members of the Alfonsine team may have also collaborated on the Bibles and the *General estoria.* However, the editorial mission handed down from Alfonso was undoubtedly Christian. For example, the section of part 1 of the *General estoria* explaining the birth of Abraham contains the following remarks:

Los arauigos an su Biblia trasladada del ebraygo como nos, como quier que demuden y ellos algunas razones a logares, e pongan y otras, fablan y destos nuestros padres dela linna; e assi ouerion sus esponedores sobrello, e aduzen

sus prueuas delos dichos que Moysen dixo enla Biblia, como lo fazemos nos
e los nuestros; e como quier que ellos anden errados en creencia, los qui la de
de Jesu Cristo non tienen, pero muchas buenas palabras e çiertas e con
razon, dixieron enel fecho dela Biblia e enlos otros saberes.

*(General estoria,* PART I, 1:85)

The Arabs have their Bible translated from Hebrew like we do, and even
though they have changed the placement of some things and added others,
in their Bible they also speak of the lineage of our fathers; and they also have
their interpreters of the Bible, who bring forth their arguments about what
Moses said in the Bible, as do we and our interpreters; and even though they
are mistaken in their belief, those who are not of the faith of Jesus Christ,
nevertheless they have said many good, certain and correct words in this
matter of the Bible and in other realms of knowledge.

The *General estoria* is a supremely political work, no doubt meant to
support Alfonso's frustrated claims to the crown of the Holy Roman
Empire. It inserts *España,* as Alfonso called his kingdom, into the grand
narrative of salvation history. The *General estoria,* along with Alfonso's
other major historiographic work, the *Estoria de Espanna,* clearly asserts
Alfonso's resemblance to the great kings of biblical history. In addition to
supporting the king's claims to the imperial crown, this lineage avowed
the divine roots of Castilian and Christian hegemony in Iberia not only
with respect to the Muslim and Jewish inhabitants of the peninsula but
also to the other Christian kingdoms such as the crown of Aragon.

Alfonso's desire to translate the Bible and then include so much of it
within his universal history surely stemmed from his vision of a common
canonical language that would not only be shared by the three cultures
coexisting in the Iberian peninsula but would also convert texts and people by linking his vernacular to salvation history. Romancing the canon
created a new royal scripture in el castellano drecho, which supported the
elevation of Castilian as a medium of intellectual communication as well
as a canonical language and a medium of spiritual reflection and communication. It is possible to see in the ambitious Alfonsine historiographic
project an attempt to produce a *castellana veritas,* or "Castilian truth" that
brought all other known truths together under its aegis, including the
biblical Hebraica veritas. With the canonization of Castilian as a language
of history and scripture, the new truth was one that could in many ways
replace the earlier texts in secular usage and perhaps even sidestep the

accusations of falsification.[27] In Alfonso's historiography, which translated the Vulgate Bible, we can see a rewriting of a master text in a language that had become the vernacular for Christians, Muslims, and Jews living in the formerly Andalusian realms of the Castilian king in the thirteenth century.

While the extant thirteenth-century Biblias romanceadas (with the exception of the biblical passages contained in the *Fazienda de Ultramar*) were based on the Vulgate, the Biblias romanceadas produced in the following centuries were translated mainly from Hebrew, basing their versions of the Pentateuch on the Masoretic texts and thus reflecting the revival of Jewish biblical scholarship in the fourteenth century.[28] Nine manuscripts from this period have survived and, as is the case for many of the thirteenth-century texts already discussed, the majority of the extant fourteenth- and fifteenth-century Bibles are now found in the Escorial Monastery Library in Spain: E3 (Monasterio I.I.3; fig. 15.1), E4 (Monasterio I.I.4), E5 (Monasterio I.I.5), E7 (Monasterio I.I.7), and E19 (Monasterio I.I.19). E3, likely copied from a complete romance Bible, is a fifteenth-century manuscript that contains texts from Genesis to 2 Maccabees and stands out from the other extant manuscripts with its Jewish liturgical notation and many illuminations. E4, also a fifteenth-century manuscript, contains Genesis through 2 Maccabees as well, but the translation of the Hebrew has been "revised somewhat on the basis of the Vulgate," according to Oliver H. Hauptmann.[29] E7, a fifteenth-century translation containing Genesis 25.17 through Kings 23.4, also appears to have been revised according to Christian biblical standards and uses Christian religious terms to translate technical terms from Jewish religious practice.[30] Unlike the other translations, as Littlefield notes, E7 often diverges from literal translation from Hebrew by paraphrasing and by the inclusion of interpretive interjections. In this respect, it resembles the earlier translations associated with the Alfonsine historiographic project.[31] E5 picks up the massoretic text where E7 leaves off and contains brief glosses, but to my knowledge has not yet been edited (though it was consulted by Llamas for his edition and study).[32] Consequently, the precise relationship between the two Biblias romanceadas remains an area for investigation.

In addition to the manuscripts conserved in the Escorial library, a partial Castilian translation of the Hebrew Bible that shares some characteristics of the translations in both E5 and E4 is contained in MS CXXIV/1–2 of the Evora Public Library in Portugal.[33] E19 contains Genesis 8 through

15.1. El Escorial, Real Monasterio de San Lorenzo, 1.1.3, fol. 2v. *Copyright Patrimonio Nacional.*

2 Kings in a translation that resembles that of E3.[34] MS 52-VIII-I of the Ajuda Library in Lisbon, a fifteenth-century copy of a fourteenth-century translation, contains versions of the Pentateuch, Joshua, and Judges that are closely related to those found in E3, as Lazar demonstrates in the comparative study in his critical edition of the manuscript.[35] The manuscript also states that the Bible belonged to the Portuguese King Alfonso V (1432–81).

The Biblioteca Nacional in Madrid houses two romance Bibles: a fourteenth-century manuscript known as the Osuna Bible (MS 10232) and a fifteenth-century manuscript (formerly in the collection of the Marquis of Santillana) containing Isaiah through Daniel, translated from Hebrew, and the Wisdom of Solomon and Ecclesiasticus, translated from Latin (MS 10288). The Osuna Bible is modeled upon a luxuriously illustrated thirteenth-century French *Bible moralisée* known as the *Biblia rica de Toledo* because it is in the library of Toledo Cathedral. The Osuna Bible, however, while containing instructions for illustration, was never illuminated.[36]

Another fifteenth-century Castilian Bible manuscript is now conserved in the Real Academia de Historia in Madrid (RAH 87). RAH 87 contains the major and minor Prophets and the two books of Maccabees, all in both Latin and Spanish, as well as Latin transcriptions of some of Jerome's prefaces and glosses deriving from Nicholas of Lyra's *Postilla*. According to Lazar and colleagues, RAH 87 represents an earlier project designed to present a complete Spanish translation of the Hebrew Bible alongside Jerome's Latin version.[37]

The mid-fifteenth-century *Biblia de Alba* (Madrid, Palacio de Liria, MS 86), or Alba Bible, is one of the most fascinating translations and one of the most beautiful Iberian Bible manuscripts to have survived to this day. Moreover, the Alba Bible is perhaps the best known of all the vernacular versions produced in medieval Spain and is often misidentified as the "first" translation of the Hebrew Bible into Spanish. In 1422, Don Luis de Guzmán, grand master of the Military Order of Calatrava, wrote to Rabbi Moses Arragel requesting a romance translation of the Hebrew Bible that would include glosses and explain divergent Christian and Jewish interpretations. Arragel at first refused the commission, but eventually accepted. Thus, Arragel, as translator, was not the author but rather the transmitter of a compendium of interpretations. Arragel prefaces his translation with a letter of fifteen "chapters," first stating his reluctance to engage in the task of translating and glossing the text, since his rabbinical exegesis might be seen as a challenge to Christianity. Arragel also recommended that his Christian reader consider his method of presentation before becoming offended. After the letter, Arragel further reassures his reader in a lengthy prologue stating that much of the gloss challenges neither Christian nor Jewish orthodoxy, and that he took care to provide only the best materials from the rabbinical and Christian traditions, having consulted with church scholars in Toledo and Salamanca. In anticipation of the inevitable conflict between Christian and rabbinical exegesis, Arragel asserts that the rabbinical materials should be understood merely as *opinión ebrea* (Hebrew opinion) and not as a refutation of Christianity.[38]

The Alba Bible, completed in 1430, was scrutinized by ecclesiastical authorities over a period of several years, became the subject of public disputation (at which Muslims, Christians, and Jews are said to have participated), and then disappeared—perhaps hidden due to the risk of confiscation—only to reappear in the library of the Duke of Alba in 1622. Some historians have wanted to see in this Bible and its production a symbol of tolerance—but a Bible of this sort could certainly have been used as a reference for anti-Jewish polemics, as was seemingly the case in the public disputation.

## Audiences and the Usage of the Biblias Romanceadas

Early decrees prohibiting the production and ownership of vernacular Bibles, such as the prohibition issued by the Council of Toulouse in 1229 and reiterated by Jaime of Aragon in 1233, appear to have had little effect on their production and dissemination. However, following the recrudescence of anti-Semitism in the fourteenth century and the violence and mass conversions of 1391, the possession of vernacular Bibles came under increasing suspicion in Iberia. As is apparent from the brief descriptions of the extant Biblias romanceadas already given, those sources that have come down to us belonged to members of royal families and the upper nobility. Indeed, some of the manuscripts now in the Escorial library belonged to the library of Isabel the Catholic, who was responsible for some of the prohibitions against ownership of vernacular Bibles. Such personages were above suspicion or beyond the reach of inquisitional persecution. The Alba family, for example, having inherited the Alba Bible commissioned by an illustrious ancestor, received special permission from the Inquisition to keep the precious manuscript in 1624:

> Don Andrés Pacheco por la gracia de Dios Obispo Inquisidor general Apostólico en los Reynos y Señoríos de su Magestad y de su Consejo. Por quanto hemos recogido una Biblia en romance manuscripta en pergamino con las figuras illuminadas concernientes a la hystoria sagrada, tradducida con orden expensas y cuidado del señor Maestre de Calatrava Don Luís de Guzmán; y por la gran confianza que tenemos de la persona del Ex^mo Señor Don Gaspar de Guzmán Conde de Olivares Caballerizo mayor y Summíller de Corps de su Magestad y de su consejo de Estado y de su gran cristiandad y celo de nuestra santa Fe Catholica; tenemos por bien de darle y entregarle la dicha Biblia en romance y licencia como por la presente le damos para que la pueda leer y tener en su casa y librería y que en ella la puedan leer también las personas que su Excelencia señalare.[39]

> Don Andrés Pacheco, by the grace of God, Bishop and General Apostolic Inquisitor in the Kingdoms and Realms of the King and his council. We have received a Bible in the vernacular, a parchment manuscript with illuminated figures concerning sacred history, translated at the expense of the lord Master of Calatrava, don Luis de Guzmán and overseen by him; due to the great

confidence that we have in his Excellency don Gaspar de Guzmán, Count of Olivares, Master of the King's Horse and Master of the King's Chamber and member of the King's privy council, as well as in his great Christianity and zeal for our holy Catholic Faith, we hold it to be right to give the said vernacular Bible back to him and give him leave, by this license, to read it and have it in his home and library, and also it can be read by such persons as his Excellency chooses.

Beyond the limited concrete information offered by the texts and codices of the fourteenth- and fifteenth-century Biblias romanceadas, the question of their intended audiences and readership is vexed. While some scholars have argued that the source languages, the ordering of books according to Jewish, Visigothic, and Roman calendars, and the presence or absence of the books of Maccabees indicate the intended recipients of these manuscripts, others have contended that all the Biblias romanceadas were, though often translated by Jews, made for Christian readers. Lazar, for example, in his 1995 edition of E3, argues that "all of the Spanish translators from Hebrew were undoubtedly Jewish, familiar with the medieval rabbinical bibles accompanied by commentaries of Rashi and David Kimhi, Nahmanides and Gersonides among others, and that their translations were commissioned by Christian patrons."[40] Littlefield, on the other hand, asserts that E4 and E7 were intended for Christian use, E5 and E19 for Jewish use, and E3 and the Alba Bible for mixed use. Moreover, as he rightly points out, echoing Morreale, the line between Christian and Jew was often blurred in the later Middle Ages, marked by conversions and reconversions as well.[41] The remarkable production of the *Biblia de Alba* demonstrates that Jewish translators undoubtedly translated biblical texts for Christian patrons in the Middle Ages, but this does not mean that all the Bibles were intended for or commissioned by Christians. Eleazar Gutwirth suggests that the renewed interest of Jewish intellectuals in the Bible also played a significant role in the production of the Biblias romanceadas.[42] Francisco J. Pueyo Mena, surveying the critical impasse, suggests that only specific historical contexts can help determine the usage of individual manuscripts.[43] Such scholarly disaccord suggests the need for further investigations into the historical circumstances of the production and readership of the Biblias romanceadas.

Given that some Jewish scholars and rabbis such as Petrus Alfonsi, Shelomoh Halevi of Burgos, who took the name of Pablo de Santa María, and Yehoshua of Lorca, later known as Jerónimo de Santa Fe, converted to Christianity only to become leading Christian ecclesiastical figures, the possibility of *converso* patrons, audiences, and translators should not be dismissed. One thing that a clerical and literate converso familiar with the rabbinical tradition could contribute to his new religious identity was his custodianship of the Hebraica veritas. Moreover, and as the disputation with rabbis held by Jerónimo de Santa Fe indicates, the rabbinical tradition was often marshaled in Christian polemics against Judaism. Immediately following his baptism in 1412, Jerónimo de Santa Fe requested permission from the antipope Benedict XIII to hold a debate in Tortosa with Jewish intellectuals. The disputations lasted for twenty months, during which Jerónimo strove to convince his interlocutors of the truth of his new faith, which he claimed was supported by rabbinical literature.[44] On the other hand, as Lazar points out, some fifteenth-century translations of biblical and rabbinical texts were likely meant for those conversos who publicly professed Christian faith and continued to practice Judaism in secret. These *conversos judaizantes* would become the targets of Inquisitional persecution.

One clue as to intended audiences and reception of the Biblias romanceadas can be found in the translations of passages where doctrinal rifts are most obvious, such as Isaiah 7:14: "Therefore the Lord himself shall give you a sign. Behold a virgin shall conceive, and bear a son and his name shall be called Emmanuel." *Virgin* is the Vulgate translation for the Hebrew *almah*, which means literally *young woman*, virgin or newly married, and has connotations of nubility.[45] E3, for example, reads, "Por tanto, dara el Señor avos señal: ahe, la virgen preñada, e parira fijo, e llamaran su nombre Emanuel" (Therefore the Lord will give you a sign, yea, the pregnant virgin, and she will give birth to a son, and they will call his name Emmanuel), which would seem to be in accordance with Christian doctrine. However, the word *virgen* is clearly a correction made to the manuscript after its original transcription. As Lazar notes in his edition, the eighteenth- or nineteenth-century hand of a cleric that made further corrections to the manuscript and inserted passages where he found missing folia also wrote in the margin of Isaiah 7: "la manceba preñada; fue mui malicisoso el que borro el n. virgen y puso manceba" (the pregnant young maid; he who erased the name virgin and put young maid was very malicious). As Lazar points out, since E3 was translated primarily from the Hebrew Bible, the original most likely used *manceba* (young woman) or *moça* (young woman) to translate the Hebrew *almah*.[46] In some of the other extant *Biblias* the translators also opted for terms other than *virgen*.

RAH 87 and the Alba Bible both contain transliterations of the Hebrew term, stating "que la alma conçibio, e parira fijo" (the *almah* conceived and will bear a son)[47] and "la alma conçebira" (the *almah* will conceive).[48] Interestingly, the *Fazienda de Ultramar,* a work undoubtedly meant for a Christian audience, also translates this term as *mançeba*.[49] What would a Christian reader, cleric or not, have seen in the use of *alma* or *mançeba* in the translation of a passage of central importance to the Christian typological relationship between the Old Testament with the New? A Christian polemicist may have found the translation useful for substantiating the accusation of Jewish tampering with the messianic prophecies of the original Hebraica veritas. On the other hand, this passage was also cited by Jews as proof of Jerome's mistranslation of Scripture when he returned to the Hebrew texts to create the Vulgate. Indeed, this particular passage was commonplace in interreligious disputations. Isidore of Seville, in his seminal polemic *On the Catholic Religion, Against the Jews* provides a justification for Jerome's choice of the word "virgin":

> Behold here is the one born of the Virgin and called "God is with us." The Jews argue over this verse, claiming that in Hebrew, the prophet doesn't speak of a *virgin* in his discourse, but of a *young woman*. The answer to them is that it would not be a miracle if a young woman—this term only denotes age—gave birth. But it would be quite an extraordinary miracle if a virgin—this term denotes the integrity of the individual—gave birth. Indeed, God said: *The Lord will give you a miracle*.[50]

Nevertheless, it is also possible that this translation indicates a Jewish audience or an audience of Judaizing conversos, as Littlefield has argued. This nontypological interpretation of Isaiah is precisely the kind of "heretical" content that the Inquisition wished to eliminate when it decreed the burning of romance Bibles in Valencia in 1497:

> Sepades que nos avemos sido ynformados que hay muchas personas en estos dichos Reynos que tienen libros escriptos en ebraico que tocan y son de la ley de judios, e de medecina, e çirujia, e de otras ciencias y artes, e asimismo brivias en romance de lo cual se esperan seguir e siguen daños.

> Know that we have been informed that many people in the said Kingdoms have books written in Hebrew that touch upon and are on the Jewish law

and on medicine and surgery, and on other sciences and arts, as well as Bibles in romance, from which damage is expected and will occur.[51]

Consequently, the local authorities were ordered to confiscate and publicly burn such books without delay.

Arragel's curious rendering of the (in)famous "horns of Moses" in Exod. 34:29—"And when Moses came down from the mount Sinai, he held the two tables of the testimony, and he knew not that his face was horned from the conversation of the Lord"—stands in contrast to the polemical implications of the translation of Isaiah in the Alba Bible and other vernacular versions: "E avino que en deçendiendo Moysen del monte Sinay con las dos tablas del testamento en su mano de Moysen, non sabia que rrespandeçia asy como rrayos rretrogrados como a manera de cuernos el cuero de su cara en fablando con el" (It so happened that when Moses was descending from Mount Sinai with the two tablets of the testament in his hand of Moses, that he did not know that the skin of his face shone with rays that bent backwards in the form of horns).[52] Here, Arragel injects a possible explanation of Jerome's translation of the verse, which describes Moses's face as horned: *cornuta esset facies*. Jerome translated *quaran*, "ray," "to send out rays," according to its Hebrew root, meaning horn, thus inspiring the iconography of a "horned" Moses that would take on demonic and antisemitic overtones.[53] In the other extant fifteenth-century Biblias romanceadas, the verse declares that Moses's face *resplandecía*, or shone with light.

As Morreale observes, "vernacular translations are bound by textual traits to the Church or the Synagogue," but "in medieval Spain it is impossible to draw a clear line of demarcation between the Church and the Synagogue. The Bible divided them and drew them together; it was the core of controversy as well as a source of mutual instruction."[54] Indeed, the Biblias romanceadas are evidence of *convivencia* and conflict between the rival yet closely related monotheistic religions of medieval Iberia. For the Inquisition and the church, however, a Bible in the common language of Jews, Christians, and Moriscos of Castile and its neighbors was a threat. The Latin Vulgate and the canonicity of Latin itself served as a marker of religious difference and exclusion. For a time, the Castilian vernacular provided a linguistic and textual space where the three "peoples of the book"—particularly Christians and Jews—might find intersections of their canonical traditions. However, the emergence of Castilian as a biblical language also occurs against the backdrop of interreligious dialogue and disputes. The castellano drecho promoted by Alfonso X in the late thirteenth century and used by fifteenth-century intellectuals such as don Luís de Guzmán and Moses Arragel became the language of law and learning, but the castellana veritas of the Biblias romanceadas was effectively silenced for all but a select few by their almost total destruction following the conquest of Granada and the Expulsion of the Jews in 1492.

## Notes

1. *Al-Andalus* and *Espanna* are geographic terms that were in use in Arabic and Castilian historiography, respectively, in the Middle Ages. At times both terms refer to the Iberian peninsula as a whole and at other times refer to specific regions in the peninsula. See José Antonio Maravall, *El concepto de España en la Edad Media* (Madrid: Instituto de Estudios Políticos, 1954).

2. For an overview of Alfonso X's cultural policies and projects, see Francisco Márquez Villanueva, *El concepto cultural alfonsí* (Madrid: MAPFRE, 1994).

3. This term appears in the prologue of Alfonso's *Libro de la ochaua espera* (Book of the Eighth Sphere), a catalog of stars. It has become the locus classicus for discussing the monarch's linguistic policies. Following Cano, Hartman, and Cárdenas, I take the term of *castellano drecho* as a description of Alfonso's rhetorical strategy and a reflection of his desire to improve upon the source text by producing lucid prose in the vernacular, rather than an assertion of grammatical and lexical normalization. See Anthony J. Cárdenas, "Alfonso X nunca escribió el *castellano drecho*," in *Actas del X Congreso de la Asociación internacional de hispanistas*, ed. Antonio Vilanova (Barcelona: PPU, 1992), pp. 151–59. When referring to Alfonso as author of the many works produced in his scriptoria, I follow Roberto González-Casanovas, who reminds us that while "Alfonso" is the author-figure in the historiographies, scientific works, and poetry from his scriptoria, this authorial name is a "convenient" shorthand that refers to multiple interactions between editors, scribes, and translators working at the king's behest. See González-Casanovas, "Book Culture in Alfonso X's Prologues: The Texts and Contexts of Wisdom," *Hispanófila* 111 (1994): 1–15, at 2.

4. Francis E. Peters, *Judaism, Christianity, and Islam: The Classical Texts and Their Interpretation* (Princeton: Princeton University Press, 1990), p. 3.

5. Ibid., p. 4.

6. For a concise introduction to the history of such accusations, see Irven Resnick, "The Falsification of Scripture and Medieval Christian and Jewish Polemics," *Medieval Encounters* 2 (1996): 344–80; and Hava Lazarus-Yafeh, *Intertwined Worlds: Medieval Islam and Bible Criticism* (Princeton: Princeton University Press, 1992).

7. *Reconquista* (reconquest) is an ideological and historical term often used by historians to describe the centuries following the fall of the Visigothic kingdom

in 711 and the expansion of the vast Umayyad Empire, a period marked by intermittent warfare between Christian and Muslim rulers of the Iberian peninsula but also by the creation of societies in which Christians, Muslims, and Jews coexisted in relatively peaceful ways. For three centuries the greater part of the peninsula was firmly under Muslim control, but, from the twelfth century onward, Muslim control of the Iberian peninsula steadily waned. Recently, historians have challenged the use of the term *reconquista* since it encodes the idea that "the Reconquest" was a single, monolithic war fought by successive generations of Christians, united by their desire to regain territory usurped by non-Christians, when in fact the historical record shows sporadic unanimity between Christian rulers and reveals that the desire for territorial and economic expansion was often as much of a driving force as religious fervor. The ideal of "reconquest" appears early in Christian Iberian chronicles, however, and the routing of Muslims in the Iberian peninsula was given the papal imprimatur of a crusade by Urban II and his successors. For an introduction to the period and to the use of the term *reconquista* by historians, see Joseph O'Callaghan, *Reconquest and Crusade in Medieval Spain* (Philadelphia: University of Pennsylvania Press 2003), chapter 1.

8. Resnick, "The Falsification of Scripture," pp. 346–51 and 372–79.

9. On the production of Bibles in other Iberian Romance vernaculars, see Serafim da Silva Neto, "Bíblia medieval portuguêsa," *Revista Filológica* Segunda Fase 1 (1955): 3–10; Margherita Morreale, "Apuntes bibliográficos para la iniciación al estudio de las traducciones bíblicas medievales en catalán," *Analecta Sacra Tarraconensia* 31 (1960): 271–90; Pere Poy, "Introducció a l'estudi històric de la Bíblia en llengua catalana," *Butlletí de l'Associació Bíblica de Catalunya* 82 (2003): 21–40; Armand Puig i Tàrrech, *Les traduccions catalanes medievals de la Bíblia: El text, lectures i història* (Barcelona: Publicacions de l'Abadia de Montserrat, Associació Bíblica de Catalunya, 2001); and Klaus Reinhardt and Horacio Santiago-Otero, *Biblioteca bíblica ibérica medieval* (Madrid: Centro de Estudios Históricos, 1986).

10. See Henry S. Gehman, "The Arabic Bible in Spain," *Speculum* 1 (1926): 219–21; Hanna E. Kassis, "A Bible for the Masses in the Middle Ages: Translating the Bible in Medieval Muslim Spain," *Annual of Medieval Studies at the CEU* 8 (2002): 207–21; and Lazarus-Yafeh, *Intertwined Worlds*, pp. 111–29.

11. Clara Foz, *El Traductor, la Iglesia y el rey: La traducción en España en los siglos xii y xiii*, trans. Enrique Folch (Barcelona: Gedisa, 2000), p. 109; and José Francisco Ruiz Casanova, *Aproximación a una historia de la traducción en España* (Madrid: Cátedra, 2000), pp. 54–73.

12. Alan D. Deyermond, *Historia de la literatura española*, vol. 1: *La Edad Media* (Barcelona: Ariel, 1992), pp. 144–49.

13. Foz, *El traductor, la Iglesia y el rey*, p. 109.

14. Ibid., p. 106; and Ruiz Casanova, *Aproximación*, pp. 64–70. On the Jewish translators in particular and the relations between the Alfonsine cultural project and "medieval Jewish translation culture," see Eleazar Gutwirth, "'*Entendudos*': Translation and Representation in the Castile of Alfonso the Learned," *Modern*

*Language Review* 93 (1998): 384–99; and Gutwirth, "Religión, historia, y las *Biblias romanceadas*," *Revista Catalana de Teologia* 13 (1988): 115–33.

15. *El traductor, la Iglesia y el rey,* p. 126.

16. Prior to these recent editions (each of which focuses on a single manuscript and will be cited further on in this chapter), scholars prepared editions based on several manuscripts. See *Biblia medieval romanceada, según los manuscritos escurialenses I-j-3, I-j-8 y I-j-6,* ed. Castro and Augustín Millares Carlo, Pentateuco (Buenos Aires: J. Peuser, 1927); and *Biblia medieval romanceada judío-cristiana, versión del Antiguo Testamento en el siglo XIV sobre los textos hebreo y latino,* ed. José Llamas, 2 vols. (Madrid: CSIC; Instituto Francisco Suárez, 1950–55).

17. Margherita Morreale, "Vernacular Scriptures in Spain," in *The Cambridge History of the Bible,* vol. 2: *The West from the Fathers to the Reformation,* ed. G. W. H. Lampe (Cambridge: Cambridge University Press, 1969), pp. 465–91, at 466.

18. Salamanca, manuscript collection of the Biblioteca Universitaria, 1997. Fernando Gómez Redondo asserts the existence of a Latin original; see his *Historia de la prosa medieval castellana I: La creación del discurso prosísitico, el entramado cortesano* (Madrid: Cátedra, 1998), pp. 112–13. Moshe Lazar, the most recent editor of the *Fazienda,* on the other hand, has argued that Almerich's original composition was in Castilian and therefore the *Fazienda* can be considered the first Romance biblical translation as well as one of the earliest literary texts in the Castilian language; "Introduction," in Almerich, Archdeacon of Antioch, *La fazienda de ultra mar: Biblia romanceada et itinéraire biblique en prose castillane du XIIe siècle,* ed. Moshe Lazar (Salamanca: Universidad de Salamanca, 1965), p. 12. Fernando Gómez Redondo contests this dating on both linguistic and historical terms. Moreover, given that under Remont's guidance the translators generally composed Latin texts, a Latin—rather than Castilian—original of the *Fazienda* would seem more likely in the Toledan context.

19. Gómez Redondo, *Historia de la prosa medieval castellana I,* p. 116. However, while Gómez Redondo asserts that the intended audience was clerical, the shift from Latin to vernacular also indicates a possible shift in intended audiences. It seems plausible to hypothesize that the original Latin version was intended for scholarly and clerical reading, while the later vernacular translation was directed at a broader audience.

20. Ibid., pp. 125–31.

21. Morreale, "Vernacular Scriptures in Spain," p. 483.

22. *Biblia Romanceada I.I.8,* ed. Mark G. Littlefield (Madison: Hispanic Seminary of Medieval Studies, 1983), p. iii.

23. Littlefield, *Biblia Romanceada,* pp. ix–x.

24. Littlefield, *Biblia Romanceada,* p. vii.

25. Roberto González-Casanovas, "The Bible as Authority in Alfonso X's General Estoria: A Rhetorist's Reading of the Prologue," in *Estudios Alfonsinos y otros escritos en homenaje a John Esten Keller y a Aníbal A. Biglieri,* ed. Nicolás Toscano Liria (New York: National Endowment for the Humanities, 1990), pp. 87–97, at 87.

26. As yet there is no complete edition of the *General estoria,* although each of the six parts have been edited separately. The most widely available edition is the partial one found in Alfonso X, *Prosa histórica,* ed. Benito Brancaforte (Madrid: Cátedra, 1984). Part 1 of the *General estoria* was edited in full. See Alfonso X, *General estoria,* ed. Antonio G. Solalinde, 2 vols. (Madrid: Centro de Estudios Históricos, 1930). The text has recently been reedited: *General estoria. Primera parte,* ed. Pedro Sánchez-Prieto Borja, 2 vols. (Madrid: Fundación José Antonio de Castro, 2001). For part 2, see *General estoria: Segunda parte,* ed. Antonio G. Solalinde, Lloyd Kasten, and V. R. B. Oelschläger, 2 vols. (Madrid: CSIC, 1957–1961). Only segments of part 3 have been published. See *General estoria: Tercera parte,* ed. Pedro Sánchez-Prieto Borja y Bautista Horcajada Diezma (Madrid: Gredos, 1994); and *Edición crítica del "Libro de Isaías" de la Tercera Parte de la "General estoria,"* ed. María del Carmen Fernández López (Alcalá de Henares: Servicio de Publicaciones de la Universidad de Alcalá de Henares, 1998). The *Concordances and texts of the royal scriptorium manuscripts of Alfonso X, el Sabio,* ed. Lloyd Kasten and John Nitti (Madison: Hispanic Seminary of Medieval Studies, 1978) make part 4 available to scholars. Wilhemina Jonxis-Henkemans has edited parts 5 and 6: *Text and Concordance of the "General estoria V." Escorial Ms R-I-10* (Madison: Hispanic Seminary of Medieval Studies, 1993); *Text and Concordance of General Estoria V, Escorial MS.I.I.2* (Madison: Hispanic Seminary of Medieval Studies, 1994); and *Text and Concordance of the "General estoria VI." Toledo Ms. 40–20* (Madison: Hispanic Seminary of Medieval Studies, 1993).

27. As Rita Copeland argues, vernacular translations could at times supplant master texts in canonical languages. While Copeland expressly excludes biblical translations from her discussion, in the case of the Alfonsine biblical translations, the intention to supplant prior texts as sources of complete history appears to be evident. See Rita Copeland, *Rhetoric, Hemeneutics, and Translation in the Middle Ages: Academic Traditions and Vernacular Texts* (Cambridge: Cambridge University Press, 1991), pp. 3, 8.

28. Morreale, "Vernacular Scriptures in Spain," p. 466.

29. *Escorial Bible I.J.4.,* vol. 2., ed. Oliver H. Hauptmann and Mark G. Littlefield (Madison: Hispanic Seminary of Medieval Studies, 1987), p. xxxiv. Hauptmann's introduction to the first volume, published in 1953, is reprinted in the 1987 edition.

30. *Escorial Bible I.I.7,* ed. Mark G. Littlefield (Madison: Hispanic Seminary of Medieval Studies, 1996), p. vii.

31. Ibid., p. vii.

32. Llamas, "Introduction," *Biblia medieval romanceada judío-cristiana.*

33. Ibid., pp. xxxiv and lv.

34. *Escorial Bible I.ii.19,* ed. Mark G. Littlefield (Madison: Hispanic Seminary of Medieval Studies, 1992), p. viii.

35. *Biblia Ladinada Escorial i.J.3,* ed. Moshe Lazar, 2 vols. (Madison: Hispanic Seminary of Medieval Studies, 1995), pp. xxi–xliv.

36. The Osuna Bible has recently been edited by Miguel C. Vivancos and Fernando Vilches Vivancos. See *La Biblia de Osuna* (San Millán: Cilengua, 2007). See also Margherita Morreale, "La 'Biblia moralizada' latino-castellana de la Biblioteca Nacional de Madrid (MS 10232)," *Spanische Forschungen der Görresgesellschaft* 29 (1975): 437–56; and *"El ms. 10.288 de la Biblioteca Nacional de Madrid. Traducción parcial castellana de la Biblia del hebreo y del latín,"* *Filología* 13 (1968): 251–87; and Mario Schiff, *La bibliothèque du Marquis de Santillane: Étude historique et bibliographique de la collection de livres manuscrits de don Iñigo López de Mendoza, 1398–1458, marqués de Santillana, conde del Real de Manzanares humaniste et auteur espagnol célèbre* (Paris: Bibliothèque de l'École des Hautes Études, 1905), pp. 240–46.

37. *Biblia romanceada Real Academia de la Historia ms 87, 15th century*, ed. Moshe Lazar, Francisco J. Pueyo Mena, and Andrés Enrique-Arias (Madison: Hispanic Seminary of Medieval Studies, 1994), pp. xvii–xx.

38. *Biblia (Antiguo Testamento) Traducida del Hebreo al Castellano por Rabi Mose Arragel de Guadalfajara*, ed. Antonio Paz y Mélia, 2 vols. (Madrid: El Duque de Berwick y de Alba; Imprenta Artística, 1920–22), 1:19. See also Wallace S. Lipton, "A Blurred Encounter in Moses Arragel's Epistle on the Alba Bible," *Modern Language Notes* 84 (1969): 298–304.

39. *Biblia (Antiguo Testamento)*, p. xxiii.

40. *Biblia ladinada Escorial I.J.3*, pp. viii and xi–xiii.

41. *Biblia Romanceada: Biblioteca Nacional de Madrid Ms. 10.288*, ed. Francisco Pueyo Mena (Madison: Hispanic Seminary of Medieval Studies, 1996), p. xxiii.

42. Gutwirth, "Religión, historia, y las *Biblias Romanceadas*."

43. *Biblia Romanceada: Biblioteca Nacional De Madrid Ms. 10.288*, p. xiv.

44. Gilbert Dahan, *The Christian Polemic Against the Jews in the Middle Ages*, trans. Jody Gladding (Notre Dame, IN: University of Notre Dame Press, 1998), pp. 38–39.

45. Francis Brown, S. R. Driver, and Charles A. Briggs, *The Brown-Driver-Briggs Hebrew and English Lexicon with an Appendix Containing the Biblical Aramaic* (Peabody, MA: Hendrickson, 1996), entry 5959.

46. *Biblia Ladinada Escorial I.J.3*, pp. 798–99.

47. *Biblia Romanceada: Real Academia De La Historia Ms. 87, 15th Century*, p. 6.

48. *Biblia (Antiguo Testamento) Traducida Del Hebreo Al Castellano Por Rabí Mose Arragel De Guadalfajara*, 2:8.

49. *La fazienda de Ultramar*, p. 163.

50. "Ecce enim quem Virgo peperit nobiscum Deus appellatur. Quo loco argumentantur Judaei quod in Hebraeo non virginem, sed juvenculam ostendat sermo propheticus parituram. Adversus quos respondetur non esse signum, si juvencula pariat, quod est aetatis. Sed hoc esse signum ad rei novitatem, si Virgo pariat, quod est integritatis. Dum enim dicit: Dominus dabit vobis signum, insinuat quoddam insigne miraculum, virginem videlicet parituram, quod procul dubio signum non esset, nisi novum existeret. Oportebat enim Christum propter insigne miraculum secundum carnem nasci de virgine." Isidori Hispalensis, *De

*Fide Catholica Ex Veteri Et Novo Testamento Contra Judaeos Ad Florentinam Sororem Suam,* PL 83:0468C. English translation from Dahan, *The Christian Polemic Against the Jews,* pp. 43–44.

51. Cited in Jesús Enciso, "Prohibiciones españolas de las versiones bíbicas en romance antes del Tridentino," *Estudios bíbícos* 3 (1944): 523–60, at 538.

52. *Biblia (Antiguo Testamento) Traducida Del Hebreo Al Castellano Por Rabi Mose Arragel De Guadalfajara,* 1:207.

53. *Brown-Driver-Briggs Hebrew and English Lexicon,* entries 7161 and 7160. For Morreale, this is an example of Arragel's desire to "harmonize" the two textual traditions; see Morreale, "Vernacular Scriptures in Spain," p. 483.

54. Morreale, "Vernacular Scriptures in Spain," pp. 469, 481.

# Glossary

ALLEGORICAL: A symbolic interpretation of a text or image.

ANAGOGICAL: A spiritual or mystical interpretation of a text or image.

ANTIPHON: Brief liturgical chant, usually sung before and after a psalm or series of psalms; the text is usually scriptural and often taken from Psalms.

ANTIPHONER (ANTIPHONARY or ANTIPHONAL): A book containing chants for the Divine Office.

ANTIPOPE: A pope not considered to be canonically elected.

APOCRYPHA: The biblical books of Ezra, Nehemiah, Tobit, Judith, Esther, and the two books of Maccabees.

ARMARIUM: Originally a book chest or cupboard; later used with the sense of "library."

BASILICA: A church endowed with special privileges by the pope.

BENEVENTAN SCRIPT: A calligraphic book hand used in southern Italy and medieval Dalmatia between the eighth and sixteenth centuries.

BIBBIE ATLANTICHE ("ATLANTIC" BIBLES): Very large format Bibles produced in Italy in the eleventh and twelfth centuries (see also Giant Bibles).

BIBLE MORALISÉE: A late medieval Bible outfitted with moralizing illustration and written commentaries.

BIBLICAL EXEGESIS: Commentary on the Bible; explanation or interpretation of a biblical text.

BREVIARY: Liturgical book containing chants, readings, and prayers for the Divine Office.

CAPITULA: 1. Chapter cues that identify the order and location of Epistle and Gospel readings; 2. short excerpts from the Bible read during the Divine Office.

CAPITULARY or CAPITULAR: A collection of brief texts, called *capitula* (chapters), organized in an annual liturgical cycle for recitation during the Divine Office.

CARTHUSIAN: Relating to the contemplative religious order governed from La Grande Chartreuse, in France.

CHAPTER: 1. Daily administrative gathering of a monastic community, so named because it included the reading of a chapter from the Benedictine Rule; 2. a short text, often from Scripture, read during the Divine Office (*capitulum*).

CHRONOGRAPHY: A description of events arranged in chronological order.

CLOISTER: A covered walkway which connects the most important buildings in a residential religious foundation.

CLUNIAC: Refers to the abbey of Cluny in Burgundy; also used to describe monastic houses elsewhere that were affiliated with it.

CODEX: A manuscript text of cut leaves bound between two covers.

CODICOLOGY: The study of the physical structure of manuscripts.

COLLECTAR: Collection of collects (prayers) for the Divine Office.

CONVERSOS: Iberian Jews or Muslims who converted to Christianity.

CORRECTORS: Scholars who revised or corrected the biblical text.

CUSTOMARIES: A written document intended to describe the customs followed within an individual monastery.

DIVINE OFFICE: Daily cycle of liturgical prayer centering on the recitation of Psalms; consists of eight services performed at different hours of the day (Matins, Lauds, Prime, Terce, Sext, None, Vespers, and Compline).

EPISTOLARY: A book or section of a book containing excerpts from the Pauline and Catholic Epistles and Acts read during the Mass and arranged in the order of annual feasts.

ESCHATOLOGY: The division of theology which addresses death and the destiny of the soul.

EVANGELISTARY: A liturgical book containing the Gospel readings (pericopes) for the Mass in the order of the church year.

FOLIOS: Codex leaves made from parchment or vellum, usually numbered on only one side.

FRIARS MINOR: Members of the Franciscan mendicant religious order.

FRIARS PREACHERS: Members of the Dominican mendicant religious order.

GALLICAN PSALTER: Jerome's revision of an earlier Latin translation of Psalms that had been made from the Greek Hexapla translation (part of the Septuagint). The Gallican Psalter is the version of Psalms found in the Vulgate.

GIANT BIBLES: Very large format Bibles produced in the eleventh and twelfth centuries (see also Bibbie atlantiche).

GLOSS: A brief explanation added to a text.

GLOSSA ORDINARIA: A synthesis of patristic and Carolingian exegesis on the entire Bible first compiled in the twelfth century.

GRADUAL: 1. Book containing the proper chants for Mass; 2. proper chant of the Mass, usually with a text from Psalms.

HEPTATEUCH: The Pentateuch combined with the historical biblical books of Joshua and Judges.

HISTORIATED INITIALS: Manuscript text initials that contain a narrative image or portrait.

HISTORICAL SENSE: The literal meaning of a biblical text, taking into account the historical context.

LECTION: General term for a liturgical reading.

LECTIONARY: Book containing liturgical readings for the Mass or office.

LESSON (from *lectio*): Liturgical reading during the office of Matins.

LIBER TRAMITIS: or Book of the Path, written in the mid eleventh century to explain the customs in use at Cluny.

MARGINALIA: Notes written into the margins of a manuscript.

MATINS: Liturgical office performed in the early hours of morning before dawn (also called Nocturns).

MEMENTO MORI: A reminder (in the form of a text or image) that all people will die.

MINUSCULE: A form of script developed in the seventh century, composed of lower-case letters.

MISSAL: A book containing chants, prayers, and readings for the Mass.

MONASTIC RULE: A written set of guidelines meant to explain how to live a contemplative religious life within a monastery.

NICOLAITISM: The practice of clerical marriage.

NOCTURN: Division of the office of Matins comprising psalmody, lessons, and responsories. *Nocturns* is also an early name for the entire office of Matins.

OBLATES: Children given to a monastery between the ages three and fourteen to be raised to become monks or nuns.

OCTATEUCH: The Pentateuch combined with the historical biblical books of Joshua, Judges, and Ruth.

ORATIONALE: Book or section of a book containing prayers for the Mass or office.

PALEOGRAPHY: The study of old handwriting.

PANDECT: A single-volume, large-format Bible.

PASCHAL TRIDUUM: The three days preceding Easter Sunday (Maundy Thursday, Good Friday, and Holy Saturday).

PATRISTIC: Refers to texts by early Christian writers.

PENTATEUCH: The biblical five books of Moses (Genesis, Exodus, Leviticus, Numbers, Deuteronomy) known to the Jews as the Torah.

PERICOPE: The technical term for a biblical reading used in the Mass.

PONTIFICAL: Liturgical book for the use of a bishop in officiating at particular ceremonies.

POSTILL (POSTILLA): A term first used in the thirteenth century for a line-by-line commentary on Scripture.

PROPER: In the context of liturgy, refers to texts designated for a particular liturgical occasion.

PSALTER: A copy of the biblical book of Psalms, in Latin translation, for liturgical use.

QUADRAGESIMA: Penitential season of Lent beginning on Ash Wednesday

QUAESTIO: A literary form in which theological or philosophical precepts were disputed.

RECENSION: A particular version or revision of a text.

REFECTORY: A room for communal eating in a religious foundation.

REGULAR CANON: A member of a noncontemplative religious order who follows a rule.

RESPONSORY: Liturgical chant for the Divine Office, composed of a respond and a verse.

ROMAN PSALTER: An early Latin translation of the biblical book of Psalms (made before Jerome's translations and revisions).

SACRAMENTARY: Liturgical book containing prayers for the use of the celebrant during Mass.

SACRISTY: The room in a church where vestments, liturgical vessels and books used in the liturgy were kept.

SANCTORALE: The calendar of saints venerated in the liturgical year.

SAPIENTIAL BOOKS: The biblical books of Ecclesiasticus, Wisdom, Proverbs, and Ecclesiastes, focusing on lessons to be drawn for pedagogical, ethical, and political purposes, and the Song of Solomon.

SCRIPTORIUM: A workshop in which manuscripts are produced.

SEPTUAGINT: A Greek translation of the Hebrew Bible with some additions that medieval commentators believed had resulted from the legendary miraculous inspiration of seventy or seventy-two translators in the third century BCE.

SIMONY: The buying and selling of ecclesiastical offices or privileges.

STUDIA GENERALIA: An early term for a university (derived from the designation *studium* for a center where Franciscans or Dominicans were sent to study).

TANAKH: Hebrew term for the canon of the Jewish Bible, including the Torah (five books of Moses), the Prophets, and the Writings.

TEMPORALE: The cycle of feasts in the church year also known as the "proper of the time," organized principally around days commemorating events in the life of Christ

TORAH: The biblical five books of Moses (Genesis, Exodus, Leviticus, Numbers, Deuteronomy); also refers to the scroll containing these five books.

TROPE: Interpolation of a newly composed text and/or melody into a pre-existing chant.

TROPOLOGICAL: A practical or moral interpretation of a text or image.

TYPOLOGY: The linking of events or individuals from one part of the Bible, often the Old Testament, to events or individuals in the Christian Scriptures.

VERSICLES: Brief chants sung in various liturgical contexts, often with scriptural texts.

VETUS LATINA ("OLD LATIN"): Collective designation for Latin translations of biblical books made in the Early Christian period, before Jerome's "Vulgate" translation.

VITA: Narrative account of a saint's life, often intended to be read aloud in the liturgy.

VULGATE: This term was used beginning in the thirteenth century for the widespread Latin translation of the Bible made in the late fourth and early fifth century, consisting partly of new translations from the Greek and Hebrew and partly of revisions of existing Greek and Latin translations.

# Contributors

Susan Boynton, associate professor of historical musicology at Columbia University, works on medieval liturgy and chant in regions of what are now Italy, France, and Spain. She is the author of *Shaping a Monastic Identity: Liturgy and History at the Imperial Abbey of Farfa, 1000–1125* (Cornell University Press, 2006), which won the Lewis Lockwood Award of the American Musicological Society, and has coedited volumes on music and childhood as well as on the Cluniac customaries. Her next book, *Silent Music: Medieval Song and the Construction of History in Eighteenth-Century Spain,* will be published by Oxford University Press in 2011.

Isabelle Cochelin is associate professor in the Department of History and Centre for Medieval Studies of the University of Toronto. She specializes in medieval monasticism and has published articles in *Revue Mabillon* and in several edited volumes on subjects such as monastic customaries, entrance into the monastery, the education of oblates, and the origins of Cluny. With Susan Boynton, she coedited *From Dead of Night to End of Day: The Medieval Customs of Cluny* (Brepols, 2005) and is coeditor of the series Disciplina Monastica (Brepols).

Emily C. Francomano, associate professor of Spanish at Georgetown University, works on vernacular literature in medieval and Early Modern Iberia and Comparative Literature. She is the author of *Wisdom and Her Lovers in Medieval and Early Modern Hispanic Literature* (Palgrave Macmillan, 2008) and articles on medieval romances, manuscript culture, folklore, and allegory. She also edited *The Riddle of Incest in Medieval Iberia* for the journal *La corónica* in 2007. Her current work in progress, "Prisons of Love: Romance, Translation, and Adaptation in the Sixteenth Century," traces the multiform translations and adaptations of late medieval Spanish romances in literary, visual, and material culture across Europe.

Richard Gyug is professor of history and medieval studies at Fordham University and a specialist in medieval liturgy, particularly in the regions of the Beneventan script. His publications include *Missale ragusinum: The Missal of Dubrovnik* (Pontifical Institute of Mediaeval Studies, 1990) and *The Diocese of Barcelona during the Black Death: The Register "Notule communium"15* (Pontifical Institute of Mediaeval Studies, 1994). Recently, he has written several studies of saints' cults and liturgy in high medieval southern Dalmatia.

Jennifer A. Harris is associate professor of Christianity: arts and letters at Saint Michael's College in the University of Toronto. She is currently completing a monograph entitled "Sancta Sanctorum: The Jerusalem Temple in the Medieval Christian Imagination." Her published articles include studies on the body as temple in the high Middle Ages, Bernard of Clairvaux's notion of place and embodiment, the sanctity of Cluny, enduring covenant in Christian discourse, and Peter Damian's architecture of the self. Her next project is a study of Christian ideas of covenant in the Middle Ages.

Laura Light writes about the history of the Latin Vulgate in the thirteenth century. She has written general articles on the history of the medieval Bible, such as "Versions et révisions du texte biblique" in *Le Moyen Age et la Bible,* ed. Pierre Riché and Guy Lobrichon, Bible de tous les temps 4 (Paris, 1984), pp. 55–93, as well as more specialized articles such as "French Bibles c.1200–30: A New Look at the Origin of the Paris Bible," in *The Early Medieval Bible: Its Production, Decoration and Use*, ed. Richard Gameson (Cambridge University Press, 1994). She was formerly medieval manuscripts cataloguer at the Houghton Library, Harvard University and published *Medieval and Renaissance Manuscripts in the Houghton Library, Harvard University*, vol. 1: *MSS Lat 3–179*, Medieval and Renaissance Texts and Studies (Binghamton, NY, 1995).

Richard Marsden is reader in Old English at the University of Nottingham, where he teaches Old English, Anglo-Saxon studies, and the history of the English language. In addition to numerous articles on Old English literature and language, he has published *The Text of the Old Testament in Anglo-Saxon England* (Cambridge University Press, 1995) and *The Cambridge Old English Reader* (Cambridge University Press, 2004), and a new edition of *The Old English Heptateuch* for the Early English Text Society (2008). He is currently coediting the medieval volume of the *New Cambridge History of the Bible*.

Stella Panayotova is the Keeper of Manuscripts and Printed Books at the Fitzwilliam Museum, Cambridge University, and the director of the Cambridge Illuminations Project, which is preparing a multivolume series of catalogs of medieval and Renaissance illuminated manuscripts in the Colleges of Cambridge and the Fitzwilliam Museum. She was the curator of *The Cambridge Illuminations* exhibition (2005) and a coeditor of the exhibition catalogue. She has completed a commentary volume for the facsimile of the fourteenth-century English Macclesfield Psalter (Thames and Hudson, October 2008) and has published the facsimile of a fifteenth-century Flemish Book of Hours (Folio Society, 2009).

Eyal Poleg, Hanadiv Postdoctoral Fellow at the Centre for the History of the Book, University of Edinburgh, studies the material culture of the late medieval and early modern Bible in England. His dissertation, "Mediations of the Bible in Late Medieval England," examined channels of transmission, such as liturgy, preaching, and layout of manuscripts, as means by which medieval audiences gained access to the Bible. He has recently prepared a critical edition of a medieval rendering of the books of Maccabees, written in the Kingdom of Jerusalem by the Abbot of the Templum Domini.

Diane J. Reilly is associate professor of art history at the Hope School of Fine Art, Indiana University. She is the author of *The Art of Reform in Eleventh-Century Flanders: Gerard of Cambrai, Richard of Saint-Vanne, and the Saint-Vaast Bible*, Studies in the History of Christian Traditions, vol. 128 (Brill, 2006), and a number of articles on the religious and political functions of medieval manuscripts. She is currently writing a book on the earliest manuscripts of the Cistercian order.

Bert Roest, fellow of the Centre for Reformation and Renaissance Studies, Toronto, and lecturer in medieval history, Radboud University Nijmegen, works on medieval and early modern mendicant intellectual culture, with a special focus on religious instruction literature, historiography, preaching, and biblical scholarship. He is the author of *Reading the Book of History: Educational Functions and Intellectual Contexts of Franciscan Historiography ca. 1220–1250* (Regenboog, 1996), *A History of Franciscan Education (c. 1210–1517)* (Brill, 2000), and *Franciscan Literature of Religious Instruction Before the Council of Trent* (Brill, 2004). He is currently writing a general history of the Poor Clares and is part of a collaborative interdisciplinary research project on exegetical culture in mendicant schools between the thirteenth and the seventeenth century.

Clive R. Sneddon is lecturer in French in the School of Modern Languages at the University of St. Andrews. He is the author of numerous studies on translation in the Middle Ages as a cultural and linguistic phenomenon; and has used translated texts to demonstrate linguistic and cultural change. Most recently he has published "À la recherche de la traduction biblique en France au XVe siècle," in Dominique Lagorgette, ed., *Littérature et linguistique diachronie-synchronie: Autour des travaux de Michèle Perret* (Éditions de l'université de Savoie, 2007), and is finalizing a book on Translating the Bible in Medieval France.

Frans van Liere is associate professor of history at Calvin College. He holds an M.Div. in theology and an M.A. and Ph.D. in medieval studies from Groningen University in the Netherlands. He published a critical edition of Andrew of Saint Victor's Bible commentary on Samuel and Kings in the Corpus Christianorum Series Latina (a translation of which will appear in the TEAMS Commentary series) and he has written several articles on twelfth-century intellectual history and fourteenth-century papal history. His critical edition of Andrew's commentary on the twelve prophets, together with Mark Zier, appeared in 2007.

Lila Yawn teaches history of art, particularly that of the Italian Middle Ages for Cornell University in Rome, John Cabot University, and the American University of Rome. Her Ph.D. dissertation, "The Giant Bible of Perugia (Biblioteca Augusta, Ms. L. 59). A Manuscript and Its Creators in Eleventh-Century Central Italy" (the University of North Carolina at Chapel Hill, 2004), is the basis of a book and several articles currently in progress and the subject of an entry in the catalogue of the exhibition *Le Bibbie atlantiche: Il libro delle Scritture tra monumentalità e rappresentazione* (2000).

# Index

# Index of Manuscripts